Chronicles of a Global City

Chronicles of a Global City

Speculative Lives and Unsettled Futures in Bengaluru

VINAY GIDWANI
MICHAEL GOLDMAN
CAROL UPADHYA
EDITORS

University of Minnesota Press
Minneapolis
London

This project was made possible with the support of the Social Science Research Grants through the University of Minnesota.

COLLEGE ᴏꜰ LIBERAL ARTS

UNIVERSITY OF MINNESOTA

Driven to Discover℠

Copyright 2024 by the Regents of the University of Minnesota

All rights reserved. No part of this publication may be reproduced, stored in a retrieval system, utilized for purposes of training artificial intelligence technologies, or transmitted, in any form or by any means, electronic, mechanical, photocopying, recording, or otherwise, without the prior written permission of the publisher.

Published by the University of Minnesota Press
111 Third Avenue South, Suite 290
Minneapolis, MN 55401–2520
http://www.upress.umn.edu

ISBN 978-1-5179-1735-7 (hc)
ISBN 978-1-5179-1736-4 (pb)

A Cataloging-in-Publication record for this book is available from the Library of Congress.

Printed in the United States of America on acid-free paper

The University of Minnesota is an equal-opportunity educator and employer.

UMP SB 2024

For Rachel, whose presence lives in these pages
and continues to guide our lives

Contents

Maps of Karnataka and Bengaluru		x
Foreword		xiii
Janaki Nair		
Note on Confidentiality		xix
Abbreviations		xxi
Introduction: Bengaluru as Urban Future		1
Carol Upadhya, Michael Goldman, and Vinay Gidwani		

Part I. Speculative Stories — 29

1 Envisioning the City — 33
Vinay Gidwani

2 The IT Juggernaut — 45
Carol Upadhya

3 Only Beautiful Plans — 53
Vinay Gidwani

4 Building the High Life — 64
Carol Upadhya

Part II. Financial Stratagems — 75

5 Capital Times in Bengaluru — 78
Vinay Gidwani

6 Low Finance in the World City — 85
Hemangini Gupta

7 The Real Estate Fix — 98
Carol Upadhya

Part III. State Speculations — 111

8 Re-placing Labor — 114
Eesha Kunduri

9 Metro Mutations — 123
Usha Rao

10 Moving Matters — 139
Shaheen Shasa

Part IV. Speculative Subjects — 153

11 From Worker to Landlord — 156
Swathi Shivanand

12 Slum Dealings — 164
Carol Upadhya

13 "Why Not Us?" — 176
Swathi Shivanand

14 The Caste of Land — 188
Carol Upadhya

Part V. Labor in the Speculative City — 197

15 Constructing Precarity — 200
Swathi Shivanand

16 Whose Streets? — 207
Vinay K. Sreenivasa

17 Chasing Targets, Making a Life — 217
Kaveri Medappa

18 Serving the New Middle Class — 229
Swathi Shivanand

Part VI. Ecologies of Speculation — 237

19 The New "Commons" — 240
Eesha Kunduri

20 Leakages of Affluence 248
Swathi Shivanand

21 Guarding the Lake 255
Priyanka Krishna

22 Reinventing the City 266
Michael Goldman

Afterword 281
Malini Ranganathan

Plate Section. Photo Essay:
Life in the Speculative City
Pierre Hauser

Plate Section. Spatial Images Depicting
Expansion of Built-up Area and Changing
Land Cover in Bengaluru, 2000–2021

Acknowledgments 287
Contributors 293
Index 295

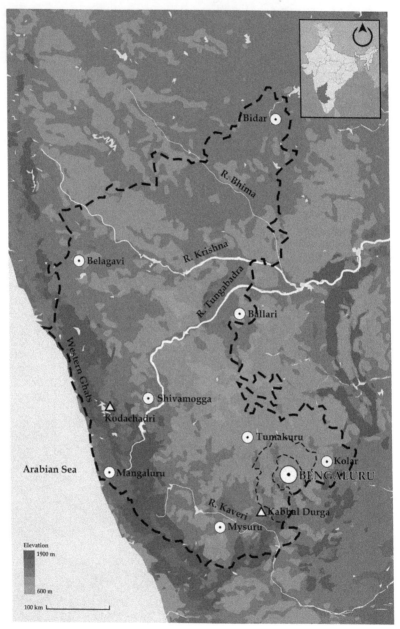

Map 1. Topographic contours of the state of Karnataka, with the city sitting atop a plateau far from flowing rivers. The inset locates Karnataka within India. Created by Deepa William.

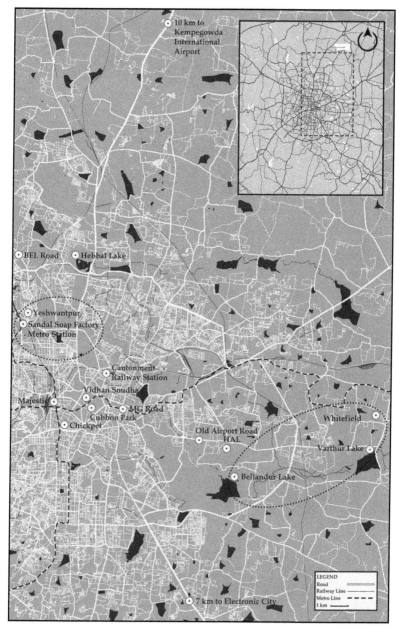

Map 2. Our two research sites, key landmarks, and the remaining water tanks of Bengaluru. The inset locates this section of the city within the larger metropolitan region. Created by Deepa William.

Foreword

Janaki Nair

Are we living through an age when the city has become history? Is that bounded spatial entity, which generated its own categories of analysis and study and sported distinctive features, now a thing of the past, as the urban expands into, colonizes, destroys, and draws on regions and resources that are well beyond the hinterland? And if so, under what strain does it place the categories with which we have long studied the city, as this deterritorialization and reterritorialization proceeds apace?

Perhaps no other Indian city allows us as intense and as telescopic a view of the process of urbanization in the new millennium as Bengaluru does. For long (in the colonial period) a civil and military station, with some lonely industrial sentinels on its edges, (the then) Bangalore escaped smokestack industrialization and retained its image as a "retirement" town par excellence. In the immediate post-independence decades the city's landscape was transformed, largely as a consequence of state-driven initiatives, as it became the favored site of capital goods industries, which served the military also through its large research and development wings while catering to a well-controlled consumer goods sector. This age of patriotic production itself produced in turn the well-planned and socially ambitious industrial township, committed to the creation of a wholly new worker-citizen. The private sector still remained a distant second in the city. If Bangalore by and large escaped the worst aspects of festering slums and blight, it was because town planning in its early stages was relatively sensitive to the needs of such—one must add—privileged workers. Still, there were signs aplenty of widespread disrespect for planning law, and for the reckless transformation of a very specific waterscape (water bodies known as tanks) in a city sited about one hundred kilometers from a perennial water source.

Beginning in the 1980s, the city dramatically departed from this phase of—still rather limited—industrialization as it oriented itself to another register, that of a global demand for immaterial production that the city was well placed to furnish. With the arrival, and the explosive growth of, deterritorialized production, Bangalore segued from being a site for the production of surplus to become a site of immaterial production and for the management of surplus, dominated by finance, banking, retail, and insurance. A small town became, in less than a decade, a metropolis. It was also detached from the region as it became plugged into a global economy, with the geographically proximate, rural hinterland merely a place to render into real estate.

We are yet to come to grips with the administrative chaos that has ensued from the growth of the urban, which is now delinked from its ties to an age of material industrial production, and suffers following the abdication of the state from its earlier redistributive responsibilities. We are yet to soberly take stock of the challenges these changes pose to planning itself, as the well-known binaries of town and country, culture and nature, legal and illegal lie in ruins. The academic incoherence that has been engendered by this explosive "end of the city" as we knew it, and the emergence now of an unbounded space, thus ironically provides a methodological opportunity. It also offers a possibility of recasting the conceptual tools that might have been appropriate to the city as a bounded, identifiable cultural, social, and physical form.

The pioneering importance of this book, structured around the concept of "speculative urbanism," lies precisely in its acceptance of this crisis as an opportunity for rethinking the urban in contemporary India. It also serves as a timely warning against the fatal neglect of the relationship between human life, activities, and energies on the one hand and the environment on the other, whose temporalities are disjunct from, or at least at an angle to, the speed with which the urban fabric is being transformed for human ends.

The book serves, too, as a critical document for our times because of its favored methodological orientation. It is a thick description, often from below, of the experience of dealing with urbanizing forces that are often exerted from afar. Its methodological innovativeness brings together more familiar stories (of dispossession) with new stories of hope and ambition (the *cheeti* or small loan schemes, modest levels of speculation on a small scale, and the [albeit self-exploitative and precarious] forms of work itself). Beneath the paralyzing scale of forces that operate on urban lives, the volume detects strategies for living, if not styles of overt defiance. Is the idea of citizenship being wrought anew in cities such as Bengaluru, where there is no doubt a robust presence of resident welfare associations, significantly marked by middle-class desire, but also the continued pursuit of social justice in the city, via people's organizations and a determined appeal to the law?

None of this detracts from the largely dystopic vision that emerges. Although India is far removed from the "planetary urbanization" once heralded by Henri Lefebvre, which has in turn inspired a small cottage industry of writing,[1] this Bengaluru-focused study enables readers via a rich empiricism to engage with the entanglements, dilemmas, predicaments, and opportunities presented by the ways in which global or national capital is deployed or withdrawn, to manipulate but also co-opt even less-endowed citizens. In the interstices of these planetary forces, some subaltern classes are endowed with the means of turning land and housing into an asset. Yet this is no celebration of native "cunning" or innately Indian "ways of being urban": if anything, the volume teaches us that beneath the planetary gentrification which is clearly taking shape, especially in the realm of real estate consumption, class lines are hardening, exaggerating the difference between the haves and have-nots for such essential services as water, power, and indeed access to the law itself. Thus, as I have pointed out elsewhere,[2] and as this work amply demonstrates, at a time when state planning is largely ineffective, it is planning itself that is offered as a service to those who can afford the gated enclave, which is also a guaranteed retreat from the city and its terrifying uncertainties. These are indeed, as Mike Davis aptly described it, the archisemiotics of class war.[3]

The book also reminds us that beneath the planetary gentrification, and despite the crushing power of the market over urbanizable land, inherited fault lines persist. We must not, for instance, allow the seeming contradiction of Bengaluru's economic miracle, which persists despite the overwhelming failures of planning, to mask the operation of the stigma of caste. In the case of Bangalore, caste foundationally deformed planning processes in the late nineteenth and early twentieth centuries. Its newer, "secularized" forms continue to determine opportunity and well-being in grotesquely uneven ways.

If anything, the secularization of caste takes many forms that render its discriminations invisible. For one, forms of eviction of the urban poor (and predominantly lower castes), whether by the state or private landlords, could occur not only by transparent legal means but also by stealth, namely, arson. Likewise, the burdens of provisioning for water fall disproportionately on the economically weaker sections of society, where lower-casteness and lower-classness are congruent. The urban poor are thus condemned to a state of "structured impermanence."

These forms of (societal) discrimination remain impervious not only to the otherwise homogenizing effect of the market but also to the forms of politics generated by representative democracy. This is another of the tectonic shifts that mark Bengaluru's passage from a small town, dominated by the public sector, to a metropolis driven by global capitalist forces. Whereas the city in the 1970s and 1980s could still boast of left-wing trade union representatives in the legislature, the seat of governance is now monopolized by those representing land and real estate interests.[4] What chance, then, of reimagining the urban in ways that foreground social justice or sustainability, or in order to redress gender/caste inequalities?

Yet Bengaluru remains a site of hope, and the close attention to two or three specific sites within this urban space generates the valuable insights of this book. Migrants may not be trading the relative "abundances" of the countryside (a mythical space of clean air, clean water, and open spaces) for the primordial squalor of the "city." The site represents the real hope of escaping the more egregious oppressions of the countryside, even if they are exchanged for quite exacting exploitation. Here there is the hope of resetting relations, of small-scale accumulation, and of relative political freedom.

With its focus on and rich embellishment of the concept of "speculative urbanism," the work implicitly emphasizes the urgency of integrating human and nonhuman elements and their discrepant temporalities in an urban reimagining, toward a cosmopolitical future. As such, it has no use for the nostalgia that is the hallmark of an increasing body of popular writing on Bangalore/Bengaluru, where a frenzied search for pasts cloaks and denies the death rattle of the city.

This book, in its very pessimism, foregrounds newly recognized imperatives that call for imagination and empathy, rather than the technoscientific fixes that currently absorb political representatives, industry captains, and the vast section of rentiers that the new urbanism has generated. Perhaps, too, this is an optimistic call for the return of a form of dirigisme, where the state once more assumes its place, not merely as the enabler of private profit and rent, but as a force that can imaginatively produce a public good and a cosmopolitical future.

Notes

1. Henri Lefebvre, "Dissolving City, Planetary Metamorphosis," in *Implosions/ Explosions: Towards a Study of Planetary Urbanization,* ed. Neil Brenner (Berlin: JOVIS, 2013), 562–71.

2. Janaki Nair, *The Promise of the Metropolis: Bangalore's Twentieth Century* (New Delhi: Oxford University Press, 2005), 162.

3. Mike Davis, *City of Quartz: Excavating the Future in Los Angeles* (Vintage Books, 1992), 231.

4. Sai Balakrishnan and Narendar Pani, "Real Estate Politicians in India," *Urban Studies* 58, no. 10 (2021): 2079–94.

Note on Confidentiality

To protect and respect the privacy and confidentiality of the many people who generously shared with us their time and thoughts, we have anonymized the exact locations of the urban and rural settlements of Bengaluru where the fieldwork on which many of the chapters are based was conducted, as well as the names of most interlocutors and organizations that participated in the study (unless referring to publicly available information). We use the real name of the larger area where our core city sites were located—Yeshwantpur—but anonymize the names of the specific neighborhoods and developments in that area where we carried out research. In the case of the peri-urban site, we use pseudonyms for the larger area where we worked as well as for the specific villages and other key places, such as the lake, mentioned in the book. Anonymized names are indicated by quotation marks on first use in each chapter.

Abbreviations

BBMP	Bruhat Bengaluru Mahanagara Palike (Greater Bengaluru Metropolitan Corporation)
BDA	Bangalore Development Authority
BJP	Bharatiya Janata Party
BMRCL	Bangalore Metro Rail Corporation Limited
CDP	Comprehensive Development Plan
CITB	City Improvement Trust Board
FDI	foreign direct investment
IPO	initial public offering
JNNURM	Jawaharlal Nehru National Urban Renewal Mission
KSDB	Karnataka Slum Development Board
MLA	Member of Legislative Assembly
MLC	Member of Legislative Council
MP	Member of Parliament
NRI	Non Resident Indian
ORR	Outer Ring Road
PRR	Peripheral Ring Road
SPV	special purpose vehicle

Introduction
Bengaluru as Urban Future
Carol Upadhya, Michael Goldman, and Vinay Gidwani

In late August and early September 2022, as we were working on the first draft of this book, the southern Indian city of Bengaluru[1] was brought to a virtual standstill by flooding caused by unseasonably heavy rains. Many roads and residential areas sank under water as lakes overflowed. An almost-finished brand-new highway connecting Bengaluru with the neighboring city of Mysuru (previously named Mysore) was submerged, and a major arterial road of the city—Outer Ring Road—was inundated, bringing traffic to a halt. The southeastern part of the city known as the IT corridor—the stretch of Outer Ring Road lined by tech parks and office buildings that forms the heart of Bengaluru's famous software industry—was the worst affected.

Pictures of fish caught from floodwaters and humorous memes proliferated on WhatsApp groups and Facebook, amid a crescendo of anguished complaints from citizens about the incompetence of the civic administration. The Outer Ring Road Companies Association wrote a strongly worded letter to the chief minister of the state of Karnataka, in which Bengaluru is located, complaining that businesses in the area had suffered a collective loss of 2.25 billion rupees (30 million USD) in just one day.[2] Videos of the city's corporate elite being rescued from their multimillion-dollar homes on tractors circulated widely through social media, while the misery of people living in informal settlements, migrant worker camps, and lower-middle-class colonies built on former paddy fields remained largely absent in media reports.

Because of their dramatically visible impact on business parks and upscale housing complexes, the floods damaged Bengaluru's brand

Figure I.1. The elevated Green Line of the Bangalore Metro cuts through the gentrifying neighborhood of Yeshwantpur. Photograph by Pierre Hauser.

image as a global IT hub. Once stories of the city's crumbling infrastructure made international news,[3] corporate elites laid the blame on incompetent and corrupt state governments, past and present, while politicians in power returned fire, alleging that it was the software companies that had constructed their campuses over stormwater drains and on the buffer zones of lakes. In response, the state government quickly announced a drive to clear the many "illegal encroachments" on channels and lakes that had impeded the natural flow of water. But only middle-class apartment buildings and the shanties of the poor were targeted for demolition—not the office complexes of big companies or the bungalows of the rich.

In August 2022, Bengaluru received more than twice the average amount of rainfall for the month, making it easy to attribute the problem to the uncontrollable effects of climate change. But the floods were nothing new. The southern and eastern parts of the city had been experiencing regular flooding since about 2005, even in normal monsoon seasons. Yet prior to the 2000s, flooding was practically unknown in Bengaluru. What had happened to make the city so vulnerable to floods?

Bengaluru is situated on a plateau, atop three main valley systems, each dotted with human-made tanks that formed a series of reservoirs linked by streams and channels. Many of these tanks were constructed in the sixteenth century or earlier, typifying the system of tank irrigation for agriculture found across much of southern India. Tanks were created by erecting dams on the undulating terrain to store water and were interconnected by channels known as *raja kaluve*, or grand canals. As rainwater accumulated in the tanks (now called lakes, although few are natural water bodies), they would overflow, the water cascading downstream through the connecting channels to fill other tanks. Some of these canals merged to form major streams feeding into rivers, and the flow of water downstream would also recharge groundwater.[4] As the city grew, successive rulers also constructed urban tanks or reservoirs to store water for domestic and other purposes, but many of Bengaluru's "lakes" began life as irrigation tanks of villages that were absorbed into the expanding city.

Beginning in the 1970s, as demand for land exploded and land values skyrocketed, developers—and even government agencies—began to fill in lake beds and channels (now referred to as stormwater drains), blocking these flows of water.[5] The formation of residential colonies on agricultural land, poorly planned infrastructure projects, and uncontrolled real estate development across the city further disrupted the simple yet effective traditional water management system.[6] Consequently, rainwater now accumulates in all the wrong places rather than being captured for future use. Moreover, water pumped from the Kaveri River three thousand feet uphill from more than ninety kilometers away is the core of Bengaluru's drinking water supply. Yet the populace increasingly relies on water pumped from the ground.[7] Overextraction has rapidly depleted the groundwater, which is also not being recharged due to extensive concretization and loss of green cover (see chapter 22).[8] Middle-class citizens have launched numerous campaigns to save Bengaluru's lakes, but the proposed solutions—such as fencing off water bodies to create privatized urban parks—more often contribute to the problem.[9]

By now, this story of disappearing lakes, blocked stormwater drains, and receding green cover is well known (and often told), although the structural shifts that led to this denouement are less visible. As Malini Ranganathan, who has been studying the city's flood risks since 2012, writes: "Beyond the inevitability of physical geography and weather, the origins of flood risk are *social*—inseparable from the history and politics of land and housing."[10]

With each round of floods and disruptions, many citizens vociferously blame the destruction of Bengaluru's system of tanks and channels on the recent history of illegal land-grabbing and organized encroachment on canals, lake beds, and wetlands by developers in connivance with politically powerful actors. The city's middle-class Twitterverse explodes with accusations: It's the greedy builders, the corrupt politicians, the lazy bureaucrats, or incompetent planners—everyone but themselves—who are responsible for the mess. Responding to the outcry, the city government springs into action, clearing a few encroachments—usually private houses whose owners have unwittingly built over long-buried and silted-up channels—and promising to cement the stormwater drains, a "solution" that will only exacerbate flooding.[11] The real estate companies that have constructed projects on wetlands or over *raja kaluve* are rarely, if ever, brought to book. But eventually, the floodwater recedes, the cleanup begins, financial damages are calculated, some relief money is distributed by the government, and the buildings targeted for demolition obtain stay orders from the court. Life returns to Bengaluru's new normal—water stagnating on the roads is replaced by the usual logjam of vehicles, belching fumes, and blaring horns.

Was all this inevitable? Is Bengaluru's spectacular environmental crisis simply the price of rapid economic development and urbanization—a series of problems that eventually will be fixed with improved infrastructure, more funding, better planning, or high-tech reengineering? Or is something fundamentally broken here—a deeply rooted systemic problem that needs to be uncovered and understood before these surface issues can be addressed? These are among the questions this book explores. As we discuss in the next section, Bengaluru's ecological degradation is inextricably entangled with the city's reinvention as a key hub of the global tech industry, bringing in investments of capital, an influx of migrant professionals and workers, and rapid real estate development.

The Worlding of Bangalore

Something happened in Bangalore before the new millennium. In 1985, Texas Instruments set up an offshore software center, importing

India's first satellite dish. The outsourcing model of back-office software development and IT-enabled services caught on quickly, as other multinational firms followed suit and Indian entrepreneurs and companies ventured into software development and other IT activities for clients in North America and Europe.

Bangalore's status as India's Silicon Plateau was bolstered by the Y2K crisis, which produced a flood of short-term contracts awarded by nervous firms across the West to Indian software outsourcing companies to help reset their computer systems. At pennies to the dollar, Indian engineers soon became the mainstay of IT systems maintenance and software development for global firms eager to outsource their software needs and dramatically reduce their costs, thus changing the nature of the industry and its workforces globally. For Bengaluru, promises of its presence in the global business world were balanced on the fulcrum of building new world-class infrastructure suitable to these globally oriented software firms.[12] When S. M. Krishna, chief minister of Karnataka between 1999 and 2004, declared his intention to turn Bangalore into a Singapore, or a global megalopolis, it was evident that the bug of urban transformation had lodged firmly in the hearts and minds of India's political leadership.[13]

These world-city aspirations were materialized in changes in urban governance, such as the relaxation of planning norms and the introduction of investment-friendly policies, in line with the neoliberal reforms that were being instituted at the national level (discussed in the following section).[14] As international investors descended on the city in search of windfall profits, local real estate firms rapidly expanded and professionalized by drawing on new sources of finance and catering to the rising demand for upmarket commercial and residential space.[15] Glitzy business parks and high-rise apartment complexes with multiple towers clustered on large sites of twenty to fifty hectares first appeared in the city during the late 1990s and early 2000s, funded mainly by investments by foreign private equity firms (especially from Wall Street).[16]

These developments created a land rush,[17] pushing up real estate prices to astronomical levels as developers, governmental agencies, and corporations competed to acquire agricultural land on the outskirts of the city as well as centrally located plots vacated by closed industries or cleared of slums.[18] Because of the huge sums of money that can be extracted from land deals, Bengaluru's real estate industry became entangled with formations of political power based on control over land.[19] The mechanisms of accumulation made possible by the expansion of real estate have also been shaped by the city's agrarian past—the monopoly over land enjoyed by particular caste and class groups, along with a complex land tenure system that makes property transactions difficult and opaque, created opportunities for rent-seeking. These layered histories of urban development reveal the complicated political economy of land and housing in the city, themes that are addressed in the following chapters.[20]

Bengaluru was at one time the fastest-growing city in Asia, and its growth has been phenomenal: the city's population swelled from 6.5 million in 2001, to 9.6 million in 2011, to an estimated 13.6 million in 2023. Much of this increase was due to the incorporation of surrounding settlements into the city as the municipal boundary was redrawn from time to time. Between 1971 and 2011 the geographical area of the Bengaluru Metropolitan Region (which includes Bangalore Urban and Bangalore Rural districts) grew four times, to 710 square kilometers (see spatial images in Plates 2.1 to 2.4, color insert), incorporating hundreds of villages and swallowing up floodplains, pastures, lakes, and drainage channels.[21] This expansion continues unabated even as Bengaluru's ecological sustainability is in grave doubt. Annual flooding is just one of several environmental crises in the city, which is notorious for its severe air pollution, traffic congestion, water shortages, and inadequate solid waste management.

The mushrooming of the business parks and steel-and-glass towers that house corporate workspaces became emblematic of the promises of globalization. By luring thousands of young people with its lucrative tech jobs as well as the burgeoning gig economy, the city is often held up as proof that liberalization works—that it creates economic mobility, or at least new aspirations for mobility. This narrative is reinforced by the proliferation of exclusive gated communities and "integrated townships," signaling the fulfillment of the unleashed desires of the newly affluent. Unlike their parents, who mostly belonged to the old middle class rooted in the public sector, Bengaluru's young professionals can afford to buy a car and their own home at a young age—also perhaps purchasing a second apartment later as an investment, ensuring their future through property ownership.[22] But what of other spaces and communities—the informal settlements of the workers who sustain the city and the lifestyles of the affluent classes,[23] as well as the rural villages that once thrived from producing food for the city?[24] These lives are thrown into turmoil by the real estate revolution, in varied and often contradictory ways.

The Speculative City Rises

The story of present-day Bengaluru starts with national—and global—economic policies that accelerated government disinvestment from state enterprises that provided public infrastructure and services, while requiring cities to attract investments from foreign finance capital and generate new revenues from user fees and land sales.[25] The discourse of the global city is marked by an opaque set of terms reflecting new financial tools designed to spirit in a flood of fresh capital to create world-class infrastructure. That is, large-scale capital flows would support the growing demand for infrastructure that can overcome the trenchant problems of a chaotic Indian city and catapult it into the realm of the global city. A world-class metro rail system will affordably relieve the streets and its travelers of the headaches of traffic jams; a well-capitalized water infrastructure will finally protect the fragile lakes and deliver water for all; and more gated communities will address the professional classes' desire for more luxurious housing to live in and/or use as a productive asset for investment. Or so goes the narrative.

The larger context of this whirlwind of change in Bengaluru is India's economic reforms of the 1990s—the neoliberal turn[26]—with its four basic, actual or aspirational, shifts: from public to private finance; from state-owned enterprises and utilities to their disinvestment and/or privatization; from a policy commitment to long-term employment to union busting and the informalization of work; and from the productive economy (making and growing) to a service-oriented and financialized (making money from money) economy. The Indian government, with the support of the World Bank and the Asian Development Bank, instituted urban reforms through, first, the Jawaharlal Nehru Urban Renewal Mission, launched in 2005—an urban policy framework that aimed to invest some national capital in cities willing to design new projects based on borrowed capital. This was followed in 2015 by the Atal Mission for Rejuvenation and

Urban Transformation, which took a similar approach to providing "water and sewage for all." The most recent avatar of urban policy is the Smart Cities Mission, which has targeted one hundred cities for rapid infrastructure upgrades, aimed at providing a "decent quality of life to its citizens" and a "clean and sustainable environment" through technology-based solutions.[27] At the center of these new economic policies is the proposition that cities are "engines of economic growth" and hence that effort and resources must be channeled into redeveloping urban spaces and developing new infrastructure to make cities attractive to capital. But this official rationale doesn't capture the tumult and volatility that waves of financialization have wrought on city life.

How have these changes affected urban governance? First, these policies stipulate that every grant or loan delivered by the central government would be a fraction of what urban projects require. State and city governments and local agencies must borrow the rest from international or domestic capital markets, with the expectation that the infrastructure built would generate its own funds to repay investors. Under these debt-induced arrangements, the city is transformed from one that ideally serves a public interest and a common social ethos by providing public space, goods, and services (however unequal in access), into one that must recover costs for every service provided.[28]

Second, under pressure from national governments and global actors to embrace this high-risk agenda, cities in India have shifted from the public provisioning of goods and services to a policy approach known as municipal entrepreneurialism,[29] based on claims that governments are too inefficient in how they provide housing, water, roads, and infrastructure. Instead of these essential goods being delivered by government agencies with (often unionized) employees, cities must recalibrate to conform to a governance model that outsources essential services and runs their agencies with fees and rents secured from the population.[30] Key policy changes included disinvestment from state enterprises (thereby freeing up valuable urban land) and the decentralization of urban administration and planning functions. In India these economic and urban governance reforms ushered in a new phase of real estate–led urban development. A crucial turning point was the central government's 2005 decision to permit 100 percent foreign direct investment in real estate ventures. This opened the floodgates to private international capital, which flowed rapidly into property development and underwrote the expansion and corporatization of India's real estate sector.

But this sea change is not unique to India. The financialization of the city, aimed at extracting value through capital circulation—from interest, dividends, rents, tolls, user fees, and short-term capital gains—is a process that is occurring worldwide.[31] When financiers lend, their shareholders and clients around the world expect top-dollar rates of return, otherwise they would invest elsewhere—toll roads in Chicago, housing projects in Madrid, tunnels in Istanbul. ("Why should we invest in risky India when we can invest in safer, high-return projects elsewhere?," investors ask.)[32] There is an imposed inevitability—and performativity—to this relationship. With promises of global capital inflows, national and local firms jump into the fray and invest in speculative land and property acquisitions. Exclusive residential towers and shopping malls, restaurant districts, business enclaves, and private schools for the nouveau riche sprout in the vicinity of large-scale infrastructure projects. As national governments retreat and small investors have only limited pools of reserves, corporate financiers (domestic and foreign) appear as the only source of much-needed capital with which to break ground for these city-expanding projects.

Thrown into this uneven power dynamic, city governments find themselves revamping their relationship with city dwellers. In the process of becoming agents of the economy rather than planners of the city, municipalities are asking inhabitants to cultivate a new sensibility as risk-taking customers and consumers. This is a far cry from an earlier belief that cities offer people a set of freedoms, rights, and amenities unavailable in the countryside. To compound matters, when land prices and home rents skyrocket as quickly and unrelentingly as they have in recent years, urban citizenship also becomes a speculative endeavor in which one must outpace the rent race to survive and stay in place. Speculation, in short, is as much an imaginative future-divining project as it is a financial one: people are compelled to recognize that they need to gamble on new ways to earn, to prosper—or merely survive—in the speculative city.

In this entrepreneurial context, it is no longer assured that national and subnational state treasuries will reliably underwrite the construction and upkeep of such infrastructure. Although the central government continues to defray the costs of infrastructure building in many instances, the social covenant has morphed. Increasingly, cities must prove that these new projects can pay for themselves through full cost recovery. The problem is that borrowing large sums of money from capital markets requires different acumen and a new power base—in terms of how to deal with actors in these capital markets and their self-designed rules of the game. Whereas in previous eras, national governments might have approached international lenders such as the World Bank and the Asian Development Bank for loans at low interest rates to finance megaprojects, individual cities are now required to borrow from these institutions as well as from capital markets.[33] But since cities have much smaller budgets than national or state governments and cannot run deficits (unlike nation-states), they are compelled to use land and public spaces as collateral for such loans. This is called "assetization of land"—because it can be securitized and traded globally as holdings that yield rents.[34] The compulsion to convert land with multiple uses, supporting diverse livelihoods, into exchangeable property often leads to the eviction of informal settlements and minoritized communities accused of encroaching on government land.[35]

After more than two decades of experimentation with global-city best practices for transforming urban agglomerations around the world into economic growth engines, the persistence of housing scarcity, compounding ecological crises, intensifying political conflicts around land, and widespread impoverishment raises the possibility that this prevalent model of urban transformation is not working as advertised. Is the solution envisioned by the global cities model itself becoming a part of the problem, and if so, why? Are cities like Bengaluru our urban future and, if so, which vector of forces is propelling this future and with what economic, societal, and ecological implications?

A Collaborative Effort

These questions led us to undertake a comparative investigation of two of Asia's fastest-growing cities, Bengaluru (India) and Jakarta (Indonesia). This research project, titled "Speculative Urbanism: Land, Labor, and Finance Capital," tracked the entanglements of global and domestic financial capital flows, real estate development, rural land-based livelihoods, and the shifting terrain of urban work and aspirations.[36] Through long-term, grounded field research we explored how the worlds of high finance and world-class infrastructure have shaped the strategies of local elites seeking new ways to invest and profit, as well as the dilemmas of ordinary working-class and rural people balancing the fear of being swept aside by the juggernaut of rapid urbanization with the desire to stay put and gain from the chaos of fast-paced change.

Market reforms, accelerating since the early 1990s, have significantly shaped urban trajectories in both countries. Like many other expanding cities in the global South, Bengaluru and Jakarta have been rapidly transformed by large, space-consuming real estate developments (new gated communities, industrial estates, residential-commercial-entertainment complexes) as well as large infrastructure projects (airports, superhighways, vast power grids), disrupting and displacing communities that function as residential and livelihood spaces for the majority of urban residents.[37] As noted above, key to the global-city approach is the conversion of land and properties into commercially generative, rent-yielding tracts using innovative administrative and financial arrangements that connect foreign and domestic investors and institutions with local counterparts. While land has been long understood as a social and ecological asset for urban and peri-urban dwellers—a prerequisite for livelihoods, communities, and biodiversity—under the global-city-making agenda land has increasingly become a speculative asset that is valued primarily for its rent-generating capacities and expected future price, a shift that has become crucial to these urban transformations. We call this multiscalar and multidimensional process "speculative urbanism," a term that we elaborate upon in the next section.

The comparison of Bengaluru and Jakarta generated valuable insights into how the global-city model of development embraced by planners and developers in both cities is working in practice. We found that the legal and extra-legal procedures by which land is acquired, and the pathways through which private and public funds are mobilized for real estate and infrastructure development, differ in notable ways due to Indonesia and India's distinct postcolonial histories and political economies. But we also discovered surprising similarities in terms of on-the-ground outcomes, raising important questions about the costs and benefits of current trajectories of urbanization in cities of the global South. Although this book does not encompass the Jakarta component of the study, valuable lessons learned from the comparison inform our discussion.[38]

Chronicles of a Global City evokes the kaleidoscopic effects of speculative urbanism in Bengaluru through an assortment of stories. Most of the research on Bengaluru was carried out in two main field sites—one in a central part of the city and the other on its swiftly expanding frontier. We focused on the processes by which land is assembled for real estate and infrastructure projects; the role of financial, business, political, and policy networks in shaping the dominant regime of urban development; and the multiple ways in which speculative urbanism transforms the lives of ordinary people, the social relations that bind them, and the environments they inhabit.

The core city site, Yeshwantpur, was selected because it was among the urban zones to be targeted for redevelopment—envisioned as the gateway to the world-class IT city. In what was once one of Bangalore's prime industrial areas, the closure of many public- and private-sector factories released large tracts of land for sale to developers. This, together with new infrastructure projects such as road-widening and a metro rail line, paved the way for high-end residential and commercial real estate projects. Our peri-urban site on the south-eastern edge of the city, which we call "Purvapur" (see the Note on Confidentiality), was chosen because it had recently become a prime site for the construction of new residential projects on land acquired from local farmers. Here, our aim was to understand the social, economic, and ecological consequences of this land transformation and rapid urbanization for agrarian livelihoods and rural communities. Our site-specific research design illustrated the ripple effects and disruptions of global-city-making for Bengaluru's working classes and its fraying urban ecologies. We found evidence of inequality, discontent, and resistance among residents, but also inventive strategies of survival and income generation. Our extensive field research revealed how the worlds of high finance and world-class infrastructure inhabit shared spaces with local elites seeking new ways to invest and profit, how government officials are creating new forms of governance based on the business of land acquisition, and how working-class and rural people are managing both the fear of being swept aside and the desire to gain ground in the chaos of fast-paced change.

This book rests on the cooperative labor of many people, including its three editors (who were also the principal investigators [PIs] of the Bengaluru component of the Speculative Urbanism project), research assistants, our postdoctoral associate, and consultants, as well as community members and our interlocutors—emphatically demonstrating that creating knowledge is a collective undertaking (see Acknowledgments). As co-PIs and editors, we tried to share the multifaceted work of research and writing equally, notwithstanding the intermittent unevenness that attends such joint endeavors. The authorship of the chapters reflects the collaborative nature of this volume. Although all the chapters carry the names of individual authors, most are the outcome of collaboration by several different team members and others in carrying out the fieldwork, analysis, and writing. Notes at the end of various chapters recognize these contributions. Most chapters draw on our extensive archive of interviews, life stories, observations, and field notes from our long duration, in-depth ethnographic research. They are also products of multiple conversations, debates, and collective thinking within the project group (and beyond) over several years. The chapters by members of the research team are supplemented by invited essays written by, or interviews with, key public intellectuals and activists in the city, to broaden the range of voices represented in the volume.

In this volume we share just a few of the many stories we collected through hundreds of interviews and interactions with many different interlocutors in and around Bengaluru. The book starts with accounts from Bengaluru's eminent movers and shakers—an architect and two prominent developers who have led the design and construction of ambitious mixed-use projects in the city. We hear their persuasive visions of urban metamorphosis in a city bursting with entrepreneurial energy and cosmopolitan aspirations, hobbled by temporary problems but on the verge of joining the ranks of the world's major conurbations. Subsequently, we encounter the voices of the city's common people—the farmers whose families have cultivated the lands around Bengaluru for generations, land now occupied by tech parks and upscale gated communities; the laborers who came from far away to build the city and keep it running; app-based delivery workers and street vendors who provision the city's residents with essential goods and services; residents of low-income neighborhoods occupying land that has suddenly become valuable; and the domestic workers whose toil sustains the lifestyles of the city's wealthy and new middle class. The stories of these various actors convey a palpable and mounting anxiety about trying to keep up, to maintain a foothold in a city driven by volatile powerful forces of speculation, dispossession, profit, ecological destruction, and constant change. The daily lives of Bengaluru's non-elite inhabitants shed new insights into what has gone wrong—into why India's Silicon Plateau, the hub of its globally famous software outsourcing industry, now reinventing itself as a "startup capital," seems incapable of solving its many urban crises.

While the accounts that populate this book are deeply embedded in the history, culture, and economy of Bengaluru, and of the state of Karnataka where it is located, we believe that the issues we explore here are of concern not only to Bangaloreans (past or present) or Indians, but also to ordinary people, policymakers, and academics across the world. The lessons from these stories are meant to travel.

Unpacking Speculative Urbanism

One way to grasp these game-changing upheavals in the lives of cities and their inhabitants—one marked by a tense coupling of financial uncertainty and galloping aspirations—is through the idea of *speculative urbanism*. As our anchoring concept for this book, it chronicles the logic and lure of "world-class" city-making that gathered force in the late twentieth century, armed with an audacious imagination of *what the new urban could be*.[39] The archipelago of artificial islands in the shape of the world map built in the Persian Gulf off the coast of Dubai is an iconic instance of the world-class city as a spectacle. Not to be outdone, Turkey has planned to make Istanbul into the "capital of the world" through a series of dramatic infrastructure projects, including the world's largest airport, the EuroAsia Tunnel linking both continents, and the Istanbul Canal linking the Mediterranean to the Black Sea. Similar schemes and designs have popped up in different national capitals around the world—a testament to the far-flung travels and traction of this discourse. The pressure is on cities to perform in this highly competitive, expensive, and outlandish global ecosystem. The relatively undiscussed underside of these ventures is: How will governments and citizens repay the investors who underwrite these grand ventures?

To help us understand the multilayered circumstances unfolding in Bengaluru, we highlight six basic characteristics of speculative urbanism, each explicated by a section of this book.

First, the idea of speculative urbanism was born from a dreamscape that emerged from elite global networks grappling with the ruptures of the neoliberal era of the 1970s and 1980s in which cities suffered from crumbling infrastructure and inadequate government (or state) support. Years of successive global-city platforms, conferences, and reports coalesced into a battle cry for warp-speed development, a *new discourse of global urbanization.* One promoter of this paradigm, McKinsey's Infrastructure Practice and the McKinsey Global Institute, wrote in 2013 that "$57 trillion will need to be spent on building and maintaining infrastructure worldwide between now and 2030," an amount "greater than the estimated value of all the world's infrastructure assets today."[40]

This is the theme of part 1 of the book, "Speculative Stories." Three chapters in the section present Bengaluru-based elites articulating a vision influenced by this globally circulating discourse of a new urban mindset and trajectory, one based on high-risk speculation with the potential for windfall gains from the construction of state-of-the-art infrastructure such as new business centers, a citywide metro rail project, new toll roads, upgraded water and sewerage systems, and amenity-full residential complexes. As the discourse declares: Set your goals high, borrow ambitiously, and the payoff will be monumental. Speculation as yarns or stories about a future-in-the-making is a vital and underemphasized aspect of this discourse. The sociologist Jens Beckert has coined the term "fictional expectations"—"the images actors form as they consider future states of the world, the way they visualize causal relations, and the ways they perceive their actions influencing outcomes"[41]—to describe the conjuring of this projected new condition. Similarly, focusing on speculation in land and property markets, D. Asher Ghertner and Robert Lake underscore how this involves the telling of "social stories through which land is narrated as a commodity to produce particular political-economic effects."[42] In this section the audacious visions of architects and real estate developers are leavened in one chapter by the critical take on this transformation narrated by a local farmer.

Also critical to this promise is the creation of new *financial tools, forms,* and *strategies,* the *second* characteristic of speculative urbanism. The corporate sector has introduced a range of instruments and contractual obligations, such as initial public offerings (IPOs), special purpose vehicles (SPVs), real estate investment trusts (REITs), and nonperforming assets (NPAs), to support expansive new investments in luxury residential complexes, business parks, and infrastructure in cities around the world, including Bengaluru. One of the global finance sector's great accomplishments of the early 2000s has been to successfully convert fixed physical infrastructure in cities worldwide into a singular *global asset class:* a Wall Street term reflecting an exciting new megamarket for investors, one that analysts claim is already an $80 trillion industry.[43] Consequently, the money pouring into Bengaluru comes partly from loans and capital investments from around the world, a phenomenon that the development banks call a win-win strategy that increases shareholder value *and* promises world-class goods and services to citizens. Hence even during the dark days of the recent global economic downturn and Covid-19 pandemic, investors such as the New York–based private equity firm Blackstone made extraordinarily high profit rates from investments in India.[44]

The chapters in part 2, "Financial Stratagems," reveal the many incarnations of finance in city life, from the newly pulsating flows of private equity capital from New York's Wall Street and Mumbai's Dalal Street to the more quotidian forms of "low finance" that support the needs of the urban low-income majority in their aspirations to cope with and earn from these changes in the urban economy. While the city throbs with hope and anxiety, many people who are unable to access formal finance find other channels to borrow money to speculate on their next opportunity. Low finance encompasses practices such as informal money lending and revolving credit groups that can underwrite a range of survival needs and family expenses. It also defrays the costs of small-scale construction of extra rooms in one's small home to rent out to migrant workers also trying to make it in the speculative city (chapter 11). By enabling participation in rental markets, low finance can be the grease that lubricates the wheel of speculation for the urban majority.

These new roles for finance capital could only have emerged with the active participation of the state in what we call *speculative governance*—the *third* characteristic of speculative urbanism.[45] For Bengaluru, some of these changes have come from the major financial agencies such as the Asian Development Bank and Japan's development aid agency (Japan International Cooperation Agency), which promote these ideas through policy-linked loans to government agencies overseeing the water utility, the sanitation network, and the metro rail transit system.[46] Some of the most significant financial-sector reforms, which have enabled nontraditional financial entities and practices to sprout and thrive in countries where they were once banned or heavily regulated, have occurred at critical moments, such as the 1997 Asian financial crisis and the 2008 global financial crisis. After such episodes, governments responded by further liberalizing rather than tightening the rules overseeing overseas finance. Not only do these reforms reflect the "tough love" conditionalities of International Monetary Fund and World Bank debt relief and loan packages; they also mimic the calls by global-urban advocates to open our cities to the "creative powers" of finance for a twenty-first-century urban transformation.

The chapters in part 3, "State Speculations," demonstrate how various state agents redesign public spaces to accommodate this financializing economy, producing new types of urban space that cater to forms of consumption and transit that privilege the elite and marginalize low-income populations. These governance practices exacerbate tensions within the context of the millions of daily bus riders and the relatively fewer metro rail commuters, proliferating private housing projects versus the dwindling of public-sector housing societies, and land-use changes that become a boon for private developers.

Next we identify a *fourth* characteristic of speculative urbanism, the emergence of a new *speculative orientation*, with corresponding modes of conduct, that pervades the everyday of city life. Life in Bengaluru today summons, even demands, an improvisational comportment—strategies of learning, as it were—that allows residents to keep up with spiraling global-city ambitions and rents in the context of dwindling state provisioning of public goods, services, and spaces.[47] To stay put if not advance, citizens must embrace speculative prospects of various kinds, mirroring the risk-laden strategies of world-class city-making and management championed by government and corporate entities. Speculation is not just a type of economic action, nor is it located only in the sphere of high finance—it is also a cultural orientation and social practice that generates new meanings and values across society.[48] Of key significance is the multivalent character of speculation: an orientation to an uncertain future that combines imagination, anticipation, risk-taking, compulsion, and the desire for mobility and material accumulation.[49] The anticipation of wealth from selling land, accumulating urban property, brokering land deals, or dabbling in informal finance permeates the atmosphere in Bengaluru—as much part of the city's promise[50] as is the startup ecosystem that is the latest avatar of the city elites' obsession with technological change.[51]

The chapters in part 4, "Speculative Subjects," illustrate how speculation encompasses the city's elite *and* ordinary residents, with differing effects for working-class and lower-caste slum dwellers, small farmers, and street vendors. They reveal how people respond to their turbulent existence by actively participating in "chains of rentiership"[52] that arise from large-scale construction projects. Such projects routinely trigger both a cascading set of displacements and speculative opportunities for gain through rental income, property brokerage, land transactions, and petty businesses.[53] Although embedded in hierarchies of power shaped by gender, class, caste, and religion, many people nevertheless find ways to join the speculative game and hope to profit from it. Families disrupted by the shuttering of nearby factories rebound by taking loans from informal moneylenders to add rooms for rent atop their modest homes. Local residents, particularly men, capitalize on the booming property market by working as brokers.[54] In short, speculative urbanism shakes up settled norms and patterns while offering room for new income-generating possibilities. But while inclusive in unexpected ways, it also results in a litany of exclusions for many segments of the working population in the process of accumulation.

The chapters in part 5, "Labor in the Speculative City," underscore a *fifth* attribute of speculative urbanism: the *precarious existence* of construction workers, domestic workers, street vendors, and gig workers, whose labor—alongside that of waste pickers, sanitation workers, security guards, restaurant employees, and many others—underwrites the lifestyles of Bengaluru's middle-class and elite residents and, less visibly, furnishes and renews the conditions of possibility for economic and social life in the city. For instance, despite the celebratory hype about the employment potential of the platform economy, the average app-based service worker must follow a punishing daily routine in the hope of earning even a living wage. More broadly, we find that the waves of small-town and rural migrants who flow into the expanding city in search of work struggle to keep up with the mounting expense of living in the city on a meager income, with pitfalls and obstacles confronting them at every turn. Laboring in the speculative city is a story of endless trials and hardship.

Rapid urban transformations produce *speculative ecologies*, the *sixth* and final attribute of speculative urbanism. We find a landscape beset by multiple environmental crises, from flooding to water scarcity, air pollution to sewage overruns, degradation of water bodies to loss of tree cover and biodiversity—all combining to add uncertainty to urban existence and placing a question mark on the sustainability of Bengaluru's urban future. The chapters in part 6, "Ecologies of Speculation," highlight the environmental foundations of urban transformation. The year 2022 seemed to be a turning point across the world in terms of extreme weather events caused by climate change: for some cities it was severe drought and heat, and for Bengaluru it was the destructive floods while suffering from a profound scarcity of drinking water. The rapid expansion of the city in just a few decades, gobbling up hundreds of villages and towns as well as floodplains, forests, pastures, watersheds, lakes, and drainage channels, has been contingent on the expectation that the IT revolution would transform the city's wealth and future. Yet, as the IT corridor was built on wetlands, with its lakes and channels paved over with expansive residential complexes replete with concrete parking lots, recreation centers, pools and sports courts, the region's ecology is flashing signs of implosion. The dream of a world-class city might be fated to drown in a torrent of sewage and floodwaters.

Bengaluru as Urban Future

To be clear: We are not suggesting that Bengaluru is somehow unique or an outlier. Yes, it has been caught in a tangled net of political wrongdoing, massive public and private debt, and the bankruptcy of farmers and small business owners. But this is also true for Madrid,

Istanbul, Jakarta, New York City, and hundreds of smaller cities across the world that suffer from similar ill effects of speculative urbanism. In short, this is not a global South problem or even an Indian one. The compulsions, and the entangled social dynamics, of financialization are unabashedly global, however uneven their effects may be. The challenge of political and social movements today is to understand the root causes behind the social inequities and environmental calamities that haunt aspiring cities like Bengaluru, and to carve out an alternative pathway based on the basic premises of ecological and social justice.[55]

Bengaluru is paradigmatic of the afflictions that bedevil city-making projects around the planet. Its transformation illustrates our main idea—speculative urbanism. The dramatic changes in rural communities and livelihoods, the urban waterscape decimated by overbuilding, the dispossession of farmers—cannot be reduced to the notion that this is what happens with urbanization, understood as a natural corollary of economic growth. Nor has Bengaluru's uncontrolled expansion been simply a response to the rising demand for housing and commercial space. Rather, it reflects speculative investments in land and real estate that have become prime loci of (profit-oriented) value extraction and capital accumulation in the midst of political-economic and cultural crosscurrents converging across the world today. While these investments are underwritten in part by flows of private equity capital and globally circulating policy prescriptions (cities as engines of growth), they are also underpinned by the murky politics of India's exploding cities, where land-grabbing and risky real estate ventures are closely entangled with hungry political power.

This book steps into the experiences and lifeworlds of a range of actors as they seek to live the speculative city. It uncovers some of the main trends at the crossroads of urbanization and financialization as a way to better understand what is unfolding in the city and its surroundings, exploring through congealed and dissident rhythms of city life what Henri Lefebvre called "the everyday."[56] A wide array of urban studies scholars working on the global South have expanded upon this approach by highlighting the agency, experiences, and knowledge of the people most often eclipsed, erased, and overshadowed in narratives of urban change. Following this method, we focus on the everyday that produces both the conditions of the lived experience in

Bengaluru and the spatial dimensions and built environment in which people live.

We make two final observations here, drawing from the voices and sentiments of city dwellers whom we interviewed. First, the power of finance and high-value urban projects cannot succeed without engaging already-existing inequalities that have cleared out space for speculation and helped to reproduce social hierarchies in space. Second, when searching for everyday critiques and alternatives, we listen to those caught in the maelstrom of speculative urbanism to learn about alternative imaginaries and practices.

The stories that you will read in the following chapters grapple with questions of urban belonging and citizenship, agrarian transformation, and how the city can become an ecologically and socially just place for all.

Notes

1. Formerly known by the anglicized name Bangalore, the city was renamed Bengaluru in 2014. In this book we use "Bengaluru" when referring to recent developments and "Bangalore" when writing about the past.

2. "August 30 Floods: IT Firms, Banks on ORR Say They Lost ₹225 Crore in a Single Day," *The Hindu*, September 3, 2022, https://www.thehindu.com /news/cities/bangalore/august-30-floods-it-firms-banks-on-orr-say-they-lost -225-crore-in-a-single-day/article65846490.ece.

3. Sameer Yasir and Emily Schmall, "In India's Tech Capital, Floods Leave Workers Riding Tractors to Work," *New York Times*, September 6, 2022, https:// www.nytimes.com/2022/09/06/world/asia/india-bangalore-floods.html.

4. Harini Nagendra, *Nature in the City: Bengaluru in the Past, Present, and Future* (New Delhi: Oxford University Press, 2016).

5. "Why Bangalore Floods—Understanding History and Location," *Citizen Matters*, October 10, 2022, https://citizenmatters.in/why-certain-areas-in -bengaluru-flood-part-2/#:~:text=However%2C%20over%20the%20last%20few ,high%20grounds%20on%20three%20sides.

6. Michael Goldman and Devika Narayan, "Water Crisis through the Analytic of Urban Transformation: An Analysis of Bangalore's Hydrosocial Regimes," *Water International* 44, no. 2 (2019): 95–114. Satellite imagery clearly reveals the rapid shrinking or disappearance of water bodies. See H. S. Sudhira, T. V. Ramachandra, and M. H. Bala Subrahmanya, "City Profile: Bangalore," *Cities* 24, no. 5 (2007): 379–90; H. A. Bharath et al., "Green to Gray: Silicon Valley of India," *Journal of Environmental Management* 206 (2018): 1287–95.

7. As the traditional water supply system was destroyed by uncontrolled

development, Bangalore began to rely on the Cauvery Water Supply Scheme for drinking water drawn from the Kaveri River (the water supply scheme retains the old anglicized name). Since this source is insufficient to meet the needs of a growing population, the city increasingly depends on groundwater extracted through borewells and distributed through private tankers controlled by a "water mafia." See Malini Ranganathan, "'Mafias' in the Waterscape: Urban Informality and Everyday Public Authority in Bangalore," *Water Alternatives* 7, no. 1 (2014): 89–105.

8. The city's green cover fell from around 68 percent in the early 1970s, to 45 percent in the late 1990s, to less than 3 percent of its total area of 741 square kilometers in 2021, according to T. V. Ramachandra of the Indian Institute of Science, who has been documenting the city's ecological degradation for many years. Devjyot Ghoshal and Nivedita Bhattacharjee, "Traffic, Water Shortages, Now Floods: The Slow Death of India's Tech Hub?," *Reuters*, September 15, 2022, https://www.reuters.com/world/india/traffic-water-shortages-now-floods-slow-death-indias-tech-hub-2022-09-15/.

9. See Jayaraj Sundaresan, "Planning as Commoning: Transformation of a Bangalore Lake," *Economic & Political Weekly* 46, no. 50 (2011): 71–79. Middle-class civic activism in Bengaluru also addresses issues of solid waste management (the perennial "garbage problem") and traffic congestion, among others. See "Sustainable Food Consumption, Urban Waste Management, and Civic Activism Lessons from Bangalore/Bengaluru, India," ed. Christine Lutringer and Shalini Randeria, special e-issue of *International Development Policy* 8, no. 2 (2017), https://doi.org/10.4000/poldev.2475. Such interventions in the city's mounting environmental problems often build on a nostalgic longing for the erstwhile "garden city." See Camille Frazier, "Urban Heat: Rising Temperatures as Critique in India's Air-Conditioned City," *City & Society* 31, no. 3 (2019): 441–61; Hemangini Gupta, "What Do We Talk about When We Talk about Heat?," *City & Society* 33, no. 3 (2021), https://doi.org/10.1111/ciso.12381.

10. Malini Ranganathan, "Why Bengaluru Is Not Immune to Floods: It's All about Land (and Money)," *Citizen Matters*, December 10, 2015, https://bengaluru.citizenmatters.in/why-bengaluru-is-not-immune-to-floods-it-s-all-about-land-and-money-17973; Leo F. Saldanha, "How Caste and Class Divisions Caused Bengaluru's Flooding," *The Wire*, September 15, 2022, https://thewire.in/rights/bengaluru-flood-caste-class.

11. Rasheed Kappan, "Bengaluru Floods: Anatomy of a Drainage System Gone Horribly Wrong," *Newslaundry*, September 13, 2022, https://www.newslaundry.com/2022/09/13/bengaluru-floods-anatomy-of-a-drainage-system-gone-horribly-wrong.

12. Janaki Nair, *The Promise of the Metropolis: Bangalore's Twentieth Century* (New Delhi: Oxford University Press, 2005).

13. Janaki Nair, "Singapore Is Not Bangalore's Destiny," *Economic and Political Weekly* 35, no. 18 (2000): 1512–14.

14. Asha Ghosh, "Public-Private or a Private Public? Promised Partnership of the Bangalore Agenda Task Force," *Economic and Political Weekly* 40, no. 47 (2005): 4914–22; James Heitzman, *Network City: Information Systems and Planning in India's Silicon Valley* (Delhi: Oxford University Press, 2003); Mathew Idiculla, "New Regimes of Private Governance: The Case of Electronics City in Peri-urban Bengaluru," *Economic and Political Weekly* 51, no. 17 (2016): 102–9.

15. Michael Goldman, "Speculative Urbanism and the Making of the Next World City," *International Journal of Urban and Regional Research* 35, no. 3 (2011): 555–81; Ludovic Halbert and Hortense Rouanet, "Filtering Risk Away: Global Finance Capital, Transcalar Territorial Networks and the (Un)Making of City-Regions: An Analysis of Business Property Development in Bangalore, India," *Regional Studies* 48, no. 3 (2014): 471–84; John Stallmeyer, *Building Bangalore: Architecture and Urban Transformation in India's Silicon Valley* (Routledge, 2010); "Bangalore's Great Transformation," *Seminar* 694 (June 2017), https://www.india-seminar.com/cd8899/cd_frame8899.html. The idea of "worlding" that we invoke here comes from Ananya Roy and Aihwa Ong, eds., *Worlding Cities: Asian Experiments in the Art of Being Global* (Malden, Mass.: Wiley-Blackwell, 2011).

16. The property boom peaked between 2012 and 2014, after which the real estate market experienced a slowdown. But the big real estate companies that emerged during the boom years remain key arbiters of Bengaluru's urban development trajectory, arguably reshaping the city in unsustainable ways.

17. Annelies Zoomers et al., "The Rush for Land in an Urbanizing World: From Land Grabbing toward Developing Safe, Resilient, and Sustainable Cities and Landscapes," *World Development* 92 (2017): 242–52. Also see Michael Levien, *Dispossession without Development: Land Grabs in Neoliberal India* (Oxford: Oxford University Press, 2018).

18. The term "slum" is employed in official laws and policies in India; hence we have retained the term here in relevant contexts.

19. Sai Balakrishnan and Narendar Pani, "Real Estate Politicians in India," *Urban Studies* 58, no. 10 (2021): 2079–94.

20. An emerging literature on "agrarian urbanism" foregrounds this dimension of urbanization in south Asia. See Shubhra Gururani, "Cities in a World of Villages: Agrarian Urbanism and the Making of India's Urbanizing Frontiers," *Urban Geography* 41, no. 7 (2020): 971–89; Malini Ranganathan, "Caste, Racialization, and the Making of Environmental Unfreedoms in Urban India," *Ethnic and Racial Studies* 45, no. 2 (2021): 257–77; Carol Upadhya and Sachinkumar Rathod, "Caste at the City's Edge: Land Struggles in Peri-urban Bengaluru," *South Asia Multidisciplinary Academic Journal* [*SAMAJ*, online] 26 (2021), http://journals.openedition.org/samaj/7134.

21. In 1991, 189 villages of Bangalore North and South districts were brought under Bangalore Urban Agglomeration, and another 110 villages were incorporated into the city in 2007 when the new municipal authority, the Greater Bangalore Municipal Corporation (now called the Greater Bengaluru Metropolitan

Corporation and commonly referred to as BBMP), was created. See Nair, *The Promise of the Metropolis*, 147.

22. Carol Upadhya, *Reengineering India: Work, Capital, and Class in an Offshore Economy* (Delhi: Oxford University Press, 2016).

23. Supriya RoyChowdhury, *City of Shadows: Slums and Informal Work in Bangalore* (Cambridge: Cambridge University Press, 2021).

24. Seema Purushothaman and Sheetal Patil, *Agrarian Change and Urbanization in Southern India: City and the Peasant* (Singapore: Springer, 2019).

25. Michael Goldman and Devika Narayan, "Through the Optics of Finance: Speculative Urbanism and the Transformation of Markets," *International Journal of Urban and Regional Research* 45, no. 2 (2021): 209–31. See also Economic and Political Weekly, *Quarter Century of Liberalization in India: Looking Back and Looking Ahead* (New Delhi: Oxford University Press, 2018); Ravinder Kaur, "World as Commodity, or How the 'Third World' Became an 'Emerging Market,'" *Comparative Studies of South Asia, Africa and the Middle East* 38, no. 2 (2018): 377–95.

26. David Harvey, *A Brief History of Neoliberalism* (New York: Oxford University Press, 2007).

27. For the Smart Cities policy, see https://smartcities.gov.in/.

28. Malini Ranganathan, "Paying for Pipes, Claiming Citizenship: Political Agency and Water Reforms at the Urban Periphery," *International Journal of Urban and Regional Research* 38, no. 2 (2014): 590–608.

29. David Harvey, "From Managerialism to Entrepreneurialism: The Transformation in Urban Governance in Late Capitalism," *Geografiska Annaler,* series B, *Human Geography* 71, no. 1 (1989): 3–17.

30. Anant Maringanti, "Urban Renewal, Fiscal Deficit, and the Politics of Decentralization: The Case of Jawaharlal Nehru Urban Renewal Mission in India," *Space and Polity* 16 (2012): 93–109; Debolina Kundu, "Urban Development Programmes in India: A Critique of JNNURM," *Social Change* 44 (2014): 615–32; Loraine Kennedy and Marie-Hélène Zérah, "The Shift to City-Centric Growth Strategies: Perspectives from Hyderabad and Mumbai," *Economic and Political Weekly* 43, no. 39 (2008): 110–17; Soumyadip Chattopadhyay, "Neoliberal Urban Transformations in Indian Cities: Paradoxes and Predicaments," *Progress in Development Studies* 17, no. 4 (2017): 307–21. For a discussion of financialization and municipal entrepreneurialism, see Joe Beswick and Joe Penny, "Demolishing the Present to Sell Off the Future? The Emergence of 'Financialized Municipal Entrepreneurialism' in London," *International Journal of Urban and Regional Research,* 42, no. 4 (2018): 612–32.

31. One hallmark of financialization is the takeover of public infrastructure and service provision (such as roads, drinking water supply, electric grids, and waste management) by financially leveraged firms, who then service debts and make profits through tolls, tariffs, and user fees. See Mariana Mazzucato, *The Value of Everything: Making and Taking the Global Economy* (New York:

Public Affairs, 2018). See also Manuel B. Aalbers, "Financial Geography III: The Financialization of the City," *Progress in Human Geography* 44, no. 3 (2019): 595–607; Brett Christophers, "Geographies of Finance I: Historical Geographies of the Crisis-Ridden Present," *Progress in Human Geography* 38, no. 2 (2014): 285–93; and Brett Christophers, "Geographies of Finance II: Crisis, Space, and Political-Economic Transformation," *Progress in Human Geography* 39, no. 2 (2015): 205–13.

32. Brett Christophers, *Our Lives in Their Portfolios: Why Asset Managers Own the World* (London: Verso, 2023).

33. Bengaluru's capital-intensive metro rail project is a case in point. The Karnataka state government and the central government have underwritten 55 percent of the construction cost. For the remainder, however, the Bangalore Metro Rail Corporation Limited (BMRCL) has had to rely on loans from entities such as the Asian Development Bank, Korea Exim Bank, and the Japan International Cooperation Agency. The third of these, for instance, loaned 37,170 million rupees (approximately 467 million USD) to BMRCL for Phase II. "Namma Metro Gets Rs 3.7k Crore Loan from Japan," *New Indian Express*, March 27, 2021, https://www.newindianexpress.com/cities/bengaluru/2021/mar/27/namma-metro-gets-rs-37k-crore-loan-from-japan-2282194.html; Ajay Sukumar and P. P. Thimmaya, "Bangalore Metro Finds Raising Low-Cost Capital Challenging," *Financial Express*, November 8, 2013, https://www.financialexpress.com/archive/bangalore-metro-finds-raising-low-cost-capital-challenging/1192162/.

34. Fulong Wu, "Land Financialisation and the Financing of Urban Development in China," *Land Use Policy*, Article 104412 (2019), https://doi.org/10.1016/j.landusepol.2019.104412; Kean Birch and Callum Ward, "Assetization and the 'New Asset Geographies,'" *Dialogues in Human Geography* (2022), https://doi.org/10.1177/20438206221130807.

35. Solomon Benjamin and Bhuvaneswari Raman, "Illegible Claims, Legal Titles, and the Worlding of Bangalore," *Revue Tiers Monde* 206 (2011): 37–54; Housing and Land Rights Network, *Forced Evictions in India in 2018: An Unabating National Crisis* (New Delhi, 2019). See also D. Asher Ghertner, "Lively Lands: The Spatial Reproduction Squeeze and the Failure of the Urban Imaginary," *International Journal of Urban and Regional Research* 44, no. 4 (2020): 561–81.

36. The editors have carried out collaborative and individual research in Bengaluru for over two decades. The "Speculative Urbanism" research project marked a capstone. Funded by the U.S.-based National Science Foundation, the project was a comparative study of real estate and finance capital, land markets, and livelihood upheavals in the urban core and peri-urban frontiers of two burgeoning Asian cities: Bengaluru, India, and Jakarta, Indonesia, conducted between 2016 and 2022.

37. Suryono Herlambang et al., "Jakarta's Great Land Transformation: Hybrid Neoliberalisation and Informality," *Urban Studies* 56, no. 4 (2019): 627–48.

38. For some outcomes from our broader comparative study of Bengaluru and Jakarta, see the theme issue "Unleashing Speculative Urbanism," guest-edited by Helga Leitner and Eric Sheppard, *Environment and Planning A: Economy and Space* 55, no. 2 (2023); also see https://www.speculativeurbanism.net/.

39. Asher Ghertner discusses the norms and practices of "world-class" aesthetics in relation to urban governance. D. Asher Ghertner, *Rule by Aesthetics: World-Class City Making in Delhi* (New York: Oxford University Press, 2015).

40. Robert Palter and Herbert Pohl, "Money Isn't Everything (But We Need $57 Trillion for Infrastructure)," *Infrastructure Journal and Project Finance Magazine* (2013), 36, 37, https://www.mckinsey.com/~/media/McKinsey/Industries /Private%20Equity%20and%20Principal%20Investors/Our%20Insights /Money%20isnt%20everything%20but%20we%20need%20$57%20trillion %20for%20infrastructure/Money_%20isnt_everything.pdf.

41. Jens Beckert, *Imagined Futures: Fictional Expectations and Capitalist Dynamics* (Cambridge, Mass.: Harvard University Press, 2016), 9.

42. D. Asher Ghertner and Robert W. Lake, "Introduction: Land Fictions: The Commodification of Land in City and Country," in *Land Fictions: The Commodification of Land in City and Country*, ed. D. Asher Ghertner and Robert W. Lake (Ithaca: Cornell University Press, 2021), 14. Also see Laura Bear, "Speculation: A Political Economy of Technologies of Imagination," *Economy and Society* 49, no. 1 (2020): 1–15.

43. G20, "Roadmap to Infrastructure as an Asset Class," Paris: OECD (2018), https://www.oecd.org/g20/roadmap_to_infrastructure_as_an_asset_class _argentina_presidency_1_0.pdf.

44. P. Sarkar, "How Blackstone Made India Its Largest Market in Asia," *Forbes India*, June 7, 2019, https://www.forbesindia.com/article/boardroom/how -blackstone-made-india-its-largest-market-in-asia/53849/1.

45. Laura Bear elaborates the concept of speculative state planning in "Making a River of Gold: Speculative State Planning, Informality, and Neoliberal Governance on the Hooghly," *Focaal: Journal of Global and Historical Anthropology* 61 (2011): 46–60.

46. Vinay Baindur and Lalitha Kamath, "Reengineering Urban Infrastructure: How the World Bank and Asian Development Bank Shape Urban Infrastructure Finance and Governance in India" (New Delhi: Bank Information Centre, 2009). For a historical perspective on financial investments in infrastructure in India, see Laura Bear, "Speculations on Infrastructure: From Colonial Public Works to a Post-colonial Global Asset Class on the Indian Railways, 1840–2017," *Economy and Society* 49, no. 1 (2020): 45–70.

47. Our formulation here has resonances with Colin McFarlane, *Learning the City: Knowledge and Translocal Assemblage* (Oxford: Wiley-Blackwell, 2011); and AbdouMaliq Simone, *Improvised Lives: Rhythms of Endurance in an Urban South* (Cambridge, UK: Polity Press, 2018).

48. Caroline Humphrey, "Real Estate Speculation: Volatile Social Forms at a Global Frontier of Capital," *Economy and Society* 49, no. 1 (2020): 120; cf. Anna L. Tsing, "Inside the Economy of Appearances," *Public Culture* 12, no. 1 (2000): 115–44.

49. Aris Komporozos-Athanasiou, *Speculative Communities: Living with Uncertainty in a Financialized World* (Chicago: University of Chicago Press, 2022).

50. Nair, *The Promise of the Metropolis*.

51. Hemangini Gupta, "Testing the Future: Gender and Technocapitalism in Start-up India," *Feminist Review* 123, no. 1 (2019): 74–88.

52. Helga Leitner and Eric Sheppard, "Towards an Epistemology for Conjunctural Inter-urban Comparison," *Cambridge Journal of Regions, Economy and Society* 13 (2020): 491–508.

53. Michael Goldman, "Dispossession by Financialization: The End(s) of Rurality in the Making of a Speculative Land Market," *Journal of Peasant Studies* 47, no. 6 (2020): 1251–77. See also Thomas Cowan, *Subaltern Frontiers: Agrarian City-Making in Gurgaon* (Delhi: Cambridge University Press, 2022); and Sushmita Pati, *Properties of Rent: Community, Capital, and Politics in Globalising Delhi* (Delhi: Cambridge University Press, 2022).

54. Vinay Gidwani and Carol Upadhya, "Articulation Work: Value Chains of Land Assembly and Real Estate Development on a Peri-urban Frontier," *Environment and Planning A: Economy and Space* 55, no. 2 (2023): 407–27, https://doi.org/10.1177/0308518X221107016.

55. See, for example, Janaki Nair, "Reimagining Bengaluru," *The Indian Express*, September 19, 2022, https://indianexpress.com/article/opinion/columns/reimagining-bengaluru-resilient-and-sutainable-urban-ethos-8158919/.

56. Henri Lefebvre, *Everyday Life in the Modern World*, trans. Sacha Rabinovitch (Allen Lane: Penguin Press, 1971).

A high-end mixed-use complex under construction on former mill land in central Bengaluru. Photograph by Pierre Hauser.

Part I
Speculative Stories

By the time Dubai and Shanghai emerged as world cities at the end of the twentieth century, leaders of Bangalore (now Bengaluru) were already envisioning, and implementing, similar modes of urban transformation. Prospects of windfall gains from the construction of state-of-the-art infrastructure, such as new business centers, shopping meccas, commuter rail projects, high-volume toll roads, upgraded water and sewerage systems, and amenity-rich residential utopias were, indubitably, powerful drivers in the rapid spread of the "global city" model. Land bankers, real estate developers, construction companies, architectural firms, labor contractors, foreign private equity, domestic lenders, big and small investors, politicians, and bureaucrats all wanted in on the game. Speculation, Gayle Rogers reminds us, is a certain kind of thinking and acting that pivots on "a charged and unruly (and sometimes unscrupulous) 'cognitive provisionality.'"[1] That is to say, the speculative drive is not entirely rational; its force originates not from the fully known but rather from the gap between what is visible in the present and what is envisioned in the future. The instinctive association of speculation in contemporary accounts with avarice, greed, gambling, and aberrant profits—all of which are evident in Bangalore's giddy metamorphosis—can obscure the fact that speculation in an important, older, sense has also been about forecasting, divining, and narrating the yet-to-come. Even in its narrower, economic, definition, imagination of the not-quite-knowable remains a key ingredient in actors' calculations of anticipated gains.

The quartet of chapters in this section on "Speculative Stories" showcase how the material and narrative dimensions of speculation are intertwined. Two of the four chapters interweave the voices of a major developer of ambitious mixed-use developments, an illustrious architect who has been the visionary behind several noteworthy construction and restoration projects, and the head of an important real estate company, describing their visions for transforming the city into a globally competitive and desirable metropolis. In "Envisioning the City" (chapter 1), the developer behind one of Bengaluru's high-profile integrated townships describes his aim as nothing less than building an "ecosystem of happiness"—a panacea for urban congestion, inadequate infrastructure, traffic logjams and soul-sucking commutes, and poor-quality lifestyles—in a self-contained smart city where services are a fingertip away, high-end shopping and cafés at one's doorstep, and workplaces and green spaces in walking distance. Our prominent architect, armed with dazzling chronicles of urban planning past and present, talks of his desire to create "dense" cities with new "public" spaces.

Speculation as contemplation, and often, as garrulous yarns intended to persuade, about that which is yet-to-materialize, is palpable in "Building the High Life" (chapter 4), where we meet a real estate developer who explains the "thought process" underlying his mixed-use gated community in "Purvapur" on Bengaluru's southeastern fringe. Happiness is once again the byword. The builder speaks of creating "a world where both wife and husband work, or the wife works and husband stays at home, but whoever lives in that home should feel pleasure and be happy." He acknowledges the complaints of customers who are skeptical of the project's construction timeline and frustrated by the lack of promised infrastructure, deflecting blame onto bureaucratic malaise and red tape. True to his persona as a salesman selling his unfinished utopia, he exhorts existing and prospective residents to think of themselves as "family" that will soon be able to enjoy their spacious, self-contained complex.

It is clear from the heady accounts of these movers and shakers who are shaping Bengaluru's cityscape that their vision of the world city is not necessarily in service of a larger design. Rather, they are creating zones of sociality where those who can afford such accommodation can find refuge to varying degrees from the trials and tribulations of everyday urban life in globalized Bengaluru. In the words of one scholar, such gated enclaves are instances of "soft secession"— new social orderings in miniature, akin to, and yet different in their makeup from, older caste- and community-based colonies in Indian cities, which "crack up" and dissipate what we imagine to be "the city."[2]

The two remaining chapters in this section offer a counterpoint to elite narratives of the world city. In "The IT Juggernaut" (chapter 2), Jagannath, a farmer who grew up in Bellandur village and was once the head of its gram panchayat (village council), condemns the speculation in land markets that has made this once quiet corner of Bengaluru into an IT hub and property hot spot, upending its agrarian ecology. Echoing "Krishna," a school principal we encounter in "Only Beautiful Plans" (chapter 3), Jagannath rehearses the suspicion among common people that the game of land is rigged: what is probabilistic for plebeians like himself is a sure thing for brokers and bigwigs in the know. For the politically powerful, they suggest, city development plans, regional master plans, and zoning guidance are official weathervanes that signal which way the winds are blowing and what future orderings of the city will look like. With foreknowledge mined from cultivated social networks, these actors are able to acquire land and property in strategic locations to maximize future gains.[3]

Other characters in "Only Beautiful Plans" detail how the eddies of rapid urbanization have disrupted rural existence. A local corporator (elected municipal representative) denounces the "tanker mafia" that is extracting groundwater unchecked in villages that surround Purvapur, in cahoots with "the system." Another resident complains about the rapid influx of outsiders into the area and how it makes her feel "unsafe." A high-level employee who works on land acquisition for a prominent real estate company is dismissive of the city's planning process and its overseeing agency, the Bangalore Development Authority, lamenting that plans are made but never implemented.

Finally, chapter 3 offers a sobering reminder that speculation is not just about anticipation of future gains. It can just as well be about anticipation of future losses and thwarting these through defensive tactics and opportunistic presentations of self. "Shamim," who makes his livelihood by sorting and selling items salvaged from the discards of local residents and businesses, exhibits a nervousness that is now commonplace among Muslims who live and work in India's cities amid increasingly strident anti-Muslim rhetoric and hostility from supporters of Hindu nationalism. Muslim migrants from West Bengal are particularly vulnerable in this fraught political environment to being branded as "Bangladeshi" infiltrators. In a poignant display of reverse nativism, Shamim defends his band of Bengali families, instead labelling a flock of migrants who have set up meager dwellings on a nearby tract of land "illegal migrants" who bring suspicion on his people's citizenship status and tarnish their hard and honest work. Rather than viewing himself and his neighbors as part of a "speculative community" bound together "on the basis of shared experiences of volatility and precarity,"[4] Shamim elects to differentiate himself, in understandable yet unsettling ways, as unfairly stigmatized and more deserving.

Notes

1. Gayle Rogers, *Speculation: A Cultural History from Aristotle to AI* (New York: Columbia University Press, 2021), 4.

2. Quinn Slobodian, *Crack-Up Capitalism: Market Radicals and the Dream of a World without Democracy* (New York: Metropolitan Books, 2023), 5.

3. D. Asher Ghertner, "When Is the State? Topology, Temporality, and the Navigation of Everyday State Space in Delhi," *Annals of the American Association of Geographers* 117, no. 3 (2017): 731–50. According to Ghertner, the "deep uncertainty that lies in the gap between the state's topographic form—its institutional hierarchy or structure of fixed posts—and its topological workings hence can function as a resource for those who are able to anticipate it or wield it toward their own ends" (745).

4. Aris Komporozos-Athanasiou, *Speculative Communities: Living with Uncertainty in a Financialized World* (Chicago: University of Chicago Press, 2022), ix.

1
Envisioning the City
Vinay Gidwani

Bengaluru's urban future is here. Or at least in prototype, if we go by the proclamations of Snehdeep Aggarwal, founder-chairman of Bhartiya Group and self-described mayor of the 125-acre integrated township of Bhartiya City, near Hebbal. Aggarwal exuberantly calls the project his "City of Joy." The guiding concept that anchors this "smart megacity"? Improbably, it is "happiness." Aggarwal's ambition is to build a city that is an "ecosystem" for happiness. As the website for Bhartiya City announces: "Happiness is in the little things. Happiness isn't momentary, it's a state of being. Happiness is not an island. The more you are surrounded by happy people, the greater your chances of being happy. Happiness is a product of all those little things coming together to form a complete environment—an ecosystem."[1] Bhartiya City's sales proposition is that happiness can be planned, and you are invited to participate.

The township's plan involves "eight precincts," promising "a seamless mix of the finest residential spaces, office towers, hotels, public realms, parks," as well as a performing arts center, state-of-the-art hospitals, and "efficient transport links to provide a complete environment for better living." The on-site K-12 standard Chaman Bhartiya School (onetime admission fee: 120,000 rupees; annual tuition fee: 165,000 rupees) styles itself as the "Maker of Leaders."[2] Under the directorship of Copenhagen-born Allan Kjaer Andersen, it pledges to "prepare children for leadership positions in the uncertain and complex world of the future" by combining "the best of Indian and Scandinavian education." Perhaps mindful of the clientele of parents who will enroll their children in the school, Andersen describes the learning environment as "joyful and stimulating without compromising academic rigour"—a goal that is realized through "projects and play-based pedagogies" in partnership with LEGO Education and

Apple Education Solutions Provider, which ensures that teachers receive "digital professional development by Apple-certified trainers."[3]

Bhartiya City's promotional materials also highlight "Financial Districts" offering offices for small and medium-size enterprises, incubator units, and flexible business space: "There's something for everyone," it reassures us, "from Multi-National Corporations to e-startups."[4] Not convinced? Here's another nudge. Workplaces at Bhartiya City will nestle in a "rural haven" of "freshly cut grass, ever-growing trees, cascading water, mellow cafes and far-reaching parks," guaranteeing that "it's not all work and no play." And that's not all. The township's website also flaunts a "High Street" containing the "best of London, Paris, Barcelona and New York"—guaranteed to make "even the most serious of shoppers giddy." Visitors will find "chic boutiques" and "expansive malls" hosting "the likes of Hermes and Louis Vuitton among other popular brands." And of course, a variety of restaurants (with no pesky street vendors to hinder your enjoyment of this urban utopia).

Oh, and let's not forget that this is after all a *smart* city. When Bhartiya City's central command center—Aggarwal calls it "the brain"—is fully up and running, life's amenities will be available at your fingertips: "Enter, an app called Whimbl. Book a show, book a table, book a court, replenish your groceries, get your car washed, you get the idea. If you are a husband responsible for the chores of your household, this simple app should make you a happy man indeed."[5] There is a nod and a wink here to the professional and tech-savvy families, with cosmopolitan gender norms, who are likely to be your neighbors—if that's the social mix you desire.

Alas, Aggarwal does not have a monopoly on happiness. The rival Embassy Springs, a 288-acre self-contained residential township in Devanahalli, advertises itself as "Bengaluru's biggest and best planned city," with a "limited edition" town center and estate plots "that are surrounded by the finest things life can offer." A mammoth sign embellishes the entrance. Emblazoned on it: "Embassy Springs— The Masterplan for Happiness."[6] In a 2017 property guide, the real estate website PropTiger.com lists Embassy Springs as one of its "Top 5 Upcoming Integrated Townships in Bengaluru." Others that make the list include Ozone Urbana Avenue (in Kannamangala), Brigade Orchards (in Devanahalli), Prestige Lakeside Habitat (in Varthur), and Bhartiya City Nikoo Homes Phase 2 (in Thanisandra).[7] Niranjan Hiranandani, managing director of the Hiranandani real estate group, praises mixed-use integrated townships as a "new urbanism"—the panacea for a plethora of urban ills, from congestion, lack of infrastructure, and increase in traffic and travel time to low-quality living spaces (see Figure 1.1).[8]

Hiranandani, who is also vice-chairman of the Ministry of Housing and Urban Development's National Real Estate Development Council, oddly makes no mention of India's rich history of integrated developments, from company towns to public-sector townships. Bhilai, Bokaro, Bhadravati, Jamshedpur, and Jaffrabad are a few that spring to mind. Whereas these were primarily intended as self-contained housing projects for employees, with various amenities ready at hand, perhaps what makes today's townships a distinctively "new-age construction" (in Hiranandani's words) is their purposeful alignment with the market logics of entrepreneurship and consumption. Contemporary mixed-use townships are premised on a postindustrial imagination, where digitally mediated service-sector jobs have overtaken manufacturing. Hence, each one, to varying degrees, promises a setting where workplace productivity can be optimized by minimizing the trade-off between labor time and leisure time. And if you're concerned about your ecological footprint, the integrated township offers a class-exclusive total environment to live your "green" values. Thus, Aggarwal imagines "a city where you will live close to your work" and perhaps commute there on bicycle, spending far less on petrol as your car slumbers in a parking lot. In fact, he believes, "Environmentalists around the world will want to hug this city for this."[9]

"Golden Springs" is a competing mixed-use project in northwest Bengaluru that has transformed the landscape of a previously down-to-earth industrial locality. Keen to obtain a firsthand sense of the architectural vision that underlay this "world-class" development—containing luxury apartments, an upscale office complex, a high-end mall, theaters, a private school, a hotel, and green space—we went to meet the man behind the concept.

"Viren," a prominent architect, is an expansive talker, with a gift for regaling listeners with fascinating trivia mined from urban lore. His stories swing buoyantly from past to present, populated by a cast of colorful characters. We meet Seshadri Iyer, the legendary Diwan

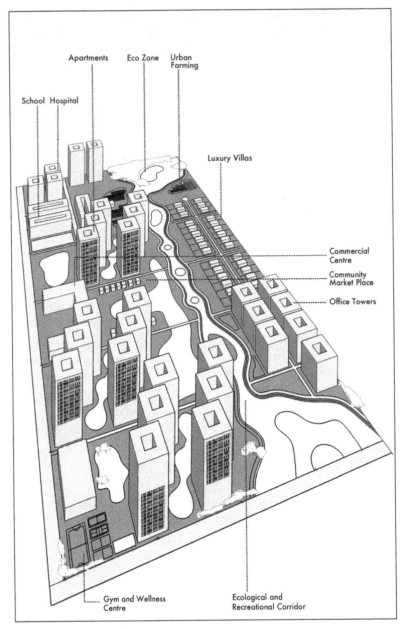

Figure 1.1. Artist's sketch of a fictional high-end "integrated township" in Bengaluru. Illustration by Deepa William.

Envisioning the City **37**

of the princely state of Mysore, who held his post from 1883 to 1901. "He was a visionary," Viren gushed, "responsible for the city's development." A follower of the "sanitary movement," which subscribed to the miasma theory of disease and gained traction in the UK in the 1840s before spreading to Europe's imperial peripheries, Iyer oversaw the formation of new residential extensions in Bangalore—in Basavangudi and Malleswaram—following the devastating plague of 1898, with wide roads, greenery, and planned layouts (in contrast to the congested inner city where most of the Indian population resided).[10] These extensions, drawing on the colonial model, replicated on the "Indian" side of the city, planned settlements like Fraser Town which already existed in the cantonment (the British or "white" settlement). Viren describes the new localities created by Iyer as "well designed and inclusive neighborhoods," eliding the fact that these modern, planned layouts later became segregated from other localities along the lines of caste and class.

Viren then adds an offhand observation about Patrick Geddes, the polymath who lived and worked as a town planner in India from 1914 to 1924 (he was also a biologist, sociologist, and philosopher). We are dazzled by Viren's chronicles of city-making but perplexed regarding why Iyer and Geddes were named side by side. Is it merely part of his freewheeling repertoire of stories? Or is he tracing a diverse, seemingly cacophonic architectural lineage to make a point? Designers have always worked at the crossroads of influences—local and nonlocal, old and new, "authentic" and "avant-garde." Architects as city designers are no different. Geddes, for instance, saw the Indian subcontinent as fertile terrain for his plans to reshape existing towns and cities. His vision of the "regional city" pivoted on harnessing the rich ecological and cultural traditions of a place, thereby enlivening what he considered the West's blunt materialism with the East's redemptive spiritualism. In south Asian cities such as Lahore, Baroda, Indore, and Lucknow, Geddes fine-tuned his method of "conservative surgery": revitalizing urban quarters by minimizing the destruction of existing buildings or the expulsion of settled populations. His method, which contrasted with the standard demolish-and-rebuild approach of British municipal engineers, rested on discovering a city's *genius loci*—the spirit of a place—and designing a plan to improve and amend a city's environment in alignment with this inherited character.[11]

Given Viren's formative role in Bengaluru's aspirational reinvention as a global city—he has been involved in some of the most defining (and, critics might say, disruptive) architectural projects in the city—Geddes struck us as an odd inspiration. And yet, as our conversation with Viren unfolded, we came to appreciate that his illustrious career personifies the tension between "world city" ideals (to be like Dubai, Singapore, or Shanghai), driven by a real estate industry catering to foreign investors and upwardly mobile professionals who expect an "international lifestyle," and aesthetic concerns over the loss of a city's unique identity or heritage. After all, the sameness of "world city" builtscapes—the repetitive parade of glass-and-steel high-rises, swanky malls, curated shopping districts with brand-name stores, and sanitized green spaces—can overwhelm the quirks and differences that impart cities their distinctiveness.

Builders and architects have navigated this tension by striving to weave traditional elements of heritage into planning layouts and structures (which then become their own niche selling proposition). Aggarwal, for example, waxes nostalgic about his own childhood in Amritsar. On his blog he writes that "it was a great revelation to me that some of the greatest cities in the world—like Barcelona, for example—had striking similarities to my own little Amritsar. Both were planned and designed in such a way that one could easily walk or cycle to schools, hospitals and even work. It then hurt me to see that most urban centres in India are unfriendly to their own people."[12]

For Aggarwal, then, Bhartiya City embodies the best of the traditional and the modern. Golden Springs, the mixed-use community designed by Viren, offers similar conveniences. But while Aggarwal the developer finds inspiration in personal memory (Amritsar of yore), Viren the architect finds it in planning history (city designers like Iyer and Geddes). And although Viren's portfolio boasts a slew of high-profile modernist projects, he has come to regard himself as a guardian of "Old Bangalore's architectural heritage." In recent years his firm has restored several iconic buildings in the city. These undertakings, ostensibly meant to interrupt the world city's gleaming monotony, are a source of great pride to him.

We wanted to know more about the making of Golden Springs, which sits on land that was previously a factory compound. After the sale of this land (described by Viren as the company's "crown jewel") to a developer in the early 2000s, Viren was hired to envision a landmark multi-use complex in this increasingly desirable area of Bengaluru. "Who or what inspired you?," we ask. According to Viren, he was most inspired by the Israeli Canadian architect Moshe Safdie's idea of "dense urbanism." Safdie, a practicing architect, city planner, and urban theorist based in Montreal, wrote a controversial book, *The City after the Automobile,* informed primarily by the North American experience of urbanization. A manifesto for a new vision of regional planning, Safdie's book called for the creation of "new centers of concentration within dispersed leafy districts." The future regional city, "a place where multiple centers of great density integrate work, commerce, culture, residence, and social services," will interweave with areas of "low-density development, expanses of single-family houses, parks, shopping, and other facilities and institutions that support the quality of life associated with the traditional green suburbs."[13] In a subsequent statement on "dense urbanism," Safdie imagines the "habitat of the future" as an integrated mixed-use development anchored by numerous towers, interconnected at multiple levels. He grandly anticipates that his approach would combine the upsides of privacy and digital communities—now standard requisites of urban living—with new possibilities for interpersonal interaction in an expanded "public realm."[14]

Because the builtscape of integrated complexes like Golden Springs—which cater to Bengaluru's elite and upper middle classes—presents a stark contrast to the staid low-rise layouts and modest architectural styles of Bengaluru's older neighborhoods, we wondered why Viren found Safdie's ideas applicable locally. His reply was cryptic. Safdie's ideas, he said, were "in the air then." (Did he mean in the cosmopolitan circuits traversed by globe-trotting architects like himself?) Viren went on to describe the milieu in Bengaluru at the turn of the millennium: "The internet bubble had ended, GE had just come into the city,[15] there was a mood of optimism in the air." "You could smell it," he said excitedly—"and you could follow the demand as land transactions quickened and legal notices filled the papers."

Expanding on this claim, Viren drops an intriguing proposition: "When you see several advertisements for real estate, that's a sign that the market has slumped. But when you see lots of legal notices in the paper regarding property cases, that means there is a 'buzz' in the

40 Vinay Gidwani

market!" His point seems to be that a surge in legal challenges around property is a sign of an active real estate market, whereas lots of ads for real estate signal a sluggish market with sellers desperate to find buyers.

Still trying to sift through Viren's sources of inspiration, we are surprised when he tells us that in models of city development, Singapore did not figure on his list. In rankings of world-class cities Singapore routinely tops the charts, but Viren dismisses it as a "dumb model" because "it is predicated on a control economy." "You need a messy model," he proclaims, "if you want it to be an analogue [to India/Bengaluru] and if you want to learn anything."

When he was commissioned to design Golden Springs, Viren laughs, he was "obsessed with the idea of mixed use and wanted a messy mixed-use model on the lines of Tokyo and Hong Kong." His thought was, "Let's not do boring!" The standard approach of real estate developers is to start with apartments. Why? Because "apartments are easy to sell," he explained, "but commercial takes time, so usually developers make the apartments first and sell them and use the money to develop the commercial property, which they lease out." To visualize the space differently, he and the developer, Hariprasad, traveled around the world to view "different properties and models of mixed-use planning." One that stood out was a "complex designed by the Mori Brothers—Roppongi Hills, in Tokyo."

The Mori Building Company claims that three principles inform its vision of city-making: developments must embody "Safety and Security," "Environment and Greenery," and "Culture and Art."[16] These principles are reflected in what Viren has tried to create at Golden Springs, a development he characterizes as an "ungated community . . . where you can just go chill, and everything is accessible in the same place." He terms it "a solution to the problem of moving around the city"—omitting to note that this "solution" is meaningful only for the select few inhabitants whose places of employment and residence happen to coincide in his planned township. To realize his messy version of "dense urbanism," Viren "mixed up the mixed use including a hotel, a school, and a hospital and not just commercial and residential properties." Declaring that this was the first such private mixed-use township in Bengaluru, he describes with evident pride how sustainability is integrated into his architectural design—

all the rainwater that falls in the complex is recycled into an artificial lake and reused.

In principle, at least. In practice, sustainability remains a distant goal. The elite residents of Golden Springs—returned NRIs (Non Resident Indians) and internationally oriented professionals—have described a litany of problems they have struggled to resolve around the operation and maintenance of the sewage and water treatment (and recycling) plants that are supposed to service the many apartment towers that populate the complex. With the Bruhat Bengaluru Mahanagara Palike (BBMP; Greater Bengaluru Metropolitan Corporation) requiring such complexes to constitute resident welfare associations to manage such facilities, residents have been forced to take on roles for which they have little or no expertise. The inhabitants of Golden Springs, for instance, have assembled a slew of agenda-based committees. This mode of civic interaction might be the kernel of a new "public realm," but hardly, one infers, the sort of community formed out of planned spaces for spontaneous encounters that architects like Safdie had in mind when they trumpet the future city.

As we trudged out of Viren's office, we were struck by the diverging desires of the world city's designers and its inhabitants. For ambitious creators like Aggarwal or Viren, integrated townships are not just amenity-rich enclaves of privacy for well-heeled professionals who desire the social homogeneity of cultured and like-minded neighbors; they are, instead, vessels for reviving and expanding the "public realm." Aggarwal, for example, boldly declares that a "good public realm is my fundamental right as is walking and breathing. No progressive society can afford to overlook this." He invokes cities like Vancouver, Barcelona, and Copenhagen, whose "very well designed public realms are a joy to the world." He constructs a chain of causality, where well-designed public space creates "happier societies" and leads to "more overall economic progress" and "healthier and longer life spans." Rehearsing the American Canadian urbanist Jane Jacobs's influential notion of "eyes on the street"[17] (without naming her), Aggarwal contends that "interactive and friendly public spaces foster pedestrian activity and thus passive surveillance; reducing the exposure to possible crimes."[18]

For the present and prospective inhabitants of townships like Bhartiya City or Golden Springs, the parks, piazzas, smart cafés, street shops, and malls as spaces of conviviality are clearly appealing. But this is only because these spaces constitute a "public realm" whose users are screened, their movements recorded and regulated, their personal safety and possessions secured from unwelcome elements. In short, this is a public realm that excludes even as it claims inspiration from templates that are more inclusive. According to Bhartiya City's website, the township's electronic "brain" will be "able to see a problem, solve it, ensure that it doesn't happen again, all before it even is a problem. Anticipation is key to the smooth running of a city. With a brain such as this, and with cameras that double up as wi-fi spots and streetlamps, we will [be able to] keep a watch on the city." Such big-brotherly talk has led some critics to compare private townships to colonial enclaves or to hold them up as specimens of "corporate urbanization"—a scenario where cities become a pockmarked geography of gated clubs characterized by the "exclusive consumption of collective goods."[19] On the inside, an affluent minority of haves; on the outside, desiring but destined only to dream, an army of have-nots. Critics of this emerging urban geography question whether the grand vision and high-minded aesthetic of a "world-class" city has finally emptied into a rhetorical specter, revealing a more baroque patchwork approach of many privately governed mini-cities and townships barricaded from the masses and shielded from "public nuisances."[20]

Residents of Golden Springs, for instance, confirmed in conversations that the self-contained nature of the development ("never having to step out if you didn't want to") was a big attraction. And with growing traffic congestion and longer commute times in Bengaluru, this is even more true for families where at least one member worked for an employer with its offices in the onsite business center. But these same residents also emphasized that a significant selling point was the fact that Golden Springs *is* a "gated community" (and not an ungated utopia, contrary to Viren's depiction)—with an army of security personnel to filter and surveil the movements of outsiders. In fact, many residents confessed to living a more or less hermetic existence in their mixed-use complex, secure in their "enclaved personhood."[21] They have only glancing familiarity with the middle- and lower-middle-class neighborhoods like "Karmikara Colony" that surround them (see chapters 11 and 20), and which supply the domestic help and maintenance personnel who sustain their idyllic habitat.

Does Bengaluru's yearning to be a "world-class" city mean that we are fated for more mixed-use developments that enlarge the public realm by making the terrain of chance encounters and conversations more guarded, exclusive, and private, where thickly monitored public spaces masquerade as urban commons? Surely, we mused, an architecture that (wittingly or not) abstracts from the caste and class fabric of quotidian life can't be the prototype of the city-yet-to-come.

Or can it?

Notes

Hemangini Gupta, Juwairia Mehkri, Michael Goldman, and Carol Upadhya contributed to this chapter.

1. Snehdeep Aggarwal, "The Mayor's Vision," https://bhartiyacity.com.

2. See "Makers of Leaders," https://chamanbhartiya.com/.

3. "Anderson's Challenging Brief," *Education World*, May 2020, https://www.educationworld.in/andersens-challenging-brief/.

4. "Masterplan," https://bhartiyacity.com/masterplan/.

5. "Intelligent Community," https://bhartiyacity.com/intelligent-community/.

6. "Highlights," https://www.embassyprojectsbangalore.com.

7. Harini Balasubramanian, "Top 5 Upcoming Integrated Townships in Bengaluru," June 18, 2017, https://www.proptiger.com/guide/post/top-5-upcoming-integrated-township-projects-in-bangalore.

8. Niranjan Hirandani, "Mixed-Use Development Is the New Urbanism," *The Hindu*, December 10, 2021, https://www.thehindu.com/real-estate/mixed-use-development-is-the-new-urbanism/article37923484.ece.

9. "Intelligent Community," https://bhartiyacity.com/intelligent-community/.

10. Sanchari Pal, "Why You Need to Learn about K. Seshadri Iyer, the Forgotten Creator of Modern Bengaluru," *The Better India*, February 21, 2017, https://www.thebetterindia.com/88222/dewan-of-mysore-seshadri-iyer-maker-of-modern-bangalore/.

11. See Volker M. Welter, *Biopolis: Patrick Geddes and the City of Life* (Cambridge: MIT Press, 2002); and Indra Munshi, *Patrick Geddes' Contribution to Sociology and Urban Planning: Vision of a City* (New Delhi: Routledge, 2022).

12. "Mayor's Blog," https://bhartiyacity.com/category/mayors-blog/.

13. Moshe Safdie, with Wendy Kohn, *The City after the Automobile* (Boulder: Westview Press, 1998), 124–25. Safdie's book had a mixed reception. The architectural critic Michael McMordie, for instance, panned his approach as "dated," writing that the "utopian dreams he offers are appealing but even more often are irrelevant." See McMordie's book review in *The Structurist* 39 (January 1999): 69.

14. Moshe Safdie and Jaron Lubin, "Dense Urbanism: The High-Rise Tower as a Building Block for the Public Realm," *CTBUH Research Paper* (Council on

Tall Buildings and Urban Habitat, 2015), https://global.ctbuh.org/resources/papers/download/2424-dense-urbanism-the-high-rise-tower-as-a-building-block-for-the-public-realm.pdf.

15. In September 2000, General Electric set up its India Technology Center in Bangalore. "GE's Technology Center Celebrates Ten Years of Innovation in India," September 16, 2010, https://www.ge.com/news/press-releases/ges-technology-center-celebrates-ten-years-innovation-india.

16. "Three Missions of Urban Design," https://www.mori.co.jp/en/urban_design/theme.html.

17. Jane Jacobs, *The Death and Life of Great American Cities* (New York: Vintage, 1992).

18. Snehdeep Aggarwal, "Public Realm: The Body and Soul of Cities," December 24, 2018, https://yourstory.com/mystory/public-realm-the-body-and-soul-of-cities-hbhqammarb/amp.

19. Ashima Sood, "Industrial Townships and the Policy Facilitation of Corporate Urbanization," *Urban Studies* 52, no. 8 (2015): 1373.

20. See, for instance, Sanjay Srivastava, *Entangled Urbanism: Slum, Gated Community, and Shopping Mall in Delhi and Gurgaon* (Delhi: Oxford University Press, 2015).

21. Devra Waldman and D. Asher Ghertner, "The Enclaved Body: Crises of Personhood and Embodied Geographies of Urban Gating," *Progress in Human Geography* 47, no. 2 (2023): 280–97.

2
The IT Juggernaut

Carol Upadhya

Among the worst-hit areas during the major floods that hit Bengaluru in August and September 2022 was Bellandur, an area in the southeastern part of the city that takes its name from Bellandur Lake—Bengaluru's largest body of water—and Bellandur village—a large agricultural settlement next to the lake. Once a fertile agricultural tract, Bellandur is now best known for its gigantic software parks, high-rise apartment complexes, and glitzy shopping malls. Real estate development in the area took off in the early 2000s, after the completion of the Outer Ring Road (ORR) that connects the IT hubs of Whitefield (home of the first tech park established in the city and of many multinational IT companies) and Electronic City (the location of Infosys and other premier Indian tech companies). The area around Bellandur, which lies along the ORR near Whitefield, began to urbanize with the rising demand for land for real estate development (see Figure 2.1).

Bellandur Lake—now heavily polluted—is often in the news for spewing foam and periodically catching on fire. The lake lies at the far end of one of the city's valley systems and serves as a catchment for huge amounts of wastewater and sewage draining from upstream areas of the city. While civic activists often blame the high pollution levels in most of Bengaluru's lakes on the paucity of sewage treatment plants and inadequate solid waste management, the larger issues of urban sprawl and rampant overdevelopment (often in violation of planning norms) less often enter public debates.[1]

Perhaps among the first to apprehend the dangers of unfettered real estate development, and to voice misgivings about the shape of Bengaluru's urban growth, is Bellandur native K. Jagannath, former president of Bellandur Gram Panchayat (elected governing body for the village). As a tech-savvy and forward-looking local politician,

Figure 2.1. Heavy flooding on Outer Ring Road, Bengaluru, September 2022. Photograph by Sudhakar D.

Jagannath had won national and state-level "best panchayat" awards.[2] But in 2002 he was in the news for other reasons—he accused Infosys—India's second-largest IT company—of trying to "grab" some of Bellandur's fertile irrigated land to construct a new campus. These rich farmlands, watered by outflow from the lake, were held mainly by small farmers who had been supplying rice, vegetables, and other produce to the city for decades.

In an interview with Kaveri Medappa in 2017, Jagannath recounted his fight with Infosys. It began with circulating rumors that IT companies were eyeing land near Bellandur to build new offices, given its convenient location near the ORR. As in other villages surrounding Bengaluru, the rising demand for land from real estate companies and land aggregators had pushed up land prices during the 1990s, and farmers had started selling their plots (see chapter 3). Wipro (another major software company) had acquired eighty acres in the area by negotiating directly with farmers, including Jagannath, who sold ten acres of his own land to the company. However, Jagannath objected to Infosys's approach: instead of offering to purchase the land from farmers, it had asked the Karnataka Industrial

Areas Development Board (KIADB) to acquire one hundred acres on its behalf.[3] The KIADB has the power to acquire land compulsorily for such projects, and the compensation it provides is usually well below market value. According to Jagannath, he had tried to meet the high-profile chairman of Infosys, N. R. Narayana Murthy, to voice their objections, but without success: "It is easier to touch the prime minister than to touch this man," he remarked sarcastically.

Jagannath explained that under the leadership of former chief minister S. M. Krishna of the Congress Party (1999–2004) the state government began using the KIADB Act to indiscriminately acquire land.[4] Farmers who got caught in the "KIADB net" were "looted" by the government and became "*paupers.*"[5] Large tracts of fertile farmland and wetlands were acquired in this way and handed over to developers and private companies, and farmers had little recourse against the power of the state.

In 2002, as this issue was simmering, Jagannath was invited to a meeting of the World Economic Forum, held in Delhi, to share his experiences as panchayat president. He used the opportunity to raise his objections to the proposed land acquisition. During a panel discussion he asserted that if agricultural land is needed for industrial development, the owners should be consulted rather than simply served with a land acquisition notification. Referring to his ongoing battle with Infosys as an example, he claimed that the company had decided unilaterally to take away farmers' lands without adequate compensation. Infosys chairman Narayana Murthy, who was in the audience, "jumped up" and began shouting, "I object!" Later he also threatened Jagannath with a defamation case. But Murthy acknowledged that Infosys had approached KIADB to acquire the land on the grounds that their project would be the "largest investment in the state."[6] Later, Infosys quietly dropped its plans to set up a new campus at Bellandur.

Although Jagannath won the battle against Infosys, developers continued to purchase or acquire agricultural lands in the area, even as he continued his struggle to save the village. Bellandur was quickly transformed from an expanse of green fields and blue water into a steel-and-glass jungle of malls, commercial complexes, and giant tech parks—such as the fifty-acre RMZ tech park, ironically named Ecospace, which was severely affected during the 2022 floods.

Reminiscing about his youth in the 1970s, Jagannath recalled that life was *"peaceful"* and *"healthy,"* the air was clean, and the water was so pure you could drink directly from the tanks. As children, they worked on the family farm every day before going to school. Bellandur Lake would dry up during the summer, turning into a playing field for children. Come rainy season, the lake would fill up again. There was never a shortage of water—the water table was at "zero level"—you only had to dig a little to find moist soil and water.

Jagannath traced Bengaluru's current crisis to its rapid industrialization in the 1970s, which attracted people from across the country. Because the Bangalore Development Authority (BDA)—tasked with town planning—could not meet the rapidly growing demand for housing, landowners and developers began to create unauthorized residential layouts on farmlands, selling plots of land to aspiring homeowners: "Illegal layouts sprouted all over, houses came up where roads should have been laid. The master plan said one thing but what happened on the ground was entirely different. Ninety-five percent of the city has grown in this manner."

Worse, lakes were destroyed by the BDA itself to make way for infrastructure such as bus stands and sports stadiums, destroying the city's water and drainage system. As the city's lakes disappeared or became polluted, they were no longer a source of clean drinking water. Fish started dying off, and hyacinth invaded many water bodies. The state government launched successive phases of the Cauvery Water Supply Scheme to bring increasing amounts of water from the distant Kaveri River to the thirsty city: "They [the government] were so invested in bringing water to the city by any means but didn't care about protecting what we already had."

Jagannath emphasized the bureaucratic miasma in the municipal government that allowed the city to develop in such a haphazard manner. He spoke about the lack of transparency and coordination between different civic agencies: "The panchayats are planning authorities, BDA is supposed to be the planning authority for the city, then BBMP [Bruhat Bengaluru Mahanagara Palike, the Greater Bengaluru Metropolitan Corporation] starts doing its own planning. On top of all this comes the KIADB, which is a *superpower* that can swallow up entire villages. It is the *nuclear weapon* of the government!" This is when real estate companies spotted an opportunity, he argued.

Jurisdictional ambiguity opened up space for the manipulation of regulations and illegitimate land-use changes. "In those days, the CDP [Comprehensive Development Plan] was not available in public places, but you could always find it in the office of a real estate company!"

Bangalore thus became a "gold mine" for builders and developers. "These same people today are in politics and hold power as MLAs [Members of the Legislative Assembly], MLCs [Members of the Legislative Council], and ministers [members of the Council of Ministers]."[7] Indeed, in 2013, twenty-three of the twenty-eight MLAs representing Bengaluru declared large land and real estate assets.[8] In 2022 at least twenty-six MLAs listed "business" or "real estate" as their sources of income. Bengaluru's MLAs are also among the richest in the country.[9] Jagannath reiterated what is common knowledge in Bengaluru—that politicians raise funds for their parties to fight elections by allocating parcels of land (acquired by KIADB) to real estate players in return for kickbacks: "This is a huge mafia."

In 2000 the BDA had begun planning the ORR, for which they wanted to acquire a large amount of land. According to Jagannath, the farmers were not consulted—they learned about the plan only after receiving land acquisition notifications. The BDA planned to take more land than it needed to build the road—five hundred meters on both sides of the new road, which would be monetized by selling the excess land to private "entrepreneurs." Jagannath began mobilizing farmers against the ORR plan. Despite protesting and filing court cases for two years, the project went ahead. Farmers received a paltry compensation of 350,000 rupees (about 7,500 USD) per acre of land acquired. Some were so angry that they simply let their land go without collecting the money, according to Jagannath.

In Bellandur, the KIADB acquired hundreds of acres of land and allocated plots to various companies and real estate developers. None of these "investments" have generated employment for local people, Jagannath asserted. Developers just build commercial complexes and rent out space to IT companies, whose employees are highly educated middle-class youth from across India.

Commenting on how the state government bent over backward to cater to the demands of the software industry by acquiring land and planning new infrastructure, Jagannath offered this insight: "The government says that only 'nonpolluting' industries would be allowed here. How are software companies nonpolluting? Have you seen the smoke that comes out of the diesel generators in these IT parks? They need uninterrupted power supply and air-conditioning, so they have these backup systems. Some 400,000 employees work in these IT campuses. Where does their drinking water come from? The sewage that comes out of those buildings, the cars they use to get to their work—isn't all this pollution?"

Most Bellandur farmers who sold or lost their land used the compensation money or sale proceeds to construct new houses or commercial buildings in the village, which they rent out to earn some income—reinventing themselves as small-scale landlords (see chapter 11). Jagannath explained, "We all sold by force. We sold due to the threat of acquisition by the KIADB or BDA. We didn't want to let go of our lands. We were living peacefully when we were farmers." Meanwhile, the water table fell drastically, from 50 feet in 1994, to 500 feet in 2005 and 1,500 feet in 2022—thanks to overextraction by the "tanker mafia" (which sells borewell water—often acquired illegally—through small tankers hitched to trucks or tractors; see chapters 3 and 21).[10] Jagannath complained that "everything has gotten worse"—now there is noise pollution, air pollution, water pollution. "We made a big mistake allowing the Outer Ring Road to come up here. Apartments, hotels, restaurants are everywhere. This village used to be dead by 9 p.m., now it is hard to tell the difference between night and day. . . . This place has become like Bangkok!" Bellandur Lake remains extremely polluted, despite a 1999 order from the Karnataka High Court directing the government to clean it up. Jagannath joked that the mosquitoes that breed there do not die very fast, and if they bite you the itch lasts for three days!

Jagannath wonders aloud what will happen to all the big software campuses and numerous apartment complexes that have come up here when there is no more water. "Only 10 percent of the city gets water from the Kaveri project." He points out that the hundreds of villages that have been incorporated into the municipality since the 1990s do not receive municipal water and depend on other sources—especially borewells and tankers: "We have created such a disaster." These are the same areas that get flooded every year as rainwater, which earlier would get captured in the tanks or groundwater reserves, runs off or stagnates on the cemented roads, its passage impeded by gigantic buildings and blocked drains.

Jagannath gradually sold off the twenty-eight acres of land that his family held at Bellandur, investing the proceeds in the construction of a house and a commercial building in the village to garner some rental income—apparently capitulating to the culture of speculative real estate that accompanies this form of urbanization. But he also purchased twenty acres of land in a rural area near Mysuru, where he grows teakwood, coconut, guava, and other plantation crops. He now spends most of his time on his farm, trying to live an eco-friendly lifestyle "in the little world I created," far from the nightmare that Bengaluru has become.

Notes

This chapter draws on an interview with Mr. Jagannath conducted by Kaveri Medappa.

1. Jayaraj Sundaresan, "Urban Planning in Vernacular Governance: Land Use Planning and Violations in Bangalore, India," *Progress in Planning* 127 (2019): 1–23.

2. T. S. Ranganna, "He Set Up a Model Panchayat and the World Noticed," *The Hindu*, October 19, 2011, https://www.thehindu.com/news/cities /bangalore/he-set-up-a-model-panchayat-and-the-world-noticed/article2552172 .ece.

3. The KIADB is a parastatal agency of the state government that is authorized to acquire land for industrial or infrastructure development—a definition that the state government has construed broadly since the mid-1990s to include commercial development such as hotels and real estate projects. The KIADB has served as the major "broker" in facilitating the transfer of agricultural land to real estate and other companies. Michael Goldman, "Speculative Urbanism and the Making of the Next World City," *International Journal of Urban and Regional Research* 35, no. 3 (2011): 555–81.

4. Janaki Nair, *The Promise of the Metropolis: Bangalore's Twentieth Century* (New Delhi: Oxford University Press, 2005).

5. The interview was conducted primarily in Kannada, and the English translations given here are by Kaveri Medappa. In the translated quotations, English words used by Jagannath while speaking in Kannada are italicized.

6. "Panchayat Leader Accuses Infosys of Land Grabbing," *The Times of India*, November 25, 2002, https://timesofindia.indiatimes.com/business/india -business/panchayat-leader-accuses-infosys-of-land-grabbing/articleshow /29366107.cms.

7. MLAs and MLCs are members of the two elected bodies that govern at the state level in India—the Legislative Assembly, or Vidhan Sabha (the lower house), and the Legislative Council, or Vidhan Parishad (the upper house), respectively.

8. Sai Balakrishnan and Narendar Pani, "Real Estate Politicians in India," *Urban Studies* 58, no. 10 (2021): 2089–90, https://doi.org/10.1177/0042098020937917.

9. Janaki Nair, "Reimagining Bengaluru," *The Indian Express*, September 20, 2022, https://indianexpress.com/article/opinion/columns/reimagining -bengaluru-resilient-and-sutainable-urban-ethos-8158919/.

10. Malini Ranganathan, "'Mafias' in the Waterscape: Urban Informality and Everyday Public Authority in Bangalore," *Water Alternatives* 7, no. 1 (2014): 89–105, https://www.water-alternatives.org/index.php/allabs/235-a7-1-6/file.

3
Only Beautiful Plans

Vinay Gidwani

Travel to Bengaluru's amoebic margins, and you are likely to encounter peri-urban locales, awkwardly attired—part country charm, part rural squalor, part city chic, part urban drab. A place that doesn't know its place. In the throes of agrarian upheaval, upended by the approaching city. Irrigation tanks and lakes that once fed paddy fields and cattle are shriveled up or bone dry. The ones that survive appear to have the consistency of sludge, with foul-smelling white froth shimmering on their surface. Erstwhile villagers, now in the municipality's care, blame it on downstream flows of untreated sewage from Bengaluru. Surreal images of Bellandur Lake on fire have gone viral. No such pyrotechnics at "Purvapur Lake," which is best known for incidents of foaming, the froth from sewage overflowing onto the adjacent road. Weeds suffocate its expanse. Plastic litter and Styrofoam blobs jam its banks. Walk the muddy, broken path at its edge and you may stumble on rotting fish carcasses. Longtime residents remember a lake with water as clear as a pristine river, home to diverse species of fish. They recall fishing excursions as children, returning home with catches of two to three kilograms that their mothers whipped up into mouth-watering fish curry dinners. Now, they say, only the rugged catfish survives in the lake's contaminated environment.

But since the lake can still charm from a distance, the array of high-end apartment complexes that surround it market the lake view as a value proposition. The proximity of the *taluk* (subdistrict) of "Purvapur" to the IT hub in Whitefield—and Purvapur's incorporation in 2007 into the "yellow zone" in the Bengaluru Revised Master Plan (RMP) 2015—has made it an alluring destination for Bengaluru's real estate developers. All the big players and several smaller ones have projects here, either sales-ready or under construction. What was a sleepy habitation of eight hundred households and three thousand inhabitants in 1980 has mushroomed into an adolescent village-town of fifty thousand residents. The road that connects Purvapur to the nearest main road into the city, which negotiates a narrow two-lane bridge over the creek that drains from the lake, has become a choke point for traffic. In this peri-urban swath there are no proper roads, no piped water, no underground drains, a barely functioning sewage treatment facility, no municipal waste management—in short, no basic infrastructure. But there are hundreds of new luxury apartments, ripe for the picking. Purvapur is a microcosm of the city's breathless incursion into its rural peripheries.

When we met the local corporator (elected member of the city's governing body, the municipal corporation), "Jyoti," in 2018, the erstwhile taluk of Purvapur had been a municipal ward for twelve years. Because she was the ward's representative, we expected her to extol the benefits of incorporation into the Bengaluru municipality. Instead, she told us that Purvapur had been better off under the gram panchayat (village government) system. The panchayat would "collect tax at the local level and use it according to the area's needs and problems." Panchayat officials were approachable and responsive: this was a sentiment, undoubtedly filtered by the selective remembrance of nostalgia, that we heard repeatedly in nearby villages that also came under the jurisdiction of the Greater Bengaluru Metropolitan Corporation (BBMP) in 2007.

Like Jyoti, other residents complained about the BBMP's bureaucracy. Water from the latest stage of the Cauvery River Project, which was supposed to provision the mushrooming apartment complexes, is yet to arrive, its fate uncertain. In the meantime, Jyoti said, apartments were trucking in their water, extracted from borewells, paying 400 rupees for every five thousand liters. "Every day a thousand tankers are going from Balagere [a nearby village] to other places." She alleged that the system is coordinated by a "tanker mafia," but her pleas to the BDA and BBMP to control groundwater extraction have fallen on deaf ears. These organs of the state, she suggests, are unreachable for ordinary people. Echoing another common lament, Jyoti says that borewells that would hit groundwater at a depth of three hundred feet in the early 2000s now strike it—if at all—at fifteen hundred feet or more. She strongly favors a law to regulate the digging of borewells (ironically, borewells subsidized by the state government to aid agriculture are now used to supply water to thirsty urban neighborhoods). She bitterly gave the example of a local farmer with multiple borewells on his five acres of land who runs a tanker business, openly defying the law that makes such sales of groundwater illegal.

Jyoti's husband interjected: "Even the Karnataka State Electricity Board is working like a mafia! They should not give the connection [to run borewell pumps] to these mafia groups. If the government officials want to stop this mafia they can do it immediately, but they don't do that. Authorities are giving permission [to dig borewells] without looking at the ground reality in the Purvapur area and the water crisis. They don't follow the rules and regulations. When concerned authorities are violating the law, what will happen to the common man?"[1]

Because lakes in the vicinity of Purvapur have dried up, shrunk, or been encroached upon over the past two decades, reliance on groundwater has exploded just as capacity to recharge has plummeted. Ironically, Jyoti's main job as an elected city official was to commission new borewells—forty-three over a two-year period!—to slake the demands of a multiplying population.

"Krishna," principal of a local school who has been very active around issues of groundwater depletion, water pollution, and overdevelopment in Purvapur, described how the BDA's plans unleashed a frenzy of change. The 1995 Comprehensive Development Plan clearly confined Purvapur and adjacent villages to the "green belt," a zone surrounding the city where the conversion of agricultural land for nonagricultural uses was strictly controlled. But in the RMP of 2015, according to Krishna (we were unable to verify this claim), the BDA revealed its plan for a Peripheral Ring Road, and that area was removed from the green belt. Krishna hinted that several politicians and big developers had gained prior knowledge of the BDA's intentions: "Around 2005, when the land around here was still marked as green belt, some politicians started buying land because they knew the land use would be changed in these parts of the city. Once they started buying agricultural land, the land values started appreciating." Illustrating the dazzling escalation in land prices in Purvapur, Krishna remarked that in 1985 their school had paid 65,000 rupees for two acres of land. In 2000, when they purchased land for the playground, three acres cost 2.5 million rupees. The present rate for the plot opposite

56 Vinay Gidwani

their school is 5,000 rupees per square foot, or 200 million rupees (around 2.5 million USD) for an acre!

Krishna indicated that some (unnamed) MLAs (Members of the Legislative Assembly) and MPs (Members of Parliament) had acquired as much as 250 acres of land in this area prior to its rezoning as "yellow belt" (where residential properties can be developed, after "conversion" of agricultural land) through *benami* transactions (purchasing plots in others' names). When asked how these transactions were possible, he pointed to their high-level political connections: "They come to know from other MLAs and ministers about the plans for land-use change in the master plan in the coming years, who advise them to invest in those areas of the city." For the politically powerful, Krishna suggested, master plans, land-use maps, and zoning guidance operate as speculative devices. Like a forecast, they show what a future arrangement of the city will look like, setting in motion an array of actions that seek to anticipate that future and leverage it for maximum gain. More perniciously, politically connected actors, including members of the local landed elite, might intervene behind the scenes in the planning process to bend it to their speculative advantage. The chain of corruption runs "from tip to toe," Krishna said with a wry smile. From high-level bureaucrats in the Revenue Department and the District Collector's office down to the revenue inspector, *tahsildar* (assistant collector), and village accountant, among others, a host of actors play a role in facilitating these transactions, he explained.

This chain of politicians and government officers, Krishna continued, also abets the aggregation of large tracts of land for the high-end real estate projects underway in and around Purvapur. It is common knowledge that the state bureaucracy has multiple faces that shift according to the supplicant's location within networks of power. Krishna narrated a typical scene in the sub-registrar's office, where land transactions are recorded:

> An agent goes into the office of the sub-registrar and says that the purchase of *x* number of acres need to be registered. The sub-registrar generally gets 20,000 rupees per acre as bribe, and the lower-level staff—typists and so on—get 10,000 rupees to be shared by all. In the evening, after working hours, the sub-registrar calculates the money he should receive for register-

ing this number of acres. All the agents also gather here after 6 p.m., and after the total land area to be registered is calculated, the agents give a box of cash to the sub-registrar.

A process that might ordinarily take months for a common person is thus concluded within days. For land bankers (see chapter 7) and real estate developers, keen to gain an edge on rivals and achieve cash flow to offset debt obligations, time *is* literally money.

Anticipation generated by the BDA's plans shakes up the landscape beyond the yellow belt in adjoining green-belt tracts. In a nearby village that still lies within the green belt, farmers have carved residential layouts out of agricultural land—a quasi-legal activity. These developments are fenced, and plots sold, without any approval from planning or civic authorities (although they may have approvals from the local panchayat), and without road connectivity, water, or drainage. Since the legal status of these layouts is ambiguous, the landowners who can get away with such practices are invariably local "big men" from the dominant Reddy caste who have networks of political connections (chapter 14).

"Prakash Reddy," a former gram panchayat member who is a member of the Bharatiya Janata Party (BJP), then in power in the state, defended this practice of making layouts in the countryside. "What should we do with that land? We can't produce anything. It has become a burden for us to cultivate because there is no labor, water, or proper value for our crops in the market." A thirty-by-forty-foot "house site" in such layouts costs 1.5 to 2 million rupees, whereas a similar (authorized) plot in the yellow belt might run at 6 million rupees or more. Thus, these quasi-legal plots are an attractive investment for middle-class urban residents and even local farmers who have sold their land. Although the plot would be registered as "B-khata" (i.e., unauthorized property) when the area is brought under the BBMP's jurisdiction, that is less of a deterrent than it might seem for buyers— several banks offer loans for the purchase of B-khata properties in Bengaluru. Moreover, the state government from time to time has "regularized" B-khata properties, bringing them on par with regular urban plots.

In addition, local landlords such as Prakash Reddy, who have a keen grasp of the legal intricacies of land administration, have managed to exploit a provision of the Karnataka Land Reforms Act (1961) that permits change of land use in the green belt for educational institutions, hospitals, libraries, sports clubs, cultural centers, temples, and other such "public purposes" (with the permission of the district collector). As a result, large tracts of agricultural land in rural villages around the city have been diverted for such uses—due in part to the speculative forces set in motion by the BDA's porous yet opaque plan-making process. Meanwhile, the rapid, unplanned development of the green belt raises the question of how much land will be left for planned uses when these areas are recategorized as yellow (residential) zones.

"Ramesh," who works on land acquisition for a prominent real estate company, was dismissive of the BDA and its planning process. In his view, the very idea of a green belt is scandalous. Designating certain areas as "no development" zones effectively burdens farmers with the task of maintaining the city's lungs while cheating them of economic opportunities (from selling land). It also pushes land deals into the domain of illegality and corruption. Ramesh described a conversation he had with the secretary of Karnataka's Urban Development Department (UDD):

> You say that you are the custodian of [the] green belt. . . . And if I am a farmer, I am required to maintain the green belt for the urban residents, but what do I as a farmer get in return? Urban residents don't think about farmers who maintain greenery. If there is a shortage of rain and the farmer is in trouble, how is the UDD helping him? . . . So how can you enforce the green belt? A farmer has to educate his children and has so many other expenses, but because of the green belt his land does not have enough value. The government is locking a private person's property for maintaining the green belt.

Ramesh's view is that the whole idea of the green belt is an administrative artifact that disadvantages farmers for the alleged environmental well-being of the urban populace. From his perspective, it is no wonder that savvy local landowners like Prakash Reddy keep finding ways to subvert zoning guidelines.

Ramesh argues that if planners truly want a green belt around the city to mitigate urban pollution, they should acquire these lands and maintain them as an ecological buffer zone. Instead, planners conspire with politicians in the land speculation game by manipulating land-use categorization, allowing powerful actors to reap windfall profits at the expense of ordinary cultivators by sharing inside information in advance of planning decisions. Ramesh termed the process of public consultation (which is required by law for the draft master plan) "an eyewash." He noted that the preliminary map showing the different zones is displayed by the BDA for thirty days at a designated government office, allowing the public to view the plan and submit objections, but the authorities are under no obligation to act on these suggestions or objections: "The objections are received only to be overruled."

Farmers in both yellow-belt and green-belt villages around Purvapur complain that cultivation is no longer remunerative because of water scarcity caused by receding lakes and falling groundwater levels—a major factor impelling land sales. "Karthik," a resident of "Hasiruhalli" village near Purvapur Lake who works in the IT sector, explained that the water crisis was accelerated by Bengaluru's explosive growth over the last two decades. Places like Hasiruhalli became sites of brickmaking ventures because the exposed beds of nearby lakes were a source of plentiful clay. With the help of earth movers, they dug deep into lake beds—creating yawning pits that restricted the flow of rainwater into the network of channels that connected the area's numerous lakes. The pits initially helped to recharge groundwater locally, but their proliferation over time led to area-wide groundwater depletion, exacerbated by the extensive digging of borewells—first for cultivation and later for extraction of water for sale to the thirsty city. Cultivation of paddy, ragi, and vegetables and fruits for the city market, as well as dairying, subsided or ceased altogether. Many farmers planted eucalyptus to earn some income, further damaging the soil and water table (it is widely believed that eucalyptus depletes groundwater and soil fertility). When even profits from eucalyptus, coconut, and areca nut plantations declined, farmers began to turn their land to nonagricultural uses or simply sold out.

Like others, Karthik pinpointed 2005 as the year the real estate boom began. He didn't blame farmers for selling their land—cultivation had become unviable, and eucalyptus yielded a crop only once in five years and not much money. In contrast, rising land values meant that selling land became the most profitable option: "Even if people sold an acre for 25 lakh rupees, the interest from FDs [fixed deposits in a bank] would be more [than their earnings from agriculture or eucalyptus]."[2] Karthik sold his own small plot in 2012 to an aggregator who was buying land for a large real estate project (see chapter 7).

The pace of change in this periphery of Bengaluru has been frenetic, and Karthik expects it to become only more so. He noted that in the RMP 2031, which was unveiled in 2018, some of the yellow-zone residential areas had been rezoned as commercial. "Real estate companies have been buying [land] and suddenly it becomes a commercial zone. How is that? Someone must have influenced these decisions, right?" Karthik shook his head. "Knowing the BDA, I'm not surprised."

Rapid urbanization in an area that is quickly losing its rural feel has brought an influx of outsiders—from middle-class professionals who have purchased newly built apartments and gated villas, to working-class migrants from poorer regions of northern Karnataka, Bihar, and West Bengal, who find livelihoods in construction, waste collection and segregation, and assorted other manual activities. Some of these migrants initially came to work in the BBMP waste segregation site near Purvapur Lake before diversifying into private recycling work.

Karthik's wife, who is clearly rattled by these demographic disruptions, tells us that their neighborhood has become unsafe. "It's scary to leave the children outside because most of the laborers [construction workers at the new developments] pass through the neighborhood." Karthik nodded, adding, "Thefts have increased." He narrated the story of a construction worker who was recently caught with "a crore [10 million] worth of jewelry and cash." Karthik laughed, "Idiot he is! He had only spent 300 rupees out of that. He didn't even run away!" Karthik also expressed concern about the "Africans living in the area" (a nearby college has many foreign students). The village where the college is located—where several erstwhile farmers have built PGs (paying guest accommodation, the local term for hostels or dormitories) to rent rooms to students—is described by locals as a "mini-Africa." According to him, villagers have been "experiencing many problems" because of these "black people." (Although unsettling, such casual racism is commonplace among middle-class Indians.)

The nativism that Karthik exudes popped up in unexpected ways in other settings. "Shamim" lives on the peripheries of a village near Purvapur. He is a Muslim migrant from Bengal whose apprenticeship in the waste trade began in Delhi at the tender age of eleven. He has been in Bengaluru for eight years, where he works as a dry-waste collection subcontractor for a BBMP employee ("Sarojini") and operates a workshop where waste is segregated. Shamim supervises forty workers. He tells us that the Sarojini and the four other BBMP employees who oversee them pay each migrant worker 10,000 rupees per month and provide some additional support for food and housing. It wasn't clear from the conversation whether the BBMP employees' subcontracting arrangements with migrants like Shamim were officially sanctioned by the municipality or if the municipal employees were simply freelancing as dry waste contractors. It's clear, though, that the setup is "informal" in the sense that there is no permanence to the arrangements and no benefits or protections for the workers. The contractors have provided Shamim with two trucks and ten auto-rickshaw tippers. The workers under Shamim start their day at 5 a.m., collecting dry waste from the apartment complexes. Next, they bring the waste back to the settlement-cum-workshop to segregate. They then take the segregated scrap for sale to different parts of the city— City Market, the ITC recycling factory, Mysore Road, and so on. The unsalable waste is dumped at a quarry-turned-landfill somewhere in Devanahalli. The men drive up to sixty kilometers one way for this. Shamim says they spend up to 3,000 rupees on diesel daily.

Migrant families like Shamim's reside in a tight cluster of *kachha* (makeshift) structures constructed of corrugated metal sheets. The settlement is on private land owned by three different Reddy farmers who rent space to the migrants, charging around 2,000 rupees per dwelling. Nearby is another settlement of approximately two dozen families. These dwellings are far more rudimentary, assembled from bamboo poles and plastic sheets (see Figure 3.1). Pointing at them, Shamim grumbled, "These people are Bangladeshis, we are Indian, we have all the documents . . . Aadhaar card, voter ID, and so on." Since these "illegals" also work in waste collection, Shamim clearly views them as a threat to his livelihood. He is also aggrieved that Bengalis

Figure 3.1. Rudimentary shelters of migrant workers near Purvapur Lake. Photograph by Pierre Hauser.

and Bangladeshis are all tarred with the same brush by politicians and local middle-class residents, who deride their presence in Bengaluru.[3] Shamim is angry that they were evicted from their previous settlement in Kudlu Gate because of such targeting. "You allow Hindi-speaking or Bengali-speaking upper-class migrants into your city to find jobs. We also work. We clean your mess. If not us, who will do it for you? Our women go to work as domestic help in the apartment complexes in and around Purvapur. I wonder what we Bengali-speaking migrants did to you and your corporator?"

The ongoing upheavals in peri-urban villages of Bengaluru are plain to see. It's a mixed picture. Longtime residents yearn for a quieter life that is destined never to return. They complain about traffic, pollution, water scarcity, loss of cultivation and tree cover, migrants, crime. Many of them, mainly from the landed castes, have made windfall profits from selling their land at prices that were once unimaginable; several have bought new plots of land farther from the advancing city for speculative gain or refuge from the suffocating press of urbanization; others have squandered their jackpots on lavish weddings and ceremonies or consumer goods; many feel duped, having sold their landholdings before property prices peaked. Others, particularly from Dalit families with little or no land, have found employment as cleaners, cooks, gardeners, security guards, and retail help, servicing the apartment complexes and schools that have proliferated in these areas; a few local Dalits, like the wealthier Reddys, have become property brokers (chapter 14).

Unwittingly, or perhaps wittingly, the planning process has created a city that repeatedly exceeds the plan's design. As Ramesh cuttingly remarked: "The planning authority [BDA] only makes beautiful plans. It does not implement them."

Notes

Sachinkumar Rathod, Kaveri Medappa, Juwairia Mehkri, Priyanka Krishna, and Carol Upadhya contributed to this chapter.

1. For a different, but complementary, account of state complicity in the over-extraction of groundwater through borewells, see D. Asher Ghertner, "When Is the State? Topology, Temporality, and the Navigation of Everyday State Space in Delhi," *Annals of the American Association of Geographers* 107, no. 3 (2017): 740.

2. In the Indian numbering system, 1 lakh = 100,000, 1 crore = 10,000,000, or 100 lakh. Property figures are typically quoted in lakhs and crores.

3. As Bengali-speaking Muslims have become more numerous in urban waste collection across major cities in India over the past two decades—a period that coincides with the rise of Hindu nationalist identity politics—popular media, police authorities, and politicians have increasingly resorted to framing them as Bangladeshis; the implication is that they are illegal migrants from Bangladesh or "infiltrators" who pose economic and security threats to the nation. Such depictions also expose these communities to extortion and abuse by state and civil society actors. See Dana Kornberg, "From Bengalis to Balmikis: The 'Caste-ification' of Muslims in Delhi's Informal Garbage Economy," *Economic & Political Weekly* 54, no. 47 (2019): 48–54. See also Rizwana Shamshad, *Bangladeshi Migrants in India: Foreigners, Refugees, or Infiltrators?* (Delhi: Oxford University Press, 2017).

4
Building the High Life

Carol Upadhya

On a bright July day in 2018, members of our research team attended an event at "Lakeview Haven," a massive luxury apartment complex located on the southeastern fringe of Bengaluru (Figure 4.1). The name of this gated community gestures to nearby "Purvapur Lake," now polluted with sewage and refuse flowing downstream from the city (see chapter 21). The function had been arranged by the promoters of the project, "Prominent Developers"—one of Bengaluru's largest real estate companies—to mark the commissioning of the first two towers. Their clients, members of the project team, and others who had contributed to the project were invited. The guests were entertained with music and dance performances on the gaily decorated stage, followed by the ribbon-cutting ceremony and lunch.

Priyanka and Sachinkumar attended the event with "Somnath," a resident of "Hasiruhalli" village who had helped the company acquire over one hundred acres of agricultural land for the project (the village is introduced in chapter 3, and Somnath's story is detailed in chapter 7). As they walked into the complex, Somnath pointed out that the old Ganesha shrine—a small surviving marker of the village life that had once been supported by this land—had been decorated. He explained, "They always pray to Ganesha before any function."

The company's chairman, "Rajiv," kicked off the proceedings with a long speech extolling the quality of the construction and the excellent facilities provided in the apartment complex. He praised his team for the speedy execution of the project:

> With the support of the entire team, we could deliver these 3,500 apartments and 250 villas, 4 clubhouses, and all these ameni-

Building the High Life **65**

Figure 4.1. Foyer of model home, "Lakeview Haven." Photograph by Pierre Hauser.

ties. . . . Today is the time to acknowledge their hard work. It is not just our team, but the owners who gave us the land, our partner who brought us to this place,[1] then the design team, the production team, the bank who had faith in us, and most important of course all of you who believed in us, who just saw a piece of land and a piece of paper and invested your life savings. . . . Our buyers, the flat owners . . . they invest because they believe in us. Without the hard work of the team and your faith it is just impossible to produce what we have within this timeline . . . in four years we have finished these two towers, even the greenery, the clubhouses.

Rajiv also assured the assembled clients that the various teething problems would be quickly resolved and that the value of their properties would surely increase over time. Then he added, seemingly as an afterthought: "Apart from all these people, some five thousand to ten thousand laborers have been working tirelessly on this project, in good weather, bad weather, sweating it out—nobody knows how much work goes into a project!" Several of these "tireless" construction workers were perched high up in the half-built towers, gazing down mutely on the proceedings.

66 Carol Upadhya

When we first visited the spacious, air-conditioned marketing office at Lakeview Haven, a sales executive showed us on a large screen a promotional video of the planned project, pointing out its key features: its strategic location close to several IT hubs, their collaboration with international brand names for the design, the various amenities provided. The twenty-five towers materialize on the screen along with pictures of lush gardens populated by happy residents, large clubhouses with state-of-the-art gyms and recreational facilities, plus a swimming pool. Shots of women relaxing on lounge chairs are followed by visuals of the "Mediterranean-style" villas. Echoing the now-popular vision of the future city as a series of fully integrated mixed-use townships (see chapter 1), he explained that all the "requirements of daily life" would be available within the walls of the gated community—a restaurant, supermarket, movie theater, medical center, bank. Residents would not need to venture outside for anything (a good thing, too, given how long it would take to travel to the nearest shopping mall on the narrow, potholed road outside).

After viewing the promotional film, we were invited to tour the tastefully decorated model homes, their living-room balconies opening onto well-manicured lawns. Parked conspicuously next to the marketing office, a tanker disgorged its load of borewell water into an underground tank. A gardener tending the carefully designed gardens—a young woman from Hasiruhalli who told us that she had lost her job as an agricultural worker as land was sold for Lakeview Haven—informed us that seven to eight tankers, at a cost of 150–200 rupees each, come each day to provide the water needed just to maintain the gardens around the marketing office. She complained about the escalating price of water (which she also needs to buy for her domestic use) and about her job, which involves working in the hot sun from 8:30 a.m. to 5 p.m. daily for just 6,000 rupees per month. But she shrugged and turned back to her work, saying, "What to do, it is my [ill] fortune."

Lakeview Haven markets its homes to software engineers and other executives who work in the nearby IT hubs of Whitefield and Sarjapur Road—a demographic that is also attracted to this area by the many "international schools" established in the nearby green belt (see chapter 3). This sprawling residential development boasts thirty-five hundred apartments in twenty-five towers, ranging in size from

2-BHK (two bedrooms, hall [living room], kitchen) of 1,200 square feet, to 3BHK of 1,655 square feet, to 4-BHK of 2,800 square feet. Also on offer are 250 premium "villas" (independent houses). In 2017 these homes sold for 65 lakh (6,500,000) to 4.5 crore (45,000,000) rupees (100,000 to 700,000 USD).[2] According to a marketing executive, this price range is well within the reach of young professionals, especially since many such families have dual incomes: "If both husband and wife are working in IT, they can easily manage the EMIs [equated monthly installments, for repayment of bank loans] on their salaries. Some may have also inherited some money, which they invest in a new house, or they might sell an old house or property in their native towns to buy a flat in Bangalore." By early 2018, twenty-five hundred units in Lakeview Haven had already been sold, reflecting the high demand for residential property in this fast-developing corner of Bengaluru. This sales executive claimed that most of their customers are "end users," although some have purchased these flats for "investment purposes," renting them out to earn some extra income while waiting for the price to appreciate (a common financial strategy of elite and middle-class families in India). However, a consultant at the function estimated that at least 20 percent of the attendees were investors. Another marketing executive claimed that such projects generally have an occupancy rate of just 70 percent, indicating that purchases of such high-end residential apartments are often speculative investments.

But Rajiv had a different view of the market. When we interviewed him at his very plush office at the company's headquarters in central Bengaluru, he reflected on how the city has changed since he was a boy. Many people come from all over India to take up employment and end up staying, he said: "They take a house on rent thinking they will work here for a while and then go back. But once they come here, they don't want to leave—the city is just sucking in people. They like the climate, there are good IT jobs. They love the city, the people. Here people are more friendly. This place is also more cosmopolitan compared to cities like Chennai . . . here you can speak any language and get away with it!"

Rajiv comes from an old trading family of Bangalore—his father and grandfather ran small shops during the "British days." Rajiv diversified the family business by becoming a builder in the 1970s: "By chance we were in the right place at the right time. Sometimes we can't even believe that we have done this [become so big]. We have built two hundred properties already in Bangalore!" Although there are many new residential projects coming up all the time, demand is always growing: "Say we are building twenty-five thousand units—we can easily find twenty-five thousand buyers. There is always a market— even if a guy has a house, he wants a bigger one. See, if you have a Maruti car, you want a Lexus. If you own a Lexus, you want a Rolls-Royce. Like that, if you have a single-bedroom house you graduate to two, then you want four. And then there are people who buy properties as an investment."

Back at the inauguration function, Rajiv continued his speech by explaining the "thought process" behind the design of the complex: "Friends, five years ago two gentlemen approached us saying, 'We have this piece of land, would you like to develop it?' One fine weekend they drove me to this place and showed me this hundred acres of land. When I saw the land, I could not imagine building up this space with an FSI [floor space index] of 3." He was alluding to the verticalization of middle-class residential housing seen in Bengaluru and other major Indian cities beginning in the 1990s. The relaxation of FSI and other planning norms allowed the construction of multiple high-rise buildings in close proximity, leading to densification as well as urban sprawl. "Nitin," the land aggregator who put together the land parcel and then became a joint development partner in the project (chapter 7), had proposed an FSI of 3, which would have allowed them to build many more units on the same plot—yielding higher profits. But Rajiv insisted that they follow an FSI of 1.5 in order to create substantial open space within the complex. He presented this decision as a sacrifice of profits to provide a better lifestyle for their clients (although property rates also reflect the extent of open space and other amenities within a residential complex):

> When I talk about space, I imagine the people living there— the housewife, children, parents—and you have to imagine that it's a pleasure for all to live here. Now you have a world where both wife and husband work, or the wife works and husband stays at home, but whoever lives in that home should feel pleasure and be happy. We also need to provide a convenient, good

lifestyle. All these things were in my mind when I saw this piece of land. I told Nitin, I have seen your land, I have walked the land, but I have a different thought process. When you look at this much space you should not think of just building verticals of one, two or three blocks, but should imagine the people living here. I thought I should create this space for people's convenience and pleasure, with [a mix of] semi-high-rise and low-rise [buildings]. Don't worry, I will get you the value, I told him.

Elaborating on how he imagined the Lakeview Haven project from the perspective of the customers, Rajiv explained:

> Because there was so much space, I thought I should divide it in half—in half you will get the tangible value and in the other the intangible value. There is a lot of intangible value which goes into a [real estate] project, it is not just about the development of land but also about the users' convenience. Intangible value is where people have space to enjoy a good life. So, we have kept the FSI to 1.5, although we could have gone much higher. We made this sacrifice so that we have 20 percent ground coverage and 80 percent open space. So, a lot of thought process went into the design, and we made this wonderful project. . . . You have all the facilities here, like a huge clubhouse for each wing.

Following this long promotional speech, clearly aimed at putting a positive spin on the project to mollify unhappy clients, Rajiv invited the "key people" who contributed to the project to come up on the stage so he could thank them. As they were assembling, he continued talking to the audience, highlighting the hard work that his "team" had put in and the difficulties they had faced, and requesting customers' "patience" and understanding for any lapses. He seemed to be acknowledging the many complaints they had received from customers about delayed delivery, the poor state of the only access road to the complex, and other such issues.

Several attendees were indeed unhappy about the problems they were facing. One told us that he had booked his flat six years earlier and had completed all the payments two years ago, but the tower in which his apartment is located was still not finished. Another buyer was apprehensive about the water supply, noting that several other large projects were coming up in the area and that all of the apartment complexes would have to rely on groundwater, since there was not yet any municipal water supply in this peri-urban area. An interior designer who had come to the function to meet potential clients confided that the ceremony is a "large PR exercise to calm the owners who are panicking because the project has been delayed by a year." He explained that he had joined a WhatsApp group started by customers to share information and concerns, so he has inside information on their discussions. Later, the members of one such WhatsApp group (there is one group for each tower) gathered near "their block" to meet in person for the first time.

When we visited the marketing office on another occasion, we asked a salesperson about the potential water problem. He explained that they had installed "high-tech systems" to conserve and maximize the available water resources—a recycling plant to supply treated sewage water to the toilets and gardens and a rainwater harvesting system to recharge the groundwater, from which drinking water will be drawn through borewells. But he admitted that the complex may have to rely indefinitely on private water tankers, which sell water extracted from more distant rural areas where groundwater is still available (the water table in this area had already fallen precipitously, as discussed in chapter 3). Another salesperson commented dismissively, "If people are so concerned about water, no one would buy any property in Bangalore, since the entire city is reeling with water problems!"

Continuing his speech, Rajiv acknowledged another "external" problem that worried many of his customers—the very narrow, potholed, and constantly congested road that provides the only access to Lakeview Haven from the city. Several flat owners we met at the ceremony worried that they would face very long commutes to work, although their offices were located just five or six kilometers away. One customer said that he plans to lease out his Lakeview Haven apartment and live in a rented flat closer to his office until the road is fixed. Prominent Developers and other real estate companies with projects coming up in the area were placing pressure on the BBMP (Greater Bengaluru Metropolitan Corporation) to widen the road—originally the main market road of the village—but little progress had been made. But Rajiv told the audience that work had already begun on converting it into a four-lane road. Indeed, notices had been issued to the shopkeepers along the road to vacate, since these small village shops would have to be demolished and relocated to widen the road. But as with most land acquisition notifications, the owners were protesting. This controversy about the road shows that Prominent Developers had received the requisite permissions and clearances to build this massive apartment complex without any consideration for connectivity or the impact on traffic congestion or air pollution—a perennial issue in Bengaluru.

Glossing over these fundamental problems in the planning of such large real estate projects, as well as the company's apparent failure to anticipate this issue, Rajiv exhorted his customers to exert pressure on the government through the political process:

> We are also looking at the external infrastructure. . . . We are facing this problem of road connectivity, but believe me, we are all working together for widening of this road. We will work with the government departments to see how we can solve this, and shortly it will be done [audience applauds]. Once this hundred-foot-wide road is done, it will be the most accessible road. We are also concerned citizens of this city . . . but people's power is the best power! We have three and a half thousand owners behind us—you are thirty-five hundred votes of this constituency, so you can also use your power—talk to the local corporator, to the MLA, to solve this problem![3]

Then, seeming to directly address customers' grievances, and disregarding the fact that such megaprojects often violate multiple planning norms and building codes, Rajiv declared:

> You see, it's very easy to criticize, to point out that this or that is not good . . . but we are all one big family. I'm not saying we are perfect—there will be problems, but whatever issues you face there is a huge team to help you sort it out. Until the last customer is satisfied, we will not rest! There will always be a small minority who will blame the builder—but remember that thousands of people have worked tirelessly to complete this project. It is no small job. . . . I request our customers to be patient with us and we will slowly do what we have to do!

Turning from these problems to again promote their accomplishments, he then shared some "good news": "Today is a fantastic day for us—our group has completed more than one hundred million square feet of built-up space as of today. . . . It is a huge job, to handle the authorities, the political system, the people on the ground—but we have been doing it because this is the work we enjoy, for us it is a passion. All my colleagues have become insane like me and work with enthusiasm. . . . With your faith we have succeeded." Emphasizing the difficulties of their work and the exceptional attributes of Lakeview Haven, Rajiv compared the production of a large real estate project with making a "blockbuster" Bollywood movie: "Making a big project like this is like producing a movie—you need a director, a producer, a villain, actors, and supporting roles. Without all these elements nothing happens. . . . According to me, Lakeview Haven is a blockbuster, and it will remain a blockbuster, not for a few weeks but for the future, for posterity." Who, we might wonder, is the hero and who is the villain in the blockbuster production that is Lakeview Haven?

Following the ribbon-cutting ceremony and the sumptuous lunch, many of the new homeowners gravitated to the swimming pool, chatting with one another while dipping their feet in the water and watching their boisterous children playing happily in the shallow end.

Notes

Sachinkumar Rathod, Priyanka Krishna, Kaveri Medappa, Hemangini Gupta, Vinay Gidwani, and Michael Goldman contributed to this chapter. The chapter also draws on Vinay Gidwani and Carol Upadhya, "Articulation Work: Value Chains of Land Assembly and Real Estate Development on a Peri-urban Frontier," *Environment and Planning A: Economy and Space* 55, no. 2 (2023): 407–27, https://doi.org/10.1177/0308518X221107016.

1. Here he is referring to "Nitin," the land aggregator who features in chapter 7.

2. In the Indian numbering system, 1 lakh = 100,000, 1 crore = 10,000,000, or 100 lakh. Since property prices and other figures are usually quoted in lakhs and crores, we retain these terms in the text.

3. This request ignores the fact that many IT professionals—most of whom are migrants to the city—are likely to be registered to vote in other states, not in Bengaluru.

Aerial view of upmarket apartment complex, Yeshwantpur. Photograph by Pierre Hauser.

Part II
Financial Stratagems

A growing body of recent scholarship traces the connections between financialization and urban development. For many scholars, the distinguishing feature of financialized capitalism is profit generation out of processes of circulation—in the form of interest, dividends, rents, tolls, tariffs, user fees, and short-term capital gains. Thus, value is extracted from urban actors either by "moving around existing resources and outputs, and gaining disproportionately from the ensuing trade"[1] (as in the case of home mortgages, potable water trucked into water-scarce apartment complexes by a "tanker mafia," or private capital investments in real estate or infrastructure projects via special purpose vehicles, or SPVs). Or, value may also be expropriated through a process of "assetization," which entails "the transformation of things into resources which generate income [namely, rent] without a sale."[2] Examples would include the takeover of public infrastructure and service provision (such as road construction, drinking water supply, electricity grids, and waste management) by financially leveraged firms, which then service debts and make profits through tolls, tariffs, and user fees. Financialization contrasts with the generation of surplus value from the production of goods and services in a traditional capitalist economy.[3]

The trio of chapters in this section touch upon the sinuous workings of financialization,[4] but they go beyond the existing literature's emphasis on global or "high finance" to highlight other circuits of finance, operating at vastly different scales, that participate in the messy fabrication of the world-class city. So, if "high finance" (international private equity) and "regional capital" (a combination of formal and informal finance) underwrite the acquisition and assembly of large land parcels, or the construction of luxury townships, exclusive gated communities, or gleaming office towers, what we term "low finance"[5] allows the city's low-income residents to withstand the gusts of uncertainty that accompany speculative urbanism, or perhaps to get into the "game" themselves (see part 4).

Each of the three classes of finance showcased in this section displays its own attendant volatilities, which the chapters here capture through the experiences of large-scale real estate, chit fund networks, and local real estate "fixers." Together, the stories reveal how the ebb and flow of capital through these separate but mutually influencing circuits has transformed the city's built environment in intended and unintended ways.

In "Capital Times in Bengaluru" (chapter 5), real estate consultants give us the inside story on the city's land boom and the frenzy of speculation that accompanied it. They explain how, after changes in the Government of India's policies in the early 2000s, a throng of foreign investors and private equity firms descended on cities like Bengaluru in search of windfall profits in the real estate sector. Initial public offerings (IPOs) and SPVs became part of popular parlance as local real estate firms tried to capitalize on the tidal wave of high finance pouring in.[6] The resulting property boom peaked between 2012 and 2014, after which—thanks to economic downturns, demonetization, and the introduction of the Real Estate (Regulation and Development) Act 2016, or RERA—the market entered a phase where the supernormal returns of yesteryears dried up.

But it would be a mistake to think that high finance has been the sole or principal driver of Bengaluru's staggering urban transformation. Everyone with the wherewithal has tried to cash in on the riptide of speculation. This is one key lesson of "Low Finance in the World City" (chapter 6), which discusses how "vernacular architectures of finance"—the *cheeti* system—are employed by low-income residents to save money for a rainy day, invest in new assets, or take a long-term lease on an apartment. For the organizers—usually women—*cheeti* groups represent a form of small-scale enterprise that builds on the dense matrix of social relations (of neighborhood, kinship, caste) that characterizes low-income localities, and which provides an independent source of income—supplementing (or sometimes supplanting) their informal-sector jobs. But for the participants, *cheetis* also meet a range of important survival needs and emergency expenses, such as managing debts or paying the rent, for low-paid informal-sector workers confronted by the ups and downs of living in the speculative city.

"The Real Estate Fix" (chapter 7) digs into the subterranean process of land assembly that is carried out by land aggregators and intermediaries, charting how finance capital (formal and informal, big and small) circulates through land as it is transformed into real estate. A large land aggregator and a local intermediary explain the intricacies and intrigues of this cumbersome process, which can be highly lucrative but is also riddled with risks.

In all, the section illustrates how multiple forms of finance are variously mobilized, organized, and deployed in the hands of elites and non-elites, which have helped to create the risk-filled opportunities of speculative urbanism.

Notes

1. Costas Lapavitsas, *Profiting without Producing: How Finance Exploits Us All* (London: Verso Books, 2013), 163.

2. Kean Birch, *We Have Never Been Neoliberal* (Winchester: Zero Books, 2015), 122.

3. Mariana Mazzucato, *The Value of Everything: Making and Taking in the Global Economy* (London: Penguin Allen Lane, 2018). Also see Llerena G. Searle, *Landscapes of Accumulation: Real Estate and the Neoliberal Imagination in Contemporary India* (Chicago: University of Chicago Press, 2016).

4. Brett Christophers, *Our Lives in Their Portfolios: Why Asset Managers Own the World* (London: Verso, 2023).

5. Ashish Kumar Sedai, Ramaa Vasudevan, and Anita Alves Pena, "Friends and Benefits? Endogenous Rotating Savings and Credit Associations as Alternative for Women's Empowerment in India," *World Development* 145 (September 2021), https://doi.org/10.1016/j.worlddev.2021.105515.

6. Michael Goldman and Devika Narayan, "Through the Optics of Finance: Speculative Urbanism and the Transformation of Markets," *International Journal of Urban and Regional Research* 45, no. 2 (2021): 209–31.

5

Capital Times in Bengaluru

Vinay Gidwani

Travel north from Bengaluru to Devanahalli and Kempegowda International Airport or south and east to Whitefield and Varthur, and it's hard to avoid the deluge of gigantic billboards featuring a parade of couples or families with suspiciously Anglo-Saxon features, all smiles, enjoying the good life at "Brigade Atmosphere," "Embassy Edge," "Godrej Reserve," "Sobha Lifestyle Legacy," or "Prestige Lakeside Habitat" (Figure 5.1). What not so long ago were cultivated lands and grazing commons, supporting an agrarian social ecology, now boast a different multispecies of crop: apartments, villas, resorts, and gated townships in different states of gestation, from the purely notional ("Coming Soon!") to preparatory earthwork to scaffolding to the ready to harvest, for use or profit.

The narrative of Bengaluru, which once styled itself as a languid "Garden City," is now all about high tech and land. Cities are, after all, imaginative geographies. The upmarket developments—luxury high-rises, gleaming malls, hip cafés, glass-and-steel office towers—steal the limelight, but away from the glare of world-class city-making, in modest neighborhoods and makeshift settlements that provision low-income housing for the working classes, change is palpable. No one who can help it wants to be left behind in the property boom. Short, squat, or skinny, it doesn't matter; dwellings of all types have grown, often sprouting rental units that warehouse seven to eight to a room, finding space to expand where it seems geometrically impossible. This fitful growth, defying architectural convention, presents a colorful contrast to the temples of modern living that dot the cityscape, but both endeavors are fueled by the same combustant: a volatile mix of anticipation, aspiration, avarice, and desire. The key

Figure 5.1. Selling the dream: advertisement for high-end apartments in Bengaluru. Photograph by Pierre Hauser.

difference between the plebeian constructions of the ordinary and the patrician dreams of the well heeled? Capital.

These are capital times in Bengaluru. The city and its peripheries have been transformed with unsettling rapidity by the flows and rhythms of capital—big, small, corporate, individual, foreign, domestic. Byzantine tales of collusion between developers, politicians, and state functionaries, with murky subplots of forced land acquisition, graft, and windfall accumulation, used to capture the headlines with regularity. Less so now. Still, it's impossible to disentangle Bengaluru's recent history of urban upheaval from the seamy currents of politics, patronage, and prospects of supernormal profits. But the main plotline is more banal, obscure, and consequential—at least in the telling of the city's real estate professionals. It has to do with economic policies and financial regulations, initial public offerings (IPOs), special purpose vehicles (SPVs), private equity and structured debt, home mortgages, land aggregation, and, yes, age-old speculative greed.

Bengaluru's land market awakened in the 1990s, in the years after India's public embrace of liberalization. Santosh, an investment executive at a top real-estate firm in the city, whom we spoke to in 2019, termed the period between 1991 and 2001 a "catch-up"—when a "controlled market" in which investment, not consumption, was viewed as the chief driver of GDP growth, yielded to a more capitalistic order that said, "Yeah, consumption is okay! You can have more credit cards, you can have more personal loans, you can consume, you can fuel growth. So, you are looking at it the American way in comparison to before, which was the socialist way." Despite this ideological shift, the spurt in land values was uneven due to jitters from the 1997 Asian financial crisis centered in Indonesia and Thailand and, a few years later, from the Y2K crisis. But some players—politicians, businessmen, builders, private financiers—sensing what was to come, made moves to gain a foothold in the land market, hoarding and grabbing land when and where opportunity arose.

The real estate boom got underway in the early 2000s. "There was pent-up demand," Santosh said, "subdued prices, and then suddenly you are triggering off something which is a multiplier. So, people investing, say in 2000, your typical multiplier between 2000 and 2008 is five to six times your capital value." This was the heyday of speculation, when fortunes were minted and the face of Bengaluru and other cities around India was irretrievably transformed: "You had a huge number of investors who believed that you could buy your second or third home and flip it around and trade it because the prices always went up." Time was money in this frenzy for property: get in early to get out ahead. Sounding almost wistful, Santosh remarked, "That has evaporated from the markets—[today] you don't have investors."

The investors, he said, fell into three categories: salaried professionals who used their bonuses to leverage loans; corporate executives at big firms who invested their more substantial bonuses in larger-ticket items; and traders with liquidity and surplus from their businesses. The Delhi–National Capital Region market was dominated by traders, the Mumbai market by executives and traders, and the Bengaluru market by salaried employees and executives, he explained. "Because of the IT boom, a number of people from the IT industry and senior positions kept buying. . . . There was no tomorrow." Santosh distinguished this speculative tendency from other forms of market behavior with disarming simplicity: "Not for end use." And he broke it down into two parts, short and long speculation. "Long speculation is a salaried goal," he explained. "It's like saying, 'I got a bonus, I will put my bonus in. I am eligible for a loan, so I will take a bank loan with a five-year position on this one.'" The trader's speculation is based on the short term. "He thinks, 'The price is going to go up in twelve months, fifteen months, eighteen months. I have my short-term surplus which I am going to shove into this.'" The salaried man may wait for construction to finish before cashing out. And the trader? He wants a quicker exit. "He says, 'I am not going to wait for this project to be completed and then hand it over. I don't have patience for that. I expect for the core in-shell to get done, I will enter the launch and then sell it.' Pre-launch to structural completion you can call it."

Bengaluru's speculative fever came to an end, according to Santosh, "somewhere between 2012, '13, '14, somewhere in that zone." The property bubble in Bengaluru didn't burst with the ferocity witnessed elsewhere—in the United States, for example, where mortgage-backed securities fired a violent home-buying frenzy and an equally precipitous crash whose economic and political effects continue to scar that country. Bengaluru's balloon just fizzled out. Investors can still find returns, but the era of supernormal profits has evaporated. What changed? Too many investors looking for exits, oversupply in the market, plummeting prices. Santosh gave the example of Golf Course Road in Gurgaon, south of Delhi, as the iconic case of irrational exuberance. Property prices there had reached 16,000 to 18,000 rupees per square foot around 2012–13. But a year later, in the 2013–14 period, people were finding it difficult to realize 9,000 to 11,000 rupees per square foot. "Almost everybody lost their shirts," Santosh said. The investors, the developers, the banks.

To understand how Bengaluru's land market went from boom to relative stagnation, it's important to grasp the macroeconomic backdrop. In 2002 India's capital market regulations were amended to permit FDI (foreign direct investment) in real estate (subject to certain restrictions), and in 2005 the floodgates were opened when 100 percent FDI was allowed in townships, housing, infrastructure, and development-oriented construction projects. This was promoted as an instrument to "generate economic activity, create new employment opportunities, and add to the available housing stock and built-up infrastructure," according to the Government of India.[1] "Gaurav," a real estate consultant who has advised many of Bengaluru's major land aggregators and developers, told us, "Funds dedicated solely to investments in real estate were set up, with money coming in from much of the world. These were routed through countries with which India had a tax treaty, such as Mauritius. There were rumors of 'round-tripping' of capital, that is, illicit incomes held in cash in India or abroad were channeled into India via this route." But there were also bona fide funds that saw participation from major players in the United States, indicating that the shortage of homes in India was increasingly seen as a major greenfield business opportunity by investors worldwide.

Local developers, established ones as well as lower-tiered, were alert to the opportunity. They started spinning fanciful tales of Bangalore's "growth story"—promising mouthwatering returns of 25–30 percent per annum to lure gullible foreign partners. FDI in real estate leapfrogged from a mere 467 million USD in 2006 to an annual average of 2.5 billion USD between 2007 and 2011. Much of this was private equity money that came through the back door. It was project-specific, transported through SPVs. On paper the terms were preferential to investors, with stock buyback agreements of dubious legality that guaranteed a profitable exit. In practice, when the market started souring, exits—barring those of some early departees—were neither smooth nor profitable.

But as Gaurav noted, foreign capital was not the only, or even principal, source of funds. Major local developers, seeking to become regional or even national players, launched IPOs to raise equity capital by issuing shares at a premium, parting with only a small fraction of their total shares. Bengaluru-based developers that had been growing rapidly since the turn of the millennium unveiled IPOs between 2006 and 2010—Sobha (2006), Brigade (2007), Puravankara (2010), and Prestige (2010). These issues were oversubscribed, reflecting the enthusiasm of investors (Sobha's IPO, the first to be launched, was oversubscribed by 104 times). With this large infusion of capital, including from foreign institutional investors, the scale and ambition of real estate projects grew manifold. According to "Vilas," manager at a major private equity fund: "From 2005, money came in from private equity and said, grow your company, buy more land, create inventory, increase your organization size. Spend money on that—no problem." He characterized the post-2005 period as *bhed chaal*—literally, sheep following each other. In retrospect, Vilas noted, "even the best of real estate funds or private equity funds never showed more than 7–8 percent profitability at the portfolio level."

IPOs brought legitimacy and a dose of transparency to the workings of the real estate business in Bengaluru and India.[2] Or as Gaurav colorfully described it, "Share prices quoted in the market, analysts hanging onto the words of real estate barons, and glitzy award functions heralded a new dawn for real estate, and it was a strange and wonderful feeling for a rather seedy industry to gain some respectability!" The euphoria that forever transformed Bengaluru's cityscape lasted until 2011, at which point "the Lehman lag" (in Santosh's words) and disappointing returns caught up with investors, who rushed to exit—only to find their planned departures clogged by sagging property prices, defiant local partners who refused to honor preferential arrangements, and the glacial workings of Indian courts.

By 2014, developers were awash in debt. The culling had begun. Cheap money dried up. Structured debt at interest rates of 13 to 15 percent, involving a network of domestic and offshore shadow bankers, replaced equity. The triple whammy of demonetization (November 2016), the imposition of a new tax regime (the Goods and Services Tax

[GST, April 2017]), and the notification of the Real Estate Regulation and Development Act (RERA, May 2017) together dealt a death blow to a great many small and medium developers. Gaurav calculated that Bengaluru had over six hundred developers in 2010; the bulk of them operated at a very modest scale but together controlled almost 70 percent of the market. By 2017 this number had shrunk to a "scarcely believable" 250.

The city's real estate development lurches on, but a sense of crisis is palpable. Gloom has clouded an industry built on sunny sentiments, as developers scramble to service mounting debts in a buyers' market with sluggish sales. Gaurav unpacked the issue. A "healthy" housing inventory, he explained, is anywhere from five to eleven months of stock; today, these stocks are running at five to seven years. Units, particularly in the (once) profitable luxury segment, have been produced at a pace that far exceeds what the market can absorb. The ripple effects are everywhere: the city's ecology has been shredded by the speculative delirium of yesteryears and the building frenzy that was its companion; unsold or unfinished apartments and villas throng Bengaluru's peripheries; and land banks, once likened to accumulating gold and held in anticipation of future demand, as far as fifty kilometers away from Bengaluru, have become a pressing liability for some owners. In this scenario, Gaurav mused, "the logical way to resolve the crisis would be to cut prices, but the slowdown has been marked by the stubborn refusal of real estate developers to do so." The dream of the speculative city persists, hoping to bend reality to its desire. Such are the afterlives of capital times.

Notes

Sanjiv Aundhe, Carol Upadhya, Michael Goldman, and Deeksha Rao contributed to this chapter.

1. Government of India, Ministry of Commerce & Industry, Department of Industrial Policy & Promotion, SIA (FC Division), Press Note 2 (2005), https://nishithdesai.com/fileadmin/user_upload/pdfs/press-note2-2005.pdf.

2. See Llerena Guiu Searle, *Landscapes of Accumulation: Real Estate and the Neoliberal Imagination in Contemporary India* (Chicago: University of Chicago Press, 2016). See also D. Asher Ghertner and Robert W. Lake, eds., *Land Fictions: The Commodification of Land in City and Country* (Ithaca: Cornell University Press, 2021).

6

Low Finance in the World City

Hemangini Gupta

In the early 2000s, vast tracts of land that housed factories and mills in Bengaluru's Peenya and Yeshwantpur areas were sold to private developers. Apartments here, situated on what was former mill land, in 2020 were being advertised at 30 million rupees (750,000 USD). Interspersed among the high-end condominiums and their accompanying leisure spaces are older, low-income communities—slums or informal settlements—typically housing domestic workers employed in the apartment buildings, service employees working in the malls and hotels, and contract sanitation workers who sweep the streets and collect trash. How do such low-income workers afford to live in these neighborhoods where their work is essential?

As a postdoctoral associate on the Speculative Urbanism project, I had recently moved back to Bengaluru and found myself looking for a small apartment to rent near these sites of my fieldwork. Unable to find anything suitable that I could afford, I ended up living in an old family home near our field sites. My own experience was a stark reminder of whom these new neighborhoods were being imagined and built for. As I lived in Bengaluru, relying on part-time workers to take care of our son and on essential workers to take away our trash, I came to understand how low-income workers without intergenerational wealth and advantages still live in the "world city." They create and engage in building financial systems to survive a reimagination and material restructuring of their neighborhood—from industrial zone to elite "world city" landscapes.

I focus here on the creation and use of local networks of finance called *cheetis* ("chit funds," or revolving credit societies). *Cheeti* literally means a "slip" or piece of paper, but in my fieldwork the term was used to refer to the act of participating in these informal circuits of finance and not to the actual voucher or receipt for the cash transactions being made, which did not physically circulate. Instead, the investments and withdrawals are tabulated in a register by the chit fund organizer and noted on WhatsApp groups by members of the *cheeti* group.

The *Cheeti*

This chapter draws from my interviews and observations in low-income and working-class neighborhoods, talking with residents about how they develop and embed themselves in vernacular architectures of finance to weather the rapidly transforming real estate markets in the city's Yeshtwantpur area. Many of the people I interviewed for this research were contract workers with erratic wages who were living in a continual condition of precarity, knowing that they could be terminated from their jobs with no notice. They relied on *cheetis* to tide them over in situations of unexpected financial need: a rent payment when wages were suspended, marriage expenses, or perhaps the purchase of a luxury item, such as gold, that could later serve as a precious commodity to pawn. *Cheetis* are an example of what we term "low finance": informal modes of finance that allow neighbors, friends, and those in trusted networks to pool their money so they can borrow from the fund when in need. As a network, *cheetis* cannot be too wide—you need to trust everyone in your group. But they also cannot be too narrow—precarious contract workers coming together with others working in similar jobs dilutes the prospects of a *cheeti's* success and therefore its utility in times of need.

From my interviewees I learned about the three main kinds of *cheetis*. The first is the *kulka* (shake, mix-up) *cheeti*, in which participants pool in a certain sum every month. For example, if a *cheeti* is planned for 10,000 rupees over ten months, the ten participating members pay 1,000 rupees each month. Every month, the names of all the members are written on individual slips of paper (chits), and a drawing is held. Whoever wins the draw gets the 10,000 rupees for that month. After a member wins, he or she exits the pool, and the remaining members continue to play until everyone has received their 10,000 rupees.

The second type of *cheeti* is the *kugo* (call out) *cheeti*, which works through bidding. Members pool in a certain sum of money every month, as in the first type, but at each meeting they can bid to borrow some amount from the fund. The highest bidder gets that amount, and the rest is divided between the others. As one of our informants explained, "Everyone has a stake in this. It is everyone's money, and we are all aware of it even when we call out an amount during *cheeti*. This is why only when someone is really desperate for money do they bid higher. Then the rest of the group understands this and stops bidding. If they continue, then it is a loss shared by all of us."

The third type of *cheeti* scheme that participants told me about is the *sangha* (group or association) *cheeti*, in which the agent of the *sangha* takes out bank loans and participants pay the interest. Usually, the *sangha* consists of fifteen members, but this might vary.

This brief outline provides an overview of how local groups of neighbors, friends, and relatives come together to create circuits of credit, but it does not encapsulate the rich affective atmosphere when a monthly *cheeti* is called. I witnessed the sharing of information and camaraderie of a *kugo cheeti* when I attended one myself, held in the small living room of the home of a *cheeti* organizer, located in a crowded lower-middle-class neighborhood in north Bengaluru.

One of my interviewees took me to the *cheeti* meeting, which was held after lunch. She led me through a narrow street with small plots of land each housing a building at least three stories high. We opened a small black iron gate and entered a tiny house with a living room that had freshly painted green walls. At first, walking into this space felt like entering a wake—somber bodies packed the space, a hushed murmur circulated through the room. The air felt tense and expectant. In the background, a large flatscreen TV played a cooking show at low volume; opposite it, three bodies were crammed into a tiny wooden sofa. Women were seated on the sofas and on large mats on the floor, chatting and catching up with one another. At one corner of the room a middle-aged man pored over long sheets of paper, furiously punching numbers into a calculator. His mother, the *cheeti* organizer, sat beside him, presiding over the gathering, greeting entering guests with a brief nod and smile.

At 4 p.m., about half an hour after we had gathered, the man finally spoke. "This is for two lakhs" (200,000 rupees), he said in a low voice as the room turned still. "It will go to one person. If nobody wants the whole amount, we will break this up further." His mother nodded, looking around the room. He called a figure. A few people raised their fingers tentatively. Some looked around the room to see who else had raised their hands. Others looked down at their phones, where they had made and stored some calculations. He began calling numbers, going higher every few minutes. Hands were raised occasionally. Only some persisted, obstinate in staying on for higher bids. Ultimately, he stopped at two lakhs. His mother nodded her head in the direction of the person who had won the amount.

The man bent down to do some calculations on his sheet of paper and then resumed almost immediately, calling a much smaller sum. The air was more relaxed now, as the calls for "3,000 rupees" and "5,000 rupees" began. A man in the back tried to bid, as did the two cousins next to me, joking to him that he had stymied their efforts at winning. The cousins then opened their WhatsApp apps on their phones and together examined the photograph of a sheet of paper dense with calculations. They pursed their lips, figuring out when they should bid. The image showed a tabulation of the amounts called, the amounts available, and who had won how much. In just about twenty minutes, the event was over. The silence shattered, and bodies relaxed as people got up to talk to the day's convenor and catch up with each other.

This brief afternoon with the *cheeti* showed me how it was created through networks of kin and caste: I was invited there by an interviewee who had joined with much of her extended family. The *cheeti* organizer spoke Telugu just as she did, and most people seemed to know each other as both extended kin and neighbors. People knew where other *cheeti* members lived; they knew their families; they spoke the same language. It was a circuit of trust that built on other prior affiliations and networks. In the next two brief scenes from fieldwork, I explore why people turn to *cheetis*, showing how histories of migration, caste, and gender shape the kinds of networks that people form and the reasons that they need to borrow.

Scene One: "RP Colony"

RP Colony seemed to disappear overnight (see chapter 12). It was an informal settlement situated on private land, housing around one hundred families. Although informal, it had existed for many decades. For more than a year I had looked down on its blue tarpaulin sheets and low cement structures from atop a flyover as my auto-rickshaw rushed over it. And then overnight, it seemed, this informal settlement was razed to the ground. Situated on an enviable slice of prime land in the center of the city, flanked by multimillion-dollar residential real estate, a community of largely Tamil-speaking Dalits had now been scattered into the larger neighborhood. The demolition was carried out at the request of the local corporator (elected municipal representative), who promised residents that he would build a modern apartment complex in place of their earlier slum housing. The demolition was met with little contest. Each family was handed 20,000 rupees (250 USD) to enable them to survive in the competitive rental market in the area while waiting for their new houses to be built.

Along the main street that connects the demolished RP Colony to the more affluent parts of the city are the tiny one- and two-bedroom units where displaced residents found rental housing while waiting for their new homes to be built. As we traced them to bare living spaces anchored by strings of clothes, we found worried residents uncertain of how long they would have to pay rent and keenly aware that they were quickly falling deeper into debt. A few kilometers away from the local corporator's office was "Mani's" house in "Kalanagar"—the first informal settlement in this area to be demolished and "redeveloped" (see chapter 12). Its residents—mostly employed in contract-based sanitation work, as he was—were now rehoused in a new multistoried apartment building.

Mani is a local leader and a well-known activist in the area who started his own social organization for the upliftment of Dalits. While Kalanagar was being reconstructed, he and his family (his wife and their three sons) navigated the costly rental markets of this rapidly developing neighborhood. His wife took loans and joined *cheeti* groups to be able to pay the deposit on a rental house and the monthly rent, while he and his neighbors all waited for the new building to be erected. Their wages were not nearly enough to cover what they had to pay in rent in this area.

Some months before I first met them, Mani and his family had moved into the new apartment. His wife proudly pointed out the running water in the taps and the shelf space above the kitchen counter.

However, the new units, built by the municipal government, were too small to house even their nuclear family. As we talked, Mani squeezed himself into the drawing room, his wife sat on the floor alongside us in the same room, while one son stood at the doorway and the younger son ran in and out through the front door. Mani had moved here with only his essentials. Nothing else fit into the house, and so all their belongings were packed into suitcases in the old rental unit, which they were still paying for, steadily accumulating their monthly debt.

Mani was born and brought up in this neighborhood—his family had moved here in the 1940s, from rural Tamil Nadu, as what he called "coolie" (daily wage) workers.[1] He used some family contacts to get a job with the municipal government, driving an auto-rickshaw that collected waste. His sons now do the same work, while Mani has graduated to a position supervising the drivers. Such sanitation work for the city government is usually contract work, and like most sanitation workers, Mani has no job security. His old slum had running water and electricity, but there was no proper drainage and water would often stagnate, causing mosquito infestations. This problem was aggravated during the rains, with leaking roofs and slush accumulating right outside the house. The residents had long protested with the local government about their living conditions, demanding a new building, and finally it seemed that their dream had come true.

Yet, while the new units were being built, Mani and others had to spend money on rental accommodation in this expensive neighborhood where they also worked. He took on significant debt to cover the house rent alone, which was 4,000 rupees a month, plus additional expenses of 1,500 rupees. As with most rental housing in Bengaluru, the advance deposit required was ten months' rent—40,000 rupees (about 500 USD)—an amount that the landlord is yet to refund Mani, since he hasn't yet vacated the apartment. The 20,000 rupees he received to cover rent while the new building was under construction proved to be woefully inadequate to meet his expenses.

As I chatted with Mani in his new flat, a massive television that took up half the wall of the main room began to dominate the conversation (Figure 6.1). Our attention kept slipping to a comedy show in Tamil, and I finally commented on how enjoyable it was to watch television since I did not have one at home myself. Mani laughed. "You don't need to have a TV," he said, suggesting that someone of

Figure 6.1. "Mani" in his small apartment in his redeveloped tenement, showing his new flatscreen TV. Photograph by Hemangini Gupta.

my caste and class status does not need such commodities to assert social status. He continued: "When we go to people's houses to collect garbage, we see what big TVs they have, so we also want to improve, we also want to have the good life." His television was not only a means of connecting him to media worlds beyond his neighborhood; it was also a potent symbol of his aspirational class and caste status, adjacent to his desire to leave the place of the slum behind.

I asked him what he meant by "good life," a phrase he used in English, breaking out of the Tamil he was speaking in. He replied, "Everything should be neat and clean. Earlier people used to look at us and say we lived in the slum; now we get respect." His aspiration for social mobility and greater respect points to the stigma commonly attached to the caste-specific work in which his family (as Dalits) are engaged—cleaning neighborhood streets of waste, manually collecting garbage, and driving the small auto-rickshaws that collect waste and transport it to garbage collection sites for disposal.

As I was leaving the building, I stopped to talk to some of Mani's neighbors. They told me that they had originally considered forming a *cheeti* for the building in which all the residents would participate. But as one woman explained, "All our men are contract workers with sanitation services. They never get paid on time; we are now waiting for two months' salary. How can we have a *cheeti* if no one has money to contribute?" Mani's wife had been forced to borrow money from her brothers in their village in Tamil Nadu, from which most residents of Kalanagar migrated some decades ago.

Meanwhile, Mani raised loans through another method—from an informal moneylender and *cheeti* organizer. He had handed over his ATM card to a local financier whom he said he knew well. The man withdraws a sum of money every month from Mani's account toward a *cheeti*, thus acting as a sort of guarantor and intermediary, since Mani is not considered a reliable borrower. This arrangement sounded risky to me, but Mani said nothing much could go wrong: his bank account never had enough money for a significant theft anyway! Mani's current outstanding loans include one for the television (for which he is being charged interest at a galloping rate—something that was not made clear to him at the time of purchase), another he had taken to cover the rent, and a third for the advance deposit paid to the landlord. The ad hoc *cheeti* arrangement, and the types of financial needs that Mani faces, are entangled with his status as a migrant to the city—with a precarious contract-based job, struggling to escape from the stigma of his caste-based livelihood and his status as a former slum dweller.

Mani is not representative of all the residents of Kalanagar. He is only able to enter a *cheeti*, that too via the mediation of a financier, because he is a relatively well connected resident in a supervisory position at his contract work who is also able to access his wife's family networks when especially needed. Other Kalanagar residents generally meet their financial needs by taking loans from informal moneylenders who charge high rates of interest. The predatory practices of these private financiers thrive on the desperation and precarity of their clients, who turn to them due to a lack of property to use as collateral for formal loans and any kind of credit history.[2]

Scene Two: Sushma's *Cheeti* Enterprise

I first heard about *cheeti* schemes from "Sushma," who was taking care of my six-month-old son. "*Cheetis* are my life!" she told me. "I've been keeping them for years! It's because of my *cheeti* that I don't pay

Low Finance in the World City **93**

a monthly rent on my house and could afford a three-year lease. I used the money I got from *cheetis* to ask my nephew to buy me these bangles from Dubai!" she exclaimed, pointing to the two golden bracelets she wore on either hand. Her husband died when she was in her thirties; he killed himself because of debt, she said. His brother, a film producer for low-budget Kannada films, had ambitious plans for a get-rich-quick scheme, and when this did not work out the entire family (who had borrowed money to invest in the scheme) was mired in debt. Unable to bear the stress of repaying various loans, Sushma's husband jumped to his death. Newly widowed and childless, Sushma left the joint family household she was living in and took up paid employment as a nanny for small children.

In Bengaluru, work as a nanny is highly precarious. As the children grow and their school hours change or they enter holiday periods, Sushma's salary varies. She earns around 6,000 rupees a month for a five-hour shift, but this income is uncertain. When employers wish to terminate her job or change her hours (and pay), she is often given as little as two days' notice. To offset the uncertainty of these financial arrangements, and because she does not have the buffer of family wealth or a partner to support her, Sushma has entered into what is locally called a lease arrangement for the one-bedroom home where she lives. As is customary in these informal lease arrangements in Bengaluru, instead of paying a monthly rent Sushma gave the landlord a lump sum of 300,000 rupees (3,500 USD) up front, which is meant to cover a three-year lease on the house. This "lease amount" (this English term is commonly used) is supposed to be returned to the tenant by the landlord in full at the end of this period unless the home has been damaged. The landlord uses this advance to invest or to pay back loans, often using it to build more rental housing—such as by constructing additional floors on an existing house (see chapter 11).

Sushma was able to assemble such a large sum for the lease amount only because she participates in a *cheeti*. In this way, through the financial infrastructure of the *cheeti*, and despite the precarity of her income, Sushma has been able to ensure stable housing in a lower-middle-class neighborhood. Her flat is well located, with access to civic infrastructure and adjacent to the more affluent areas where she finds work as a caregiver. In addition, she is not forced to negotiate with the landlord every month when she cannot afford to pay rent (like so many other tenants); instead, her accommodation is guaranteed for the three-year period of the lease.

Sushma's home is a neat one-bedroom apartment in a small building accessible through a swinging gate. When I visited her, she directed my attention to the narrow street with houses all overlooking each other: "It's very safe for a single woman," she said. In her living room she has a bed and a washing machine, and an inner room is stacked with plastic chairs. Each room has just enough space for one piece of furniture, so Sushma and I sat facing each other on the bed while her neighbor, who came down to chat with us, stood in the doorway. Her neighbor—also single—has now joined a *cheeti* scheme through Sushma's introduction. Sushma exclaimed: "We are both like this, *independent!*" She uttered the word "independent" in English. It gestured not just to her ability to find and participate in networks, but to expand them for her friends and to shape an enjoyable life in this neat and self-contained home. Her residence is a few minutes' walk away from a large, enclosed water body—Sankey Tank—which she visits with her friends every evening for a leisurely stroll and chat.

In Sushma's neighborhood, houses on either side of the small street look into each other, and people stand on balconies watching over the children playing on the street. People know what others are doing at home and are conscious of comings and goings; this visibility is what makes Sushma feel safe here as a single woman. She can afford her place here in this desirable area because her *cheeti* provided her with the money needed to enter into a lease arrangement. But her participation in a *cheeti* is also supported by her residence in this neighborhood. The dense sociality of her streets and neighbors is precisely what enables Sushma's *cheeti*.

Sushma pulled people into her *cheeti* scheme by drawing on her relatives and friends from the immediate neighborhood and by finding someone with a good reputation and financial acumen willing to run it. As we walked over to the monthly calling of her *cheeti*, she pointed out other members' homes that we passed. Her aunt's family has the door open, so we wave; there is a niece in another, also preparing to come to the *cheeti* meeting. As Sushma describes it, the most important criterion for joining a *cheeti* is that the members must know each other—trust is key. If strangers join the group and do not contribute after they have drawn money, the entire group bears the loss. To join a *cheeti* group, an aspiring participant must have a guarantor from within the group who will take responsibility for them and ensure they make their payments on time. Usually those who run the *cheeti* do not bring in members they do not know. The most common reason for defaulting on the payments is when someone dies, in which case the *cheeti* manager has to pay the amount owed to the group.

Sushma's *cheeti* group met all these conditions. It is composed of members she herself cobbled together, including relatives (cousins, aunts, and nieces), neighbors, and friends. Most members share the same caste, class, and gender identity; they also all speak Telugu. I witnessed how these commonalities and networks shaped the social bonds and level of trust in the *cheeti*. Cousins sat together, some whispering to each other before calling an amount. Others shared an accounting sheet on a WhatsApp thread and made some calculations to track how the *cheeti* was being divided.

In Sushma's group, the *cheeti* money is mostly used for personal shopping—saris, jewelry, wedding expenses—and to pay children's school fees (a major expense for most families), as well as for lease arrangements for single women to maintain their neighborhood and class status despite their precarious work. Most women participants in *cheeti* groups are from Reddy or Naidu (middle-ranking agrarian castes) communities of Andhra and economically belong to the lower middle class. They live in localities close to areas undergoing urban flux due to rapid real estate development. Unlike the Dalit sanitation workers of Mani's community, these women are not dependent on their local corporator for decent housing. Instead, they draw on existing social networks and intergenerational wealth to share the resources that enable their class aspirations and upward mobility.

Given Sushma's doubly precarious position—as a single woman with no regular financial support and as an informal worker—I wondered what would happen to her as she aged and stopped working. Or even what her plans might be after the three-year lease on her house ran out. Near the end of my fieldwork, Sushma decided to stop working as a nanny. Through some contacts, she had discovered a young woman who had moved to Bengaluru for work and needed a respectable place to live. Her parents did not want her to live in a hostel among strangers, and so Sushma had offered a mattress in her house with breakfast and dinner included to earn some rental income. She then found another young woman in a similar circumstance and brought her in as a second renter. The tiny one-bedroom was now providing Sushma with the income she needed to cover her monthly expenses.

The most obvious value of participating in a *cheeti* scheme is to borrow money to offset debt, but *cheetis* also enable forms of urban sociality and the possibility of fulfilling urban, middle-class desires. They also, more concretely, allow precarious workers to survive in the current real estate market. How would the "world city" maintain its facade if its sanitation workers did not live alongside gated communities and affluent neighborhoods? How would the city's professional middle classes thrive if nannies could not get to work at a half-hour notice? How would neighborhoods be reimagined apart from an industrial past if corporators negotiating private contracts could not raze older settlements and construct brand-new apartment buildings for affluent residents (in the process, shifting the costs of housing a displaced population onto poor residents)? In life, as in work, Bengaluru's lower-income precarious workers labor hard to provide the essential services and material adjustments required to keep alive the "world city." The *cheetis* in which they participate, then, are not for their survival and well-being alone, but offer the integral, vernacular source of finance necessary to fabricate the grand scale of the "world city" imaginary.

Notes

Thanks to Deeksha M. Rao and Juwairia Mehkri, who participated in fieldwork on the research that supports this essay.

1. In Kannada and other south Indian languages, *kuli* means "labor," "worker," or "wage" (especially referring to daily wage work). The word has come into English as *coolie*.

2. Household debt experienced a boom between 2004 and 2014, including both market-based and interpersonal loans, as did the diversity and number of lenders. See Isabelle Guérin and G. Venkatasubramanian, "The Socio-Economy of Debt: Revisiting Debt Bondage in Times of Financialization," *Geoforum* 137 (2022): 174–84, https://doi.org/10.1016/j.geoforum.2020.05.020.

An innovative financial diaries–based research study conducted in a rural district near Bengaluru among low-income workers in the informal sector found a preference for loans from microfinance institutions (MFIs) over *cheetis*, although these loans had very high rates of interest and stringent repayment rules. See Rajalaxmi Kamath and Smita Ramanathan, "Informal Businesses and Micro-credit—Evidence from Financial Diaries: A Study in Ramanagaram, India," *IIMB Management Review* 27, no. 3 (2015): 149–58, https://doi.org/10.1016/j.iimb.2015.05.002. In general, MFIs are necessary sources of lending for those engaged in business and with routine and daily financial needs.

7
The Real Estate Fix

Carol Upadhya

Sitting in his plush modern office in north Bengaluru, located just behind a new hotel built by his company on Outer Ring Road, "Nitin" (whom we met briefly in chapter 4) tells us his rags-to-riches story. He is from an ordinary Bunt (a landowning agrarian and business caste) family of Mangaluru (a city in coastal Karnataka, formerly called Mangalore) and moved to Bangalore after finishing college in the early 1990s. He started his business career by opening a small restaurant serving Mangalorean cuisine ("We Bunts are famous for our eateries," he explains). As it became popular, he opened branches of the restaurant in other cities. Next, he built a three-star hotel, which also expanded into a chain of several hotels across Karnataka. Most recently, he tells us proudly, he completed two five-star hotel projects and has another in the pipeline, along with a couple of residential real estate projects in Bengaluru and Mangaluru.

In relating this story, Nitin skipped over the part of his career for which he is best known and because of which we had requested an interview with him. Nitin is one of Bangalore's biggest land aggregators, and it is through this activity that he made his name and money. He mentions land aggregation only after we ask him how he got into the real estate business.

He started doing land aggregation in 1995, alongside running his restaurant, by creating a few layouts—residential projects, usually carved out of agricultural land, offering plots of land for sale—on the fringes of the city. Making a layout requires negotiating with farmers to buy land; managing the complicated legal and administrative processes of land transfer, conversion, and consolidation; and then selling the plots. Having gained some experience in buying and assembling land, Nitin realized the potential of providing this service to developers at a time when Bangalore was rapidly expanding and the real estate industry was taking off. He claims to have been one of the first to get into this lucrative but risky activity. He grew his business by working with most of the major real estate companies in the city, and later expanded into real estate development himself: "My strong area is land banking—acquisition of the land, completing all the formalities for converting from agricultural to nonagricultural, and so on."

Nitin built his business by purchasing small plots of land in villages surrounding Bangalore and aggregating them into larger parcels to offer to real estate companies. He takes care of all the legal and bureaucratic steps needed to convert agricultural land into unencumbered urban property: "The developer wants land with clear title; only once it is clear will they make a deal. So, responsibility for the land is mine up to that point, then after we give it to the developer, it is theirs." Land aggregators often employ retired government officers who are familiar with the land administration system; their role is to overcome bureaucratic hurdles in this process. Nitin's aggregation business thus does more than simply acquiring many parcels of land and assembling them together—it fundamentally transforms the land from one form (agricultural holding) into another (urban property, ready for investment or development). Once a parcel is consolidated, "clean" (unencumbered), and ready for sale, it may be purchased by a real estate developer outright, or the developer may enter into a joint development agreement (JDA) with Nitin's company.[1]

Nitin's success as a land aggregator was due in part to his ability to anticipate in which direction the city would grow and identify areas where farmers may be willing to sell. As he explained the process, the first step is to identify areas where land might be in demand by developers—future real estate "hot spots." Anticipating the city's outward expansion, land aggregators such as Nitin as well as real estate companies have created "land banks" as much as fifty kilometers from the city. Because the process of land aggregation can take up to eight years, "we look ahead and see where the city might develop."

Once they have identified a target area, the aggregator informs local brokers that they are interested in buying land: "There are a lot of agents in the villages," and they only have to "spread the word" and agents will "bring" prospective sellers. But the process of purchasing numerous contiguous plots to create a large parcel of land is lengthy and painstaking, with each deal being individually negotiated: "You need to convince the farmers one by one. They all have a different mentality; you have to adjust to their mentality. With some you can spend less money, others need more. . . . Then we have to look at their family situation, so there should not be any problems with the land deal." Here Nitin is referring to the complications that often arise in land deals, such as disputes within the family or the sudden appearance of a long-lost relative who claims to have an interest in the property.

"Wherever we are acquiring land," he continues "we must have two or three people in the local area to help . . . someone in whom people have faith and who we can trust as well." These sub-aggregators do most of the legwork—negotiating with landowners, handling the paperwork, dealing with government officials, and so on. But Nitin claimed that he also must build direct personal relations with landowners to gain their trust. Representing himself as a friend to farmers, he claimed, "Farmers have a lot of faith in me. In 1995 I acquired twelve hundred plots in north Bangalore and made a housing society—even now farmers are asking me [for help]. It's a matter of building relations."

Nitin had been eyeing the "Purvapur" area on the southeastern fringe of Bengaluru for some time (see chapters 3 and 4), which he believed would soon become a prime area for real estate development. He wanted to acquire a parcel there large enough to be attractive to a major developer. In 2005 he started acquiring land through local brokers, but by his own admission he could not make much progress. Then, in 2009 he met "Somnath" of "Hasiruhalli," who agreed to help him assemble land. As an educated and well-off local man from a landowning family of the village, Somnath was ideal for the job. According to Somnath, it was because he was a son of the village that he could gain the trust of the farmers and convince them to sell. Moreover, he belonged to the powerful Reddy community, which owned most of the land in Hasiruhalli. Because Somnath was college educated and had experience working in the private sector and running his own small businesses, he also had the social skills and confidence to work with a successful and worldly urban land aggregator such as Nitin.

Over the course of several long interviews in his modest office located on the busy main road running through Hasiruhalli (and up to "Lakeview Haven"; see chapter 4), Somnath explained how he arduously assembled a contiguous parcel of over one hundred acres. On a creased and worn copy of the village revenue map, he showed us the rough target area he had first marked out. Then he consulted the land records in the Revenue Department office to identify the owners of each plot within the boundary he had drawn. The next step was to carry out a "background check" on each of these families to understand their financial and social situations, based on which he gauged their willingness to sell. Finally, he redrew the boundary of the target area to include about one hundred plots he thought he would be able to acquire, leaving out those held by "difficult" landowners. The result was an odd-shaped project area: "People used to make fun of me, saying that I'm creating an amoeba!," he joked. Somnath then approached the owners of each plot to offer a deal, starting low and negotiating up as needed. Nitin had set a target price of 1 to 1.5 crore (10 to 15 million) rupees per acre—much higher than the prevailing price in 2007 of around 15 lakh rupees (1,500,000 rupees). Each deal had to be individually negotiated by Somnath, directly or through a broker, which meant that the sale price varied according to the family's financial situation or staying power. Many smaller landowners sold early and at lower prices because they needed quick money to clear debts or to pay for urgent expenses, while more substantial landowners had the financial means to hold out for a higher price. In the end, according to Nitin, they paid between 1.25 and 2.3 crore (12.5 to 23 million rupees) per acre. However, it was rumored that some owners received as much as 4 crore. After consolidating the parcel, Nitin's company formed a JDA with the real estate company Prominent Ventures, which developed the Lakeview Haven apartment complex on the land (Figure 7.1).[2]

Explaining why a local man such as Somnath is so important in the process of land assembly, Nitin noted, "Somnath knows everyone in the village, he knows the family tree and the situation of the family, so there would not be any problems with the land deal. Wherever we are acquiring land, we must have two or three people in the local area to help. It must be someone in whom people have faith, and he should be trustworthy for us also."

Elaborating on his strategy, Somnath explained that he would

Figure 7.1. View of "Lakeview Haven" gated community under construction. Photograph by Pierre Hauser.

first investigate the "family background" of each owner, which helped him decide what kind of inducement might convince them to sell. Because he was familiar with the financial situation and family problems of most of his neighbors, he could find the right leverage to convince them to part with their land: "I knew what each family wanted or needed and so could persuade them to sell their land at the right price." Illustrating his tactics, Somnath told us about an owner who had adamantly refused to sell his land: "Since I don't know *goondaism* [gangsterism or strong-arm tactics], I tried offering more money. In the end, I had to give some of my own land in exchange for theirs." He closed the deal by offering thirty *gunta* (one *gunta* is equal to around one hundred square meters) of his own valuable roadside land in exchange for the landowner's twenty *gunta*, which was "locked" in the middle of the project area. The point of telling us this story was also to illustrate his commitment to completing the project by any means, even by sacrificing his own land.

Somnath attributes his success in aggregating such a large parcel of land to his "inheritance," meaning the family and caste connections he enjoys because he belongs to a landowning Reddy family of

Hasiruhalli. He emphasized that his family is well known and maintains good relations with other villagers. Describing himself as a very accessible and amicable person, Somnath claimed that—except for one or two farmers—everyone "cooperated" with him: "People love to work with me; my achievement is that the owners' satisfaction is 100 percent." An unspoken element of this "cooperation" was caste—it is no accident that most of the farmers who sold their land for the project were also Reddys. Indeed, the target land parcel excluded lands held by Dalits, which are commonly thought to be too encumbered with legal cases and other problems to establish clear title.

One of Somnath's main tasks was to mediate the family disputes that frequently arise when landowners are approached with an offer to sell their land. Since multiple relatives have a legal interest in agricultural land (regarded as "ancestral property" under Indian law), Somnath had to trace all the relatives who might have a claim to the land and convince them to sign off on the deal. Because there are usually multiple claimants for the same parcel of land, numerous signatures must be obtained on the sale documents to ensure clear title. While around 100 families sold land for the project, Somnath said that he had collected a total of 500 to 750 signatures.

After completing each negotiation, Somnath was also responsible for handling the bureaucratic processes of turning land into real estate: applying to the District Commissioner's office for official "conversion" of the plot from agricultural to nonagricultural use, transferring the land from the registers of the Revenue Department to the municipal land records, and getting the sale deed registered, among several other steps. Local intermediaries like Somnath are essential to manage these procedures because they possess the local knowledge and social networks needed to navigate the land administration and district bureaucracy, as well as to negotiate the "fees" that must be paid to fixers and various officials.

While lower-level intermediaries such as Somnath are crucial for dealing with the local administration, land aggregators also need to manage the state machinery at higher levels to successfully aggregate a large parcel of land. Aggregators at Nitin's level cultivate connections with powerful bureaucrats (such as the District Commissioner and the secretaries of key state government departments) and state-level politicians (such as the local MLA [Member of Legislative Assembly],

MP [Member of Parliament], and ministers in the state government), whose support is crucial in acquiring land. Nitin also draws on his networks in developing his "vision" of the city's growth, such as by extracting inside information about the alignment of a planned highway or the location of a new infrastructure project. When we asked Nitin whether political connections are necessary to succeed in this business, he at first denied it, claiming that he does not know "anyone like that." But on further probing, he admitted, laughing: "Yes, you know, politicians are always involved, these things are always there, but I don't want to disclose them."

Indeed, Nitin's restaurant is a favorite haunt of important politicians and high-level bureaucrats in Bengaluru, known as a place where important people meet to cement deals, both political and financial. As a well-connected, longtime resident of the city wryly observed: "In the evenings you will see overweight men dressed in crisp white shirts and gold chains having drinks and dinner at Nitin's restaurant." To raise money to finance land acquisition, aggregators also invite their patrons to invest in their business, an attractive offer given that land is often used for laundering illicit "black money" into "white." The close relation between land transactions and political money—particularly to fund elections, which requires large amounts of "unaccounted money" (cash that circulates outside the banking system to funnel to voters and election campaigns)—is part of popular "common sense" in Karnataka. As an aggregator said, "Land is a great parking place for money," a role that has contributed to the land boom in peri-urban Bengaluru since the early 2000s.

Somnath represents himself as a benevolent local leader rather than a middleman brokering deals for profit. He claims that he agreed to help Nitin because he believed that Hasiruhalli would inevitably get swallowed up by the expanding city, one way or another, and so he wanted to ensure that the residents would benefit from these changes. He also cited rumors that the Bangalore Development Authority was planning to acquire some land in the village for a housing project, which meant that those farmers would lose their land for compensation much lower than what the market would yield. He believed that he could get landowners a better deal if they sold their land to Nitin, and indeed it was the threat of compulsory land acquisition (a rumor that some say was floated by Somnath himself) that persuaded some owners to sell. Somnath spoke often about his moral responsibility to his community, claiming that he was motivated not by greed but by a desire to help his fellow villagers by fetching them a good price, which in turn would "develop" the village. He even asserted that he had not made much money through this work, but in the same breath admitted that he was not in the business to "do charity." Indeed, the wealth he had accumulated was visible to all: he built a fancy new farmhouse in a mango orchard on the outskirts of the village, drives a BMW, owns a petrol station, and started an elite private school. He also owns two villas in Lakeview Haven, which he received as part of his payment for the mediation work.

Elaborating on his sense of obligation to his community and his indifference toward material wealth, Somnath spoke about his spiritual inclinations. Citing the Bhagavad Gita, which teaches that if you act with honesty and the right attitude you cannot fail, he said that he would not approach owners with the intention of "conquering" (persuading them to sell) but would first try to "understand their needs." He also asserted that he never forced anyone to sell—whenever he ran into problems they would "automatically" and "miraculously" get resolved. Somnath's self-presentation as a religious, moral, and public-minded person seemed to be directed at creating a veneer of respect and legitimacy while pursuing activities that are often seen as underhanded or nefarious. Land brokering, or "real estate business" (the English term is used also while speaking in Kannada), is popularly viewed as an unsavory activity because of its associations with goondaism, corruption, and black money. Indeed, Somnath refused the label of "real estate person" and presented himself as the opposite of the "brokers" and other dubious characters that populate the booming land markets around Bengaluru.

But several local people presented a rather different picture of Somnath's role in acquiring land, which they believe contributed to the demise of the agrarian economy. They spoke about the pressure tactics his brokers employed to induce farmers to sell and the negative consequences of land sales—the quarrels that had broken families apart and the corrupting influence of new money. Said one farmer, "Ever since they started selling land and have money, people have changed for the worse. Land is simply perceived as how much money it can fetch in the market, and as soon as people get a good price, they sell it." A woman from a neighboring village blamed Somnath directly for "ruining people's lives." "Rajesh," an old friend of Somnath's, said resignedly: "We all knew when we sold that it is a loss, but what to do? We are forced to sell. Like how people smoke cigarettes despite knowing that it is harmful to health."

Even Somnath, despite his talk about bringing development and wealth to the village, decried the acquisition of land all around Bengaluru by big real estate companies, which among other ill effects was draining rural areas of water: "Like the Britishers, these big builders are coming. As individuals we cannot do anything. Our children will starve [if we refuse to sell]. . . . To dig a borewell to a depth of a thousand feet, you need close to 3 lakh [300,000] rupees. How can farmers live like this?" Indeed, many farmers in Hasiruhalli agreed to sell their land because they saw no future in agriculture—largely because of the falling water table and dried-up lakes (as discussed in chapter 3). It seemed sensible to realize the monetary value of their land and use the proceeds to buy cheaper agricultural land elsewhere—deals that Somnath sometimes helped negotiate. For the price of one acre of land here one can get five to six acres elsewhere, according to Somnath. The inflow of money from land sales thus percolates outward as landowners invest in land farther from the city, enlivening land markets in more distant villages. Other residents of Hasiruhalli who sold land invested the proceeds in rental properties in the city or in small businesses.

This kind of large-scale land aggregation in rural areas around Bengaluru has had a dramatic impact on local land markets—driving up prices astronomically. Nitin spoke about one of his projects where they paid 35–40 lakh rupees (75,000 to 90,000 USD) per acre from 2004 to 2006, 60–65 lakh in 2007, 1 crore in 2009 (200,000 USD), and later as much as 2.5 crore. By the time they completed the acquisition, the land was worth 5–6 crore per acre, he said. Residents of Hasiruhalli similarly spoke about the sharp increase in land prices, from just 4–5 lakh rupees (9,000 to 10,000 USD) per acre in 2000 to 10 crore (155,000 USD) in 2017. The insatiable thirst for land for real estate ventures means that capital is poured into rural economies through many small, local-level transactions, leading to ripple effects that push up land prices and create new speculative land markets—as farmers invest their windfall profits in land in other districts and as aggregators move ever farther from the city to build up their land banks.

The intermediaries who are at the center of these markets are also the major beneficiaries of this urban transition, taking a cut of each transaction through commissions, fees, or margins as land changes hands multiple times. Real estate companies profit from selling the properties they create on the land, although their fortunes are subject to market fluctuations and other macroeconomic conditions. The original landowners, too, usually reap substantial benefits by disposing of their land at inflated prices, although the price they receive is always a fraction of the land value after it is transformed into real estate. Often forgotten in this land rush is the fate of the agricultural workers employed on the farms, the tenant farmers who lease land for cultivation, and the many other (mostly landless) households whose rural livelihoods have been erased by surging urbanization. These displaced and marginalized families have few livelihood options, while those who accumulate wealth from selling their land can always find ways to invest their money or pursue other businesses.

Like land brokering, land aggregation is viewed as a rather unsavory business, entangled as it is in corruption, "rowdyism," and black money. Indeed, one of the key functions of land aggregators seems to be to shield professional real estate companies, which strive to present a clean image to their middle-class and affluent clients, from the seamier aspects of the business—pressuring farmers to sell, lubricating the movement of documents through the government machinery, and converting black money into white as it flows through land. As "Viren," the architect we met in chapter 1, explained: "There is a different level of thuggery required to pull out land, and big developers don't engage with this. So, these people do it, package the land, and pass it on." It is perhaps for this reason that Nitin emphasized in our interview that he is no longer into land banking: "I am sixty years old—I have been doing this work for thirty-five to forty years. I can't keep doing this. It is difficult work. You have to go to the villages personally to convince people. I am not taking up new projects. I am now just doing a lot of charity."

Nitin's narration of his life story reflects the trajectory of other land aggregators in Bangalore, who, after becoming very wealthy from this business, moved up the value chain to become real estate developers or small builders. Once they have accumulated enough capital, they try to build more respectable reputations. Nitin says that his focus now is on the hospitality sector, and he has groomed his son to take over the business by sending him to an expensive hotel management course in Switzerland—leaving him free to focus on his "charitable" activities.

Notes

Hemangini Gupta, Sachinkumar Rathod, Priyanka Krishna, Kaveri Medappa, Vinay Gidwani, and Michael Goldman contributed to this chapter. The chapter draws on Vinay Gidwani and Carol Upadhya, "Articulation Work: Value Chains of Land Assembly and Real Estate Development on a Peri-urban Frontier," *Environment and Planning A: Economy and Space* 55, no. 2 (2023): 407–27, https://doi.org/10.1177/0308518X221107016.

1. In a JDA, the developer puts up the capital and takes care of planning and execution of the project, while the land that is contributed by the landowner or aggregator is their share of the equity.

2. In this JDA the equity share was 30:70 between the aggregator and the developer, which means that the land was valued at 30 percent of the total capital. The revenue and liabilities are split in the same proportion.

Metro construction work underway on MG Road in 2019, next to the Parade Ground and Cariappa Memorial Park (military areas in the city). From the film *Our Metropolis* by Gautam Sonti and Usha Rao, 2014.

Part III
State Speculations

Moving beyond lofty architectural visions and the unsettling rhythms of capital, this section plots the historical and spatial contours of Bengaluru's momentous transformation, evoking alternative imaginations of "futures past" (historian Reinhart Koselleck's term for paths that were once present but not taken)[1] as well as the frictions generated by colliding ideals of urban life. Once known as a "public-sector city,"[2] Bengaluru has been recast as the "IT city" and utterly transformed by post-reform policies of deindustrialization together with the rise of new service industries. As urban real estate becomes the profitable focus of the new economy, land-flush industries like public-sector factories, once the mainstay of the city's economy, have been closed and their land sold to private ventures primarily interested in capitalizing on skyrocketing land values. The state and central governments have facilitated and brokered these public land conversions, turning urban spaces and enterprises that once provided livelihoods to many city residents into tradable assets for the real estate and financial sectors. As this transformation occurs across the region, finance capital—both domestic and foreign—becomes emboldened, and the "public" city is reshaped in the service of private capital.

Chapter 8, "Re-placing Labor," shows how a receding industrial past laid the conditions of possibility—material and aspirational—for present-day Bengaluru, as told through the voices of former trade union activists and the chairperson of a public sector undertaking (PSU). These interlocutors emphasize the crucial role of the public sector in shaping the city and its emerging middle classes in the decades following Indian independence, while narrating the declining political power and social influence of organized labor in recent years.[3] Despite a recent strike by contract workers employed in one of the few remaining PSUs, Indian Telephone Industries, which points to a

112 Part III. State Speculations

residual working-class consciousness and activism in Bengaluru, the stories related by key figures of this earlier era illustrate the new reality of contractualization of labor, precarious employment, and the dilution of the social value of the "public" in Bengaluru's civic life.

Few interventions have had as significant an impact on the city as the ongoing metro rail project, promoted as Namma Metro (Our Metro). While supporters celebrate it as the answer to Bengaluru's infamous traffic congestion and unwieldy commutes, critics have expressed fears over its adverse economic and environmental impacts. "Metro Mutations" (chapter 9) offers an intimate account of the disruptions and destruction of livelihoods and landscapes as the Bangalore Metro Rail Corporation Limited (BMRCL) expands its lines, cutting through existing roads, commercial areas, residential neighborhoods, and parks. This government-owned company aims to cover the high costs of building and operating the metro by creating a "speculative ecosystem" centered around capturing maximum value from land. In practice, this involves monetizing the real estate it has acquired using the power of eminent domain (often in a callous, roughshod manner) by expanding commercial spaces in and around stations and marketing them as "retail destinations." These interventions have fundamentally altered the normative character of historic urban zones such as MG Road, making public spaces less accessible to "uncivil" elements. The chapter also gestures to the temporal and spatial disruptions induced by the metro as it dislodges people from their livelihoods and accustomed routines on the "promise" of a better urban future.[4]

"Moving Matters" (chapter 10) provides a stark contrast to the story of Namma Metro, poignantly underscoring the importance of affordable mass transit to people's livelihoods and aspirations. The chapter shows that when market metrics come to guide budgetary allocations, state finance can diminish or dry up, with adverse consequences for ordinary citizens. In this case, the adoption of a new revenue generation model based on cost recovery from users by the Bangalore Metropolitan Transport Corporation (BMTC) drove up fares, making bus journeys prohibitively expensive and undercutting the economic security of many workers. Pushback by civil society groups has been modestly successful in thwarting the state's market-friendly impulses, but troubling questions about the government's priorities remain. The chapter shows that the Karnataka state government could have found funds to offset BMTC's losses and roll back the fare hikes, thus preserving broad access to a pivotal public good, but it lacked political will as it was beholden to a "neoliberal" revenue model.[5]

Thus, the push to formulate high-visibility infrastructure projects based on land monetization has induced state and city governments to opt for expensive transport systems like metro rail systems,[6] leaving more common and affordable forms of transit such as bus systems to languish.[7] These policy decisions illustrate the growing dominance of what Laura Bear terms "speculative state planning,"[8] where market mechanisms deployed for public investment in urban infrastructure and services are revealed as speculative financial strategies that have driven state and municipal governments into deep debt.

Notes

1. Reinhart Koselleck, *Futures Past: On the Semantics of Historical Time* (New York: Columbia University Press, 2004).

2. Janaki Nair, *The Promise of the Metropolis: Bangalore's Twentieth Century* (New Delhi: Oxford University Press, 2005).

3. Supriya RoyChowdhury, "Public Sector Restructuring and Democracy: The State, Labour, and Trade Unions in India," *The Journal of Development Studies*, 39, no. 3 (2003): 29–50; Dilip Subramanian, *Telecommunications Industry in India: State, Business, and Labour in a Global Economy* (New Delhi: Social Science Press, 2010).

4. Nikhil Anand, Akhil Gupta, and Hannah Appel, eds., *The Promise of Infrastructure* (Durham: Duke University Press, 2018).

5. Loraine Kennedy, "The Politics and Changing Paradigm of Megaproject Development in Metropolitan Cities," *Habitat International* 45, part 3 (2015): 163–68.

6. Isher Judge Ahluwalia, "Urban Governance in India," *Journal of Urban Affairs* 41, no. 1 (2019): 83–102.

7. Dinesh Mohan, "Mythologies, Metro Rail Systems and Future Urban Transport," *Economic and Political Weekly* 43, no. 4 (2008): 41–53; Geetam Tiwari, "Metro Rail and the City: Derailing Public Transport," *Economic and Political Weekly* 48, no. 48 (2013): 65–76.

8. Laura Bear, "Making a River of Gold: Speculative State Planning, Informality, and Neoliberal Governance on the Hooghly," *Focaal: Journal of Global and Historical Anthropology* 61 (2011): 46–60.

8
Re-placing Labor
Eesha Kunduri

In the colonial period, when the southern districts of present-day Karnataka state were part of the princely state of Mysore, Bangalore witnessed a state-led industrialization drive.[1] The state granted land to industrialists to set up manufacturing units in the city. Some of today's core city areas—Rajajinagar, Yeshwantpur, and Cottonpet—were once industrial hubs hosting government factories such as Government Soap Factory and Mysore Lamps, and textile mills such as Binny Mills, Raja Mills, and Minerva Mills. Remembering the colonial-style buildings, "Comrade Chandan" (as members of leftist organizations often call one another), a former worker and union member at Minerva Mills, remarked on the importance of the textile mills to the identity of central Bangalore: "They constructed our buildings without pillars in those days! The roof was made of teak wood. *Aa reeti adhbutha vaagittu* [The plan for the mill was incredible]. . . . This [the mill lands] was Bangalore."

Building on the legacy of a flourishing industrial city, the postindependence period saw the establishment of several public sector undertakings (PSUs) in Bangalore, most on agricultural land acquired in the public interest, according to the prominent trade unionist Michael Fernandes, a retired employee of the well-known and still functioning public-sector company Indian Telephone Industries Limited (ITI). The setting up of public-sector industries in Bengaluru was the main impetus behind the city's economic development from the 1960s. "Most of the original, earlier, bigger, and very prestigious industries were set up here," Fernandes remarked in an interview. "Communications and electronics for defense and for commercial use, and then machine tools, then aeronautics or aerospace came for defense again, and then earthmoving equipment. So very, very prestigious industries were established here. And for that reason, we seem[ed] to be leading

114

Figure 8.1. Apartment complex built on former mill land, Rajajinagar. Photograph by Pierre Hauser.

the whole show." Fernandes noted that Bengaluru was referred to as the "capital of public-sector industries" due to the presence in the city of five major PSUs,[2] in addition to numerous other government and private factories and scientific and technical establishments. Research laboratories and organizations such as the National Aerospace Laboratories, Defence Research and Development Organisation, Electronics and Radar Development Establishment, Indian Space Research Organisation, and Central Power Research Institute were clustered around the PSUs—earning Bengaluru the appellation of India's "Science City."

Fernandes, who joined ITI as a technical apprentice in 1955 and went on to become an assistant executive engineer, estimated that in the 1980s, around 75,000 workers—about 15 percent of Bangalore's population—were employed in these PSUs. This figure roughly accords with historian Janaki Nair's estimate of over 80,000 workers employed in PSUs from the early 1980s until 1991.[3] Statistics from ITI's personnel department reveal that 15,920 workers were employed in 1991, a sharp decline from 19,496 in 1980.[4] The year 1991 marks the moment when public-sector workers started to be retrenched, as economic reforms prompted a paradigm shift toward dilution of industrial and labor policies, deregulation, and disinvestment and privatization of public-sector enterprises.[5] Beginning in 1958, Fernandes was a member of the ITI Employees' Union (a politically independent plant-level union), at various points in time serving as general secretary, vice-president, and president.[6] His role as a union leader often overlapped with his tenure as an officer of the company, and Fernandes proudly claimed to "know both sides": "I know the company as a company, and I know the union side of my existence."

Fernandes also played a prominent leadership role as the main spokesman for a major seventy-seven-day strike of public-sector engineering workers that took place in the city from December 1980 to March 1981. The strike, which galvanized about 125,000 workers from across the city and beyond, united union leadership across political lines in its demand for wage parity across PSUs in the city. As Fernandes recounted, "Bangalore was a pay-setter for wage revision in the public-sector industries." Unlike the revision of pay for government employees, which usually takes place every ten years, wage revisions in Bangalore's PSUs were as frequent as every three years, based on negotiations between trade unions and the companies. Because of these frequent wage revisions, pay scales in these PSUs came close to parity with those at some private-sector companies in Bangalore. "There was a new atmosphere created, largely due to trade union militancy . . . whereby the wage increases [in Bangalore's PSUs] became substantial," Fernandes remarked.

Although the strike was principally about parity in wages and emoluments among the city's PSU workers, it needs to be understood in a far broader context—the politics of urban industrial workers, which had local, regional, and national implications. Though the negotiations eventually failed, the 1981 strike has been described as the "longest and costliest conflict in the history of the public sector in India."[7] It represents a period in India's industrial history when public-sector industrial workers and their trade unions exercised political clout and agency—power that dwindled with the shift toward the contractualization of employment and more flexible labor regimes beginning from the 1990s.[8] As Fernandes observed on the challenges of unionizing contractual workers, "The bargaining capacity of unions has declined, since it is not easy to organize contract workers. When contract workers are doing the same work alongside permanent workers at a much lower cost to the company, they [contract workers] are scared to lose what [wages] they are getting. The organized workers also find it difficult [to organize contractual workers]."

Aside from employing a significant proportion of the city's population and constituting a benchmark for wages in the city, Bangalore's PSUs fueled its urban development. Residential townships were developed by public-sector enterprises to provide housing for almost all their employees across different job categories. Some of these "integrated townships" were located close to the factories where their residents were employed. For those located elsewhere in the city, the company provided transportation for the workers to reach their workplaces. These townships were self-contained units, designed to provide a good quality of life for employees and their families, with adequate space for residential, commercial, and recreational use. Several PSUs created hospitals, schools, and other infrastructural amenities for their workers, which were also made available to the public.[9] As

"Praveena," a public-relations manager with a PSU, noted, "These schools, colleges, and hospitals don't just serve our employees. They serve the neighborhood also."

"Vinod," a former PSU chairman and managing director, commented, "The prosperity of the city certainly grew as a result of the presence of the public sector, but it was sort of a slow osmosis." Elaborating on this, he said that PSU managements made substantial investments of money and time to create and manage infrastructural facilities, even as the city's municipal corporation disavowed responsibility for their upkeep. This commitment, in his view, diverted the focus of PSU managements away from matters of enterprise productivity and efficiency and toward running these facilities. "Looking back, I do not know whether it was the right way of doing things, because what it meant was that the city . . . felt that they had no responsibility to provide the infrastructure or the facilities for this growing [PSU] labor population."

Diagnosing the uneven and haphazard nature of urban development in Bangalore beyond the planned PSU townships (and other areas controlled by government authorities, such as the Army and Air Force), an urban planner and former adviser to the Karnataka state government emphasized that the public sector "played an important role in the overall economic development of the city, as well as urban development. From the 1970s and 1980s, the services sector began growing—it all happened in the private sector mostly, IT and other services. Unlike the public sector, these companies didn't provide housing, and they set up their units anywhere and everywhere. It was not planned development in that sense."

Moreover, PSUs offered high-paying jobs with significant periodic wage revisions, in contrast to the current industrial scenario dominated by low-paid and insecure jobs in industries such as ready-made garments, and lucrative but equally precarious jobs in the IT and the ITES (IT enabled services) sectors. In the remaining PSUs, such as ITI, formerly stable jobs have largely been replaced by contractual arrangements, which provides flexibility to employers almost to hire and fire at will. Such contractual arrangements also pose challenges for labor organizing, as Fernandes observed.

Notwithstanding such challenges, during the Covid-19 lockdown in 2020, contract workers in ITI came together to form the Karnataka

General Labour Union (KGLU)–ITI Unit to protest against non-payment of wages and to demand benefits due to them under existing labor laws.[10] The KGLU–ITI Unit, affiliated with the All India Central Council of Trade Unions, has been staging a peaceful sit-in protest outside the ITI gates since December 1, 2021, in response to the termination of about eighty contract workers. The protesters are also objecting to the dishonoring of a settlement between the KGLU and the ITI management for reinstatement of sacked workers.[11] Despite the Karnataka High Court's judgment in April 2023 upholding the settlement as binding on the management and directing conciliation proceedings, ITI management has failed to comply with the order.[12] At the time of writing this chapter, the agitation had not been called off.

Nearly half of the terminated workers are from marginalized caste backgrounds, and several of them are also women.[13] This is noteworthy, because historically PSUs have played a prominent role in creating urban employment not just for the able-bodied upper-caste male worker but also for workers from Scheduled Castes, Scheduled Tribes, and Other Backward Classes through policies of affirmative action.[14] The PSUs also fostered social mobility through their high wages and employment security and by providing a good education to employees' children, some of whom went on to join the software industry or other white-collar employment—propelling them into the middle class. Fernandes reckoned that a PSU job in the 1950s paid about double the wage of a comparable private-sector job at the time, creating a ripple effect that contributed to the expansion of Bangalore's middle class. This dynamic also drove other economic activities in the city. "Many people working in a similar job in a private-sector company would not have been able to build or own their own house," he observed, "but public-sector workers have managed to do that. And that has also created jobs—you know, it is a chain effect."

Bengaluru's thriving IT sector drew significantly on the skilled industrial, scientific, and technical workforce that was fostered by the PSUs and scientific establishments (especially the Indian Space Research Organisation) of the pre-liberalization era. According to Vinod, "They provided a trained workforce, particularly in the case of electronics industries. A lot of middle managers, a lot of young engineers in their first ten years of their careers, were taken by these private companies—multinationals and also Indian companies. They provided the nucleus for these new industries, new enterprises, to man some of their essential functions." C. Balakrishnan, a former trade unionist with Bharat Electronics Limited, concurred, noting that the IT industry was able to profitably leverage the "scientific, technological, managerial intelligentsia" created by the city's PSUs.[15]

Bangalore's history of industrialization driven by public investment points to a period when a different configuration and vision of urbanization was possible—a time when industrial space and the industrial workforce featured in the imagination of the city through state patronage of manufacturing. Housing for employees was a natural corollary to setting up public-sector enterprises. In Vinod's assessment, "There was a feeling in those days, and I think to some extent it continues, that being a government-owned company . . . [it] should act like an ideal employer. Of course, the definition of ideal . . . was left to each one to decide. . . . From the workers' point of view, it meant that they should be paid well, they should have housing, they should have transportation, they should be fed well. And, you know, the idea was to generate employment, therefore overstaffing was accepted as one of the responsibilities of [the] public sector."[16]

This view of Bangalore as a public-sector industrial city has steadily diminished, replaced first by the "IT city" and then by a speculative city, where the land on which public-sector enterprises once stood has become highly valued real estate. Decades ago, the government acquired land from farmers at minimal compensation to build infrastructure and industries; today those same tracts have been transformed into "prime land." "The public sector is today under attack from its own parents, if I may call the government its parent," Fernandes fumed. "They [the government] are themselves interested in seeing an end to these public industries. . . . Land outside the city becomes a part of the heart of the city and now its value has multiplied not by tens or hundreds but by thousands." As industries proclaimed "losses," they were permitted by the government to close. This "freed-up" land was then sold to real estate developers who built shopping malls, gated apartment complexes, and shimmering office towers that now stand tall in place of factories and mills. Commenting on this transition, Comrade Chandan observed, "Now land is the main resource to make money out of. An industry needs so much work—you have to set up the factory, find workers, pay them, sell the products, and run the business. But in the case of land, none of this work is needed. All that has to be done is to divide it into plots and sell it. You receive many times the money you spent on it. These days, because of a scarcity of land, apartments are built—the land is the same, but on that common piece of land [the developer] makes money out of all the houses built on it [on multiple floors]."

It is easy to forget that today's Bengaluru, marked by large-scale investments in real estate and global flows of finance capital that seek to transform it into a world-class metropolis, stands on the back of a vibrant industrial city that was animated by the public sector. Even as property speculation leverages and assetizes the physical infrastructure of the industrial city, it neither generates much employment nor creates social infrastructure of the kind nurtured by the industrial city. But the ongoing, long-drawn-out agitation by ITI's contract workers, in an effort to hold the city's public sector accountable for unfair labor practices and to its promise of being a "model employer,"[17] signals a critical moment for reclaiming the public-sector industrial city.

Notes

The author is grateful to H. Jacob Carlson and Kaveri Medappa for their extensive fieldwork and rich notes on which this chapter is based.

1. This chapter primarily draws on interviews conducted by H. Jacob Carlson during 2009 and 2010 as part of a research project led by Michael Goldman, with retired public-sector unit managers and employees, current public-sector employees, trade union leaders, city planning officials, and IT workers in Bangalore. See H. Jacob Carlson, "Model Employers and Model Cities? Bangalore's Public Sector and the Rise of the Neoliberal City," *Urban Geography* 39, no. 5 (2018): 726–45. The chapter also draws on interviews with former union leaders in the Yeshwantpur area conducted by Kaveri Medappa in April 2018 as part of the Speculative Urbanism project.

2. These were, in addition to ITI, Bharat Electronics Limited, Bharat Earth Movers Limited, Hindustan Aeronautics Limited, and Hindustan Machine Tools Limited.

3. Janaki Nair, *The Promise of the Metropolis: Bangalore's Twentieth Century* (New Delhi: Oxford University Press, 2005), 83, 127.

4. Dilip Subramanian, *Telecommunications Industry in India: State, Business and Labour in a Global Economy* (New York: Routledge, 2018), 387–88.

5. Amit Bhaduri and Deepak Nayyar, *The Intelligent Person's Guide to Liberalization* (New Delhi: Penguin Books, 1996), 34–35, 40–43; Chirashree

Dasgupta, *State and Capital in Independent India: Institutions and Accumulation* (New Delhi: Cambridge University Press, 2016), 260.

6. Subramanian, *Telecommunications Industry in India*, 421–32.

7. Dilip Subramanian, "Bangalore Public Sector Strike, 1980–81: A Critical Appraisal. I: The Settlements of 1973 and 1978," *Economic & Political Weekly* 32, no. 15 (1997): 768.

8. During the decades of state-led economic development in India, i.e., the *dirigiste* period (1950s to 1970s), the political interests of workers were defended by trade unions, even as they were restricted to the formal factory sector and experienced state repression. The shift toward neoliberal policies during the 1980s and 1990s led to the casualization of the workforce and the informalization of formal-sector employment, creating a pool of "flexible" labor that is devoid of employment benefits and protections. These shifts have also undermined the bargaining power of labor. See Dasgupta, *State and Capital*, 260.

9. Carlson, "Model Employers."

10. Akash Bhattacharya et al., "Fact Finding Report on the Unlawful Termination of Workers at ITI, Bengaluru" (All India People's Forum, February 2022), http://aipf.online/2022/03/09/fact-finding-report-on-the-unlawful-termination -of-workers-at-iti-bengaluru/.

11. The author is grateful to Clifton D' Rozario and Akash Bhattacharya of the All India Central Council of Trade Unions for clarifying details about the ITI contract workers' struggle.

12. Maitreyi Krishnan, "Victory for Struggle of ITI Workers," *Workers Resistance,* June 2023, https://www.aicctu.org/workers-resistance/v1/workers -resistance-june-2023/victory-struggle-iti-workers; Malini Ranganathan, "At Indian Telephone Industries in Bengaluru, Workers Fight a Battle Seen across the Public Sector," *The Wire,* December 8, 2021, https://thewire.in/labour/indian -telephone-industries-bengaluru-workers.

13. Bhattacharya et al., "Fact Finding Report."

14. Subramanian, *Telecommunications Industry in India*.

15. Carlson, "Model Employers," 741.

16. Carlson, 742.

17. See KGLU's Charter of Demands to ITI Management in Bhattacharya et al., "Fact Finding Report," 18–19.

9
Metro Mutations

Usha Rao

The Bangalore Metro Rail, known as Namma Metro (Our Metro), is in a state of perpetual construction. One cannot escape its ubiquitous presence as it spreads, crisscrossing the city east to west and north to south. While metro riders enjoy a seamless commute, city roads are choked with mud-splattered green sheets that sometimes carry the apology, "Metro Work in Progress. Regret Inconvenience." Borers and drillers have been diligently working their way through the belly of the city to prepare the ground for a future that runs on the metro.

Since its commencement in 2008, environmentalists, city dwellers, and project-affected individuals have criticized the Bangalore Metro Rail Corporation Limited (BMRCL) for its lack of transparency, its high-handedness with the public and land losers, its callous de-greening of the city, and its penchant for snatching public spaces without considering the long-term adverse impact on communities. The metro is also applauded as a winner by supporters, who see the costs borne by some as a necessary sacrifice for an *aaram* (easy and comfortable) city commute. Surely, there is another side to the "success" story?[1]

Decoding the Morning Ride

"Suresh," like many other commuters in Bengaluru, is delighted with the metro. He works as a team leader in a prominent IT firm on Mahatma Gandhi Road (MG Road), in the city's Central Business District (CBD) approximately fifteen kilometers from his home in south Bengaluru. The run into MG Road takes him about an hour, a little less than it would by road on a good traffic day. Suresh prefers to use the metro, as it promises comfort and certainty: "The interior is stress-free and comfortable—it avoids the mess on the roads. I'm

123

also sure that I will reach my office at a certain time." His words echo those of BMRCL's managing director, who claimed (in his conversation with me in 2017) that the metro commuter is more productive as "he reaches office in a good mood." "A productive professional makes for a productive city," he added.[2]

The metro announced itself as a world-class mass transit system that would rid Bengaluru, the IT hub, of its unbecoming traffic congestion. However, beneath the flashy headline about easing city commutes, the small print tells another story. Apart from the fast and air-conditioned ride it provides, the metro has other kinds of impacts on city spaces that are often excluded from accounts of its achievements.

The radial transport corridors and main transport arteries in Bengaluru, in alignment with the metro's planned development, were designated as "mutation corridor zones" at its inception, meaning that these areas are intended for high-density growth of commercial and residential properties. For instance, along the metro line, small shops and residences change hands and become high-value real estate, bringing in large developers. This is enabled by an enhancement of the floor-area ratio from two to five floors along the alignment for densifying land use.[3] Although it is reported that this concept may be scrapped from the Provisional Revised Master Plan 2031, it has already transformed lives and spaces in the city.[4] The famous *jinke mane*, a majestic old home embellished with deer sculptures, was a familiar landmark on the heavily tree-lined Kanakapura Road, one of the oldest routes leading south out of Bengaluru toward Mysuru. Today, the vicinity of the ruins of this home is a dense hub of commercial properties that bears no resemblance to what stood there before the commencement of the metro line. The nature of the city along the alignment does not merely change in its form but undergoes a deep and drastic transformation in use.

The company that builds and runs the metro rail system, BMRCL, is empowered to acquire private homes and establishments, public parks, stretches of road lined with trees, and sometimes an entire playground in the "public interest" (Figure 9.1). BMRCL is a special purpose vehicle (SPV). Its organizational status allows it to operate outside the ambit of local politics and democratic processes, in terms of deciding the alignment and acquiring land. Land acquisition carries the weight of the state and central governments, which are both rep-

Figure 9.1. Demolition to make way for construction of metro line, MKK Road, 2009. From the film *Our Metropolis*, by Gautam Sonti and Usha Rao, 2014.

resented on the company's board. Individuals or city governance bodies have little say in decisions, despite citizens' groups like Hasiru Usiru and Environment Support Group (see chapters 10 and 22) pushing for more transparency and a participative approach.[5] The design and nature of use of the acquired lands is determined by BMRCL and its retinue of contractors in consultation with its financial partners.

When land is acquired for a public project such as Namma Metro, private property owners may benefit from a satisfactory settlement, but the public is never compensated for the loss of commons or public spaces, even though the fallout affects the lives of people in the immediate vicinity and beyond. And tenants, who account for most occupants along old commercial stretches in the city, are provided with inadequate allowances for relocation and often lose access to business areas they have helped to build up.

As can be seen on the major business streets of CMH Road and MG Road, locally owned or small establishments give way to chain stores and branded retailers. Public land that is acquired is leased out to private developers and enterprises for commercial purposes, thus making it unavailable and inaccessible for free use.[6] The metro brings about a "mutation" that transforms the *meaning* and *use* of space in fundamental ways, especially in the vicinity of stations.

Land—whether private or public—is transformed into high-value real estate that produces a "new" city along the alignment. The increased floor-area ratios not only encourage vertical growth but enhance the possibility of extracting value through rentals. Places along the line begin to acquire a familiar look, which historian Arif Dirlik refers to as a "generic local" that evokes cityscapes from elsewhere (see chapter 1).[7] A recent report mentions that the new Airport Line is expected to convert lands (often referred to as "empty" or "barren") along the alignment into commercial hubs.[8] The transformation of space and urban densification are not incidental but intrinsic to the financial logic of the metro.

The Elephant on MG Road

I get my first glimpse of trees when the metro inches up into the light from Cubbon Park station. The commuter can imbibe the city's charms ensconced in air-conditioned comfort. The spectacular sight of copper pods in full bloom comes into view on one side as we glide up and above MG Road and its dense traffic. On the other side are rows of buildings—some glassy and glinting in the evening sun, the remainder quietly resigned to being torn down. Sringar Complex, the once bustling shopping center, is overrun with weeds and miniature trees staking one last claim before its impending demolition gives way to yet another swanky building.

The Voice announces the arrival at "Mahatma Gan*dh*i Road" with his peculiar emphasis on the last syllable. I walk out—and almost into a fake elephant decked in traditional Dussehra finery. Spectacular but out of place in a CBD station bursting with commercial hoardings. Across the road, over the tops of endless cars, the southern entrance to the station stands where the old Plaza Theatre—a major city landmark—once stood. A shiny luxury watch showroom has replaced the charmingly scruffy India Coffee House, a cooperative that was run by workers since the 1950s. Ballooning rents pushed them out and into a smaller place on Church Street, which runs parallel to MG Road. I sometimes spot an old waiter dressed in white with the customary *topi* (cap) leaning against the wall of the Deccan Herald building (which houses Bengaluru's favorite daily) close to his old premises. A specter calling attention to the past.

At the window seat in India Coffee House, one could watch passersby while steeped in the chatter of journalists, students, and shoppers and the clatter of chipped crockery. Stepping outside, I could take in the city's past and present in one swift sweep of the eyes. MG Road unified two threads of Bangalore's history. On the eastern side, the steeples of Trinity Church consecrated in 1852 for the British regiment stationed in Bangalore Cantonment, on the western horizon behind a line of old evergreens, the domes of Vidhana Soudha, the State Legislature of Karnataka that seemed to return the gaze of the colonial edifice. Forming a green and magenta arc above the road was the walkway, popularly referred to as the "MG Road boulevard," the protagonist of this tale. Today, the heavy metro pillars dominate the view.

In its British days, MG Road was called "South Parade" and was the main drag of the "white" city that abutted the Parade Ground of the Bangalore Cantonment, established in the early 1800s.[9] The promenade that ran along and above its length was a hot spot where genteel residents could "take the air." Post-independence, South Parade was renamed MG Road, but the old promenade was retained and came to be called "the boulevard." Shorn of its colonial elite, the nondescript yet pretty path became a favorite of amblers, vendors, "idlers," students, courting couples, and working folk who traversed the city on foot. One could savor the pleasures of loitering and slowing down time, shuffle slowly under the magenta bougainvillea munching peanuts from a paper cone, tripping over a broken tile, all the while ignoring the occasional drunk supine on a bench, and blissfully unaware of the stench from the public toilet below.

When the boulevard was dug up in 2007 to prepare for the metro construction, there was outrage, primarily from middle-class Bangaloreans who saw it as an attack on the character of MG Road. BMRCL promised to develop in its place a "new cultural landmark" and "public space." After the dust settled, the Metro Rangoli Center was unveiled. It houses a gallery, a small auditorium (both of which are hired out for events and exhibitions), a play area, and a swath of kiosks and stalls that are rented out to vendors.[10]

How public is the Rangoli Complex? The once open boulevard has been revamped into a curated walkway that bears little resemblance to its bougainvillea-adorned predecessor in terms of the possibilities of use, overall design, and aesthetic. Hoovina Haadi (the flowery path) is fenced and maintained by a real estate company. It is policed by private security, disallows "uncivil" behavior like smoking, peddling food stuff, and "loitering," and does not tolerate nap takers on benches—all of which were some of the charms of the old path. A prominent restaurant chain has opened its outlet and promises coffee and *thindi* (snacks) restaurant style for a pretty price. It is now inaccessible to the peanut vendor, the flaneur, or the college student in search of a bench to contemplate the meaning of life.

Signage, narratives about the metro, and maps of the Rangoli Center direct the viewer through the space—*where* to walk, *how* to walk, *where* and *what* to consume. While the MG Road boulevard may not have been equally accessible for *all* Bangaloreans, it remained a "common" space in use and practice. The takeover by the metro transformed it into "property" and commodified it under the ownership of the BMRCL. In place of the joys of directionless meandering and contemplation, its "new" design invites a *certain kind* of orderly public that is willing to be directed through its spaces and partake of what is on offer.

Spectral Sightings, April 20, 2017

It is late afternoon. The customary crowds that throng the station on a weekend are missing. Down the stairs, past the watchful eye of the security guard, I walk from the Church Street end of the metro station toward the MG Road exit and into the expansive lobby. The cold and empty hall with its high ceiling amplifies the beeps of security wands and the clack of heels. I notice some men setting up stalls in the empty space to the right of the doorway. Two of them are busy displaying an assortment of handcrafted bags with ethnic embroidery. A thin crowd passes by them. In the far end, untouched by the extravagant lighting in the central space, is a small dusty window. It beckons me to its ill-lit corner. I move toward it.

It begins gently—a whirring in my ear that turns to a steady clicking ticking sound that grows louder with every step drowning the sounds of the station. A clock strikes a majestic baritone *ding* three times. The slow rhythm of a swinging pendulum grows louder.

Metro Mutations **129**

A room is now forming around me. The gray stone floor is bare and cold through my thin slippers. As I drift into the past, the murky glass blooms into a generous window with a deep blue trim. Etched on it is the legend—Phoenix Watch Works.

It is a bright day in this land of memory. A steady stream of traffic moves along MG Road. A hand-drum vendor can be heard through the open window playing his beat to the pace of pedestrians passing through. A wild wind suddenly blows in and flips the pages of a 2008 calendar hanging alongside fading photographs on a white-washed wall. One colored print stands out: a young man with an impressive moustache and a blue brass-buttoned blazer atop a Bullet motorcycle. The giant wall clock tick tocks at the far end, marking the seconds.

Mr. Ramchander Sharma is bent over his worktable. He is a dapper man in his seventies, dressed in khaki pants and a spotless white shirt, with a magnifying lens glued to his eye. His moustache continues to hold its majestic twirl. Mr. Sharma is absorbed in the delicate mechanics of a wristwatch. The table is cluttered with tools—some acquired by his father in the 1930s when Phoenix Watch Works first opened its doors. "My father was a horologist," Mr. Sharma tells me. "He repaired watches and clocks of all kinds, especially imported ones that were popular with British residents and the who's who of that time." Mr. Sharma works on while chattering. On his wrists are multiple watches. "I wear them together so that I can check if they are all working fine after repairs," he clarifies in his clipped English, almost in anticipation of my question.

The shop has accumulated layers of history and its attendant dust, sheaves of old journals, and piles of watch parts and tools. A long broom stands in readiness to clear cobwebs. At the rear end of the room is a massive worktable loaded with metal tools that his father had imported from Switzerland.

Mr. Sharma has practically grown up in Phoenix Watch Works, which stood next to the Plaza Theatre. He remembers the flow of fashionable customers in the 1940s, both Indian and "foreign"—British and American soldiers, and the occasional Italians who frequented the establishments on South Parade, for R & R—films at Plaza Theatre, dance floors at Funnels (now the headquarters of Deccan Herald), drink and conversation at the innumerable bars in the area.

Mr. Sharma's life has centered around this end of MG Road. As a schoolboy he did a daily run for his father and his clients, fetching flasks of coffee from India Coffee House a few meters down the road. More than fifty years later, he maintains his coffee routine. Every day at 11 a.m. he turns the key on the massive old lock and walks down the street, past Plaza Theatre and the office of *Deccan Herald* on his way to his bank. Once his business is concluded he takes a customary break at the India Coffee House, where he has a steaming cup with his old friend Len Shepard, an elderly Anglo-Indian gentleman who continues to live in the neighborhood. This has been his routine as the proprietor of Phoenix ever since he can remember. His work, leisure, friendships, and sense of self are rooted in the South Parade of his childhood.

The sky darkens. The calendar skips ahead by a couple of years. It is the dead of night but dense with activity. Trailers are ferrying metal parts for metro construction. In the light of a single lamp, a frail-looking Mr. Sharma is packing his tools, sifting through papers. The window near his work desk has been smashed. Mr. Sharma is trying to salvage his things before the demolition machine chomps through his shop. He and his sons are working at a frantic speed, as scarcely a few hours remain before daylight. After BMRCL acquired Plaza Theatre in 2010, Mr. Sharma was given barely any time to clear out material and memory accumulated over seven decades. Although the Sharmas had been occupants for over seventy years, Mr. Sharma received only a relocation allowance as his compensation because he was a tenant in the building.

Day breaks. Phoenix is a mass of rubble. The horologist's tool lies wounded on its side among the fragmented bricks. The shop's gray stone floor has been pulverized. Stuck in the rubble is the photograph with the young Ramchander in a blue blazer, gazing at the camera with pride and confidence.

"Madam—no taking photo! *Chaliye, chaliye* [Move, move]." A booming voice jolts me out of the world of Phoenix Watch Works. I am back in the white light of the station—an irate guard is waving me on with his baton. As I walk out into MG Road, I spot an A4-sized notice announcing the opening of bids for rentals at the station. Next to it, a blank wall with its tiny grubby window. Phoenix had returned to the dust.

Waiting for the "Commuter-Consumer"

Halasuru Metro station is the pause between two hectic stops—Trinity Station on MG Road and Indiranagar. The western entrance opens out onto a chipped and worn footpath which hosts a perennial pool of stagnant water. Set back from the road is an eatery selling north Indian snacks. Abutting it is a ragged space occupied by parked motorcycles. This marks the spot where Mr. Manjunath's ancestral home once stood. His grandfather arrived in Bangalore as a construction worker who helped to build, among other things, the Vidhana Soudha. The family was forced to give up the house and move to make way for the Ulsoor Metro station. The compensation, though adequate, did not blunt the loss of a home built on the family's hard labor. Across the road, almost stuck to the metro stairway, is the dust-coated facade of a once-majestic structure with characteristic tile and wrought iron window grills—the remains of someone's home that managed to survive the metro.

The station is a favorite roosting spot for local pigeons that gather in large numbers on the roofs and along the grimy glass windows. The floor is splattered with white spots which are occasionally mopped by the skeleton housekeeping staff. Unlike the glossy floors and interiors of stations in the more upmarket areas of MG Road and Indiranagar or those adjoining malls, Ulsoor is a "low-footfall" location. According to the BMRCL project manager, all stations are "cost centers."[11] The revenue from ridership and rentals at the Halasuru station does not justify the cost of hiring extra staff needed to keep it squeaky clean.

Today, there are hardly any "locals" on the platform—only a handful of students and a family traveling to visit cousins at the southern tip of the Purple Line. Although they are close to the station, the brothers who run the eighty-year-old Sumangali Stationery Store bring back supplies from the old city on their scooter, as the metro restricts the amount of merchandise that can be carried by commuters.

The station interiors echo hollowly, waiting for retail stalls to claim their place, in contrast to the cramped and bustling market a stone's throw away. Ulsoor's Bazaar Street and its neighboring lanes are teeming with shops that sell everything from colored birds to precious jewelry. For most of the day, the station is quiet and empty. In one corner I spot a sign, "Space for ATM." Although it was expected that Halasuru station would have less traffic than its two neighboring

132 Usha Rao

ones, what warrants its large footprint? It appears that the extensive space that ingested homes, corners of temples, and shops was acquired in anticipation of future revenues.

One day, while I sat inside the station control room with "Ashok," the rookie station controller, a young woman walked in to sign the register. Ashok introduced her as the retail development officer for Halasuru, who is responsible for seeking out, publicizing, and attracting bids for rentals inside the station. Rentals and footfalls are essential for turning stations into profit centers. The logic of retail within stations is simply stated as convenience for the commuter to "pick up his daily needs." However, contrary to this claim by the former managing director, the shops that do come up inside are not basic grocery or fresh produce stores. The preference is for established food and beverage brands like Café Coffee Day, Nandini milk parlors, Domino's Pizza, and Chai Point, shops for gifts and knick-knacks, aggregator cabs, and other chain retailers.[12]

Retail rentals go through tendering and bidding and are processed through a bureaucratic setup that ultimately determines what the commuter-consumer is "offered." How the station space is designed and what is "on offer" may have more to do with financial considerations and the needs of business partners of BMRCL than the wish list of commuters or of the community where the station is located.[13] For instance, the real estate developer Embassy Group agreed to invest 1.4 billion rupees (approximately 16.8 million USD) to build the Bettahalasur station on the Airport Line, even before the work began. In return, they retain the right to use a part of the station for advertising, and for developing retail and commercial spaces.[14]

Despite the hot denials made by officials in the early days, the conjoining of retail rentals and metro lines has been publicly acknowledged as part of the design and financial model of the metro. Stations are expected to become "retail destinations." This is apparent on the Green Line, which has three prominent retail destination stations—the high-end Orion and Mantri Malls and, more recently, IKEA, the Swedish brand, which has set up shop at the tail end of the line. Corporate partnerships and investments are exchanged for retail space within and abutting stations.

Halasuru, according to this blueprint, must languish and wait for commuter-consumers to arrive. Perhaps this will materialize sometime in the future after the neighborhood undergoes the required "mutation" that increases footfalls. Until the coming of that future, it remains a convivial spot for the local pigeons to gather.

Spectacle and Speculation

The Bengaluru Metro is a massive financial project that is being built at spectacular cost, sourced mostly through international capital as long-term "low-interest" loans. The first phase, of forty-two kilometers, cost upward of 116 billion rupees (approximately 1.5 billion USD), with delays causing considerable cost escalation. The ongoing seventy-two-kilometer network of Phase II is expected to be completed at an approximate cost of 307 billion rupees (3.8 billion USD).[15] A significant part of the finance for all phases has come from international agencies such as the Asian Development Bank and Japan International Cooperation Agency (JICA). The latter loaned 37,170 million rupees (467 million USD) to BMRCL for Phase II.[16]

The metro goes beyond connectivity, or fast and convenient commutes. Its "reach" (to use metro terminology) stretches into the realm of finance, international lenders, and real estate consortia. It is entwined with larger processes of land transformation, real estate markets, and global finance that continue to reshape landscapes and cities around the world. The metro serves multiple constituencies— governments at all levels, corporates, developers, and city residents who aspire for a world-class commuter system.

The high cost of building and running the metro is not covered by revenues from ridership. In Bengaluru, buses carry six times as many people as the metro—approximately three million commuters travel by bus every day compared to 500,000 by the metro (see chapter 10).

The rationale for this high investment is that more Bangaloreans are expected to use the metro in the future, after the network becomes more extensive. This logic does not seem to factor in any analysis of ridership trends, or issues such as poor last-mile connectivity that keep potential commuters in their vehicles and on the road. Studies like those by Dinesh Mohan and Geetam Tiwari of IIT Delhi, which have pointed to the limitations of the Delhi Metro to serve the majority of the city's population, seem to have had little or no influence.[17] The metro continues to expand unfettered.

If ridership revenues are not significant, what then is the profit stream? It flows from the value of commercial properties and rentals within and around spaces owned by BMRCL. The project is financed through "land value capture," a world-wide model that was used for the Delhi Metro and subsequently became a blueprint for BMRCL as well as for metros in other Indian cities.[18] Underscoring the dependence on retail, in March 2022 BMRCL decided to monetize its real estate by expanding commercial spaces in stations to 2.2 lakh (220,000) square feet from the current 21,000 square feet.[19]

While the expanding metro brings in more spaces and places under its alignment, there are indications of ruination—both literal and metaphorical. The relations between management and workers (who run and maintain the trains) has been tense over issues of benefits, working conditions, and union recognition (which is key to accessing a range of labor rights). Besides, the contract workers who perform important functions like housekeeping and security allege irregularities in pay and leave practices. Within the BMRCL Employees Union there are whispers about corrupt practices that may be escalating the costs of running and building the metro. They allege that kickbacks from construction tenders and rental bids are fattening private purses and leading to "below specs" construction standards.

A case in point is the appearance of the "honeycomb"—a rough patch on the track that stalled metro service on the busy Purple Line in 2018.[20] The leader of the Employees Union, "Swamy," continues his attempt to file a public interest litigation (PIL) against what he calls rampant corruption that is filling individuals' pockets and, in his words, "eating away" taxpayers' money.[21]

The Unbounded City

The metro continues to proliferate with new lines and alignments, forging into the hinterland, building the city as it goes. Aggressive land banking is underway on Kanakapura Road in the southern rim of Bengaluru—edges of erstwhile villages, tree lines, and fields have been swallowed up.[22] Meanwhile, landowners anticipate returns on their fields that will become part of yet another line. Perhaps the inevitable shift away from agrarian land-based occupations and its attendant social fabric will generate potential commuters who will be compelled to ride the line to seek employment in the belly of the city. Like the metro itself, all of this is in the realm of speculation.[23]

BMRCL has claimed a portion of the surrounding reserve forest (a part of an elephant corridor) to house its Anjanapura depot on the Green Line, thus incorporating the peri-urban wilderness into the urban fold, despite the dangers this step may pose.[24] The hardship caused by recent floods and soaring temperatures in the city—attributed to the massive loss of tree cover—will fade quickly from public memory. The metro dips into water sources deep in the ground and runs on electricity generated at the Sharavati Hydro Station in the heart of the lush Malanad forests, four hundred kilometers from Bengaluru. Where are the limits to this city and its metro? While we wait for the future, we are already hitting against the ecological limits in the here and now.

Notes

1. For this essay I drew on field notes compiled during my ethnographic research on the Bangalore Metro Rail project. The vignettes presented here are based on my interviews with metro officials (2017 onward), conversations with activists and city dwellers, "gossip" sessions, interviews with members of the yet-to-be-recognized BMRCL Employees Union, and my observations between 2008 and 2022.

2. The idea that a comfortable ride makes commuters more productive is etched into official "metro talk." This is echoed by the Delhi Metro Rail Corporation (DMRC) architect featured in Rashmi Sadana's book *Metronama: Scenes from the Delhi Metro* (New Delhi: Roli Books, 2022), 156.

3. Kushala S., "No More a Bridge Too FAR: Bonanza Awaits Builders," *Bangalore Mirror,* January 24, 2015, https://bangaloremirror.indiatimes.com/bangalore /cover-story/Metro-track-lines-Floor-Area-Ratio-BMRCL-Siddaramaiah -government-Namma-Metro-Pradeep-Singh-Kharola-metro-corridor /heroesshow/45997079.cms.

4. A mutation corridor is an area designated in the master plan where virtually blanket permission is granted to property owners to build commercial structures, although the area might be zoned for residential or other uses. This provision for certain arterial roads in Bengaluru's Comprehensive Development Plan 2015 was the source of much controversy because it led to the rapid commercialization of residential areas. See "Bengaluru: New Master Plan Axes 'Mutation Corridors,'" *New Indian Express,* December 18, 2017, www .newindianexpress.com/cities/bengaluru/2017/dec/18/bengaluru-new-master -plan-axes-mutation-corridors-1729999.html; Collaborative for Advancement of

136 Usha Rao

Studies in Urbanism through Mixed Media, "The Bangalore Metro: For . . . ?," December 2007, https://casumm.files.wordpress.com/2008/02/metro-booklet -dec-2007-16-2-08.pdf.

5. See the Environment Support Group website for details on campaigns and litigation: https://esgindia.org/new/tag/bangalore-metro/.

6. Randhawa discusses the transformation of land in the context of the Delhi Metro. Pritpal Randhawa, "Beyond Mass Transit," *Economic & Political Weekly* 47, no. 16 (April 21, 2012): 25–29.

7. "Global aesthetic" refers to a generic look that is shared across many cities. Arif Dirlik, "Architectures of Global Modernity, Colonialism, and Places," *Modern Chinese Literature and Culture* 17, no. 1 (January 2005): 33–61.

8. Of course, there are no "barren lands"—it is agricultural fields or common lands that will be acquired. The managing director of BMRCL, Anjum Parvez, confirmed the expected real estate boom in 2021: "The real impact can be seen along the Airport Road corridor as a lot of land is available there. IT parks, office spaces, and residential flats are all moving there." Rasheed Kappan, "Namma Metro—One Slow Decade," *Deccan Herald*, October 10, 2021, https://www.deccanherald.com/india/namma-metro-one-slow-decade-1039132.html.

9. See Fazlul M. Hasan, *Bangalore through the Centuries* (Bangalore: Historical Publications, 1970).

10. See the report in *The Hindu* on the new Metro Boulevard, which cost approximately 50 million rupees to construct. "Eatery among Attractions on M.G. Road Boulevard," *The Hindu*, April 8, 2013, https://www.thehindu.com /news/cities/bangalore/Eatery-among-attractions-on-MG-Road-boulevard /article12188860.ece.

11. For the details on retail and stations, I have drawn on my conversations with the project manager who requested to remain anonymous (February 2018) and the then managing director of BMRCL, Mr. Kharola (November 2017).

12. Bengaluru follows the Delhi Metro model discussed by Matti Siemiatycki, "Message in a Metro: Building Urban Rail Infrastructure and Image in Delhi, India," *International Journal of Urban and Regional Research* 30, no. 2 (June 2006): 277–92.

13. Sadana notes the processes and constituencies that decide the design and nature of the station with reference to the Delhi Metro. Rashmi Sadana, "'We Are Visioning It': Aspirational Planning and the Material Landscapes of Delhi's Metro," *City & Society* 30, no. 2 (2018): 186–209.

14. S. Lalitha, "Bettahalasur Station Back on KR Puram-Kempegowda International Airport Metro Line," *New Indian Express*, July 3, 2023, https://www .newindianexpress.com/states/karnataka/2023/Jul/03/bettahalasur-station -back-on-kr-puram-kempegowda-international-airport-metro-line-2590803 .html.

15. Suchit Kidiyoor, "Cost of Namma Metro Phase II Increased by ₹4,290

Crore," *The Hindu,* April 10, 2022, https://www.thehindu.com/news/cities
/bangalore/cost-of-namma-metro-phase-ii-increased-by4290-crore/article
65309493.ece.

16. The Delhi Metro has also been financed by JICA. See Sadana, *Metronama,*
109. The Agence Française de Development has loaned BMRCL 200 million
euros for Phase II (BMRCL Annual Report 2020–2021, 106). See the report
for more details on loans from international agencies. Ajay Sukumaran, "Bangalore Metro Finds Raising Low-Cost Capital Challenging," *Financial Express,* November 8, 2013, https://www.financialexpress.com/archive/bangalore
-metro-finds-raising-low-cost-capital-challenging/1192162/; Express News Service, "Namma Metro Gets Rs 3.7k Crore Loan from Japan," *New Indian Express,*
March 27, 2021, https://www.newindianexpress.com/cities/bengaluru/2021/mar
/27/namma-metro-gets-rs-37k-crore-loan-from-japan-2282194.html.

17. Dinesh Mohan, *Mythologies, Metros, and Future Urban Transport* (New
Delhi: Indian Institute of Technology Delhi, 2008); Geetam Tiwari, "Metro Rail
and the City Derailing Public Transport," *Economic & Political Weekly,* November 30, 2013, 65–76.

18. Bérénice Bon, "A New Mega Project Model and a New Funding Model:
Traveling Concepts and Local Adaptations around the Delhi Metro," *Habitat
International* 45, part 3 (January 2015): 223–30, https://www.researchgate.net
/publication/263894095.

19. Chiranjeevi Kulkarni, "Metro Seeks to Boost Non-fare Revenue as Operation Costs Soar," *Deccan Herald,* March 10, 2022, https://www.deccanherald
.com/india/karnataka/bengaluru/metro-seeks-to-boost-non-fare-revenue-as
-operation-costs-soar-1089858.html#. Value capture finance and rentals through
commercial property development form part of BMRCL's revenue-raising
model. Sridhar Vivan, "Pandemic Blues: Namma Metro's Revenue Takes a
Hit," *Bangalore Mirror,* July 26, 2022, https://bangaloremirror.indiatimes.com
/bangalore/others/pandemic-blues-namma-metros-revenue-takes-a-hit
/articleshow/93120011.cms.

20. P. Kumaran, "Six Years into Operation, Metro Pillar at Trinity Station Develops Major Fault," *Bangalore Mirror,* December 13, 2018, https://
bangaloremirror.indiatimes.com/bangalore/others/six-years-into-operation
-metro-pillar-at-trinity-station-develops-major-fault/articleshow/67067778
.cms. In an interview with a railway expert I learned that the "honeycomb" was
an indication of poor-quality construction and insufficient curing.

21. These observations are based on my extensive interviews with members of
the BMRCL Employees Union. The stories about corruption and misdemeanors of "officers" are what Taussig refers to as a "public secret," as workers seem
to know what not to know. Michael Taussig, *Defacement: Public Secrecy and the
Labor of the Defensive* (Stanford: Stanford University Press, 1999), 2.

22. Swetha R. Dhanaka, "Branding Urbanization in Karnataka: Information

Flows and the 'Right to the City to Come' in Peri-urban Areas" (paper presented at workshop "Bangalore's Great Transformation," National Institute of Advanced Studies, Bengaluru, June 24–25, 2016).

23. My research so far has not looked at the impact of the new lines on communities in the peri-urban area, but this is in the cards.

24. "BMRCL Applies for Forest Clearance to Access Anjanapura Depot," *The Hindu,* April 30, 2019, https://www.thehindu.com/news/cities/bangalore /bmrcl-applies-for-forest-clearance-to-access-anjanapura-depot/article26996518 .ece; Kulkarni Chiranjeevi, "Metro Line to Anjanapura Inaugurated, to Be Opened for Public from Friday," *Deccan Herald,* January 15, 2021, https://www .deccanherald.com/india/karnataka/bengaluru/metro-line-to-anjanapura -inaugurated-to-be-opened-for-public-from-friday-939009.html#.

10
Moving Matters

Shaheen Shasa

Manjubai is a domestic worker who lives in the Jai Bheemeshwari Nagar slum rehabilitation quarters in Laggere, in northwest Bengaluru. She earns 4,000 rupees (50 USD) per month. She struggles to pay for her children's school fees and uniforms. A nutritious meal for her children is a luxury. Traveling to and from the middle-class neighborhood of Rajajinagar, where she works, is inconvenient and expensive. To save money for her children's needs, she tries her best to cut down on her travel expenses. Buses from her neighborhood, located on the edge of the city, are infrequent, so she must walk three kilometers to Nandini Layout to catch a bus. But instead of taking the bus from there, which would cost her 40 rupees per day, she walks to the next stop and boards the bus at Saraswathipuram to save 10 rupees.

Lakshmi is a sanitation worker with the city corporation who lives in Anjanapura. She is a single mother with three children. Her day starts while the rest of the city still sleeps. She leaves home as early as 4 a.m. Often the streetlights are out, and the condition of the road is bad. If she misses a bus, she can't get to work on time. At times she spends 30 rupees extra on an auto-rickshaw to reach the bus stop on time. Lakshmi's monthly salary is 14,000 rupees. If she does not report to work by 6 a.m., she will lose the day's pay. She struggles to cover the house rent, electricity and water bills, school fees, nutritious food for the family—all basic needs—within this budget. The high cost of travel is a burden for her. At a public hearing on the affordability of bus services in Bengaluru, she lamented that the city wouldn't be clean without the toil of workers like her, but the city does not take care of them by providing adequate public transport.

Municipal sanitation workers in Bengaluru earn around 11,000 rupees per month. Housekeeping staff, who work in apartments, offices, or shopping complexes, also earn 10,000 to 11,000 per month,

Figure 10.1. Bus terminal in central Bengaluru. Photograph by Pierre Hauser.

while the salary of a worker at a ready-made garments factory is around 7,000 rupees. Construction workers earn 8,000 to 10,000 rupees (100 to 125 USD) on average. With these low levels of income, many workers in the city cannot afford the high cost of mobility.

Bus fares in Bengaluru are the highest for any city in India. A trip of two to four kilometers by bus costs 10 rupees, a six-kilometer trip costs 15 rupees, and a trip of eight to fourteen kilometers costs 20 rupees. The average trip by bus (twelve kilometers, according to the city's Comprehensive Mobility Plan 2020) costs 20 rupees, which translates to a monthly expense of 1,040 rupees for most commuters. A monthly bus pass costs 1,050 rupees. Since travel cannot be avoided, many like Manjubai walk longer distances to reduce travel costs, confine themselves to employment opportunities within walking or affordable distances, or cut down on essential needs such as health or education.

Bangalore Metropolitan Transport Corporation (BMTC), the city's public transport undertaking, apparently does not take factors such as affordability or equity into consideration when setting the ticket fares. Instead, the operating logic for BMTC, mandated by the state government, is to recover the entire cost of its operations from ticket revenues. The Government of Karnataka prescribed a fare-revision formula for transport corporations in Karnataka (including BMTC) in September 2000, linking fares exclusively to fuel price and staff salaries (which form the bulk of their operational costs). The formula allows these corporations to raise fares whenever the combined effects of increase in fuel prices and staff salaries exceed 0.25 rupees per passenger kilometer. The objective of this rule was to allow the transport corporations to reduce their losses and financial burden due to fare subsidies. However, no significant fare revision has taken place in recent years due to staunch public opposition.

In 2009 the state government started a special service for the poor called Atal Sarige. The service, which offered fares at a 50 percent discount, operated twenty to twenty-five buses on ten to fourteen routes connecting particular areas where the poor are concentrated (such as slum rehabilitation projects, usually built on the outskirts of the city) to specific destinations. Before the Covid-19 pandemic, twenty buses were running on eleven routes under this scheme. While the lower fares eased the burden on commuters, many found even these fares unaffordable. With just one or two buses on each route, the frequency was quite low, and with just a handful of routes, service coverage of the city was extremely limited. Such special services will always remain limited and deficient unless more resources are committed. There were many more areas that the service did not connect than those it did. Besides, the poor don't live only in slum rehabilitation housing, nor do they travel to just one or two destinations. The Atal Sarige service reflects an impoverished imagination of how the poor commute or the quality of life that they should have in the city.

The Slum Board quarters in Sadaramangala, near Whitefield in the southeastern corner of the city, includes eight hundred rehabilitation housing units. The project was built by the Karnataka Slum Development Board (KSDB) for people displaced from Netaji Slum, which was centrally located in the city, in the Bamboo Bazar area in Shivajinagar. While there is a wide main road less than one kilometer from the housing complex, the availability of public transport is erratic. The area is served by just two bus routes going to two major market and transport hubs in the city, Shivajinagar and K. R. Market, at 7 a.m. and 9.30 a.m. But the residents complain that these buses are neither regular nor reliable. So, they are forced to rely on auto-rickshaws, costing anywhere from 30 to 100 rupees, to get to points from where they can catch buses to their destinations. In the evenings, too, the buses to Sadaramangala often run only up to points three to four kilometers away, from where riders must walk back home or catch auto-rickshaws. This makes it an ordeal to get home in the evenings, especially for young women who commute to work. And as it gets late, auto-rickshaw operators start charging more money. Residents say they must travel to access livelihood opportunities and to earn money, so they are forced to depend on autos even when they are unaffordable. Sometimes, at the end of the day, they are left with no money for dinner and sleep on an empty stomach because they have spent so much on transport. Even to go to hospitals for medical treatment, residents of Sadaramangala are dependent on autos because of the lack of bus services during the day. They do have the option of using trains, but it is a two-kilometer walk to Hoodi railway station, and trains are infrequent.

Sadaramangala is not an exception. There are many such KSDB quarters dotting the city's fringes, constructed for the relocation and resettlement of slum residents whose centrally located informal settlements were demolished (see chapter 12). Most of these areas have connectivity problems like Sadaramangala. However, the service gaps are not limited to such settlements or the city peripheries alone. BMTC operates high-frequency services on all arterial roads and many other main roads (starting from the central hubs in the city) and along the ring roads between hubs such as Kengeri, Banashankari, Domlur, and Hebbal. But there are many areas along these roads, away from the main roads, where bus services are negligible or simply absent, cutting across all types of neighborhoods and settlements.

While these are the ground realities in the city, the BMTC is mandated to sustain itself from its own revenues, which means its focus is on cost recovery from users rather than providing an affordable public service. This reflects the larger neoliberal or market-driven economic policy framework introduced in India in the early 1990s. Under this policy regime, financial performance (revenues, profit and loss, operational efficiency) became the overriding concern of public service undertakings. In the name of better management and improved quality of services, the Bangalore Transport Service, which until 1997 operated as a division of the Karnataka State Road Transport Corporation, was reconstituted as the Bangalore Metropolitan Transport Corporation. From that time, profit and loss and revenue flows have been the primary criteria by which its performance is assessed. Inevitably, they also became the governing considerations for ticket pricing, service provisioning, and operations.

This is not to say that BMTC does not provide a useful service. Far from it. BMTC is the transportation lifeline for the majority of Bengaluru's residents. Before the pandemic some 3.5 million people were traveling by BMTC buses daily. This number stood at around 2.8 million in 2023, after a significant drop in ridership during the pandemic. Even when travel is expensive and unaffordable for low- and low-middle-income commuters, BMTC buses are less expensive than most other options in the city. With its fleet of around six thousand buses, BMTC runs more than two thousand routes and provides connectivity along all major roads to most parts of the city. But, as noted, there are gaps in service in many areas as well. The stories of Manjubai and Sadaramangala are thus the story of the multitudes who fall through the cracks of a transport system that is designed and operated with flawed priorities. It's the story of the systemic deficiencies in how a city plans for the mobility of its residents.

What role does transport play in the city, in making the city, in making the lives of people in the city? Is it a public service that the state ought to provide to all residents? What is fair pricing for such an essential service? Should it be free, should it be priced at levels affordable for low-income working-class communities, should it be priced to recover costs and turn profits? How does transport provisioning and the cost of mobility affect people's lives? How does it shape the city itself? These questions are at the heart of the mobility crisis in Bengaluru, one of the most rapidly growing cities in the world and one of the most congested cities in India and Asia. The public discourse on transport in the city is still dominated by questions of traffic congestion, caused by the explosion in private vehicles on the roads, and the inadequacies of public transportation. What is often missed are the human and social dimensions of mobility, especially public transportation, as the enabler of lives and livelihoods, as a gateway to opportunities, and as central to the city's economic development and the vitality of its cultural and political fabric.

Bengaluru Bus Prayanikara Vedike (BBPV; Bengaluru Bus Commuter Forum)—commonly referred to as "the Vedike"—a coalition of workers unions, slum residents organizations, and activists, has been striving to highlight these multiple dimensions of mobility and the importance of affordable and accessible bus-based mass transit to urban and working-class lives. The Vedike builds on the work of earlier civil society networks in the city, such as Hasiru Usiru, which in the early 2000s challenged the idea of building the city's way out of congestion through infrastructure-heavy projects such as road widening, overpasses, and signal-free corridors—all "solutions" oriented to private vehicles.

Although the still-under-construction metro rail system is promoted as the best mass transport option, groups such as Hasiru Usiru and the Vedike have consistently questioned whether the high costs of the metro system—and the severe disruptions it has meant for the city (see chapter 9)—can be justified and whether it is a viable transport solution for Bengaluru. Experts and citizens have pointed to the misdirected planning process and the high economic and social costs of constructing the metro. The project has also entailed the displacement of many residents and the forcible acquisition of properties, giving rise to multiple waves of protests. Civil society groups in Bengaluru and other Indian cities argue that buses—the primary public transport across urban centers—as well as cycling and walking are the most sustainable and equitable mobility options. While policymakers, bureaucrats, and politicians pay lip service to these ideas and tinker with minor improvements here and there, the major focus and funding in Bengaluru continues to be on road infrastructure and metro rail, neither of which can provide affordable, accessible, or sustainable transport solutions for the city at large.

This is the backdrop against which the Vedike has been campaigning for lower bus fares to make public transport more affordable for large sections of the working population. The Vedike also advocates for the introduction of more buses (of different sizes) and a redesigned route network to provide better connectivity in all parts of the city (including interior areas, the outskirts, and narrow roads). Another demand is to give priority to buses on the road (through bus priority lanes, priority at signals, and so on) so that they can move faster.

Affordable mobility and lower fares are the Vedike's longest-

Photo Essay
Life in the Speculative City
Pierre Hauser

Plate 1.1. The visual field of Bengaluru is saturated with billboards advertising the peaceful and comfortable lifestyle promised by luxury high-rise apartment complexes. Here we see Phoenix One Bangalore West, built on a seventeen-acre property acquired from a closed factory in Rajajinagar, where apartments sell for 40 to 65 million rupees, or 500,000 to 800,000 USD (chapter 8).

Plate 1.2. Millions of construction workers have come to Bengaluru from across the country to build the city's tech parks and apartment complexes. Most are circular migrants, staying on or near their work sites only for as long as they are employed, and returning to their villages in Hyderabad-Karnataka or northern or eastern India every few months. Construction work in this high-tech city is low paid and marked by arduous and risky manual labor (chapter 15).

Plate 1.3. On the southeastern edge of Bengaluru, the twenty-nine-story towers of "Lakeview Haven" rise from the fertile soil of agricultural land which until recently provided a bountiful livelihood to farmers (chapters 3, 4, and 5).

Plate 1.4. In low-income neighborhoods across the city, owners take out loans to construct multistory buildings on their modest plots, creating rental housing to earn extra income. These modest units cater mainly to migrant workers who move to the city to work in its burgeoning but precarious service economy (chapter 11).

Plate 1.5. The privatized spaces of Bengaluru's new malls and entertainment complexes, surveilled and monitored, offer a substitute for the shrinking public spaces of the city—at least for elites and the middle classes. No loitering permitted! (chapters 1 and 19).

Plate 1.6. "RP Colony," a small working-class housing cluster in Yeshwantpur, is squeezed between new real estate projects sprouting all around it. Finally, the residents are squeezed out, forced to vacate the land and accept tiny one-bedroom apartments as rehabilitation housing after their houses are demolished. The photos show the settlement before and after demolition (chapter 12).

Plate 1.7. This image of people waiting at a bus stop in Whitefield underscores the importance of affordable bus transit for Bengaluru's residents and workers who are essential to the city's economic and cultural fabric but find themselves struggling to cope with transportation costs in an increasingly expensive city (chapters 9 and 10).

Plate 1.8. Travel to Bengaluru's agrarian margins and you are likely to encounter peri-urban locales like this, in the throes of upheaval, upended by the city's rapid expansion. The conversion of ancestral farmlands into real estate has brought far-reaching social, economic, and ecological consequences (chapters 3 and 14).

Plate 1.9. Street vendors provide a large range of amenities to the city's middle-class and working-class inhabitants, but as property values soar and the aesthetic sensibilities of residents shift they find themselves increasingly vulnerable to eviction from public spaces (such as pavements and roadsides) that serve as their sites of business (chapter 16).

Plate 1.10. Once vibrant and the linchpin of a thriving rural economy, "Purvapur Lake" on Bengaluru's southeastern periphery lies in a state of disrepair – depleted, reeling from pollution, overgrown with hyacinth and algae. That has not deterred apartment complexes from extolling the "lake view" in their marketing campaigns (chapters 3 and 21).

Plate 1.11. Farmers from dominant caste communities, who have made windfall gains from selling land to real estate developers, have routinely invested profits in building cheap rental housing for workers in low-end service jobs that cater to the lifestyles of affluent residents in the nearby high-tech enclaves of Whitefield and Sarjapur.

Plate 1.12. A residential layout carved out of agricultural land—harbinger of Bengaluru's future? (chapter 7)

Spatial Images Depicting Expansion of Built-up Area and Changing Land Cover in Bengaluru, 2000–2021

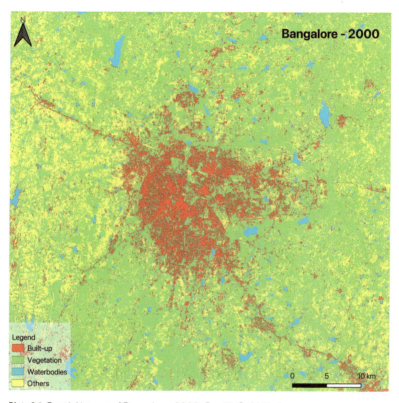

Plate 2.1. Spatial image of Bangalore, 2000. Credit: Gubbi Labs.

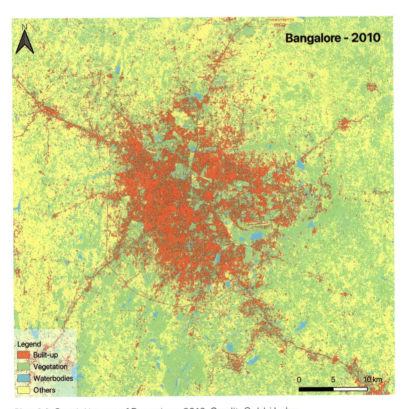

Plate 2.2. Spatial image of Bangalore, 2010. Credit: Gubbi Labs.

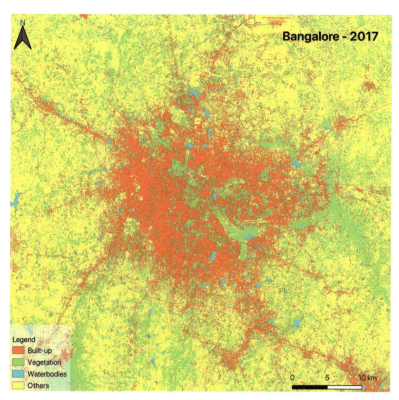

Plate 2.3. Spatial image of Bengaluru, 2017. Credit: Gubbi Labs.

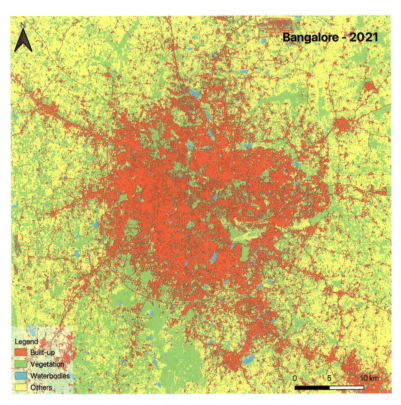

Plate 2.4. Spatial image of Bengaluru, 2021. Credit: Gubbi Labs.

standing demands but also the most intransigent ones. The Vedike was formed in 2013 after the BMTC increased the fares for its ordinary services substantially (an increase of 30 to 70 percent, depending on travel distance). Workers' unions, slum communities, student groups, women's groups, and other constituents came together to demand not only a reversal in the fare hike but also that the fares should be brought down to levels that are affordable for working-class communities. When the campaign took to the streets and bus stands with demonstrations, most commuters echoed the concern about unaffordable fares. But street protests ran for months, to no avail. They were eventually called off when the Vedike recognized that this would be a long-term struggle requiring different strategies.

Since 2013, reducing fares has become a perennial demand and advocacy agenda for the Vedike. Every year, its members lobby the BMTC and the government, and advocate through media and other campaigns, about the need for affordable transport and lower bus fares. Whenever fare hikes are proposed, protests and media campaigns are organized to oppose them. While further fare hikes have not been imposed since 2013, thanks in part to these efforts, the original demand of reducing fares to more affordable levels remains unfulfilled.

When BMTC announced the massive fare hikes in 2013–14 it had run up losses of 1.5 billion rupees (about 25 million USD), but the allocations for transportation infrastructure in the state budget that fiscal year included items such as 3 billion rupees for the widening of Bannerghatta Road and Sarjapur Road (two main arterial roads leading out of the city to the south) and 3.5 billion rupees for two elevated roads to ease traffic on major corridors in the city.[1] The 1.5 billion rupees required to offset BMTC's losses and keep the fare unchanged was a mere 1.3 percent of the total budget for Bengaluru in the state budget.[2] If it had the political will, the government could have easily found funds to offset BMTC's losses and roll back the fare hikes. So, when activists and citizens protest fare hikes they are up against not a resource crunch so much as an economic ideology that pushes for public expenditure cuts and cost recovery from users—in this case commuters—while sanctioning heavy borrowing for infrastructure projects that benefit only a small proportion of the city's residents.

BMTC's losses have grown since then. With increased fares, bus travel became more expensive than riding two-wheelers (scooters and motorcycles), making them the preferred option for many. The opening of metro rail operations along existing bus corridors and the entry of ride aggregator services provided additional options for a segment of bus users. These have contributed to a decline in ridership over the last decade. The losses have been further aggravated by the increase in fuel prices and the effects of the pandemic and lockdowns. The state government was forced to step in to pay salaries to staff during this period. Because of delays in salary payments and compensation to staff who died due to Covid, as well as alleged discrimination and harassment at the depot, BMTC staff went on strike twice during the pandemic. One strike ran for a full two weeks. With the dismissal of some during the strike, and others quitting or retiring, BMTC is also facing a staff crunch. But the government has not allowed BMTC to hire more workers, because that would increase the salary bill. During the pandemic, BMTC's service levels were down to half of the pre-pandemic levels. Post-pandemic, without enough staff, BMTC is unable to return to its original service levels or expand its fleet. Even in late 2022, well after the city's return to a semblance of normality, BMTC was still not operating most of its air-conditioned fleet because it is more cost-effective to keep the buses idle given their high operational costs. The corporation is in such a bind that it is thinking of introducing conductor-less buses to cut costs. But with the high commuter volumes in the city, especially during peak hours, the feasibility of such an arrangement is doubtful.

Following sustained public campaigns by the Vedike and other citizens' groups, the government began making budgetary allocations to help BMTC procure more buses. BMTC also started acquiring an electric bus fleet on a lease model, utilizing central government funding meant to promote electric mobility. Thus, there has been a gradual increase in the size of the fleet. Although the lease model for electric buses is a risk to the public service model, it offers an opportunity for BMTC to add to its fleet.

In 2019 the concept of a bus priority lane was successfully piloted on a twenty-kilometer stretch of the Outer Ring Road (ORR), one of the most notoriously congested roads in the city (despite being one of the widest). This led to a significant improvement in travel time and ridership. Since then, bus priority lanes were planned for all high-traffic corridors to address the severe problem of congestion. It is noteworthy that this decision was made after the government's proposal, floated in 2017–18, to construct elevated corridors across the city met with widespread public opposition. These corridors, intended to facilitate the free movement of traffic at enormous cost, were strongly contested by the Vedike and other citizens' groups. The campaign against elevated corridors also promoted more buses and bus lanes, which would cost much less, as a better alternative.

The introduction of bus priority lanes was a big step in the right direction, but the project has not progressed much since the announcements. None of the other high-density traffic corridors have bus priority lanes. As traffic started picking up on the ORR with the waning of the pandemic, metro construction along that corridor also took off, taking away a big chunk of the road space. Now, motorists who use the ORR, clogging the road with their vehicles, are blaming the bus lane—which moves the maximum number of people using the least road space—for congestion! Equitable access to road space and priority on the road for buses is still an uphill struggle in the city.

With financial support and priority focus from the government, BMTC could easily address all the deficiencies and gaps in its service and serve the city and its people better. With an allocation of just 1 percent of the state budget, BMTC could provide free public transport in the city.[3] With half of that or a little more, fares can be cut in half or made free for women and vulnerable social groups.

But the city's mobility plans still focus on new infrastructure such as elevated corridors, with no steps being taken to curb the use of private vehicles. Further extensions to the metro have been announced despite Phase I falling well short of projected ridership. Construction of a metro line connecting south Bengaluru to Kempegowda International Airport was started during the pandemic at a cost of 960 crore (over 9 billion) rupees. With that amount of money, BMTC could run its buses for free for twenty-five years! Those who continue to argue in favor of the metro say that it will move much higher volumes of commuters faster (a moot claim) and that it's not the government paying for it but loans from international financial agencies (such as the Asian Development Bank; see chapter 9). However, with the largest metro rail network in India (over 370 kilometers) and over two decades of operation, Delhi Metro has not yet reached its projected ridership levels. With dedicated bus lanes and high-frequency services on all main roads, and an optimized route network with better first and last mile connectivity, BMTC could provide a reasonably comparable performance to the metro at a much lower cost—moreover, international loans are merely delayed payments with interest, to be made from the public exchequer in installments over several years (Karnataka's outstanding debt in 2021–22 stood at 4.6 trillion rupees, or 60 billion USD).

The pandemic plunged working-class households into deeper poverty, further aggravating the crisis of affordable mobility. The Vedike met workers and communities to build a firsthand understanding of the situation and to spread awareness about fare reductions and free travel schemes that have been instituted in other states. After interacting with people across the city, it became evident that many are living under serious economic stress. Many workers lost their jobs or were working fewer days and cannot afford the bus fares. For many, their lives are circumscribed by the three- to four-kilometer distance they can walk or the 10-rupee distance they can access by bus. The Covid-19 crisis was a period when the city most needed affordable mobility, but this was also the period when BMTC was forced to run significantly fewer services to reduce costs.

To bring these issues into the public domain, the Vedike, along with several workers unions and community groups, organized a public hearing where people from underserved communities testified about the challenges they face with transport. Manjubai, Lakshmi, and many others recounted their struggles with commuting in the city. Affordability and availability were common concerns of all who testified at the hearing. Kausalya, a community worker from Chamrajpet, narrated her experience of traveling in Tamil Nadu state when she went to visit her family. She was surprised that when she tried to buy a ticket on the bus the conductor returned her money, telling her that travel is free for women. At the hearing she asked why Karnataka cannot provide the same benefits to women—are they not also people?[4]

Selvi, a domestic worker from Kadirenahalli, spoke about how difficult she finds it to pay for transport from the 3,000 rupees that she earns by working in two houses. Munilakshmi, a street vendor from Vijayanagar, spoke about how small vendors find it difficult to make regular trips to the market by bus with their meager earnings.

She also recounted the struggles her son and other students face due to the restrictive terms of use for student passes. Multiple participants spoke about how, in their neighborhoods, families have to spend substantial amounts to send their children to schools and colleges due to the unavailability of buses, and how children (especially girls) are consequently dropping out of school. Varsha, a student from Anekal, an urban division adjacent to Bengaluru but covered by BMTC, complained that even though there are subsidized passes for students, without adequate bus services in her neighborhood they are forced to use other means for travel, making the student benefit unusable. Karunakar, a representative from the transgender community, said that many transgender people, shunned by their families, earn their living by begging on streets and find autos prohibitively expensive. Karunakar said that a free travel scheme would benefit her community too.

After listening to the testimonies, a citizens' jury consisting of social workers, academics, and people's representatives concluded that access to high-quality, affordable bus services in the city is tightly linked to the well-being of people and their access to education, health care, and gainful employment, as well as to the empowerment of girls and women. Noting how buses contribute to reducing congestion, air pollution, and greenhouse gas emissions, the jury said that those who use public transport are not taking a public service but *doing* a public service. They pointed out that the positive externalities of the bus should be recognized and compensated, through either free or subsidized bus services. The jury also stated that free travel for women would go a long way in improving their physical and emotional well-being by providing them a safe and dignified commute, and that such measures would contribute to gradually dissolving the deep-seated patriarchy in society.

Citing these arguments, in the run-up to the announcement of the state budget in 2022 and 2023 the Vedike campaigned for subsidized fares for all and free travel for women and other vulnerable communities. In a press meet during the 2023 election campaign, Isaac Amruthraj—convenor of Slum Janara Sanghatane, a statewide organization of slum dwellers allied with the Vedike—pointed out that women are often the primary earners in slums and that a free travel scheme for women would provide a significant economic fillip for families living in slums, estimated to be 40 percent of the state's urban population.

In the budget presented in February 2023, the state government announced free bus passes for 3 million women working in the organized sector and for 800,000 girl students across the state.[5] But this scheme, if implemented, would not have benefited women who, like Manjubai (like the majority of workers), are employed in the unorganized sector. Considering that the state has over 34 million women and a student population of 5.5 million (in secondary school and above),[6] and that women in the unorganized sector face greater economic insecurity than those in the organized sector, the government's announcements appear to have been a hastily formulated public-relations gambit aimed at mobilizing support ahead of the May 2023 state elections.

There is a large constituency of people who struggle every day for want of affordable public transport. But their voices are still not powerful enough to resonate in the corridors of power, nor do they become important enough to be an election agenda item. There are signs of hope, though, in the gradually growing pockets of support within the general public, the bureaucracy, media, and civil society for bus-based solutions for Bengaluru that would allow for better and affordable mobility. An ongoing campaign against an overpass and road-widening project spearheaded by the primarily middle-class residents of Malleswaram has supported the demand for more bus services as the answer to urban congestion. As one of the jury members pointed out at the Vedike's public hearing, there is no question that a well-functioning, high-quality, affordable bus service is essential for a decent, humane, and sustainable city, for improved quality of life, and for economic development in the city. Why this does not form the center of policy decisions is the real question, and one to which the usual plea of lack of funds cannot be a serious answer.

On August 15, 2022, its twenty-fifth anniversary of becoming a separate transport corporation for the city of Bengaluru, BMTC ran all its services for free. That day, 6.5 million people rode on the bus, in contrast to its average daily ridership of 2.8 million. Granted, it was India's Independence Day, a holiday, when many people have free time to travel around the city. Still, it's an indication of what free or affordable travel might portend for the city.

Notes

This chapter draws on my experiences working with BBPV. I acknowledge its members and volunteers, Vinay Sreenivasa of Alternative Law Forum, Leo Saldanha and Bhargavi Rao of Environment Support Group, and Hasiru Usiru (a precursor platform to BBPV), all of whom have contributed to my understanding of the urban.

1. "Karnataka Budget 2013–2014: Hitting the Poll Road," *DNA*, July 13 2013, https://www.dnaindia.com/bangalore/report-karnataka-budget-2013-2014 -hitting-the-poll-road-1860642.

2. "Karnataka Budget 2013–14—Highlights," *EcopackIndia*, July 12, 2013, https://ecopack.co.in/2013/07/12/karnataka-budget-2013-14-highlights/.

3. Karnataka's budget for 2022–23 was 204,587 crore rupees; BMTC's traffic revenue in 2019–20 was 1,807 crore and losses 540 crore, totaling just about 1 percent of the budget (1 crore = 10 million).

4. A similar scheme providing free travel for women was introduced by the new state government of Karnataka, which was elected in May 2023. The "Shakti Yojane" scheme, launched in June 2023, provides for free travel for all women and members of the transgender community resident in Karnataka on all non-premium public buses across the state. It is estimated that the scheme will cost the state 40.5 billion rupees annually, and the BMTC 7.7 billion rupees annually. See "Shakti Scheme for Free Bus Travel: A Look at the Finances of Karnataka Transport Bodies," *Indian Express*, June 19, 2023, https://indianexpress.com/article/explained/shakti-scheme-free-bus-travel-finances -karnataka-transport-8671672/. Following the launch of the scheme, the daily ridership on BMTC buses increased from around 2.8 million to 3.5 million during the first week of operation. This figure includes not only an increase in the number of women commuters traveling free of cost but also of male and paying commuters. Sanika Athavale, "Karnataka 'Shakti' Scheme: 50 Lakh to 55 Lakh Women Avail Free Bus Ride Daily, 3.6 Crore in 8 Days," *Times of India*, June 20, 2023, https://timesofindia.indiatimes.com/city/bengaluru/karnataka -shakti-scheme-50-lakh-to-55-lakh-women-avail-free-bus-ride-daily-3-6-crore -in-8-days/articleshow/101119863.cms.

5. Karnataka 2023–24 Budget Speech, February 17, 2023, p. 46, https://finance.karnataka.gov.in/storage/pdf-files/1_BUDGET%20SPEECH(Eng).pdf.

6. Government of India, Ministry of Education, Department of School Education and Literacy, "Report on Unified District Information System for Education (UDISE+), 2020–21," https://udiseplus.gov.in/assets/img/dcf2021 /UDISE_Report_2021_22.pdf; Government of India, Ministry of Education, "All India Survey on Higher Education (AISHE) Final Report 2020–21," https://aishe.gov.in/aishe/viewDocument.action;jsessionid=FCE11C585C1C903 AF44963204AA3BE5B?documentId=322.

Basic accommodation built in "BC Colony" for rent to single male migrant workers; up to ten workers may share these small apartments with toilet facilities outside. Photograph by Pierre Hauser.

Part IV
Speculative Subjects

In this section we explore how urban spaces and communities rooted in the "old Bangalore" have been engulfed by, and sometimes participate in, the real estate revolution. These four chapters also highlight the crafting of new "speculative subjects" as ordinary people grapple with the currents of change that swept through their communities: a low-income community in a central area of the city that is demolished and rebuilt in the name of upgradation and beautification—a form of dispossession that is strongly opposed by housing rights activists who demand equal property rights for Dalits; an old working-class locality where modest homes are transformed into middle-class apartments to earn rental income in response to the increasing precarity of employment; and an urbanizing village where both upper-caste landlords and Dalits attempt to make money by acting as intermediaries in the booming land market.

Chapter 11 tells the story of "Karmikara Colony," a modest working-class neighborhood in Yeshwantpur—a former industrial area that has become a real estate hot spot. The colony has undergone a palpable makeover in the last twenty years as retired factory workers and their families turn to rent to supplement other, often more precarious, sources of income. Rudimentary dwellings have been expanded and upgraded to create new rental units, catering to rising demand for housing from migrant workers.[1] The upsurge in petty landlordism has catalyzed its own sub-industry of property brokers and fixers, who find and vet prospective tenants. The upgrading of Karmikara Colony reflects the assetization of (previously much less valuable) small plots of urban land and homes, as owners seek to profit from the burgeoning rental market. These incremental constructions allow residents to recalibrate housing needs as families expand, or simply, generate a dose of valuable rental income as cities undergo a "spatial reproduction

154 Part IV. Speculative Subjects

squeeze."[2] As discussed in part 2, "low finance"—such as loans from private moneylenders or advance deposits on rent given by tenants to landlords—can provide timely injections of capital that enable ordinary residents to engage in forms of "autoconstruction,"[3] which, over time, may entirely transform the face of urban settlements. But this story also highlights the forging of new imaginations, middle-class aspirations, and risk-laden livelihoods as the neighborhood is transformed by incremental building activities, reflecting on a smaller scale the "worlding" that the wider locality is undergoing.

Chapter 12, "Slum Dealings," tells the tale of "RP Colony," an old Dalit settlement also located in Yeshwantpur. Residents express mixed reactions to the proposed demolition and redevelopment of their informal settlement, whose "owner" wanted to reclaim the contested land on which it stood after it became more valuable. The chapter records the yearnings and anxieties of displaced residents as they waited for the flats to be built, going into debt to pay rents and preserve place-based livelihoods in the interim.[4] Despite the uncertainty and financial risk involved, many community members also embrace the dream of a better life that the slum redevelopment project seemed to offer.[5]

In "'Why Not Us?'" (chapter 13), a leader of Slum Janandolana-Karnataka, a statewide movement of slum dwellers, chafes at the state's casteist neglect of Dalit demands for land. Narasimhamurthy traces the efforts of city-based Dalit and housing rights organizations to contest the dispossession of the urban poor and assert their rights to urban land on par with the middle classes and corporates. He denounces the government's discriminatory policy of providing replacement housing in multistory tenements (as described in chapter 12) in slum rehabilitation and redevelopment projects rather than granting the preferred house sites, as well as the restrictions imposed on the sale of the new apartments by the beneficiaries. This denial of full property rights, according to Narasimhamurthy, diminishes the ability of slum residents—in contrast to their middle-class counterparts—to build rental units or otherwise profit from the booming property market in Bengaluru. The chapter points to the growing significance of property as the basis for urban citizenship, and speculative investment as a key source of income, across the social spectrum.[6]

Chapter 14, "The Caste of Land," returns us to Bengaluru's peri-urban frontier, where, as previous chapters show, rural land is being converted into urban real estate in various ways—especially through the formation of "revenue layouts" offering house sites for sale, catering mainly to middle-class investors.[7] While members of major land-owning castes have been the primary movers and beneficiaries of this process, converting land illicitly often in connivance with powerful politicians and bureaucrats, this chapter provides an unexpected twist. It shows how local Dalit youth have also participated in the booming real estate market, not only in pursuit of upward mobility but also as a means of resisting caste oppression. Dalit activists in urbanizing villages have fought against the illegal conversion and transfer of agricultural and common lands by dominant-caste Reddy landlords and brokers into the public domain, even as many also make their livings as land market intermediaries.

Notes

1. Cf. Thomas Cowan, "The Urban Village, Agrarian Transformation, and Rentier Capitalism in Gurgaon, India," *Antipode* 50, no. 5 (2018): 1244–66.

2. D. Asher Ghertner, "Lively Lands: The Spatial Reproduction Squeeze and the Failure of the Urban Imaginary," *International Journal of Urban and Regional Research* 44, no. 4 (2020): 561–81.

3. Teresa Caldeira, "Peripheral Urbanization: Autoconstruction, Transversal Logics, and Politics in Cities of the Global South," *Environment and Planning D: Society and Space* 35, no. 1 (2017): 3–20.

4. Malini Ranganathan, "Caste, Racialization, and the Making of Environmental Unfreedoms in Urban India," *Ethnic and Racial Studies* 45, no. 2 (2021): 257–77.

5. Ghertner argues that slum residents may also invest in the dominant vision of a global city. D. Asher Ghertner, *Rule by Aesthetics: World-Class City Making in Delhi* (New York: Oxford University Press, 2015).

6. Ananya Roy, "Dis/possessive Collectivism: Property and Personhood at City's End," *Geoforum* 80 (March 2017): A1–A11.

7. Jayaraj Sundaresan, "Urban Planning in Vernacular Governance: Land Use Planning and Violations in Bangalore, India," *Progress in Planning* 127 (2017): 1–23. Cf. Ozan Karaman et al., "Plot by Plot: Plotting Urbanism as an Ordinary Process of Urbanisation," *Antipode* 52, no. 4 (2020): 1122–51.

11
From Worker to Landlord
Swathi Shivanand

Starting in the early 2000s, residents of working-class neighborhoods in the old industrial area of Yeshwantpur, such as "Karmikara Colony," began to build up on their small properties to create rental units. Residents of the area attribute the feverish building activity of these decades to the changing landscape of the larger neighborhood—the development of new transportation infrastructure and the mushrooming of upscale residential and commercial complexes—that transformed the area into an important transport node and valuable real estate. Owners of even modest plots or houses capitalized on the increased demand for housing presented by these changes by investing in the construction of rental housing. On offer at Karmikara Colony are mostly 1- and 2-BHK (bedroom, hall, kitchen) apartments and smaller single-room units. These are built to cater to the growing stream of white- and blue-collar workers—especially migrants—who move into the area to take jobs in the burgeoning service economy.

Since its establishment in 1964, Karmikara Colony has transformed from a modest, low-rise locality into a densely built neighborhood, dotted with narrow three- and four-story buildings. Most of these buildings have been constructed up to the property line, leaving little space between them. Such developments in Karmikara Colony are illustrative of the ordinary but widespread changes taking place in similar neighborhoods across Bengaluru. Spurred on by large-scale investments in infrastructure and real estate in the city, residential localities—from working- and middle-class to affluent—have become sites of individual speculation as homeowners create rental units, often by building onto existing structures, to earn regular income from their properties.

156

From Worker to Landlord 157

Figure 11.1. Old and new houses in "Karmikara Colony," showing redevelopment of this working-class locality. Photograph by Pierre Hauser.

The colony was established in the 1960s by the erstwhile City Improvement Trust Board (CITB) (which became the Bangalore Development Authority [BDA] in 1976) to provide housing for about 150 working-class families who were relocated from a nearby slum that was demolished. The (male) allottees, many of whom were employed in the factories of Yeshwantpur, were allocated sites measuring thirty by forty feet with basic, single-story cement houses (Figure 11.1). The houses were granted on a thirty-year-lease basis, for which they had to pay 30.50 rupees per month to the government. After the lease period expired, allottees could apply for registration of the property in their names, giving them clear title. The relatively secure property rights enjoyed by most owners in Karmikara Colony played an important role in this transformation of the colony, since the papers allowed them to apply for bank loans to finance construction.

At the time of allocation, the government assured allottees that they would not be evicted for failure to keep up with the lease payments. Gopal, a former factory worker and a long-term resident of the colony, recalled that a community leader had demanded that the CITB add this no-eviction clause to the lease agreement. Indeed, most residents could ill afford the monthly payments. As "Raju," a senior resident of the neighborhood, remarked, "How could they [residents] pay so much money every month? In those days, my father worked in the [nearby] mills and earned just 16 rupees per month." Over the years, as the children of the original allottees got employed and household incomes increased, most families were able to pay off their dues as a lump sum when the thirty-year lease period ended in the mid-1990s. These payments enabled them to apply for registration of the property in their names.

After receiving titles to their properties, many owners in Karmikara Colony sold their sites for 2 to 3 million rupees and used the money to purchase property in more peripheral areas of the city where they could buy larger plots. This phase of rapid turnover of property ownership in the colony coincided with a steep rise in property values in Yeshwantpur, as industries closed and their land was sold for real estate development (chapter 9). However, at least two-thirds of the owners held onto their properties and transformed themselves into small rentier landlords—building up on their existing houses or constructing new multistory buildings to create several rental units.

"Ramakrishna," one such owner, has a three-story (G+2, or ground floor plus two upper floors) building in the colony, constructed on his original small site. Soon after he completed his training at an Indian Technical Institute, Ramakrishna got a job at the Kirloskar factory in 1964, where he worked until his retirement. In the same year, his father—who had worked in "defense under the British"—was allotted a site in the colony. In August 1964 the family of five moved into the CITB house. The property was later divided between Ramakrishna and his brother, and both built multistory structures on their tiny sites.

In 2003, Ramakrishna constructed a single-story house on his portion of the land, financed from his savings and loans from friends. The following year he built two additional floors to create rental units. This construction was financed from bank loans and his retirement benefits. Ramakrishna now lives on the ground floor with his wife, son, daughter-in-law, and grandchildren, and two tenant families live on the upper floors. Although his units are two-bedroom apartments, the rent is on the lower side (7,000 rupees) because of their small size. According to a local real estate agent, the rents that apartments in Karmikara Colony command depend on their size and whether they are old or newly constructed. Rents in the locality can go up to

12,000 to 20,000 rupees per month for a two-bedroom apartment, and as much as 25,000 rupees per month for a 3-BHK apartment—comparable to those in more solidly middle-class neighborhoods.

Given this range of rents and varying size of apartments, the colony has two kinds of tenants—white-collar professionals employed in jobs such as software engineering, teaching, and banking, many of whom work in the new office complexes nearby; and blue-collar workers such as domestic help and auto-rickshaw drivers, who typically rent cheaper units costing 6,000 to 8,000 rupees per month.

Given the small plot sizes and narrow roads in the colony, a top priority for landlords is to optimize the use of the available space to maximize their returns. Consequently, one finds many buildings constructed with little or no setback, and in some cases sharing a common wall. Parking space is out of the question on most streets. While a few owners purchased adjacent sites and consolidated them to create larger plots, the same logic of utilizing almost the entire site for the built-up area prevails even for the larger plots. Thus, the small size of the original sites (thirty by forty feet) has shaped how the colony has transformed—although it has undergone a process of "gentrification,"[1] it retains its original layout, preventing it from scaling up to resemble a truly middle-class locality with larger plot sizes and wider roads.

In Bengaluru, tenants are typically required to pay large security deposits in advance, usually ranging from five months' to ten months' rent. Landlords often put these large deposits to work by channeling the cash into moneylending or property businesses. Indeed, home ownership, moneylending, and small-scale landlordism are interlinked activities, as Ramakrishna explained: "People who own a house and a house site might take out a bank loan using the house as collateral, and then use the money to construct another house on the site. Then, they take a loan on the new property and use that money to lend it to people at double or triple the rate of interest they are paying the bank. In this way, they not only multiply their assets but also have a lucrative business."

However, not every small landlord profits from such investments. In Karmikara Colony we heard many stories of families whose ventures into the small-scale rental economy failed, leaving them with no choice but to sell their plots. One resident recalled how his longtime neighbors vacated their house overnight after they could not repay the loans they had taken to construct a building. Owners such as Ramakrishna, who had permanent jobs in factories with assured retirement benefits, were more successful in turning their bit-sized plots into rental properties that yield regular returns on their investments.

However, not all homeowners in the colony had access to such retirement benefits or substantial savings on which they could draw to build rental units. These owners financed construction by taking informal loans from moneylenders or by drawing from *cheetis* (rotating credit groups; see chapter 6). Another common strategy is to offer a tenant the apartment on a long-term "lease" of two to three years. In such agreements, the tenant pays the equivalent of two to three years' rent up front and lives rent-free during the lease period, after which the full amount is returned by the landlord. This lump sum "lease" payment functions as an informal loan given by the tenant to the landlord, who in many cases uses the money to complete the construction. The lease for a 1-BHK flat could range from 600,000 to 700,000 rupees (7,500 to 8,750 USD) for three years.

While these informal financing options help owners build up on their properties or pay off accumulated debts, they come with varying levels of risk. Lease arrangements are considered the least-risky option, since once the lease period is over and the money is paid back, the landlord has a completed unit that can be given out for a monthly rent. But the risk here is that the tenant is not obliged to vacate the flat until the lease amount is returned. The least-desirable option is a loan from a private moneylender, which carries high interest rates, but some owners in Karmikara Colony were forced to turn to such informal financiers to complete their construction projects.

The speculative nature of such small-scale rentiership was highlighted during the Covid-19 crisis. For many small landlords in Karmikara Colony, rent was their main or sole source of household income. After a strict lockdown was imposed in March 2020 across India, the rental economy in the colony took a serious hit (as in most of the city), because many tenants returned to their hometowns having lost their jobs or shifted to remote work. In 2021, scores of "To Let" boards could be seen hanging on the gates of buildings, indicating that many of these rental units were still vacant. Real estate agents confirmed that some owners had slashed their rents in the hope of attracting new tenants. Many landlords could ill afford to keep their rental units unoccupied, because they needed the rental incomes to support themselves or to pay off outstanding loans. Those who could afford to keep their units vacant, however, refused to reduce rents.

The speculative economy that has emerged around housing even in modest localities such as Karmikara Colony has also spawned the ubiquitous figure of the real estate agent. Agents are invariably local, since brokering rental agreements requires detailed local knowledge of a neighborhood, its buildings, and their owners. Real estate agents perform the vital task of connecting landlords to prospective tenants, and they also help to filter "socially unacceptable" tenants out of the area's rental market. Especially where tenants have no prior kinship or other social connections in the area, the real estate broker steps in to mediate these property transactions, matching the "right" tenant with the "right" landlord and earning a commission in the process.

Speaking to real estate agents gives us a glimpse into how tenants are judged and what kinds of people are allowed entry into the neighborhood. According to one agent, "Jairam," the rents and "security deposits" quoted by landlords depend on the social status or identity of the prospective tenant. For instance, they might demand only five to six months' rent as advance from bank officials, since they move frequently and are considered trustworthy tenants. The standard deposit required is ten months' rent, but for "risky" cases they may ask for "double" (i.e., 200,000 rupees advance for a unit costing 10,000 rupees per month).

Further, because of the densely built environment in Karmikara Colony, landlords are choosy about the kind of tenants they will accept. Jairam listed some of these conditions: no dogs or young children (both of which can be noisy); no cars (which would block entry to the house); and only small families (two to four members is ideal, because larger households would lead to water scarcity). Landlords also do not prefer people working in "finance" or with their own business, because they do not have steady incomes. Single women living alone are always under suspicion, since they could have questionable moral standards. Unmarried men, or men who have migrated to the city for work without their families, commonly known as "bachelors," are another category that most landlords avoid because they are considered "rowdy" or "untrustworthy." As in most Indian cities, Muslims are the most avoided category of tenants, as "Srivatsa," a tailor who also works as a real estate agent, confirmed: "No owner likes to give houses on rent to Muslims. If we do take them to see the house, the owners flatly refuse, and we don't ask them for reasons."[2]

Like the small landlord who may not rely solely on rental income, the local real estate agent also has other ways of making money. Many intermediaries in the rental market are part-time agents, supplementing their incomes from their regular jobs with real estate work. Jairam, for example, is an auto-rickshaw driver who also works as a broker in the colony. His close understanding of the social matrix of the locality, the particularities of available properties, and the many requirements of their owners facilitates his mediation work. But with the rapid expansion of rental housing in Bengaluru across the economic spectrum, some real estate agents have tried to make a small business out of this work. "Manoranjan," a full-time broker, said, "This work is like a lottery. There may be days when you make lots of money, and other days when not a single deal comes through. Even if you work very hard, there is no guarantee of earnings." Asked how he sustains himself on brokering alone, he replied, "I have my own house. I get rents monthly to meet household expenses, so that is how I'm able to do this as a permanent business." Manoranjan is an old resident of the neighborhood, and his embeddedness offers him a significant advantage in leveraging networks of homeowners and other brokers to find suitable housing for potential tenants.

For real estate agents, risk is endemic to their occupation. Small-scale agents who deal primarily with rental housing but who also broker the occasional property transaction invest considerable time and money in managing transactions with uncertain outcomes. "Kishore," a real estate broker working in another working-class locality, explained that he needs to spend at least 1,000 rupees even to negotiate a deal: "I have to wear a nice shirt, pants, watch. . . . I have to be tip-top. I can't go to meet clients wearing sandals, I must wear shoes. . . . If I wear good perfume and go, some clients will take me directly to their dining table and start talking. . . . Only if our valuation is high do we get good clients." The "valuation" of the broker also depends on how he travels around the city: "If the client sees me come in an auto, my valuation plummets. An Ola or Uber cab is an essential means of transport."

Like several landlords in Karmikara Colony, Kishore used to work in a nearby factory. He was a foreman on a "good salary" until he lost his job when the unit was shifted out of Yeshwantpur. He then started a taxi business with his brother, taking out a loan to buy six cars and employing drivers. However, competition soon drove him out of business. He was forced to sell all but one of the cars, which his brother drives as a taxi. Next, Kishore ventured into real estate brokering—he explained that he wanted to have his own business and earn more money. Despite the risks and heavy investments needed to mediate real estate transactions, Kishore argued that "one good deal can give you a lifetime's salary."

The dream of the deal that can "set you up for life" resonates with the investments made by small property owners in becoming rentier landlords. The belief that easy money can be made from property circulates widely in Bengaluru's speculative economy—and not only in the entrepreneurial world of venture capital–funded start-ups. Real estate brokers like Kishore and small-scale landlords like Ramakrishna have come to understand that property and land have become the major source of value generation in the city. They want their share of this new wealth by tapping into the booming property market, no matter how small the scale, and will pour all their resources into risky investments in the hope of handsome profits and a stable and prosperous future.

Notes

Kaveri Medappa contributed to this chapter.

1. Ghertner argues that the concept of gentrification does not apply well to southern contexts, because it refers to the reinvestment of capital in already capitalized urban spaces with well-established property regimes. In contrast, these processes usually reflect the "initial rounds of the capitalist production of space" in postcolonial cities such as Bengaluru which have distinct "property and planning systems, legal frameworks, and histories of land development." D. Asher Ghertner, "India's Urban Revolution: Geographies of Displacement beyond Gentrification," *Environment and Planning A: Economy and Space* 46, no. 7 (2014): 1555.

2. Discrimination against Muslims in rental housing markets has a long history in India, a situation that has been worsened by the rise of "communal" or sectarian politics and Hindu nationalist ideology since the 1990s. This has reinforced a pattern of residential segregation and the formation of Muslim-only localities in most cities. See Naveen Bharathi, Deepak Malghan, and Andaleeb Rahman, "Neighbourhood-Scale Residential Segregation in Indian Metros," *Economic & Political Weekly* 54, no. 30 (2019): 64–70.

12
Slum Dealings
Carol Upadhya

As we walked from Yeshwantpur Circle toward "RP Colony"—an informal settlement we encountered in chapter 6—one day in early March 2018, we noticed that tall blue barricades had been put up all around the site—a clear sign of construction activity. The name board that used to stand at the entrance to the settlement had disappeared, replaced by a newly constructed, whitewashed boundary wall. Just inside the entrance, a new board announced, "This property belongs to Manjunath." Where once a small informal settlement of many *kacha* ("raw" or unfinished) houses tightly clustered together stood (Figure 12.1), we now could see only a flat stretch of empty, brown land. The only familiar sight was the old woman standing near the entrance, selling peanuts and other small snacks from her cart. About halfway inside the site another blue fence loomed, suggesting that the property had been divided into parts.

We spotted four men sitting and chatting in auto-rickshaws parked nearby. One was a familiar face—"Rajiv," the self-proclaimed leader of the slum whom we had met on an earlier visit. He stepped out of the rickshaw, smiling, and greeted us. In response to our queries about what had happened to the settlement, he informed us that all the houses had been razed two months before to make way for a slum redevelopment project. Pointing to the construction workers milling around at the far end of the site, he proudly explained that the BBMP (Greater Bangalore Metropolitan Corporation) had already started constructing new houses for the residents of RP Colony, "free of cost." After long negotiations, the residents had reached an agreement with the landowner, "Manjunath," who "wrote half the land in the people's names." Speaking in Kannada, Rajiv said, "Our people are happy that at last they will get proper homes, after living in small, cramped houses with no facilities. . . . We will get a *lift, shower,* and

Figure 12.1. "RP Colony," an informal settlement, prior to its demolition for a redevelopment project. Photograph by Pierre Hauser.

tiles," he declared, as the other men nodded in agreement. Rajiv told us that the government was constructing two four-floor buildings, with a total of 120 "1-BHK" (bedroom-hall-kitchen) flats. Each eligible family would be allotted an apartment of 280 square feet to replace their bulldozed "sheet houses" (made of corrugated metal or asbestos roofing).

To learn more about the history of RP Colony and these recent events, we spoke to "Devika"—a flower vendor who had lived in the settlement since birth. Even after the demolition, Devika could be found in front of the neighborhood temple, sitting on a plastic chair under the shade of a garden umbrella, mounds of jasmine garlands, *kanakambara* (firecracker flowers), and button roses on the table in front of her. According to her, the colony—now around seventy years old—was built on the farmland of one "Ram Prakash" (hence the "RP" in RP Colony). He had allowed agricultural laborers working on his farm to build their houses on the site. Devika's mother, who belonged to a village near Bangalore, was among the original settlers. Later, Ram Prakash brought more agricultural workers from Tamil Nadu, who also settled down in the colony. Over the years, other families moved in as well, and RP Colony grew into a compact settlement inhabited mainly by Tamil- and Kannada-speaking Dalits. The colony, built on about one acre of land, consisted of about 120 small *kacha* houses, without indoor toilets or water connections.

Devika fondly recalls growing up in what was earlier a rural locale, now utterly transformed. Pointing to the broad road in front of the temple, she tells us that in her youth it had been just a single-lane road where trucks would park to load and unload goods for the nearby wholesale market. Cars were a rare sight: "Whenever a car passed by, we came running out to see it," she recalled, smiling. Much later, an overpass was built adjacent to RP Colony to ease the increasingly heavy flow of traffic from the city to Tumkur Road—the major artery running through Yeshwantpur and connecting with the highway to Mumbai. Once a sleepy district road, this corridor had become a prime site for infrastructure and real estate investment from around the year 2010. The road was widened by demolishing many shops and homes along the way, and an elevated corridor and metro rail line were built running above it. High-end apartment complexes, shopping malls, and five-star hotels, along with an office tower called "World Trade Center," quickly materialized on both sides of Tumkur Road—leaving small, informal settlements like RP Colony sandwiched between steel-and-glass towers on small pieces of land. Looking up at the high-rises just across the road, Devika observed, *"Ella change aagide illi, aadre naav change aagilla. Namhatra dudd ilvalla"* (Everything has changed here, only we [residents of RP Colony] did not change. You see, we don't have money).

But change soon came to RP Colony as well, despite the opposition of some residents. During our conversation with Rajiv and his friends, two younger men—leaning on another auto-rickshaw parked a bit farther away—were listening quietly. Recognizing Ganesh—also a resident of RP Colony and a driver employed in a public-sector factory—we asked them if they were happy about the slum redevelopment project. Pointing to Rajiv with his eyes, his friend Samuel whispered, *"Seri illa avaru, bari duddugaagi"* (He is not straight, it's only for money [that he is doing this work]). Clearly, they did not trust this "leader" who had helped the local MLA (Member of the Legislative Assembly) and corporator (local representative) persuade the residents to accept the slum redevelopment plan. Samuel feared that the new buildings would be poorly constructed (like most government-built slum redevelopment and rehabilitation projects): "What if something happens to these houses? We will have to go back to these people and beg again. . . . But who knows if these same people [the MLA and corporator] will be in office then. Where would we turn then?" Despite these misgivings, the redevelopment plans had gone ahead. The residents were now scattered around the city, living in rented accommodation while waiting for their new houses to be built.

The history of RP Colony—from its beginnings as a rural labor settlement, later becoming an urban slum with some degree of tenurial security for the residents, to its demolition to make way for new housing—encapsulates, on a small scale, the pattern of speculative urbanism that is transforming the city on a broader scale. As this story shows, the disruptive currents of soaring land values and intensifying conflicts around rights to land and housing often destabilize urban poor communities—even as they may also invest in the promises of "development" that the globalizing city seems to offer.

Beginning in the 1950s, as Bangalore expanded into its rural hinterlands and the city government acquired agricultural lands for industries, housing colonies, and public infrastructure, villages became urban neighborhoods, and small Dalit settlements (like RP Colony) were reclassified as slums. The demise of agriculture in the Yeshwantpur area forced the residents into urban informal employment—the men working as auto-rickshaw or taxi drivers, casual manual laborers, or construction workers, the women earning modest incomes as street vendors or from domestic work. After Yeshwantpur was incorporated into the municipality in the 1960s, RP Colony was designated a "notified slum." This declaration conferred certain rights on the residents (in particular, they could not be evicted without compensation), giving them a sense of security—despite periodic efforts by Manjunath and the city government to evict them.[1]

Manjunath claimed to own the site on which RP Colony stood, because it was (he said) part of the property he had inherited from Ram Prakash, his grandfather. However, the legal status of the land was murky—various court cases by different claimants were pending, and conflicting government orders had been issued over the years. According to a local politician, the land was actually "government land" since it had been granted to Ram Prakash by the state. At some point in the 1980s the BBMP had issued a land acquisition notification against part of the land for an infrastructure project. A local trust had filed a court case claiming that the land had been granted to them by the government. And at one point the Karnataka Slum Development Board (KSDB) had planned a slum redevelopment project on the site. Incensed by what he viewed as interference in his "private property" by politicians and the government, Manjunath fumed: "Many years ago, the MLA began work on the site [for a slum redevelopment project] without proper procedure and without my knowledge. This is my land! A Slum Board engineer even put out a tender to build permanent houses for the people here. How can he call for a tender to build on private land?"

These cross-cutting claims allowed RP Colony to remain undisturbed for many years, despite the residents periodically facing pressure to vacate. Manjunath's father had filed a legal case to affirm his ownership of the property, but the petition languished in court. Manjunath then took up the cause. He is a licensed lawyer who spends most of his time fighting his own cases to reclaim his grandfather's extensive landholdings around Yeshwantpur. Apart from legal tactics, he tried other strategies to dislodge the residents of RP Colony, from sending *goondas* (henchmen) to threaten them, to offering to rehouse them in a KSDB slum rehabilitation project on the outskirts of the city.[2] He was very bitter about their refusal to accept these "free, beautiful houses" offered by the government. In recounting this incident, he blamed the "ungrateful" slum residents for blocking the development of the city: "How can people be allowed to stay in these central places just because they insist on it? People should make way for development and be happy with whatever they are given by the government!" But the residents staunchly resisted this offer, knowing full well the difficulties of living in such colonies—where many other slum residents have been relocated—far from their places of employment and sociality, and where adequate schools, health care, and transportation are usually absent (see chapter 10). They were also fairly confident that their tenurial rights were firm enough to forestall eviction. Not only was the settlement a notified slum, but most occupants also held *parichaya patras* (identification papers) issued by the KSDB in the 1990s.

In 2015, Manjunath finally succeeded in obtaining a court order affirming that the land was his private property. But he still could not sell or develop the land as long as it remained occupied by the slum, nor could he find a legal means of having the residents evicted. So, he entered into negotiations with the RP Colony residents, brokered by the local corporator, "Narayana," who wanted to rid his ward of unsightly slums to better align it with rapidly globalizing Yeshwantpur. His goal was to make the ward *swaccha, sundara, aarogya* (clean, beautiful, healthy). Accordingly, he formulated a plan to "develop" all the slums in his constituency, drawing on KSDB redevelopment schemes to replace the "poor huts" of residents with "proper houses" in multistory buildings. The local MLA, "Anand," shared Narayana's ambition to create a "slumless constituency" and supported his efforts. These politicians mediated between Manjunath and the RP Colony residents (represented only by Rajiv), finally reaching a compromise. Manjunath agreed to part with almost half the land, which would be used to construct new housing for the residents, while retaining the other half free of interference.

Although many residents were content with the agreement, others felt that their views had not been heard. Some questioned Rajiv's authority to represent them: "Leader? Have we voted for him?" However, Rajiv played a key role in persuading the residents to accept the deal, telling them that they could not continue living "as their grandfathers did" and urging them to think about their children's future. Key to convincing the residents was the fact that Narayana had already completed a similar redevelopment project in a neighboring slum, "Kalanagar"—a small settlement of forty-five houses. People in these two localities knew one another, so the RP Colony residents could see what their new homes would be like if they agreed to the project. Devika, the flower vendor, said: "Water used to enter our houses when it rained. . . . Who will say no when they are told that they will be given better houses?" Several residents remained skeptical that the project would ever materialize, but eventually they yielded: "*Oppilla, madam, oppsidru*" (We did not agree, madam, we were made to agree!), exclaimed Ganesh.

Thus, the redevelopment plan went ahead. Manjunath handed over 15,000 square feet of land to the BBMP—the agency responsible for building the new tenements—while retaining a plot of 22,000 square feet adjoining the main road. The project—at an anticipated cost of 80 million rupees (about 1.1 million USD)—was funded from a special BBMP fund earmarked for the welfare of SC/ST (Scheduled Castes and Scheduled Tribes) communities. Anand also supported the project by drawing on his special MLA fund meant for development projects in his constituency.

As soon as the agreement was signed, Manjunath constructed a boundary wall to separate his land from the plot earmarked for the new buildings—the one we spotted on our first visit to the cleared site. The residents were given just one week to vacate their houses before the demolition began. They asked Manjunath for permission to put up temporary structures on his portion of the site while the construction of the new building was underway, to save on the expenses of renting houses. They also wanted to stay on the site because they did not trust Manjunath. Samuel said, "What if tomorrow Manjunath kicks us out from here and says all this land is his and doesn't allow us to come back?" Manjunath, in turn, did not trust the residents: "What if they don't vacate even after the construction? What if the government money stops coming and the building work is stuck? What shall I do then?" Because of this impasse, the residents were forced to find alternative accommodation for the duration of the construction. The new buildings were supposed to be completed within two years, but with the advent of the Covid pandemic and the severe lockdown that was imposed across India in March 2020, work was considerably delayed—adding to their expenses.

Most RP Colony families moved to rented apartments nearby during the construction period, incurring expenditure of 5,000 to 6,000 rupees per month in addition to the advance payment of ten months' rent that is customary in Bengaluru. Although they could have found cheaper accommodation farther away, most chose to stay close to the colony and their places of work. Narayana gave each family 20,000 rupees to help with their expenses during the period of relocation, but this amount was clearly insufficient to cover their extra costs. Samuel remarked, "What is 20,000 rupees? It doesn't even pay three month's rent, let alone help with rental expenses for a year. It's not even enough to pay the advance of many houses."

Given this sudden escalation in their household expenses, most families were forced to take out informal loans from local moneylenders or relatives. Others obtained "gold loans" by pledging their jewelry to banks or jewelry shops, or they borrowed from their *cheetis* (revolving credit groups; see chapter 6). Manjunath was dismissive about the burden of debt that the redevelopment scheme imposed on the "beneficiaries," asserting that it was a "good lesson" for "slum people," who would now have to work harder to cover their expenses rather than just idling away their time. Samuel, who works as a supervisor on construction sites, complained that his family's expenses had increased many times over: "We somehow manage because I have a stable job and get a monthly salary. What about people who don't have such work? How do they pay rent? There are people here who find it impossible to gather even 2,000 rupees in a month."

Vasavi is a cobbler whose family was among the original settlers of RP Colony. A year after the demolition, we found her living with her husband and two school-age children in a rented apartment near the colony. Apart from her husband's small monthly pension, as income they had only her earnings from the small cobbler's shop that she rents near the overpass. They were spending 4,000 rupees monthly on rent and had paid 40,000 rupees as advance. To cover these expenses, she had taken a loan of 10,000 rupees from a local moneylender at a high rate of interest. Like other residents of RP Colony, she was managing her household by juggling loans—taking new loans to pay off previous ones. She was resigned to the situation: "What can we do now? We have to pay rent, which we could have lived without. I would have been happier living in a hut than a rented house, with the burden of loans I have to pay off." Asked how her family might benefit from the housing project, she responded, laughing: "My only hope right now is to live in a place without having to pay rent. We have trusted them to construct a house, we will have to wait and see." Although his family was relatively better off and managing to pay rent, Ganesh said, *"Rent katbeku, adakke hotte swalpa uriyathe"* (Now that I have to pay rent, my stomach burns a bit)—a Kannada expression indicating a feeling of anxiety or helplessness.

The residents of nearby Kalanagar had been living in the redeveloped housing for about a year at the time RP Colony was demolished. While the burden of rent was lifted when they moved into their new homes, they now faced additional, unanticipated expenses such as higher electricity bills. And they suddenly received a large water bill for the building for the entire year, which the residents had to collectively pay. "Rajeswari" was in charge of collecting money from her neighbors to cover this unexpected payment, which was a difficult task: "If I don't pay the bill, they will cut the supply, and then from where do we get water? Before [in the original settlement] we had a borewell and a tank [for storing water] as well. Now we don't have these." In addition, the residents are required to pay a monthly maintenance fee to cover collective costs such as the elevator and lighting in the common areas of the building.

Despite these issues, many Kalanagar residents were generally happy with the new flats, especially compared to their earlier living situation. "Mani," the leader of the colony—whom we met in chapter 6—explained that the space occupied by their settlement had been shrinking over the years, as new buildings encroached on the land from all sides: "Like dogs and their little pups in a kennel, we had to stay squeezed all together in our little homes." Although the new flats are also small (260 square feet) and insufficient for their families, they are larger than their old houses. Rajeswari said, "We make it work. Compared to the space we had before, this is better." Many residents viewed amenities such as indoor toilets and piped water as improvements. And, "at least we are not flooded every year!"

However, many residents complained that their households cannot be accommodated in the new apartments, especially "joint families" where adult sons and their families live together with their parents. Consequently, some family members must give up their claim to the flat and move out—a situation that often leads to conflicts within the family. In Kalanagar, several families had resolved this issue by deciding that one brother would become the "owner" of the flat by paying the other brothers or claimants to give up their rights. Explaining this arrangement, Rajeswari said, "Why should one sibling have to live in a rented house while the other gets to live in their own house?" But major fights would erupt when the family could not reach an agreement. Such a conflict had fractured Rajeswari's own family: "Our eldest brother took 3 lakhs from my other brother and moved out. Before he left, he severed all ties with the rest of the family, saying we don't exist anymore to him—that he no longer has any brother, sister, or parents. He does not speak to us anymore. I have seen this kind of family dispute in nearly five houses. I am sure it will happen with others as well."

Many residents of these former slums pointed to other drawbacks of slum rehabilitation and redevelopment projects that provide apartments in multistory buildings, contrasting them negatively with the preferred "sites and services" model in which beneficiaries receive small plots of land on which they can build their own houses (as the leader of a housing rights organization, Narasimhamurthy, explains in chapter 13). In the old settlement there was always a possibility of expanding their houses by constructing additional floors. Several residents outlined their foiled plans to build up incrementally on their houses to accommodate all the brothers as they got married and formed their own families. Indeed, several families in RP Colony had already constructed additional floors on their houses, which in some cases were rented out to earn extra income. Such investments were a total loss to these families when the slum was demolished.

Anticipating these difficulties, several residents of RP Colony were thinking of selling their new flats or renting them out, using the proceeds to buy or rent larger houses in a less expensive part of the city. (Most did not openly admit to such plans, since under the terms of the allotment they are not allowed to sell or rent out the new flats.) Selling the property would also prevent family conflicts from erupting, since the money could be divided among all those who had a claim on the property. But some residents planned to live in the new flats although it meant that some family members would eventually have to move out: "It's one's own house, in the city center, where no one has to pay rent! Who would let go of something like that?"

The redevelopment of RP Colony and Kalanagar upended the lives of the "beneficiaries." These schemes certainly provided them with more solid houses, but with conditional property rights (since they cannot be sold legally), limiting their utility as financial assets. Many families were plunged further into debt by the scheme at the same time that their main source of social security—family ties—started to unravel. The residents were well aware of what they had lost, especially in comparison with what Manjunath stood to gain by recovering part of the land as his personal freehold property. Samuel and Ganesh spoke sarcastically about how much money Manjunath would make from the deal, simply because he could establish legal ownership of the highly contested piece of land where they had been living for three generations! Based on current property prices in the area, they calculated that his portion of the land would sell for

230 million rupees (around 3 million USD). And Manjunath owned several other properties in the vicinity—most acquired by filing court cases to "recover" land that he claimed had belonged to his grandfather. They estimated his total net worth at 100 crore rupees (15 million USD).

Manjunath's windfall profits would surely be shared with those who helped negotiate the deal—the corporator, the MLA, the slum leader—as well as with various government officials who facilitate the approval of such projects. Others who stood to benefit, to varying degrees, from the conversion of this small plot of land into a lucrative piece of real estate include the building contractor (in this case, Narayana's brother); the small landlords who rented out accommodation to the displaced residents; the informal financiers who lent money to the cash-strapped residents; and the real estate company or investor that ultimately purchases the "freed up" land. The list could go on. This tiny piece of land, serendipitously located close to booming Tumkur Road, was made to yield enormous value by a simple court order that ignored the tenurial rights of the residents who had lived there for several decades, in favor of the principle of "private property." But the redevelopment housing, built on the same land, can never produce similar wealth for the new occupants because they are not deemed full "owners" by the state (see chapter 13). Such are the ironies, and outcomes, of the speculative city for Bengaluru's marginalized and poor communities.

While waiting for the completion of the new buildings, Samuel was living with his brother in an eight-by-ten-foot room, paying 3,000 rupees per month as rent. Complaining about this uncomfortable accommodation, he observed: "The toilet in our village home in Tamil Nadu is bigger than this. . . . It's so small the two of us find it difficult to sleep at the same time!" Moreover, the landlord was very strict, always telling them not to do something or the other. Samuel missed the freedom they had enjoyed in their old twelve-by-twenty-two-foot house in RP Colony: "We had a bachelor pad—my friends often visited, we would listen to music and party all night. We felt free!"

As evening closed in on the day we first discovered that RP Colony had been demolished, only Samuel and Ganesh remained chatting with us in the middle of the emptied plot. A few dogs with scruffy collars approached us, sniffing. Ganesh commented that since everyone had moved out, the dogs were now going hungry. "When we all lived here, someone or the other would feed the dogs—now they have to look outside for food."

Notes

Hemangini Gupta, Kaveri Medappa, Deeksha M. Rao, and Revathi Kondu contributed to this chapter.

1. For residents of informal settlements in Bengaluru, security of tenure falls on a continuum, depending on the type of official recognition and documentation they hold. See A. Krishna, E. Rains, and E. Wibbels, "Negotiating Informality—Ambiguity, Intermediation, and a Patchwork of Outcomes in Slums of Bengaluru," *Journal of Development Studies* 56, no. 11 (2020): 1983–99. In Karnataka, residents of "notified slums" (declared under the Karnataka Slum Area Improvement and Clearance Act, 1973) and "recognized slums" (recognized by other government bodies for various purposes)—which tend to be older slums—hold official documents such as possession certificates, lease-cum-ownership papers, or identity cards that provide a measure of tenurial security or protection against eviction. *Hakku patra* (literally, "document of rights") is a certificate of occupancy given to beneficiaries of housing schemes or residents of notified informal settlements which provides conditional tenurial rights. *Parichaya patra*—the type of document held by the residents of RP Colony—is an identification certificate issued by the Karnataka Slum Development Board that does not grant tenurial rights but provides proof of residence and therefore eligibility for rehabilitation schemes and compensation in case of eviction. Slum residents carefully hold onto such documents because they are aware of their importance in their struggles to "stay put." Liza Weinstein, *The Durable Slum: Dharavi and the Right to Stay Put in Globalizing Mumbai* (Hyderabad: Orient BlackSwan, 2014).

2. Several types of slum relocation and redevelopment schemes have been floated by different state and municipal agencies in India. When slums are demolished and rebuilt on the same site, it is referred to as "redevelopment." Projects where residents are removed to another site and provided with new housing are known as "slum rehabilitation."

13

"Why Not Us?"

Swathi Shivanand

When land—essential for living and for livelihood—becomes real estate, the battle over who is entitled to a plot of land in the city acquires moral dimensions. Should only those who can afford to buy a house site or an apartment be regarded as legitimate urban citizens? What about the urban poor or migrant workers, particularly from marginalized communities? Where is the space for them to make a home in the city? Has the "right to the city"[1] been reduced to narrow legal criteria and paperwork—residence proof, land titles, sale deed?

Where the pursuit of world-city aspirations has meant that slum residents, who constitute nearly one-third of Bengaluru's population, live under the threat of evictions and displacement, such forceful moral articulations challenge the understanding of land as only real estate, and of the settlements of the poor as illegal "encroachments" and unsightly blots on the gentrifying landscape (chapter 12). Instead, slum residents and their organizations argue for a right to the city by foregrounding their contribution as the labor that builds and sustains the city. This contribution, they argue, makes them eligible to claim the right to ownership, thereby dissociating ownership from financial capacities and formal titles.

Such claim-making is important because residents of slums are mostly employed or self-employed in the urban informal economy, in poorly paid and insecure occupations—trapping them in a cycle of poverty.[2] Because they lack secure land tenure, slum residents live a precarious existence, constantly under the threat of eviction so that the government or private owners can recover the valuable land they occupy.[3] The state government, through agencies such as the Karnataka Slum Development Board (KSDB), has instituted various slum redevelopment schemes in the name of providing better housing to the urban poor. But such programs usually entail resettlement and "rehabilitation" in remote places on the outskirts of the city, far from their places of work, which lack basic services such as schools, hospitals, and transportation (see chapter 10). As Bengaluru has pursued its world-city aspirations, the position of the urban poor has become even more precarious.

This situation has prompted slum residents in Bengaluru to organize to demand secure housing and land rights in the city over the years. One of the most prominent organizations in Karnataka is Slum Janandolana Karnataka (SJK), a statewide movement of slum dwellers. A. Narasimhamurthy is the state convenor (leader) of SJK. Through several long interviews in 2019 and 2022, he laid bare the matrix of power, caste discrimination, and deprivation that excludes slum residents from reaping the benefits of Bengaluru's booming economy. His narrative kept returning to the question of land: Who has a right to land, to property, to the city itself?

Since the 1990s, a major form of exclusion of the urban poor have been the slum "improvement"[4] schemes that are embedded within neoliberal urban policies such as the Jawaharlal Nehru National Urban Renewal Mission (JNNURM).[5] Marking a break from earlier government practices of developing popular "sites and services" schemes and allotting plots of land (as in the case of "Karmikara Colony"; see chapter 11), these programs have focused on providing housing in multistory buildings, either on the same site as the demolished slum ("in situ") or at a "rehabilitation" site.[6] Narasimhamurthy explained that in such tenement schemes, allottees have no right to the land: "The culture of providing houses in tenements for the urban poor is a recent trend. . . . Before that, house sites were being allocated. Depending on their financial situation, they would build a hut or a house of their dreams. This dream has been taken away by the government."

Worse, the "beneficiaries" of these housing schemes are not allowed to make any changes to their homes, nor can they sell them or rent them out (see chapter 12). Such apartments are meant only for the "use" of the allottee and do not constitute an asset that could be used to generate income or wealth, thereby excluding slum residents from the speculative land economy. This can happen in three ways: first, they are denied full property rights and so cannot access credit by using property as collateral; second, slum housing schemes restrict the sale of allotted houses for fifteen to twenty years; and third, the absence of clear title and the small sizes of the homes limits their capacity to expand and build rental units. If Bengaluru's lively rental housing market has induced many middle-class homeowners to undertake expansions and improvements to create rental units to earn extra income (see chapter 11), these housing-only schemes have restricted beneficiaries of slum redevelopment schemes from participating in the market: "We can't construct such [multistory] rental housing in slums. We are struggling to accommodate our own families already. Only if we have surplus can we give something out for rent," Narasimhamurthy noted. Slum rights organizations have demanded that families with two or more children should be provided with two houses instead of one, but this demand has not been taken seriously.

In addition, low-cost housing schemes now have mandatory "beneficiary contributions," a mechanism through which the state attempts to recover some of the costs from the beneficiaries. The premise behind making such contributions mandatory is also the logic of self-responsibility—the notion that a plot of land or a house for the poor should not be given free but must be paid for, so that the beneficiary feels a "sense of ownership." Following this logic, nearly all low-income housing schemes now require the beneficiary to pay 10 to 60 percent of the cost of the plot or apartment being allotted.[7]

Yet these subsidized housing schemes push urban poor communities into debt because to finance the mandatory beneficiary contributions, individuals take loans from microfinance companies and banks. For instance, for Scheduled Caste (SC, or Dalit) communities, a maximum of only 3.5 lakh rupees (4,200 USD) is available from existing government schemes for housing finance, and the remaining funds must be borrowed. "The state tells us that you anyway pay rent of 4,000 to 5,000 rupees per month. So instead, if you pay this amount to a bank [as interest], in about five years you will have your own house." However, unlike middle-class residents, the urban poor cannot use their property to earn rental income, which could be used to pay off loans. In curtailing opportunities to monetize their houses or land or to create assets in the form of additional housing units, the state limits the possibilities of achieving financial stability and upward mobility for slum residents.

Slum rights organizations in Bengaluru have generally accepted this principle of beneficiary contributions as a necessary evil, said Narasimhamurthy. The hope is that by participating in such housing schemes, the urban poor would at least get a foothold in Bengaluru's valuable real estate market. But these hopes sit uneasily with the recognition of the larger political economy of land and corruption that undergirds slum housing schemes, making it unlikely that the state would return to offering land ownership to slum residents in the near future. "We ask for a site, they insist on giving us houses. Why? Because they have profits to make. There are contractors and political parties that benefit from this arrangement [by undertaking construction of multistory buildings under redevelopment or rehabilitation schemes]. They lobby a lot for this [the housing schemes]. . . . The government's housing plans are a business. It is a business of poverty. They are not interested in our development," Narasimhamurthy asserted. In 2019 the state government declared that it would pass a law to end the widespread corruption in housing schemes,[8] but, he observed, this legislation is yet to see the light of day.

In response to demands from slum residents' organizations for land ownership, successive governments have often argued that there is no land available to allot to the urban poor. Contesting this argument, Narasimhamurthy pointed out, "Be it revenue [government] lands or lands on the outskirts of the city, there is a lot of land available. But the state, in their slum rehabilitation schemes, always gives us flats in tenements. The government is hesitating to let certain castes access these lands or to give them ownership." Here he was referring to the fact that most slum residents in the city belong to lower-caste and Dalit communities, and denying ownership of land is thus to deny the historically marginalized a right to the city.

To substantiate his argument that there indeed is land available that could be distributed to the poor, Narasimhamurthy referred to the findings of the Joint Legislature Committee on Encroachments in Bangalore Urban District Committee (published in what is popularly known as the A.T. Ramaswamy Committee Report). The committee found that nearly twenty-seven thousand acres of government land in Bangalore Urban district had been "encroached" (by builders, politicians, and other powerful people) and recommended its retrieval.[9] After the publication of the report in 2006, slum rights organizations began to demand that some of the land identified as encroached be granted to slum residents. The state government, in response, committed to setting aside 248 acres for the benefit of slum residents.

"Initially, the government said that they would cover 50 percent of the market value of the land while the residents must pay for the rest. We fought against this requirement and managed to have it waived," Narasimhamurthy explained. But by the time the waiver came in, government agencies such as the Bangalore Development Authority had annexed about one hundred acres of this land to create middle-class layouts in the city. The remaining lands that were allotted to slum residents were scattered across the peripheries of the city and were of poor quality. The struggle for the one hundred acres continues.

Another reason for the state's refusal to grant freehold land to slum residents lies in the larger policy framework for urban development, which hinges on the monetization of public land and properties. Narasimhamurthy pointed out that after the Fiscal Responsibility and Budget Management Act was passed in 2002, urban local bodies (ULBs) are assigned credit ratings based (among other criteria) on the property they hold, which often includes land occupied by informal settlements. The credit rating determines the capacity of municipalities to obtain loans from multinational agencies and global banks for development projects. The less land a ULB controls, the lower the credit rating. This is why ULBs such as the BBMP do not want to transfer land to the KSDB for slum redevelopment schemes. Nor do they allow the KSDB to give *hakku patras* (possession certificates) or title deeds to slum residents, because that would mean land going out of their hands. Although the state government announced in March 2021 that it would hand out title deeds to more than three hundred thousand households,[10] it turned out that titles would be granted only on land that would not affect the BBMP's credit rating, Narasimhamurthy explained.

For Narasimhamurthy, these procedures and decisions—using urban land as collateral for loans, usurping land intended to benefit urban poor communities for middle-class and corporate interests, not providing land titles to slum residents—are all part of a larger pattern of "government speculation." Behind the reluctance of the Karnataka state government to provide land to the urban poor lies a complicated history of the transformation of urban land into real estate, and the ways in which the city's economy, politics, and governance have become enmeshed with the real estate business. This transformation has been gradual in some cases, as when agricultural land gives way to large, gated complexes or residential layouts over several years (see chapters 7 and 14). In other cases, the transformation has taken the form of violent dispossession.

The early 2000s saw many instances of slums "catching" fire in Bengaluru. These incidents were so frequent that a fact-finding committee, drawn from several human rights organizations in the city, was set up to investigate. The committee found that these fires had been intentionally set and that they represented an escalation of threats that slum residents had already been facing to pressure them to vacate the land. All the incidents were concentrated in one electoral constituency.[11] Narasimhamurthy explained these fires as a "land-grabbing tactic." He pointed out that many such fires took place in central parts of the city, such as near Cantonment Railway Station, next to Vidhan Soudha, and near Majestic (a central area of the city and the location of the main railway and bus stations). In an interview with a media outlet, Narasimhamurthy claimed that when S. M. Krishna was chief minister, in the early 2000s, many slums faced demolition because Bangalore was hosting international events and games. He further asserted that nearly twenty slums were set on fire every week.[12] Intentional fires that destroyed the lives and belongings of the urban poor were an important part of the overall strategy of dispossession from land in the city.

Because of these incidents, the issue of land-grabbing entered public discourse in Bengaluru in the early 2000s, shaping the response of civil society to the situation of the urban poor. The fact-finding exercise on slum fires led to the establishment of the Slum Dwellers of Karnataka Joint Action Committee, comprising left, Dalit, and nongovernmental organizations, which examined amendments to the Karnataka Slum Areas (Improvement and Clearance) Act, 1973. This period also saw the establishment of an urban resource center that works on issues of housing and slum rights, Janasahayog: "For about ten years [late 1990s to early 2000s] we worked in the Joint Action Committee, which was primarily focused on Bengaluru," recalled Narasimhamurthy. "The reason for this was simple—Bengaluru is where most of the slums were located, and most instances of land-grabbing were in the city."

Later they began to feel a need to form a wider coalition of slum residents across the state. "Dalit and left organizations would enter into negotiations with the state on our behalf, but without including us. There was no representation of slum residents. We did not think this was right," Narasimhamurthy explained.[13] In the two years leading up to the formation of Slum Janandolana Karnataka, they conducted information gathering exercises in slums across the state. A *padayatra* (political march on foot) on land rights was held, in which participants covered five thousand kilometers over about thirty districts. In 2009, following widespread discussions with people from slums, it was decided to form SJK. The organization was launched officially on January 6, 2010: "This day has historical significance attached to it. It was the day when Dr. B. R. Ambedkar [Dalit leader and icon of Dalit liberation] introduced the concept of 'reservation' at the Depressed Classes Conference held in Assam on January 6, 1929," said Narasimhamurthy.

Prior to SJK's formation, the Joint Action Committee had been successful in negotiating for amendments to the Karnataka Slum Areas (Improvement and Clearance) Act 1973 in the year 2002, which vested the KSDB with the power to transfer land to slum residents and undertake improvements. In 2010 they also succeeded in getting the name of the board changed from Karnataka Slum Clearance Board to Karnataka Slum Development Board, a significant ideological and practical victory. SJK also fought against the government's efforts to introduce public-private participation in the slum policies and programs, and they participated in consultations on proposed amendments to the act in 2018.

In addition, SJK was involved in efforts to ensure that an unprecedented 20 percent of funds allocated to urban local bodies by the state government should be reserved for the development of slums. The movement was also successful in forcing the state to waive the interest on installments slum residents had to pay under the Valmiki Ambedkar Awas Yojana and other housing schemes sponsored by the Department of Urban Development and Housing. They fought for land to be reserved through land bank schemes for deprived urban communities. Protest campaigns held over four years for the regularization of slums finally culminated in an amendment to the Karnataka Land Revenue Act, 1964, allowing individuals residing without authorization on government land to be granted possession of the land under certain conditions (Figure 13.1).[14]

Figure 13.1. Inauguration of a rally organized as part of the state-level convention of Slum Janandolana Karnataka, Tumkur, Karnataka, March 25, 2017, attended by people from across the state. The theme of the convention was, "We don't need slum-free cities! We need equitable and discrimination-free cities!" Photo credit: Janasahayog, Bengaluru.

If the struggle for land rights for slum residents has been a key part of the work of movements such as SJK, dissemination of information on the relevant laws and policies to slum residents has also been a priority: "Amongst us, it is common to just preserve the *hakku patra*, thinking I have the house, who will come and ask me? So, we find that in older slums, where households were given *hakku patras* decades ago, people still don't have an absolute sale [title] deed. The validity of the *hakku patra* would also have expired," Narasimhamurthy observed.

Hakku patra is a possession certificate granted to recognize occupancy of land, under certain conditions, but it does not confer full property rights. Usually these documents carry a conditional period of validity, such as ten to fifteen years, after which the holder can seek regularization of possession from relevant state agencies.[15] But converting a *hakku patra* to a title deed is a tricky and onerous process, requiring documents that attest to one's lineage: "Suppose the *hakku patra* was given to my grandfather Hanumanthappa. I will first have to prove I am Hanumanthappa's grandson, for which my family tree, my father's and grandfather's death certificates, and other documents will be required. We won't have any of these, because when someone dies we just do rituals and leave it at that. All this work of getting death certificates, having the family tree made [a legal document], and so on would be undertaken only if people have some farm property. That is why we are trying to spread awareness and get *hakku patras* registered at the sub-registrar's office now," Narasimhamurthy declared.

Yet the transformation of land into real estate has resulted in another form of dispossession, which Narasimhamurthy repeatedly called (in English) "evictions." He spoke about several cases where people holding clear titles but residing in slums located in prime real estate locations have been subjected to market-led "evictions." "This is not forcible eviction [by the state]," he explained, "but in some circumstances when people are in financial distress, buyers coerce the urban poor to sell their land. They tell them that they can use the money to buy land elsewhere or to build a house in their village. Among our people, some will have some health problems, a daughter's marriage to be arranged, or some other difficult situation requiring quick money, and so sell."

Such "evictions" are taking place in various parts of the city, such as Kanakapura Road, Magadi Road, and Malleswaram, where upper-caste communities such as Gowdas, Lingayats, and Brahmins are buying up properties, Narasimhamurthy claimed. He gave the example of slums around Old Airport Road, where members of dominant caste communities such as Reddys and Naidus have bought land from Holeyas and Madigas (SC communities) and were now benefiting from the booming demand for rental housing in the area. But in former slum areas that have been redeveloped and become more like lower-middle-class localities, they are easily identifiable as "SC colonies" because of their names (such as Ambedkar Nagar and AK Colony). This label curtails opportunities for building rental units, since non-SC people would prefer not to live in such areas, according to Narasimhamurthy.

If market-led dispossession of Dalits in Bengaluru is taking place in various parts of the city, Narasimhamurthy points to other dimensions of caste in the operation of rental markets: "If SCs want to give houses for rent, nobody will come. Only if you belong to the touchable category, people will come for rent." The identity of a homeowner is always well known among the neighbors and real estate agents. And even if an SC landlord offers their house for a lower rent, potential tenants are dissuaded by rumors that the house is not *"vaastu* compliant."[16] Upper-caste residents also tell brokers not to find tenants for "our houses," said Narasimhamurthy, or they try to buy our (the Dalit community's) houses for more than the market value to keep us out of the market.

Even as slum rights movements have demanded unconditional ownership of land in the city, Narasimhamurthy's observations highlight the ways in which the operations of caste, the land market, and the state converge within a speculative real estate economy to reinforce—and capitalize on—oppressive structures of caste and class inequality. With the transformation of land into real estate and the movement of the state toward privatized "affordable housing" schemes, the "dream" of the urban poor of owning a small plot of land in the speculative city has become a receding aspiration. Given that a large section of the urban poor belong to historically deprived Scheduled Caste and Scheduled Tribe communities, their lack of access to land and housing in the city and inability to participate in the speculative economy of the city perpetuates the caste-based logic of segregation. The spatial organization of Bengaluru has come to resemble what Isaac Arul Selva, another well-known slum rights activist, has often called the *agrahara-keri* division—a traditional division in villages between Brahmin and Dalit colonies.

Notes

This chapter is based on interviews conducted with Mr. A. Narasimhamurthy at his office by members of the Speculative Urbanism project team. Translations and transcriptions from Kannada into English were provided by Kaveri Medappa, Deeksha M. Rao, and Swathi Shivanand.

1. Henri Lefebvre, *The Production of Space* (Oxford: Blackwell, 1991).

2. Supriya RoyChowdhury, *City of Shadows: Slums and Informal Work in Bangalore* (New Delhi: Cambridge University Press, 2021).

3. On the complexities of land tenure rights in informal settlements, see Solomon Benjamin, "Occupancy Urbanism: Radicalizing Politics and Economy beyond Policy and Programmes," *International Journal of Urban and Regional Research* 32, no. 3 (2008): 719–729; Anirudh Krishna, Emily Rains, and Erik Wibbels, "Negotiating Informality—Ambiguity, Intermediation, and a Patchwork of Outcomes in Slums of Bengaluru," *Journal of Development Studies* 56, no. 11 (2020): 1983–1999.

4. See Malini Ranganathan, "Rule by Difference: Empire, Liberalism, and the Legacies of Urban 'Improvement,'" *Environment and Planning A* 50, no. 7 (2018): 1386–1406.

5. The JNNURM was introduced in 2005 by the central government then controlled by the Congress Party–led United Progress Alliance. The policy was one of the cornerstones of India's economic liberalization agenda. This large debt-financed program pumped some 20 billion US dollars into urban renewal and infrastructure projects—most implemented through public-private partnerships—with the aim of attracting global capital investments. Since then, slum development schemes have promoted subsidized housing in multistory buildings rather than sites-and-services schemes. Such housing projects often entail the relocation and "rehabilitation" of slum residents in poor-quality housing on urban peripheries. See Lalitha Kamath, "New Policy Paradigms and Actual Practices in Slum Housing: The Case of Housing Projects in Bengaluru," *Economic & Political Weekly* 47, nos. 47–48 (2012): 76–86; and Karen Coelho, "Tenements, Ghettos, or Neighbourhoods? Outcomes of Slum-Clearance Interventions in Chennai," *Review of Development & Change* 21, no. 1 (2016): 111–36.

6. In sites-and-services schemes, planned layouts are created and basic amenities such as roads, water connection, and drainage are provided, but beneficiaries must construct their own houses—for which they may receive low-interest loans.

7. Prajwal Suvarna, "Housing for All: Who Is Left Behind," *Deccan Herald*, February 27, 2022, https://www.deccanherald.com/specials/insight/housing-for -all-who-is-left-behind-1085506.html.

8. Times News Network, "Govt Housing Schemes: New Legislation to End Corruption," *Times of India*, December 12, 2019, https://timesofindia.indiatimes .com/city/bengaluru/govt-housing-schemes-new-legislation-to-end-corruption /articleshow/72485340.cms.

9. Karnataka Legislature, Joint House Committee, Encroachment of Government Lands in Bangalore City/Urban District: Interim Report Part 1, February 1, 2007, https://advgen.kar.nic.in/pdf/atr/PART%201%20ENGLISH.pdf.

10. "Title Deeds: Fee Waiver for Slum Dwellers," *The Hindu*, March 28, 2021, https://www.thehindu.com/news/national/karnataka/title-deeds-fee-waiver -for-slum-dwellers/article34180835.ece; "Karnataka Govt. to Grant Title Deeds to Over 16 Lakh Slum Dwellers," *The Hindu*, August 20, 2020, https://www .thehindu.com/news/national/karnataka/govt-to-grant-title-deeds-to-over-16 -lakh-slum-dwellers/article32407212.ece.

11. People's Union for Civil Liberties, People's Democratic Forum, Slum Jagatthu, AIDWA, Madiga Misalarti Horata Samiti, Students Federation of India, Democratic Youth Federation of India, Pedestrian Pictures, APSA, Vimochana and Alternative Law Forum. "Slums under Fire: A Fact-Finding Report on the Slum Fires in Bangalore," February 2006, https://www.scribd.com /document/192471097/Final-Slum-Fire-Fact-Finding-Report.

12. Yogesh S., "Political Parties Have Looked at Slum Dwellers as Vote Bank: Narasimhamurthy," *Indian Cultural Forum*, April 25, 2018, https://indianculturalforum.in/2018/04/25/political-parties-have-looked-at-slum-dwellers-as-vote-bank-narasimhamurthy/.

13. Because a large proportion of people living in slums are Dalits, Dalit organizations have often been at the forefront of these struggles for land and housing rights.

14. Among the many caveats included in the new clause was that land within eighteen kilometers of the Bengaluru city limits should not be granted.

15. The *hakku patra* does not have the same legal validity as a sale deed, which is the most valid proof of property ownership in India. At most, the holder of a *hakku patra* may receive some compensation or rehabilitation housing if they are displaced. A *hakku patra* may also be canceled by the relevant authority. These documents cannot be used to seek loans from banks, in most cases. The uncertainty surrounding the kind of property rights conferred by the *hakku patra* disincentivizes holders from improving their dwellings, especially if their settlement is in a prime location where the land might be acquired for an infrastructure project. According to Narasimhamurthy, *hakku patra* have typically been distributed to the poor periodically to commemorate some important event such as the twenty-fifth anniversary of Indian independence.

16. This refers to the revival or reinvention of the traditional Indian system of architecture (based on an ancient text, the Vaastu Shashtra) by contemporary developers. Many buyers insist that the apartments or houses be compliant with the principles of *vaastu*.

14
The Caste of Land

Carol Upadhya

On one of the first field visits by our research team to the southeastern fringe of Bengaluru, in April 2017, Kaveri Medappa and I had a chance encounter with two individuals who became key interlocutors for our research.[1] As we were driving around the area noting the transformation of agricultural land into "urban" uses, we spotted four men walking into an empty plot of land adjacent to the road. Thinking that they might be discussing a land deal, we approached them. We discovered that two of the men were indeed local land brokers. "Shekhar," a young man, and his uncle "Nagappa" were showing a plot of land for sale to potential customers. After we explained our interest in learning about real estate development in peri-urban villages, they agreed to speak with us and we settled down on the steps of a closed shop to chat. With little prompting, Shekhar and Nagappa began telling us about the rampant "land-grabbing" that was occurring in the area, and especially how members of the powerful Reddy community were "encroaching" on government land (Reddys are the major landowning and agriculturalist caste in this area).

Offering to show us an example, Shekhar and Nagappa took us to see a cricket field that had been carved out of *gomala* land (village common land meant for grazing animals and other livelihood activities, open to use by all villagers). According to them, a local farmer had bribed the village accountant to falsely list the land as his personal property. Having thus "grabbed" the land, he planted eucalyptus trees on it, but when that venture failed (due to the declining water table; see chapter 3) he turned it into a cricket ground. The "owner" now rents out the grounds to "techies" (software engineers) working in nearby IT parks who come to play on the weekends.

As Sachinkumar Rathod (another team member) carried out fieldwork in this area over the next two years, he documented many similar stories of "land-grabbing" (the English term is commonly used even while speaking in Kannada). He also learned about the opposition being mounted by local Dalits against what they viewed as the illegal appropriation of land by Reddys. In these rapidly urbanizing villages, struggles around land are deeply marked by caste. Shekhar and Nagappa often spoke about how, as land values soared, Dalit families had lost their land to local landlords or affluent "outsiders." While a significant proportion of agricultural land had been sold by farmers to real estate developers or land aggregators (see chapters 4 and 7), they highlighted other routes through which private agricultural holdings and common lands were being converted to nonagricultural purposes or real estate ventures. One of the most common is the (usually unauthorized) formation of "revenue layouts" offering house sites for sale, which are attractive investments for many middle-class urban households. Such plots of land are popularly viewed as lucrative investments, since they are less expensive than land in central city areas. Moreover, everyone says that "land values always go up."[2]

The appropriation of *gomala* lands and agricultural land belonging to poor families by local landlords and political leaders is a common story in villages all around Bengaluru. Rural land markets have been enlivened by the spatial extension of the city into its hinterlands and declining agricultural productivity, attracting speculative investors to buy or "grab" land. Nagappa often spoke angrily about the "land mafia" that operates with the connivance of powerful politicians and bureaucrats. According to him, everyone from ministers, department secretaries, MLAs, and the District Commissioner (top state officials and elected leaders), down to the local revenue inspector, *tahsildar,* and village accountant (local officers), is part of the "network" of corruption that facilitates what is popularly termed "land-grabbing." "This new mafia is making crores of rupees," Nagappa exclaimed.[3]

Shekhar and other local Dalit activists have contested this process by carefully documenting such cases, especially highlighting the role of Reddy landlords and politicians. Nagappa could recite from memory the survey numbers of all the contested plots of land in his village and recount the details and perpetrators of each case. He especially highlighted the illegal transfer of Scheduled Caste "assigned lands" (lands granted by the government to rural poor and Scheduled Caste households under land-distribution schemes) and encroachments on *gomala* lands to create layouts or for other money-making ventures such as the construction of marriage halls. Nagappa displayed thick files of documents he had collected to build his cases, which he hoped to present to government authorities to force them to take legal action against the perpetrators.

For Shekhar, the issue of land-grabbing was personal: he was drawn into it by a dispute in which his own family was embroiled with a local landlord, "Subba Reddy." Shekhar's father had taken a loan from Subba Reddy, pledging his land as surety by creating a general power of attorney (GPA)[4] in Reddy's name. Reddy then used the GPA to claim the property as his own. Shekhar's father filed a lawsuit against him, but the case languished in court for years until Shekhar took it up and finally won. Fighting his father's case made Shekhar realize how widespread land-grabbing was in his locality, and he started helping other Dalit families reclaim land that they had lost through fraud or manipulation.

"Santosh," a Dalit activist from a neighboring village, was also engaged in the struggle against land-grabbing. He explained that politically connected landowners in his village had obtained advance knowledge about future real estate and infrastructure projects and started buying up land from Dalits and marginal farmers in anticipation of rising prices. When offered what seemed like a good price, many Dalits sold their small holdings, only to discover later that the same plots were being resold at a profit: "If a piece of land was worth 1 crore [10 million rupees], they gave the Dalits 20 lakhs [2 million rupees]." When asked why Dalits would sell at this low price, he responded, "We wouldn't have seen so much money, right?" Even his own family sold 2.5 acres to a developer in 2007: "Back then, we didn't know what was happening, but now things are becoming clear." Feeling cheated, Dalits began to file lawsuits to reclaim their property, citing the law that prohibits the sale or transfer of assigned lands.

Like the story of Shekhar's family, Santosh pointed to moneylending as a key modality through which Dalit lands have fallen into the hands of rich landlords. Marginal farmers often pledge their land as collateral when taking private loans, later losing it when they are unable to repay the debt. "Like this," Santosh said, "the poor farmers give away their lands to the rich, who then sell it for crores. The rich become richer, and we are becoming poorer" (Figure 14.1).

Figure 14.1. House of a rich Reddy landlord, "Purvapur" village. Photograph by Pierre Hauser.

Another land-grabbing tactic mentioned by Santosh is the practice of giving bribes to Revenue Department officials to falsify land records. Criticizing such officers for their venality, he said, *"Duddu maadod onde guri"* (Their only motive is to make money). Santosh argued that with enough money, "anything can be done with land"; that is, wealthy and well-connected people can easily persuade government officials to ignore land-use violations or alter documents.

Dalit rights organizations (of which there are several in Bengaluru) have been involved in struggles around land across the city—especially in campaigning for the rights of residents living in informal settlements in addition to social justice issues (chapter 13). Although they belong to different organizations, Santosh and Shekhar expressed similar views on this issue. Santosh became emotional while describing his first encounter with Dalit activists—he felt that at last he had found people who were articulating what he felt as a Dalit. He credits "DPA" (a pseudonym for a prominent Dalit organization in Karnataka) for giving him the confidence and ability to approach government offices and "get work done." When he visits the BBMP ward office or the local panchayat office, he is able to access the documents he needs quickly because the officers know and respect him: "DPA is my everything, my strength."

One day, Shekhar and several other village residents attended a meeting with the recently appointed Deputy Commissioner (DC), arranged by the state president of DPA, to voice their concerns. The leader explained each case to the DC one by one—atrocities against Dalits, the need for basic infrastructure in Dalit colonies, allocation of house sites, encroachment of common lands—and handed over files of paperwork to support their claims. The DC questioned the junior officers present about these cases, who became increasingly uncomfortable. In the end, he directed them to "take action against these illegal activities."

Shekhar explained that Dalit organizations have gained some influence with the government over the years: "Ambedkar is like a railway engine, and we are like railway compartments. When we go through Dalit organizations, our land-related work will be done immediately. Otherwise, it is very difficult."[5] But here Shekhar is referring not only to the struggle against land-grabbing but also (and especially) to his work as a land broker.

Activists such as Shekhar, even as they oppose the illicit appropriation of land by upper-caste landlords and real estate interests, make their living as land brokers. Indeed, these activities are not as contradictory as they might first appear but are closely intertwined. Shekhar, who went to college and had planned to become a software engineer, explained that he was drawn into the land business through his involvement in his father's court case and his efforts to help other Dalits recover their land. By working on these cases, he learned about the complex legal framework governing rural land and the technicalities of land sales, which gave him the confidence to work as a "real estate agent"—a more respectable term for broker. Conversely, Nagappa attributed his deep understanding of Revenue Department procedures to his fifteen years of experience as a broker, which in turn has enabled him to compile detailed evidence of land-grabbing.

The spectacular profits that can be made from trading in land—legally or otherwise—have enticed many people in peri-urban villages to act as brokers, full- or part-time, arranging land deals and handling the byzantine paperwork involved in land transactions. Most of the big brokers in these peri-urban villages are Reddys, but Dalits have also entered the "real estate business"—a phrase commonly used even while speaking in Kannada to signal all kinds of activities related to the land market. While Reddy brokers generally corner the larger land deals, Dalit agents handle smaller transactions such as sales of house sites, or they mediate family property disputes. In the course of their work, Dalit brokers such as Shekhar spend much time at local government offices and courts, where they track down files, negotiate with officials, and engage "touts" to help move files. Their familiarity with these bureaucratic spaces helps them to access the documents needed to file legal cases against illicit land sales or encroachments.

These seemingly conflicting activities—fighting against land-grabbing and brokering land deals—converge in other ways as well. Shekhar explained that when he comes across a case of illicit transfer of Scheduled Caste–assigned land, he approaches the original owners and offers to file a court case on their behalf. If they agree, he covers the costs of litigation himself, and if he wins he keeps part of the recovered land as his payment. Thus, while Shekhar is passionate about exposing the nefarious activities of local landlords and big politicians, pursuing such cases also forms part of his "real estate business."

Shekhar's entrepreneurial flair in finding ways to prosper from the fight against land-grabbing suggests that the struggle of these Dalit activists is not only about caste inequality or social injustice. Rather, their desire is to participate on an equal footing in the booming land market, from which they have been largely excluded. For example, after successfully recovering his father's property, Shekhar promptly sold it to Subba Reddy's son for 1 crore rupees—despite the deep attachment that his family had to this land which represented their earlier important status as the village Thoti (village watchman).

One day, when the research team visited their house in Purvapur village in July 2019, Shekhar and Nagappa related the story of their Chalavadi community (a Scheduled Caste). In the days of the Mysore kingdom, they explained, one Chalavadi family in each village held the hereditary post of Thoti. The Thoti was the local representative of the king, responsible for collecting taxes, making official announcements, and guarding the village. In return, Shekhar's family had received 2.5 acres of *inam* (grant) land. Shekhar then brought out a beautifully crafted instrument called *gantebattalu*, carefully wrapped in cloth, which he had inherited from his grandfather. This ornate brass bell and ladle connected by a chain was a symbol of the authority of the Thoti. Standing up proudly and grasping the handle while ringing the bell, he demonstrated how the Thoti would go around the village collecting the grain due as tax to the monarch, measured by the large spoon.

Shekhar and his family, like most Dalits, may have fallen from the exalted position once held by his forebears as village watchman and representative of the king, who he claimed honored the Chalavadi caste above all others. The gradual dissipation of whatever small plots of grant land they held had reduced Dalits to dependence on upper-caste farmers for employment as agricultural workers. But with the recent land market boom, some Dalits have found new ways to reassert their dignity, pursue economic mobility, and contest their political marginalization—not only as activists but also as land market intermediaries and real estate developers. Rather than acquiescing in their marginalization, Dalit activists push back against the accumulation of land by powerful groups as a way of asserting their right to take part in and prosper from this new speculative economy—echoing the argument of city-based Dalit and housing rights activists such as Narasimhamurthy (chapter 13).

Indeed, Shekhar has expanded his business beyond brokering by replicating one of the key strategies of the Reddy "land-grabbers" he condemns—he has created his own layout on "greenbelt land" where he sells house sites. When asked about this venture, he declared angrily, "If Reddys do illegal things it's okay, but if Dalits do the same it infuriates them." But he is confident that he will not face legal problems—he says that all the papers are in order and there is no "*dispute*" on the land. Moreover, there is little risk to the buyers because the sites can later be regularized through the Akrama-Sakrama scheme.[6] Shekhar pursues his real estate and political activities from his "office"—a small shack constructed in this layout, where he also spends evenings playing cards with his friends.

Notes

Kaveri Medappa, Sachinkumar Rathod, Juwairia Mehkri, and Hemangini Gupta contributed to this chapter, which also draws on Carol Upadhya and Sachinkumar Rathod, "Caste at the City's Edge: Land Struggles in Peri-urban

Bengaluru," *South Asia Multidisciplinary Academic Journal* 26 (2021), http:// journals.openedition.org/samaj/7134.

1. See the introduction to this book for an explanation of the research project and description of the research team for the Speculative Urbanism project. Different team members carried out research in this site at different times.

2. These housing developments are known as "revenue layouts" because they are formed on agricultural land, which is governed by the Revenue Department. Until recently, agricultural land in Karnataka could not be converted to other uses without special permission from the authorities. However, this practice of converting revenue land into layouts—exploiting various loopholes in the law or using underhanded practices—is ubiquitous in Bengaluru, especially because such property can later be regularized.

3. Indeed, land-grabbing was a major public issue in Bengaluru in the 1990s, as numerous encroachments and illegal constructions on government land (including water bodies) were seen as a cause of environmental degradation. A committee headed by an MLA, A. T. Ramaswamy, was appointed to investigate the matter (Joint House Committee, Karnataka Legislature 2006, 2007). Its report found that politicians had participated in land-grabbing at all levels and across party lines. Dalit organizations in Bengaluru have been actively monitoring cases of land-grabbing while also fighting for the rights of residents of informal settlements on government land (see chapter 13).

4. The term "GPA" is commonly used in vernacular speech. Although it is technically not a legal instrument for land transactions, the GPA is widely used to cement informal land deals through brokers.

5. Dr. B. R. Ambedkar led the movement against untouchability in the early twentieth century. He was also a key leader of India's struggle for independence and an architect of the Indian constitution. Ambedkar is an icon for Dalits across India.

6. The much-debated Akrama-Sakrama ("illegal-legal") scheme in Karnataka allows for the regularization of properties created or purchased in violation of laws, planning norms, or building bylaws, on payment of a fee.

Portrait of a worker on a large construction site, Bengaluru. Photograph by Pierre Hauser.

Part V
Labor in the Speculative City

Whose labor enables the world-class city to arise and function? The chapters in this section vividly highlight the ubiquitous yet often invisible forms of work that underwrite the desired amenities and lifestyles of the city's middle-class and affluent residents. They reveal the struggles, aspirations, and livelihood uncertainties of construction workers, street vendors, domestic helpers, and gig workers as they strive to earn, save, and secure dignity while dealing with mistreatment and wage theft by employers, insecure housing amid rapidly rising property values, threats of eviction from their places of livelihood, punishing work schedules, and various other contingencies and forms of prejudice. Together, these stories showcase the ambivalence of working-class people as they try to carve out aspirational lives in a city that needs them but doesn't acknowledge or support them.

"Constructing Precarity" (chapter 15) contains richly detailed stories of construction workers who toil in obscurity and lead uncertain lives, and who are routinely defenseless in a city that wants their labor but offers little in return. An elderly migrant worker, "Amba," who worked for over thirty years as a construction laborer but now finds herself spent by the daily grind and unwanted by employers, bitterly remarks, "No matter how hard I worked, how much I prayed and reposed faith in Shiva, he has only given me *kashta* [difficulties]. This life has not seen any *sukha* [comfort]."[1] So, why do workers continue to flock to jobs in sectors like construction where an injury or bout of illness can render you dispensable? "Basava," who hails from a poor, low-caste peasant community, reveals that despite the tribulations of working in the city, it trumps the alternative of working as an indentured laborer in his native, drought-prone region of Hyderabad-Karnataka.

Street vendors, who purvey a dazzling array of wares and services at low cost, are ubiquitous in India's cities. Informal vending is a form of self-enterprise that supports thousands of livelihoods in Bengaluru because of relatively low barriers to entry, a degree of occupational autonomy (no bosses or supervisors who constantly harangue), and a certain amount of flexibility in work rhythms (which is particularly important to women who have social reproductive obligations). But rapidly escalating land prices and incomes in the speculative city have lubricated a middle-class sensibility and altered the character of localities that were previously working-class or mixed-income communities. Attitudes of residents and city authorities have shifted accordingly—to the detriment of street vendors who have long provided a range of amenities to the city's inhabitants.[2] "Whose Streets?" (chapter 16) narrates the plight of Bengaluru's vendors as they fight harassment by police and municipal staff, and struggle to preserve pavements, roadside spaces, and other public areas as sites of business, despite the Indian Parliament's passage of the Street Vendors Act of 2014, which prohibits unilateral evictions. A vendor, fed up with abuse from a neighborhood's residents, angrily exclaims, "We were here long before the houses came, when these were just empty sites. Many of these residents have bought things from us for so long. But now they want space for their cars, so we must leave, is it? Don't they have any humanity?" Rising sectarian tensions in Bengaluru over the last decade and politically motivated threats of economic boycott have made the already insecure livelihoods of vendors even more so for Muslim vendors.

In "Chasing Targets, Making a Life" (chapter 17) we spend a day with a young delivery worker, "Ajay," as he navigates boredom, expectation, traffic, and the remorseless discipline of clock-time to deliver food orders to the city's affluent residents on his motorbike. Despite the razor-thin margins of his gig work in the burgeoning "platform economy,"[3] Ajay brings a gung-ho attitude to life—pursuing bonuses on his app, exploring other sources of income in parallel, and speculating on a better future that he believes will come.

While new on-demand app services of all kinds employ a burgeoning pool of workers in precarious jobs to serve the city's middle classes, a much older form of service work persists in a state of uneasy flux. Who cooks and cleans for Bengaluru's growing middle-class population, many of them recent arrivals to the city? How do domestic helpers experience the giddy upheaval in the city's demographics?

"Serving the New Middle Classes" (chapter 18) confronts these questions, revealing the travails and traversals of domestic workers as they cope with changing employment relationships and moral expectations. One says with a note of bafflement, "They don't value money. If I happen to arrive a little late, they would have ordered food from outside."

Notes

1. We are reminded here of political economist and philosopher Karl Marx's denunciation almost 150 years ago of the abysmal conditions in which workers toil: "In its blind, unrestrainable passion, its were-wolf hunger for surplus labour, capital oversteps not only the moral, but even the merely physical maximum bounds limits of the working day. It usurps the time for growth, development, and healthy maintenance of the body." *Marx & Engels Collected Works, Volume 35, Karl Marx—Capital Volume 1* (London: Lawrence & Wishart, 2010), 270–71.

2. See Lekha Adavi, Darshana Mitra, and Vinay Sreenivasa, "Contestations Over Public Space," *Seminar* 694, https://www.india-seminar.com/2017/694/694_lekha_adavi_at_al.htm#top. Jonathan Shapiro Anjaria, in *Slow Boil: Street Food, Rights, and Public Space in Mumbai* (Stanford: Stanford University Press, 2016), provides a rich ethnographic account of how street vendors in a major Indian city organize and invent to defend their rights to urban space against neighborhood associations and city authorities who want vendors off cluttered sidewalks.

3. Bhavani Seetharaman, Joyojeet Pal, and Julie Hui, "Delivery Work and the Experience of Social Isolation," *Proceedings of the ACM on Human-Computer Interactions 5*, no. CSCW-1 (2021): 1–17. On the rise of platform capitalism, see K. Sabeel Rahman and Kathleen Thelen, "The Rise of the Platform Business Model and the Transformation of Twenty-First-Century Capitalism," *Politics and Society* 27, no. 2 (2019): 177–204.

15

Constructing Precarity

Swathi Shivanand

For anyone coming up the unpaved road to "JB Nagar" settlement in Laggere—a site in northwest Bengaluru to which a number of slum communities from across the city have been relocated—"Amba" was a permanent fixture. She sat in the same spot under the shade of a large tree every day, stitching colorful patchwork quilted blankets. Now well into her sixties, the former construction worker had no choice but to return to making these traditional quilts, a skill she had learned from her foremothers. Her aging, depleted body had been deemed unproductive by an industry constantly looking for young blood and bodies.

One afternoon, as I sat with her trying to piece together the story of her life as a migrant construction worker, I asked her how long she had done *gaare kelasa* (construction work). It seemed to trigger some latent rage. "See, I will do any kind of work. . . . I have been asking so many people for construction work. They say even people who look strong and healthy are not getting work, *amma* [mother], so who will call you? So! Only the strong ones should live, is it? Should people like me go die? If only those with strength to work, those whose bodies are built well, if only they are called to work, those of us who have grown soft, what should we do? That god has given this body, this soul, a stomach that needs to be fed, what should we do?"

God and fate often turned up in conversations with Amba, to whom life had dealt the cruel hands of both patriarchy and poverty. Originally from a village in Yadgir district of northern Karnataka, Amba had lived through the severe drought of the early 1970s when her parents struggled to find work and food. They had survived by eating fodder meant for goats. When she was a young girl she was

Constructing Precarity **201**

married off to a man who had some agricultural land to his name, but he had taken to drinking and gambled away the land—claiming that it was his property so he could do whatever he wanted with it. Having lost all means of income in the late 1990s, Amba and her husband moved with their three children to Bangalore, at the suggestion of a relative who said they could find work in the city. Amba and her children started to work on construction sites, and she soon became the main earner for her family. Her alcoholic husband remained uninterested in work and then fell ill with cancer and died. But given that women construction workers earned as little as 25 rupees per day when she started in the late 1990s, and children even less, she barely managed to make ends meet. Occasional assistance in the form of food and other essentials (but not a share in property) from her natal family helped to sustain life in the city when her children were young.

Distress migration, triggered by loss of farmlands, alcoholic husbands, and the inability to look after very young children, was a recurring theme in the lives of many residents of JB Nagar whom I interviewed during fieldwork in 2017. Like Amba, many of the earliest migrant households were effectively headed by women, who had been pushed to take over the responsibilities of surviving, given absent (natal) families or husbands. They arrived in Bengaluru from the poor and neglected region of Hyderabad-Karnataka and eventually became part of the growing unskilled workforce in the construction industry. This was the period when "labor catchment areas" for Bengaluru had shifted away from neighboring districts toward northern parts of Karnataka and east to Andhra Pradesh and Tamil Nadu. The city's need for a constant supply of low-paid and docile workers to fuel the construction boom led to the creation of new labor catchment areas in regions previously unconnected to Bengaluru through channels of migration (Figure 15.1).

When these early migrants—fifty to sixty households, including Amba's—arrived in the late 1990s they squatted on land near a government school in Laggere, on the outskirts of the city. They put up huts, gradually filling up a nearby lakebed with construction debris to create solid ground. In the early 2000s, land values in the area had started to rise and these families began to receive threats from local gangsters, acting on behalf of local politicians, who wanted them to vacate the land. On February 18, 2006, when the adults were away at

Figure 15.1. Women workers and their children at a construction site, Bengaluru. Photograph by Pierre Hauser.

work, some miscreants set the huts on fire after locking up the children in a room inside the nearby school. All their belongings were destroyed in that fire. "For fifteen days, we sat on the footpath, not going to work, living off whatever charity some organizations and individuals bestowed on us. We had no clothes, no vessels, no shelter over our heads," Amba recalled. This was the period when the city saw a spate of similar cases of slums set on fire. A fact-finding report produced by civil society organizations suggested that the fires were a strategy deployed for "land-grabbing," a phenomenon that was rampant in the city's peripheries where land was steadily rising in speculative value (see chapters 7, 13, and 14).

In the years after the fire, these settlers moved farther away from the city, to a site used for dumping construction debris, where they rebuilt their settlement. It grew in size as more migrants came and settled in. Pointing to the buildings around us and the elevated portion of the Outer Ring Road that runs above the settlement, Amba said, "Laggere has become Laggere because of us. When we first came here, it was like a forest, everything growing wild, there were just hillocks everywhere. Only after we settled down here did all these roads and buildings come up." With consistent support from activists associated with the city-based slum rights organization Janasahyog (see chapter 13), residents of JB Nagar were allotted houses through a scheme of the Karnataka Slum Development Board. When we first met, Amba was living with her youngest son, also a construction worker, and his wife, in one of these small one-room houses.

The presence of these migrants who stayed put in the city despite its hostilities has, over time, enabled many other households from the Hyderabad-Karnataka region to migrate to the city to work on construction sites. Amba, her house, and whatever networks she had became the first shelter for many from her extended family and village who came to Bengaluru to find work. The mother of "Basava" was one such relative who migrated through Amba's connections. Abject poverty had driven her to put her youngest child, Basava, to work as a bonded laborer—the practice called *jeeta*—in a landlord's house in her village while she migrated to Bengaluru. Unable to bear the burden of *jeeta* work, Basava ran away. His mother searched high and low for him for several months, begged for assistance from government departments, and finally managed to locate him. After that, she did not return to Bengaluru and decided to stay in the village looking after her son and subsisting by doing odd jobs. But fate dealt a cruel blow. She died when the vegetable truck she was traveling in had an accident. Basava then went to Bengaluru to stay with his older siblings and joined the construction workforce as a young child, in the late 1990s. Now in his late twenties, he told me about the circumstances that led him to the city.

"At that time, the *mestris* [labor contractors] would hesitate to employ children like me. I was a child who had just arrived in Bengaluru and didn't know the work properly. But I started work as a helper, carrying cement. I couldn't even lift bricks. By the end of each day, my arms and legs would just give up and I would have no strength at all. I was sick of Bengaluru and just wanted to go back to my village. If my mother had not died, then maybe I would never have had to come here."

Although his earliest memories of the city are scarred by the loss of his mother and the consequent blistering toil he had to undertake, Basava is enthusiastic about the possibilities for small levels of accumulation that working in the construction sector offers. Wages have increased in the two decades since the first set of migrants arrived in the city. As unskilled workers, women and men earn about 250 and 400 rupees per day, respectively; for semiskilled work, wages can go up to 800. Pooling his savings together with those of his brothers, Basava has purchased agricultural land in his village, rebuilt their village home, and helped to pay for weddings for himself and his brothers.

It is these opportunities to earn more money than they ever could in the village that has enabled people like Basava, who are from poor, lower-caste peasant communities, to reject oppressive practices such as *jeeta*. "When people have to repay debts or need money urgently, they don't opt for bonded labor anymore. People now know that they can come to Bengaluru and earn some money quickly, then return to the village and pay off their debts." Basava told me how construction work in Bengaluru has turned into a strategy for transforming rural lives. The availability of such work in the city seems to act as a sort of fail-safe mechanism to cover any possible losses in ventures undertaken in the village: "My relatives leased land for 50,000 rupees per year, but it rained so heavily that they lost three-quarters of their standing crop. Whatever they were able to harvest was not enough to even cover their investment. They had also taken the initial 50,000 rupees investment on loan. If they keep losing crops like this for two years, they get into deep debt. Then they will come to Bengaluru to work and pay off their debts." Such losses in risky agricultural ventures are often the basis for intermittent, circular migration into the construction industry.

But for those looking for regular work in the construction industry, like Basava, building steady relationships with *mestris* is crucial. Basava reeled off all the requirements needed to ensure regular work: "*Mestris* tell us which site to go to. If you are friends with them, if you work well, then you will keep getting work. If you are slow and don't work fast enough, they will not call you back. But you also have to work with neatness. You can't just be fast and not neat. If you get into an accident by any chance, then again you won't be called back." These different conditions that workers must fulfill is a reminder of how much the constancy of work is dependent on the skill, agility, and plain good luck of the worker to not fall victim to accidents.

Even though many construction workers told me that work is readily available and that they could enter and exit the labor force when they wanted, they also know that a workplace accident could end opportunities for work permanently. Besides, construction work can only be undertaken for a short span of one's life. Making as much money as quickly as possible in this risky, body-depleting venture is the goal. "This is very rough work. We cannot work beyond the age of forty-five to fifty years here," Basava told me. Before making this comment, he was explaining how most young construction workers in the settlement prefer working with unlicensed contractors because they can get paid anywhere between 700 and 1,000 rupees per day. "With licensed contractors, the *kuli* [daily wage] is less, say about 500–600 rupees, because they have all their papers in order. But if you meet with an accident, they have insurance and you can get money. That's not possible with an unlicensed contractor. If any injury or even death happens, no one will care and you won't get any money," he said. It seemed to me that in the speculative city, unorganized and unsupported workers gamble their bodies away for a few hundred rupees more in the hope of greater accumulative possibilities.

The ephemeral nature of work in the construction industry has been sustained by design. Although the Building and Other Construction Workers (Regulation of Employment and Conditions of Service) Act, 1996 mandates benefits such as pension, accident insurance, health care, and support for children's education, none of the workers I spoke to were able to access these schemes. To get these benefits, workers must register with the BOCW (Building and Other Construction Workers) Board, and such registration requires a licensed contractor to provide an employment certificate stating that the worker has worked with him for a period of ninety continuous days. Even if the worker did work with a licensed contractor for this period, no contractor is willing to take the risk of giving such a certificate out of fear that he would be held liable for any future accidents.

For Basava, all this means he will eventually return to the village, hoping he will have accumulated enough as a construction worker to spend the rest of his life in some comfort. For Amba, however, the expulsion from the workforce has meant an excessive dependence on her children, with whom she has difficult relationships. As the sole earning member of the family, supporting her alcoholic and sick husband out of a sense of wifely obligation, and as a poorly paid unskilled woman worker, Amba's possibilities of accumulation were restricted during her working life, compared to able-bodied, male-headed households. "No matter how hard I worked, how much I prayed and reposed faith in Shiva, he has only given me *kashta* [difficulties]. This life has not seen any *sukha* [comfort]," she once told me.

From the late 1980s on, the emerging speculative city spread its tentacles far and wide, drawing in people for their laboring bodies with the lure of better wages than a depleted countryside could offer. But after the thirty-odd years that Amba labored as a construction worker in the city, she had no option but to return to her village when her elder son passed away from alcoholism-related health complications. She now earns some money by deploying her ancestral skills in making patchwork quilts and selling them for a pittance. She remains hopeful that her grandson will do better by her than her disappointing sons.

Note

This chapter draws on fieldwork carried out by Swathi Shivanand for her doctoral thesis, which explored the twentieth-century histories of development in southern India, in particular the erstwhile state of Hyderabad-Deccan and contemporary Karnataka.

16

Whose Streets?

Vinay K. Sreenivasa

One Monday evening, I came home just as it was about to rain. "Thank god you managed to reach home dry," my mother exclaimed. And as she said that it started pouring. A few minutes later, at dinner, she asked, "Wonder what happened to 'Lakshmi' and 'Kaveri'? Tomorrow is Gowri Pooja—they'll have good business for the festival. But in such rain, what will happen to them?" Lakshmi and Kaveri, sisters, are street vendors who have been serving our residential area for years. They come in the evenings, around 7 p.m., three to four days a week, with their pushcarts, to sell fruits, vegetables, and, around festival time, flowers. That night it was 8:30 p.m., and they were yet to come. Suddenly we heard a cry, "*Amma, hoovathandiddeevi!*" (Mother, we have flowers!). I rushed to the door. We saw Lakshmi and Kaveri, standing in the pouring rain, a tarpaulin covering the merchandise on their carts. Kaveri was holding an umbrella but was soaked. Lakshmi, who was just using a plastic sheet to shield her head, was thoroughly drenched. We hurriedly purchased some flowers and fruits so they could leave. I invited them in to take shelter. "It's okay, *anna* [brother]," Lakshmi replied. "We are anyway drenched, at least if we go home fast, we can dry ourselves and eat something." This has happened many times. Sometimes they will come in, but often they just continue on their route in the rain, saying, "It's normal for us, *anna*, what can we do?"

As I was thinking about the difficult conditions Lakshmi and Kaveri have to endure to eke out their livelihoods, I was reminded of another evening a few days earlier. As India celebrated seventy-five years of independence (the Amrutha Mahotsava) on August 15, 2022, a coalition of civil society groups launched a campaign to remember the country's forgotten women freedom fighters. An event was organized at the Vijayanagar street vendor market in Bengaluru. Because of my

207

association with the Bengaluru Jilla Beedhi Vyapari Sanghatanegala Okkuta (Federation of Street Vendors Unions of Bangalore District), I was also invited. Speaking at the event, "Janaki," a street vendor, said, "We are proud of the fact that we are celebrating seventy-five years of an independent India. Proud of the fact that we have developed so much. However, we feel bad that we street vendors still do not have the freedom to undertake street vending peacefully. Every now and then we face evictions, we face harassment. Where is the freedom for us?" Mr. S. Babu, the president of the union, observed in his speech: "This event has been organized to remember the sacrifices of ordinary Indians during the freedom struggle. Working-class people like us. We are happy that the efforts of the working class are being recognized. Similarly, we ask that the role of street vendors in today's economy also be recognized. We feel that even after seventy-five years of independence, our children do not have the freedom to get a good education. Only those with money can afford a good education. What about our children? Where is the promised goal of equality?"

What is the harassment of street vendors that Janaki spoke about? There are basically two types of street vendors. One type is mobile vendors like Lakshmi who go from road to road, selling their wares from pushcarts. The other type is stationary vendors, those who stay at one place to sell their goods, often sitting on the footpath, as sidewalks are called in India (Figure 16.1). Stationary vendors face a lot more harassment than mobile vendors. The police, local municipality officials, and sometimes resident welfare associations (RWAs) try to have them evicted.[1] Police officials often collect bribes from them. Vendors are always unsure if they will be allowed to vend the next day in the same spot.

Take, for instance, the plight of vendors in Kaverinagar, a residential area in Bengaluru where both middle-class and working-class people live. One morning, after receiving a call telling me that the police were coming to remove the vendors, I rushed over. The area has a huge water pipeline running through it and a narrow park at surface level above the pipeline. A tarred road runs along one side, with houses and shops on the other side. Around thirty to forty vendors used to stand by the road beside the park, selling fruits, vegetables, and flowers from their carts. They had been vending in this place since around 2005. Over time, since this was the only large market in an area

Figure 16.1. Roadside stalls of street vendors in Bengaluru, covered for the night. Photograph by Pierre Hauser.

where there were no supermarkets, business improved. The vendors had erected some poles and tarpaulins to make shelters. However, a local politician who had bought a house on the same road, opposite the market, had tried many times to have them evicted. Apparently, he disliked having the market across from his house. Some vendors believe that visitors to his house told him that the market made the area seem like a slum, and this injured his pride. Another vendor told me that one day the local politician came home in an auto-rickshaw and asked the vendors for change to pay the driver. When they refused, he felt slighted. Another time, when he had convinced the BBMP (the municipal authority) to evict them, the newly elected MLA of the area stopped the eviction.

All these events took place before the vendors were unionized in 2014. Although these vendors became part of our union, the local politician never stopped looking for ways to dislodge them. In 2014, several members of an RWA filed a public interest litigation in the High Court of Karnataka, asking that "encroachments" on footpaths be removed across Bengaluru.[2] The High Court, in an interim order, directed the BBMP to remove encroachments. While a few shops and

210 Vinay K. Sreenivasa

some other sites were targeted, street vendors were singled out in several areas. On September 5, the BBMP—already under pressure from the local politician—evicted the vendors in Kaverinagar. Our union was unable to stop the BBMP's actions in the morning, but that afternoon we met with the mayor of Bengaluru, Ms. Shantakumari, to update her about the eviction and point out that it was in violation of the national Street Vendors Act of 2014. The mayor immediately called the area municipal engineer and took him to task. The vendors were able to resume selling their goods. Deeply relieved, "Kavita"— an affected vendor—exclaimed, "I was really worried what we would do! I had spent a few thousand rupees buying these fruits, and if we were not allowed to sell them here, they would have ripened and gone to waste." Another vendor chimed in, "It's not just today's goods. If they evict us, what about tomorrow, our future? We don't have big savings like big people. Only if we work today can we eat today."

But their relief was short-lived. In December of the same year, the area municipal engineer returned with police and evicted the vendors, claiming that their presence on the road would damage the water pipeline several feet below. This on a road where buses travel frequently, and trucks are regularly parked! The vendors called the local corporator. His phone was switched off. One of them rushed to the corporator's house on a motorbike. He wasn't home, which angered the vendors. "Manjunath," an elderly coconut vendor, raged, "Where are these people when we need them? He must have known this was happening, that's why he has disappeared, the coward!" Despite our efforts to speak to the municipal authorities and the police, we were unable to halt the evictions. The vendors were frustrated and irate, and some of them were close to tears.

Over the next few weeks, we filed a Right to Information application with the police, asking for copies of the complaint they had allegedly received from the Bangalore Water Supply and Sewerage Board (BWSSB) asking for the vendors to be evicted. It turned out there was no such complaint. We met with BWSSB and BBMP officials as well as the police and submitted memoranda about the case to them. We met the corporator and MLA again and requested their intervention. All to no avail. Some vendors were allowed to carry out their business at a spot some distance away, but not all. Others took up miscellaneous jobs—one took a shop on rent, but soon closed it since the business didn't generate enough revenue to cover the rent, let alone provide a living income. We are unsure how the majority survived. Generally, after being evicted, if vendors are not able to return to their occupation fast enough, they stop attending union meetings, so it is difficult to track what happens to them.

The Kaverinagar eviction took place although Parliament had passed the historic Street Vendors (Protection of Livelihoods and Regulation of Street Vending) Act, 2014, section 3(3) of which states that until a survey of all existing vendors is conducted, no vendor may be evicted. The act is also clear that there can be no unilateral evictions. First a notice must be issued to vendors and an alternate site of commerce selected in consultation with them. But none of these rules were followed in this case. It is possible that many in the Bengaluru administrative machinery were unaware of the act, which had been recently passed. But even after the union highlighted the violations, the plea to restore street vending in the area was not considered. In 2022, eight years after the passage of the law, several officers of the BBMP and the police continued to plead ignorance about the act and its provisions. This lack of awareness suggests deliberate neglect of this vital issue within the higher rungs of the bureaucracy.

Not all vendor evictions follow Kaverinagar's script. Nor do all result in a complete "wash-out" (a term vendors use to describe an eviction). For instance, in Gandhinagar, after a new Circle Inspector[3] took over at Upparpet Police Station, he evicted around two hundred vendors. The vendors spoke to him and tried to negotiate. They informed the local MLA. But nothing happened. Finally, the union met the area's Deputy Commissioner of Police and argued that the eviction was a violation of the Street Vendors Act. The Circle Inspector was then directed to allow the vendors to renew their business.

Krishnanandanagar is an area in northwest Bengaluru that houses several garment factories. A street vendors' market there caters chiefly to the garment workers when they walk home from work. The market opens at 3:30 p.m. and continues until around 7:30 p.m. Vegetables are sold in small heaps called *guddes*. The vegetables sold are of relatively low quality and price, since garment workers cannot afford anything more. Even bananas are sold in bunches of two to three, for the same reason. When this market began, the area had only a few houses. Street vendors sat along the edges of roads, spreading their wares on mats in front of them. A few vendors had carts. Eventually, as middle-class families bought sites in the area, built houses, and moved in, they wanted space to park their vehicles and not the hustle-bustle of vending. In an attempt to force out the vendors, some home-owners started abusing them. A resident even poured water from their balcony on them. The vendors did not block anyone's house or disturb the residents, but the newly formed RWA approached the corporator and MLA to have them removed. This angered the vendors. "Santosh" voiced their indignation: "We were here long before the houses came," he thundered, "when these were just empty sites. Many of the residents have bought things from us for so long. But now they want space for their cars, so we must leave? Why couldn't they build houses with parking facilities inside? Don't they have any humanity?"

In response, our union organized a meeting with the RWA, which the corporator reluctantly agreed to chair. But the meeting was not very successful. The corporator suggested an alternate site for the vendors on an adjacent main road, but they were afraid of using that site because of the heavy truck traffic. We mapped the existing road used by vendors and compared it to the main road. Our measurements showed that the main road didn't have sufficient space to accommodate all vendors. Moreover, it was not a pedestrian-friendly road, which meant that the customer traffic would be low. Eventually, because of pressure from the union, the RWA's threat fizzled out and vendors continued selling at their original location.

This tussle between car-parking and street vending is symptomatic of contestations around public space in Bengaluru and other cities of India. While streets are an urban commons meant to serve all, police and municipal officials are always more comfortable with streets being used for free parking rather than for livelihood activities such as vending. (Bengaluru has periodically considered a paid parking policy for public roads, but this proposal is always met with opposition and has never been implemented.) The case of Krishnanandanagar illustrates how middle-class and affluent residents of Bengaluru tend to regard the road space in front of their homes as theirs, rather than part of a commons or public space. In another example, in Koramangala, an upscale neighborhood in southeastern Bengaluru, a wide foot-path borders a park. Several food vendors operated there until they were evicted because local residents did not like the smell of chicken momos and chicken fried rice wafting into their homes—or at least this is what we were told by the police!

I could tell many more stories of such battles. When vendors are unionized, it's easier to stall evictions, obtain a stay order from courts, or negotiate their return after a "wash-out." But none of these outcomes are guaranteed. Evictions demonstrate how precarious the lives of street vendors are, even after the passage of a national law to protect their rights. They can never be sure that their place of vending will not be removed someday. And if it does get cleared, they can never be sure that they can get it back.

Despite the unrelenting precarity of their existence, street vendors contribute immeasurably to India's cities. It is popularly acknowledged that *santhes* (open village markets) were transformed into street vending as urban areas grew. Across India, street vendors offer a wide range of goods and services to the general public. While fruits, vegetables, flowers, and food items are the most well-known, vendors sell a variety of other goods, including clothes and undergarments. Brooms, utensils, watches, stationery, and books are some other goods they purvey. Vendors also provide essential services on the roads. One of the most popular services is that of cobblers, who repair shoes and other leather goods. Roadside barbers who give haircuts and shaves at a fraction of what it would cost in beauty salons are also commonplace, particularly in northern India. But vendors provide services ranging from knife sharpening, umbrella repair, and tailoring to astrology!

Street vendors benefit the city in multiple ways. Mobile vendors deliver fruits and vegetables and other services to the doorstep, a cell phone call away, thus easing the burden for senior citizens and disabled residents who might find it difficult to go to the shops. Stationary vendors provide a range of commodities of varying quality at lower cost, catering to different income levels. Many autorickshaw drivers and other working-class people eat food prepared by street vendors because it is fresh and cheap, easily available, and the quantity much larger than what is available at *darshinis* (basic roadside eateries). Similarly, people from various parts of Bengaluru come to Shivajinagar and Malleswaram to buy clothes from street vendors because it's cheaper than buying from shops.

In addition, the presence of street vendors, and therefore customers, make streets safer for all. "Abdul," a vendor in Shivajinagar, points out that when the area's vendors were evicted in 2010 the footpaths around the bus stand degenerated into public urinals. "But when vendors are present, the footpaths are always clean," he says. In fact, after the Kaverinagar eviction, a police constable told the vendors, "As long as all of you were on the street, we didn't have a single incident of chain snatching [robbing of necklaces], but now that you are gone chain snatching has started in the late evenings." "Samir," another vendor from Shivajinagar, asks, "Why are we looked down upon like this, when we contribute so much to the city? Because of us customers can get stuff at low rates, wholesale suppliers get business. We contribute to the economy, we ensure streets are safer. Why, then, are we looked down on?"

"Ahmed," a seventy-year-old vendor, goes door-to-door on Infantry Road selling fresh coconut. Items such as jackfruit, *thatinungu* (ice-apple/toddy palm), and *bhoo-chakregadde*[4] are sold only by street vendors. The same is true of many repair services. Why is this so? The reasons are simple. These activities require substantial labor and are often messy. Anyone who has seen tender coconut sellers will have noted that their shirts are always soiled. It is no easy job to handle a *macchu* (an implement used to open the fresh coconut). Similarly, cobblers are primarily Dalits. An enduring legacy of the caste system is that it is largely uneducated, landless, migrant Dalits who perform the vital service of making and maintaining footwear. In the absence of this underappreciated service, if someone's expensive footwear were to get damaged it would simply have to be discarded. (It is worth adding that cobblers are typically worse off socioeconomically than other street vendors, and many are also homeless.)

Aside from providing services to the wider population, street vending has several upsides for vendors too. It is a form of livelihood that can be pursued irrespective of one's education, without much capital investment, and it involves less toil than other alternatives such as construction work. This is why many older workers and women who quit garment factory work—and even some college graduates—take up street vending. The barriers to entry are relatively low. One might argue as well that livelihoods like street vending have prevented the country's unemployment crisis from being even more severe than it is. Indeed, a large proportion of India's urban population depends on self-employment in the unorganized sector.[5]

Despite the passing of the Street Vendors Act of 2014, and despite the multitude of benefits street vending provides to the residents of Bengaluru, vending remains a highly insecure livelihood—particularly in an aspiring "global city" that is acutely oriented to rising property values and real estate development. BBMP finally conducted a survey, as required by law, and issued ID cards to around twenty thousand vendors in Bengaluru. Of course, the number of vendors is far greater. While those with ID cards have indeed received some manner of protection, there are thousands more whose daily existence remains deeply uncertain.

The recent rise of sectarian politics in Karnataka has also made vendors wary. In many markets, Hindu and Muslim vendors work together; in fact, in a few areas most vendors are Muslims. But there have been no conflicts between the two groups until recently, when *hindutva* activists—supported by the former BJP-led state government—began to provoke anti-Muslim sentiments and intercommunity conflicts. The calls by right-wing Hindu groups to boycott Muslim vendors at temple fairs in Karnataka in 2022[6] and 2023[7] alarmed Muslim vendors in Bengaluru, who were also threatened with a boycott in 2022. However, the intervention of a local politician ensured that the boycott did not materialize.[8]

This political tumult has deepened the precarity of street vendors in the city. "Ramu," a vendor in our union, summarized the situation: "We have more challenges than before. With increasing traffic, malls, and everything, the threats to our livelihoods have increased. We had no weapons in our arsenal earlier, but now we at least have the law. This doesn't mean the threats have disappeared, but we at least have one weapon. But what we need is security. The insecurity around whether we will be able to continue vending is a cause of huge stress for us and for our families. That's why none of us want our children to take up this job. This has to end with us."

Notes

This chapter is based on my experiences working with the Bengaluru Jilla Beedhi Vyapari Sanghatanegala Okkuta, a federation of street vendor unions affiliated with the All India Central Council of Trade Unions (AICCTU). I have been associated with the AICCTU since its inception. Much of the information in this chapter is due to the collective work of the federation. I am indebted to the president, Mr. S. Babu, and other office-bearers—Mr. Swamy, Ms. Shashikala, Ms. Vanajakshi, Mr. Syed Zameer, and Mr. Fayaz Ali—and the comradeship of fellow advocate Lekha K.G. I also thank advocates Clifton D'Rozario and Maitreyi K. of AICCTU, who taught me about the law and collective work and who continue to inspire me with their work and commitment.

1. In Indian cities, middle-class RWAs often engage in legal battles against informal settlements and street vendors in their neighborhoods. On the politics of RWAs in Bengaluru, see Lalitha Kamath and M. Vijayabaskar, "Middle-Class and Slum-Based Collective Action in Bangalore: Contestations and Convergences in a Time of Market Reforms," *Journal of South Asian Development* 9, no. 2 (2014): 147–71.

2. Niranjan Kaggere, "Designer Moves HC for Safer Footpath," *Bangalore Mirror*, February 24, 2014, https://bangaloremirror.indiatimes.com/bangalore /cover-story/public-interest-litigation-jenny-pinto-bbmp-footpaths-high-court -chief-justice-d-h-waghela-chief-minister-siddaramaiah-advertising-sign-boards /articleshow/30913164.cms. See also "BBMP Told to Clear Footpath Encroachments within 3 Months," *Times of India*, July 24, 2014, https://timesofindia .indiatimes.com/city/bengaluru/bbmp-told-to-clear-footpath-encroachments -within-3-months/articleshow/38948031.cms.

3. Senior inspector in charge of a "circle" of several police stations.

4. This is a special snack sold only by street vendors in southern India; its name could be translated as "earth-sugar tuber." There is debate about its botanical name, whether it is a stem or root, and even which tree or plant it comes from.

5. National Commission for Enterprises in the Unorganised Sector (NCEUS), "Report on Conditions of Work and Promotion of Livelihoods in the Unorganized Sector" (New Delhi, 2007), https://msme.gov.in/national -commission-enterprises-un-organised-sectornceus.

6. "Temple Fairs and the Saga of Economic Boycott: Dakshina Kannada," *Sabrangindia*, January 23, 2023, https://www.sabrangindia.in/article/temple -fairs-and-saga-economic-boycott-dakshina-kannada.

7. Prajwal Bhat, "Karnataka: Muslim Traders Barred from Bappanadu Temple Fair for Second Year in a Row," *News Minute*, April 7, 2023, https://www .thenewsminute.com/article/karnataka-muslim-traders-barred-bappanadu -temple-fair-second-year-row-175598.

8. "'We live in a secular country and everyone is free to do business': BJP MLA Snubs Demand to Ban Muslim Traders in Bengaluru Religious Festival," *Indian Express*, November 29, 2022, https://indianexpress.com/article/cities /bangalore/bjp-mla-snubs-demand-to-ban-muslim-traders-8296764/.

17
Chasing Targets, Making a Life

Kaveri Medappa

It was a Thursday in late January 2020. I was both excited and nervous anticipating the day ahead of me when I got out of bed at 6:30 that morning. It was the day "Ajay" and I had picked for me to shadow him in his work as a food delivery "partner" of Zomato, a popular app-based food delivery service in India. In the five months of knowing twenty-four-year-old Ajay, our frequent meetings and telephone conversations had made him an important part of my PhD project—an ethnographic study that sought to learn about the experiences of digitally mediated work and life among app-based food delivery workers and cab drivers in Bengaluru. To gain a better understanding of such work, I had asked Ajay if I could ride with him on his motor scooter for an entire day as he went about his work. Ajay, very kindly, had agreed.

This chapter chronicles the thirteen hours I spent with Ajay as we waited for, picked up, and dropped off food orders. Shadowing Ajay allowed me to observe closely, and to some extent feel for myself, the anticipation, frustration, risks, indignities, and fatigue involved in app-based food delivery work. As much as the day revolved around Ajay chasing "targets" to earn his living, it also offered a peek into the various labors, aspirations, and solidarities that went into gig workers' attempts to carve out livelihoods in the city.

On-demand food delivery businesses like Zomato, Swiggy, and Uber Eats expanded in most major Indian cities between 2015 and 2017. Zomato and Swiggy are the largest food delivery apps in India currently. In 2019, Zomato had an estimated 250,000 delivery "partners," similar to Swiggy's (their main competitor) delivery fleet. I met more than seventy food delivery workers during my ten months of fieldwork, a majority of them in the eighteen-to-thirty age group.

Like Ajay, most "delivery boys" (as both the general public and delivery workers themselves referred to them) had been moving from one dead-end job to the other, all characterized by low salaries not exceeding 15,000 rupees (around 200 USD) per month. Expectations of higher incomes had motivated most of my research participants to take up this work. Drawn by the very attractive piece rates and incentives offered by these delivery platforms, youngsters like Ajay had quit their (mostly informal-sector) jobs and entered app-based work.

"It's Thursday. Come to the Raghavendra Swamy Temple by 7:30. We will go to the temple and start from there. And bring your helmet," Ajay had told me. When I reached the temple a bit after 7:30 a.m., I spotted Ajay driving toward me wearing his red Zomato T-shirt, which matched the vermilion mark between his eyebrows. The temple visit had been completed and it was time to start work.

7:45 a.m. We were waiting at a popular vegetarian fast-food joint. Two men wearing Zomato tees and carrying backpacks sat on its outside ledge staring at their phones. One of them was Ajay's friend "Raghu." Half-smiling at Ajay, his curious eyes darted between Ajay and me. Ajay asked him in Kannada, *"Esht-aaythu, anna?"* (How many did you finish, *anna?*). (In Kannada, *anna* means "older brother.") "One," he replied. Ajay introduced me as a "student doing research on Zomato and Swiggy," and they both chuckled as Ajay told him that I planned to spend the entire day with him to see how they work. Addressing me, Raghu said, "They keep changing incentives every week. The 900 rupees daily *minimum income guarantee*[1] is not there anymore. What was there last week is not there this week. Usually, in other jobs, income stays the same or goes up. But in this job, our *payment* keeps decreasing. How should we manage our *commitments* like this? They think we can keep reducing our expenditure as and when they change their mind!"

Raghu was older than Ajay, probably in his early thirties, and worked full-time for Zomato like Ajay. Remuneration in food delivery work, as in most other on-demand platforms, is based on a piece-rate and target-incentive model. In January 2020 every completed order fetched 30 rupees, which increased by a few rupees if the delivery distance exceeded 5.5 kilometers. Meeting targets—completing a certain number of orders—made workers eligible for (but did not guarantee) the "incentive" component of pay, because earning incentives was tied

Chasing Targets, Making a Life **219**

to adhering to several other *"rules"* laid down by the company. These rules included a strict cap on order cancellations (zero or one); "mandatory" lunch and dinner peak-hour logins, especially on Sundays; weekend attendance; "good" customer ratings; and a minimum number of weekly log-in hours (usually thirty). Although app-based work is often seen as "flexible" and as providing workers with "choice," making labor relations more egalitarian, the numerous rules governing the work process and earnings tell a different story. Coupled with this, as Raghu grumbled, working conditions had become more demanding over time, and unilateral cuts to remuneration had become the norm. The increasing gap between what these app-based delivery companies promised and what "partners" earned after repeated rate cuts led to a "strike" in September 2019, which was how I first met Ajay. Zomato delivery workers in many localities in Bengaluru and a few other cities in India had logged off work for several days in protest against Zomato's decision to slash incentives. Despite the protests, the incentive cuts were implemented.

8:15 a.m. Time moves slowly while waiting for orders. Ajay suddenly remembered that he sometimes gets an order at a famous dosa joint from a particular customer on Thursdays. "Madam, come, let's go try there." Within five minutes we were at the dosa center, and a young boy who worked in the kitchen there came out to greet Ajay. No orders. I used the time to jot down notes, but something Ajay said caught my attention. Ajay was advising the young boy, who had migrated from Davangere district in Karnataka, to "dream": "If you don't want to leave this job, it's your wish, but don't stop dreaming. It's the only thing we don't have to pay tax for," he told the boy, who smiled absent-mindedly while toying with Ajay's accelerator. The boy ran back inside saying a quick goodbye as soon as he heard his boss calling out for him.

Ajay and I chatted about Zomato having expanded the delivery location *"boundary"* for delivery workers after its purchase of UberEats—Uber's food delivery arm—earlier that month. The older delivery radius of approximately five kilometers had been expanded to include three more neighboring localities, which meant that deliveries could now be at distances as much as twenty kilometers. The remuneration pattern remained the same—around 30 rupees per order and 1 rupee extra for every ten meters exceeding 5.5 kilometers. "What do you think of this?," I asked Ajay. "Places that we don't know . . . addresses which we don't know," he said, pointing to the implications of an expanded delivery area when every second wasted looking for addresses during peak hours meant not completing orders quickly, and not receiving another order, thus being far from reaching the daily target.

9:30 a.m. Two hours since Ajay logged in, and he was yet to receive his first order. I could sense his growing frustration. We went to yet another restaurant to try his luck. Seeing no other Zomato workers there, he said hopefully, "I'm the only one now, I should get the next order." As we inhaled copious amounts of dust standing by a main road in peak hour traffic, Ajay told me about his years growing up. His father was a pushcart vegetable vendor who died in a road accident when Ajay was eleven years old. His mother passed away four years later. Ajay grew up in an orphanage, and his school education was sponsored by the institution. "Those were good days. We got food, we were sent to school, we got love [preethi], we had comfortable beds to sleep on. I slept on a double bed. Even if it was jail, it was a happy jail," he said. A few years after his mother died, his father's creditors threatened to take their three-acre farmland that Ajay's father had given as collateral for loans. Ajay started in the pre-university course (11th and 12th standards) after completing school (10th standard), but he discontinued during the second year because he had to start earning money to look after his younger brother: "That is when my life became about carrying one responsibility after another. I worked, earned money, paid off the creditors, and saved our land. There is no work I have not done [laughs]. Construction work, tea shop, marketing, courier, selling vegetables, money-lending business, doing supervisor jobs, ella maadideeni! [I have done everything!] I am all my younger brother has. I want to make him a lawyer like Ambedkar, but he wants to become an engineer [chuckles]," said Ajay as he refreshed his app again.

More minutes passed. "Appa devre!" (Oh god!), he exclaimed looking up at the sky, thanking god because he had finally landed his first order—at 9:50 a.m. Soon after Ajay had collected the food and placed it in the faded red Zomato bag placed between his feet on the scooter, the app demanded that he upload a selfie within sixty seconds. He placed the bag on the seat, pulled it closer to him, tamed his hair, and

Chasing Targets, Making a Life **221**

clicked a selfie. If the selfie did not show the food bag and Ajay's red Zomato T-shirt, his ID could be temporarily blocked.

As we began to ride to our first destination, I saw Ajay trying to reach the driver support center. He tapped several numbers into a screen, staring down at his phone instead of paying attention to the road. He drove by steering only with his right hand, his left hand focused on connecting to call support and keying in details. He had to enter several numbers before he could speak with someone, and each time he looked at the screen the scooter slowed down or veered dangerously close to other vehicles. Finally, he pressed an option that threw up multiple choices and was able to speak to someone. But I soon realized then that he was not talking to call support but had called a close friend, also a Zomato delivery worker, to vent about his "drop location" being thirteen kilometers away and his earnings only 90 rupees for the delivery. "*Map area* has enlarged, so they say I have to deliver. I won't get orders from there, so I'll have to come back *khaali* [empty-handed/without an order] from there," he grumbled to his friend. Platforms did not then compensate drivers for returning to their "zone" after a delivery.

As we were riding, Ajay suddenly turned the scooter around, mumbling about "*danger*" ahead: "*Aiyo!* Police! My vehicle insurance has lapsed, and I have some twenty cases of signal jumping. If I were alone, I would ride fast and escape. But I can't take that risk with you. Plus, if they see I have a woman sitting behind me, they will stop me for sure, thinking 'what is this *delivery boy* doing with a woman behind him'!" I had a hard time locating the police, who appeared to me as white specks very far away, while Ajay had spotted them from some two hundred meters away. To avoid getting pulled over, we rode on the wrong side of the road and then entered what seemed to be a peri-urban area, indicated by a sudden reduction in traffic, noise, and air pollution. Cows grazed on green patches of land. This hardly felt like the city, and I wondered why anyone would order one *masala dosa* and two *vadas* from so far away.[2] Are these customers even aware of the distance from which their food travels to them? Finally, in the middle of what seemed like a village, we reached a large apartment complex. As we checked in at the security kiosk, a young man with a large green Grofers bag (a grocery delivery app) also "made entry."

Somewhat puzzled and concerned by Ajay's lack of motor vehicle insurance, given that his livelihood depended on riding a two-wheeler, I asked him why he had not renewed the policy. When he said that the premium was 2,000 rupees, I suggested that he could save a portion of his earnings toward this. In response he said, "Madam, I'll tell you some numbers, keep adding them up." He started listing his monthly expenses—5,000 rupees for *cheeti kaasu* (monthly payment to a *cheeti* group—see chapter 6), 3,000 rupees for EMIs (equated monthly installments) to repay the loan on the motor scooter, 600 rupees for phone EMIs, and some interest payments for "hand [informal] loans." While reeling off these numbers Ajay would pause every now and then to ask me, *"Esht aaythu?"* (How much does it add up to?). Then he mentioned his household expenses, his brother's school fees, and the costs of fuel and servicing the scooter at least twice a month. The total came to around 23,000 rupees. "On average, if I work six days a week for a *minimum* of twelve hours, I get close to 25,000 per month [gross]. And there are other expenses which may come up suddenly—temple visits, doctors' fees, family ceremonies, and so on. Now tell me how I will save to pay my insurance?" He mentioned that he had been saving some money every month toward unforeseen expenses, but reminded me of his brother's recent hospital admission to get treated for dengue fever. He had spent more than his savings to pay the private hospital bill.

10:45 a.m. First delivery completed an hour after we had picked up the food. As Ajay had predicted, we rode back thirteen kilometers "empty." We calculated that he had spent 40 rupees for fuel on this order, so his net earnings were just 50 rupees. Just as we were entering Ajay's work zone he received another order. The restaurant was nearby, but the drop location was eight kilometers away. Ajay once again rode on the wrong side of the road. "Any way that saves petrol is our way!" he proclaimed jovially as we drove into a large, upscale gated community. We took five minutes just to reach the "make entry" point at the security gate and then had to ride to Tower P from Tower A. He mumbled to me, "Sometimes these security people act like they own us, *esht kopa baruthe!* [how angry I get!]" for being ordered around by security staff or for the unnecessary delays they create for delivery workers for whom every minute matters. I accompanied Ajay into the building to make the delivery. We reached the seventh floor and rang the doorbell. No response. We could hear a TV playing loudly inside, so we waited a few more minutes. After around ten minutes, a young man got out of the elevator and took the food packet from Ajay without even looking at his face. Ajay said "Have a good day, sir" in a soft tone, a tone that I hadn't heard him use since that morning. The man just nodded his head, took a quick look at me, and shut the door. As we rode across many speed bumps making our way out, Ajay grumbled about the time and fuel they have to waste going "round and round" in these apartment complexes. "And these damned *humps* break my back!" he exclaimed angrily.

At 11:30 a.m. we finally stopped to eat breakfast at a small home-run restaurant that Ajay knew. He had already received his third order for the day. As we ate, Ajay chatted with the friendly owner who was contemplating partnering with Zomato. "With the 20 percent commission I have to pay them I will have to increase prices," the owner said. "And if you want your hotel to be shown on top, you have to pay them more," added Ajay. "Who will pay 60 rupees for a plate of *idli-sambar*?[3] People already grumble that they have to pay 30 rupees. And I just about meet expenses and make some profit to get by." Although his business was running satisfactorily, he was tempted by Zomato's promise that his sales would increase if he used their service. His wafer-thin margins discouraged him from becoming a "restaurant partner," but he also expressed insecurity about his decision as he noted that more and more small, independent eateries in the locality were partnering with Swiggy or Zomato.

On our way to our next delivery, I noticed that Ajay was not following the map on his phone. We were in the older part of Ajay's neighborhood, and the class distinction between the old and the new parts were very visible as we rode through very narrow streets where small houses stuck to each other and absent-minded cows sauntered about. As he handed over the food packet to a woman, Ajay requested her, "Please give five-star rating, madam." As we rode back, he explained, "In this work, we have to gulp shame. Some people feel embarrassed to ask for ratings, but every five-star rating gives me 10 rupees. Not everyone has this *ratings bonus*. Ten such ratings and I earn 100 rupees. That's one and half liters of petrol, and I can make four to five deliveries with that. I have to make all these calculations, madam. What to do, *life-e-lekkachara!* [What is life but calculations!]."

Ajay would often wave to friends he spotted on the road who were also doing delivery work. Sometimes they would ride slowly alongside one another while they caught up on how many orders they had gotten, how many hours they had been logged in for, and where they were headed to next—before zooming off to pick up or drop a food order. These moments of sociality punctuated the monotony of delivery work. Ajay was also constantly on the phone chatting to friends, often greeting them with *"Esht aaythu?"* (How many did you finish?). In the more than thirteen hours I spent with Ajay that day, I did not see him even for a minute without at least one earphone attached to his ear.

Delivery workers in Bengaluru have created area-based WhatsApp or Telegram groups to communicate with each other, and it is common for them to talk to friends as they ride around the city. These practices not only create a sense of community and keep workers' spirits up, but they are also a source of social support in dealing with the risks of app-based work. Indeed, delivery app companies take little responsibility for risks and emergencies such as accidents, run-ins with the police, vehicles getting towed away, drunk or rowdy customers refusing to pay money for the food, or getting mugged—leaving gig workers to devise their own mechanisms of ensuring safety for themselves.

1:40 p.m. Another order, another sprawling apartment complex. "This apartment is a little strict, so wait outside," Ajay told me. I was relieved to spot steps in front of a store and eagerly walked toward them, caring little about the thick layer of dust on them. All I wanted was to rest my sore lower back against something solid. It was evident why Ajay, all of twenty-four years, had developed chronic backache. I looked down at my beige trousers to find lines of brownish-gray wherever they had creased. Rubbing my eyes felt like I was rubbing them with sandpaper thanks to the dust that had settled all over my body, including on my fingers and face. This reminded me of how several delivery workers had called this a job "without a *future*." "How long can we work like this, roaming the streets, drinking dust and pollution every day?" While heading back, Ajay and I spoke about the heat and wondered how bad April and May will be if January is like this. *"Navella baradgettogideevi madam* [These conditions have hardened us]. I have lost all my *glamour,"* Ajay joked. Later, he showed me a picture of himself with a clean-shaven face and pointing to his skin tone said chuckling, "See how nice-looking I was!"

Our eighth order came at around 2:45 p.m. 36 rupees. As we reached yet another large apartment complex, the security guard rudely instructed Ajay to stop outside the gate because he needed to take his photograph. By then the Zomato app also demanded another selfie from Ajay. Ajay told the guard in Hindi, his tone a mixture of annoyance and slight anxiety, *"Ek minute bhaiyya, idhar mera selfie lena hain"* (Wait a minute, brother, here I have to take a selfie). After sending Zomato the selfie, Ajay posed for a picture for the security guard. I saw a board for MyGate, a popular app for security solutions, hanging on the tall gates of this apartment complex. When Ajay went inside the upscale building, I sat down on a ledge in front of the apartment complex. I was immediately instructed by the security guard to get up from where I was sitting and sit on another side. I was getting irritated at the way we were being ordered around. While riding back I asked Ajay how he felt about being spoken to so rudely, and he replied cryptically, quoting a popular Kannada saying, "Madam, it doesn't matter if the cloth flies to the thorn or if the thorn gets stuck on a cloth. In the end it is the thorn that gets blamed. So, it's better I do whatever they ask me to."

It was close to 3:30 p.m., and my hunger pangs were intensifying. Ajay, too, was hungry and suggested going for lunch. "Yes, I could eat," I told Ajay coolly, trying to contain my excitement at the thought of food finally hitting my stomach. I entered a restaurant, and the pictures of food displayed on its board never looked more appetizing to me. Just as I turned to wait for Ajay, he announced, "Madam, *order banthu* [another order has come]. Ice cream. Let's go." I let out a sigh as I dragged myself away from the restaurant. At close to 4 p.m., when the hunger pangs of customers had been taken care of and mine had died a slow death, we finally had the chance to eat. As we were served food, Ajay's friend from Zomato, "Bhaskar" *anna*, joined us. I had met him once before, also in the protest against Zomato in September 2019. Bhaskar *anna* was having a bad day—he had been allocated only three orders since 9 a.m. "I have earned 90 rupees so far. Out of that 50 goes for petrol. *Bejaar aaguthe ee kelsa maadakke* [I feel sad/frustrated to do this work]."

Ajay consoled him saying that he was also not having a particularly great day and was yet to touch the first target (ten orders) despite being logged in for about eight and a half hours. Feeling *bejaar* (a Kannada word commonly used to express sadness/melancholy/frustration) was an inescapable part of being a delivery worker. Sliding incomes, periodically slashed incentives, hours of unremunerated time spent waiting for orders, motorbikes getting towed, missed targets, rude and arrogant customers, and the despotic blocking of their IDs by companies like Zomato with little scope to dispute such treatment were among the reasons workers felt *bejaar*. But friends and coworkers often lifted each other's spirits and provided the emotional support they needed to keep going.

However, despite the many disappointments and risks in platform work, several delivery and driver "partners" described app-based work as an "addiction": *"Aiyo! Idu apheeem thara!"* (This work is like opium!), an Uber driver once remarked. The unpredictability of orders and earnings kept workers hooked as they anticipated that the next hour may be better than the previous one, that the dinner peak might turn out to be less "dull" than the lunch peak, or that tomorrow's earnings might be better than today's. Workers stayed logged in for longer and longer hours in the hope of hearing that ear-splitting alert on their phones indicating a new order. In 2019, the generous rates and incentives with which these businesses had first lured workers to these jobs had long disappeared. With delivery platforms ruthlessly slashing rates and incentives, workers had little "choice" but to chase targets by spending long hours at work to try to make earlier levels of income.

As we were eating lunch, Ajay got an order from the same restaurant. That was Ajay's tenth order, and with that we had completed the first target. This meant that Ajay was eligible for 250 rupees as incentive pay, provided he logged in for the dinner peak that night and did not cancel any orders.

6:10 p.m. Another order. By then I was getting exhausted from all the riding around and the monotony of picking up and delivering orders—even though I was not the one doing the labor of driving the scooter and walking to collect and deliver orders. After delivering our twelfth order at 7 p.m., Ajay was out of cash and made a few calls to friends to borrow some money. We met a friend who lent him 200 rupees. Such financial "adjustments" among coworkers and friends occur almost daily. It is common for delivery workers like Ajay to discuss their credit scores (CIBIL scores, which workers often pronounced as "*civil scores*") and to be preoccupied with keeping up with loan EMIs, as defaulting on loans would lower their CIBIL scores and foreclose the possibility of getting more loans. Apart from informal "hand loans" and *cheetis,* workers were often steeped in debt to make up for their steadily falling incomes. These included loans offered by private financial businesses and fintech apps to which platform businesses refer their "partners." Drivers are also often indebted to one of many loan apps on the Google Play Store, which charge extremely high interest rates (more than 30 percent for a seven-day loan tenure), usually based on sharing one's Aadhar card (national identity card) details plus any other form of personal identification. Our discussion of loans reminded Ajay of his overdue credit card payments. As if making a mental note, he said, "I will tell them I don't have the money to keep paying their high interests and ask for a *final settlement* when they call next."

Thirteenth order, 8:10 p.m. Ajay's calf muscles were hurting and he had started asking customers in buildings without lifts to "please come down halfway to meet him on the stairs." He had to be careful while making these requests so as to not ruin his customer rating scores. Ajay called customers as soon as we reached their houses and decided whether to make this request based on their tone. I was exhausted too and would have given anything to be able to lie down and rest my back. I had a sharp pain in my lower back, my upper thighs had gone numb, and I was covered in the fumes and dust of the city from head to toe. Ajay had to make two more orders to reach his second target, upon which he could earn 400 rupees as incentive. I asked him if he was tired. "I am, but it's a *waste* to go home now with only two more orders to complete the *second target.*" On our way to deliver the order, Ajay got a call informing him that a close friend's daughter had been admitted in the hospital. Ajay stopped by a popular chain supermarket to buy some fruit to give to his friend's daughter. He swiped his overdrawn credit card and bought apples, oranges, and kiwis.

After our thirteenth delivery at close to 9 p.m., we decided that I should go home. Ajay had been logged in for more than thirteen hours, and he had earned 550 rupees from all his deliveries. I asked him if he will work tomorrow with his leg and back hurting. "I have to. My scooter EMI is due for the past two months, and I have to pay at least one month's EMI to keep my vehicle with me," he said. "My *commitments* have increased after coming to this job. Who knew they would cut rates and incentives like this? They made us trust them and then slit our throats *[nambsi kath kuythaare]*. Expenses have increased, incomes have decreased. I have to find ways to cut down on my expenses," he explained.

After reaching home and taking a shower, I called Ajay to thank him. He had finally logged out after reaching the second target. He had completed fifteen orders in a little more than fourteen hours. His order earnings had reached 640 rupees, and he had received 400 rupees as an incentive, bringing his total gross earnings for the day to 1,040 rupees. *"Mosa illa alva madam?"* (It's not bad, no madam?), he queried, his voice perkier than when I had left him an hour ago. After deducting expenses, he had made 700 rupees for the day. I said something about his daily earnings being less than minimum wage, considering that he had exceeded the standard eight or nine working hours a day. *"Aiyo, mayy-dam!* Show me which factory or office follows all these rules. If they did, why would I need this *vanavaasa?"* (The word *vanavaasa*, inspired by the Indian epic Ramayana, is used in everyday parlance to refer to a prolonged period of hardship/pain). After a few more minutes of chatting, he ended the call saying, "Goodnight, madam, I know you are also waiting to sleep. Tomorrow is Friday. Weekend. Let's see, hopefully I will reach the *third* or *fourth target."*

Notes

This chapter is based on in-person ethnographic fieldwork that I carried out between June 2019 and March 2020 in Bengaluru for my PhD project. Shadowing workers for part or the whole of their workday was one of the research methods I used to better understand app-based worker experiences. Fieldwork was carried out solely by me, and conversations with workers and other interlocutors took place in Kannada and Hindi.

1. When not translated into English, quotations from conversations with my participants are provided with English glosses. Within translated quotations, italicized words or phrases in English are English words or phrases that workers regularly used while speaking in Kannada or Hindi. Translations from Kannada and Hindi to English are mine.

2. These are popular breakfast and snack dishes in South India.

3. Another popular breakfast dish.

18
Serving the New Middle Class

Swathi Shivanand

The arrival of the new apartment complexes around "Karmikara Colony" did not initially entice "Lalitha" into expanding her geography of work. While many other women in her neighborhood transitioned into working for households in these towering buildings, Lalitha stayed resolutely faithful to her longtime employers in the old, elite neighborhood of Malleswaram in whose houses she had begun her journey as a domestic worker and where she had transitioned to working as a cook.

"They are rich only in name," she said when we asked her why she did not work in the new apartment buildings. She recounted an instance when she had agreed to work in a "Punjabi" household for a monthly salary of 5,000 rupees (about 30 USD), but fifteen days after the end of the month she had not been paid. When Lalitha asked for her salary, her employer gave her only 2,500 rupees and said that she would be paid the full amount only if she came to work twice a day (terms that had not been agreed to initially). Lalitha promptly told her employer to find someone else and quit the next day. "They didn't even give me money for the fifteen extra days I had worked, and I didn't go back to ask for it," she said in disgust.

For Lalitha, such treatment at the hands of this employer at "Golden Springs" apartments was a complete contrast with her longtime "Brahmin" employer in Malleswaram (see chapters 2 and 20). Over the twenty years she had been working in the Malleswaram household, the employer-employee arrangement had evolved into a patron-client relationship, where her employer's assistance extended to other parts of Lalitha's life: "They have helped my family a lot, and whatever we are today is because of them. They educated my children.

Whatever problem I've had, I've told them about it, and they've helped me. My children and I have eaten their food," Lalitha said, using the colloquial phrase "eaten their food" to refer to what she considered their benevolence. This relationship with her Brahmin employer was so important for Lalitha that if the timings for a potential cooking job at other houses clashed with her timings at this house, she refused these opportunities. Instead, she would refer her relatives (sister or daughter-in-law) or acquaintances to these workplaces.

From working at seven to eight houses when she first started domestic work, Lalitha had settled into three houses where she worked regularly and only cooked. This is typical of older women domestic workers who work in three or four houses, in contrast to newer and younger domestic workers whose bodies allow them to work in as many as seven or eight houses. Working in multiple houses is essential for most domestic workers because they are only employed part-time, typically working one to two hours in each house, and do not have access to any social security benefits. The wages earned in one house are so low that it is not enough to sustain life in the city. Most domestic workers either do the work of cleaning houses (sweeping, mopping, washing utensils and clothes) or cook for the household. Cooking is better paid and more valued than housework, perhaps because it involves less manual labor and is considered more skilled work.

For Lalitha, the way her employers treated her was central to her calculations and desire to continue to work in these households. She spoke about another employer—who had moved from Malleswaram to one of the large apartment complexes around Karmikara Colony—who helped her by posting flyers in her building to advertise her availability for domestic work. These relationships of patronage, with their attendant benefits and dignities, are crucial considerations for working-class women like Lalitha when deciding where to labor.

Another domestic worker in Karmikara Colony, "Sharda," who had been working for about two decades for a family in Malleswaram, told us that she found her job in that house comfortable. While the apartment complexes seem luxurious, the payment is often low, at about 2,000 rupees, she said. Another reason she gave for not choosing to work in the new apartments was that most people there are renters and could leave anytime: "What will I do if they say they are leaving the house and going elsewhere? I know I won't lose the Malleswaram houses." Such explanations for why households in older, elite neighborhoods such as Malleswaram are preferred over new apartment complexes reveal how domestic workers make employment choices based on who they think are more permanent residents in the city.

Lalitha and Sharda belong to an older generation of domestic workers in Karmikara Colony, an area that has typically serviced the elite and upper-caste residents of neighboring Malleswaram. Over the years, as the new style of apartment complexes built by large real estate companies started to come up all around the colony, many women residents have been drawn to domestic work for the residents of these apartments—largely professionals and business families from different parts of India. Conversations with several residents of the colony indicate that women undertake domestic work for various reasons—to augment household incomes, or because they are the primary earners, or to become financially independent.

In the areas where these workers live, people often expressed the notion that the arrival of modern apartment complexes had improved the locality. This improvement included the increase in opportunities for domestic work, which allowed women to earn more than previously possible. One Karmikara Colony resident claimed that domestic workers could now earn up to 10,000 rupees per house: "Sometimes I feel you can earn more money in these kinds of work [domestic work] than after studying for so many years and struggling to find jobs."

However, such perceptions of high earnings were misplaced. Women typically earned around 2,500 rupees a month in each household (so, if they worked in four homes, they could earn 10,000 rupees—less than the prescribed minimum wage in Karnataka for most jobs). Even this income could be precarious, as the amount of work expected of a domestic worker could keep increasing without a commensurate increase in wages. "Nalini's" experience with her employer revealed the exploitation that is built into this unregulated domestic work in the informal sector. Her employer, a resident of a large apartment complex, had loaned her a sum of money as an "advance" (Nalini could not recall the exact amount, which is not surprising given that illiteracy or low levels of education are common among women domestic workers). Nalini said that for three years her employer deducted 5,000 rupees per month from her salary against this advance, paying her only 1,000 rupees. Although Nalini felt that she had repaid the loan amount in

232 Swathi Shivanand

full, her employer disagreed, claiming that she still had an outstanding sum to repay. Meanwhile, Nalini's workload had steadily increased. From sweeping, swabbing, and washing vessels and clothes, her tasks multiplied to encompass cooking, walking and bathing the employer's dog, and even putting out the coupon for the milk delivery man the next day. All these tasks meant Nalini could leave the workplace only by 8 p.m. every day. When Nalini finally quit her job, her employer repeatedly sent her driver to coax Nalini into returning to work.

Nalini's experience of exploitation as a domestic worker is not uncommon. Several factors contribute to the devaluation of her labor. Domestic work is dominated by poorly educated and low-income women and is largely unregulated. Wages are further depressed because women's income is usually considered secondary within a household. Further, the fact that in domestic work the workplace is a home—a place of caregiving and not a factory shop floor or other such worksite—has meant that female domestic workers are not recognized as workers. Although it is paid, domestic work is considered an extension of women's ordinary care work, carrying with it expectations that women workers would treat the employer's home as their own by providing endlessly extendable labor. In India, where the culture of servitude has a long history, defining the relationship of patronage between "servant" and employer, could we see Nalini's quitting her job as her refusal of a new, undesirable kind of servitude that was expected of her from her employer?[1] Without the attendant benefits of patronage, the relationship between Nalini and her employer was purely one of exploitation. Could we say that, when she finally quit, Nalini sought to reorder the relationship to one of an employer-employee wage relation?

Although Nalini may have refused work in an exploitative workplace, a look at the daily schedules of domestic workers reveals the large extent of toil that marks their day. While she was working in this household, Nalini used to wake up at 4 a.m. to finish her own household chores, which included washing, cooking, and getting the children ready for school. Once she reached the employer's house at 10 a.m., she would take the dog out for a walk, make juice and breakfast for the employer, sweep and mop the floors, and wash the kitchen utensils, finishing by noon. After cooking lunch for the employer and cleaning up after the meal, Nalini returned home at 3 p.m. to do additional household chores, feed her children, attend to their needs, and drop them off for their after-school classes. She would then return to her employer's house by 6 p.m., serve her juice, cook dinner, put the dog's bed in her bedroom, put out the milk coupon, and finally leave at 8 p.m. When she returned home, she would immediately set about cooking dinner for her family and finish any remaining domestic work.

Nalini's tightly choreographed daily schedule is all too common among domestic workers. The daily routines several of them narrated to us demonstrate how the clock dictates their days. Of course, this "double burden" is not new for women who carry out unpaid labor at home and are also employed in paid work. Work in the export-oriented ready-made garment industry, the other common source of employment for women in Karmikara Colony (and in Bengaluru generally), also demands strict adherence to the clock. However, domestic work allows a measure of "flexibility" that "accommodates" women's reproductive labor and caregiving responsibilities in ways not possible for garment workers employed in factories, with their inflexible shift timings. Women in domestic work are able to return home in the afternoons to cook lunch and take care of children; at times they can adjust their schedules to take care of ailing family members. This "flexibility," it should be noted, does not diminish the quantum of work undertaken in a single day; instead, work expands to fill the entire day.

While opportunities for domestic work have grown enormously with the unbridled growth of the city and has become a key source of employment for women, such employment remains almost entirely informal, with all the uncertainties and precarity of such work. Unlike the garment worker, who if employed in an export-oriented factory will be paid at least the minimum wage and provided state-mandated benefits such as health insurance and contributions to retirement schemes, domestic workers have only their bodies to draw upon for their income and security. The specter of their dispensability is ever-present. As Lalitha pointed out: "What do we get when we stop working? As long as our hands and legs are strong, we can eat from our earnings. After that? We think that we worked here for twenty-five years, there for thirty years, but when we cannot work anymore, they say goodbye to us and will have someone in our place the next day. We don't even get holidays, no increment, no bonus. The government has done nothing for us."

Her words, spoken in 2017, were prescient—during the Covid-19 outbreak and subsequent lockdowns, Lalitha was unemployed for two years. Her employer in Malleswaram had passed away, her second employer had left the country, and her third employer had reduced her schedule to two days a week. Her husband had also passed away, and she and her daughter struggled to pay rent for the house they had moved into during the second lockdown, forcing them to pawn her daughter's gold jewelry to pay part of the advance on rent required by the landlord. From a monthly income of 12,000 rupees before the pandemic, Lalitha's earnings had dwindled to nothing during the lockdowns. When we met her again in late 2021, Lalitha had just started working as a cook in a nearby apartment building, where her job was to prepare food twice a day for a family of four. When reminded that she used to prefer to work at houses in Malleswaram, she said that this is still her preference, but now she has no choice but to seek employment with the affluent households in these towering complexes.

Lalitha also explained how she must navigate through the apartment's security system. She has to allow her bag to be checked while exiting, cameras follow workers like her everywhere, and she must sign a daily log while entering and exiting the apartment. Elaborate security apparatuses, which service personnel must negotiate to enter and exit gated residential complexes, have become a common, even expected, feature of middle- and upper-middle-class life in these residential enclaves that provide an exclusive space for affluent city dwellers to separate themselves from other social classes (Figure 18.1). They are also symptomatic of the vast economic and cultural divide between domestic workers and their well-heeled employers, who often do not speak the local language of Kannada.

"I work on the twenty-eighth floor in an apartment building with twenty-nine floors. They apparently bought the flat for 3 crore [30 million] rupees (around 450,000 USD) and spent another 30 lakh [3 million] rupees on interior decoration," Lalitha said. The family where she is now employed is of mixed regional backgrounds, and only the father speaks Kannada well. "They don't value money," she said. "If I happen to arrive a little late, they would have ordered food from outside. The children don't even finish their food and throw away the leftovers," she exclaimed. Lalitha's evaluation of her new employers and workplace also reveals the discomforts of witnessing the rapidly changing social composition and mores of the middle-class households that employ her.

Figure 18.1. Security guard at entrance to a high-end mixed-use complex, central Bengaluru. Photograph by Pierre Hauser.

The transformation of the landscape around Karmikara Colony has different meanings for older domestic workers such as Lalitha. Apartment complexes signify changes not merely in the built form but also in the social relationships that were fostered by the old bungalows of Malleswaram. While relationships between employers and domestic workers in old middle-class neighborhoods were also unequal and exploitative, they were marked by a degree of mutual dependence and intimacy—in contrast to the more impersonal terms of employment in the new gated communities. Lalitha's transition from the elite neighborhood of Malleswaram to the enclaved spaces of apartment complexes also illustrates the changes taking place in the realm of informal work, as workers negotiate the loss of somewhat stable, older patron-client relations and grapple with their entry into distantiated work spaces.

Notes

This chapter draws on fieldwork conducted by Hemangini Gupta, Kaveri Medappa, and Swathi Shivanand.

1. See Raka Ray and Seemin Qayum, *Cultures of Servitude: Modernity, Domesticity, and Class in India* (Stanford: Stanford University Press, 2009).

"Purvapur Lake" foaming due to severe water pollution. Photograph by Pierre Hauser.

Part VI
Ecologies of Speculation

The foundation of any cityscape is the environment, which includes the social practices of the people who manage the commons of the city and its surrounding and foundational ecological terrain. The commons can range from managed pastures, forests, and water storage tanks on the rural periphery to open-air markets and vibrant commercial street life in the city center. As a city of lakes atop the Mysore plateau, Bengaluru exists because of its history of constructing and maintaining a complex infrastructure of hundreds of water bodies connected by channels flowing across the undulating terrain. Its vitality depends upon the community-based maintenance work of watersheds, wetlands, aquifers, and catchment areas in the green belt surrounding the city.[1] But because of rapid urban expansion over the past few decades and building and infrastructure projects that completely ignored or built over much of this infrastructure, today the city is starved of water yet also periodically flooded by it—a twin dynamic that marks the limits to the future of the city.[2]

This section details the detrimental environmental impacts of rapid urbanization on the city's intricate waterscape. It explores this crisis from four perspectives. "The New 'Commons'" (chapter 19) describes the fragile coexistence of residents of a lower-middle-class settlement, "Karmikara Colony," with the recently built high-rise complex that abuts it. The conversion of a public playground in the colony into a fenced urban park is one source of tension. "Leakages of Affluence" (chapter 20) reveals how wastewater runoff and sewage overflow from the gated community into this older locality has become an additional flashpoint. These incidents have convinced the lower-income inhabitants of Karmikara Colony that their powerful, wealthier, and inconsiderate neighbors can swing outcomes in their favor with the connivance of bureaucrats and politicians.

238 Part VI. Ecologies of Speculation

"Guarding the Lake" (chapter 21) takes us back to "Purvapur," where the lake, once central to life here, is in utter disrepair thanks to unfettered urbanization. Choked with hyacinth and toxic runoff, the lake regularly spews clouds of chemical-smelling white froth, as if protesting its abuse. While residents worry about the existential loss of their tank and the perceived ire of the lake goddess, its traditional guardian, a group of middle-class activists wants to clean up and revitalize it as an urban lake, fenced to keep out "encroachers" (and thereby traditional livelihood users as well) and encircled by a jogging path to provide a recreational space for exhausted IT employees. The contests around "Purvapur Lake" highlight not only the ailing state of Bengaluru's once-vibrant water bodies but also the question of who should have a say in the repair and upkeep of the city's lakes.

The section concludes with "Reinventing the City" (chapter 22), an interview with well-known environment activists Bhargavi Rao and Leo Saldanha of Environment Support Group, who offer their reflections on what has gone awry with the city and how it might be salvaged through the democratization of city governance, with neighborhood representatives empowered to equitably direct the trajectory of Bengaluru's social, political, and ecological future.

The chapters in this section demonstrate that when the environmental foundation of the city is devalued—treated as sites for the dumping of waste or free for extraction, regarded as valuable only as a revenue-generating asset or collateral for debt—ecologies become highly volatile and produce life-altering ruptures. When city leaders mandate "forever growth" without considering the characteristics of nature, they may have created a future of irreparable damage. These chapters highlight the importance of understanding the city's complex socio-ecological history, the value of the practices of managing or governing the commons throughout recent history, and the importance of deliberative democracy as a road map for future sustainability and social justice.

Notes

1. Harini Nagendra, *Nature in the City: Bengaluru in the Past, Present, and Future* (New Delhi: Oxford University Press, 2016); Amrita Sen, Hita Unnikrishnan, and Harini Nagendra, "Restoration of Urban Water Commons: Navigating Social-Ecological Fault Lines and Inequities," *Ecological Restoration*

39, nos. 1–2 (2021): 120–29; R. D'Souza and H. Nagendra, "Changes in Public Commons as a Consequence of Urbanization: The Agara Lake in Bangalore, India," *Environmental Management* 47, no. 5 (2011): 840–50; Eesha Shah, "Telling Otherwise: A Historical Anthropology of Tank Irrigation Technology in South India," *Technology and Culture* 49, no. 3 (2008): 652–74.

2. Malini Ranganathan, "Storm Drains as Assemblages: The Political Ecology of Flood Risk in Post-colonial Bangalore," *Antipode* 47, no. 5 (2015): 1300–1320; Shubhra Gururani, "Making Land out of Water: Ecologies of Urbanism, Property, and Loss," in *Death and Life of Nature in Asian Cities*, ed. Anne Rademacher and K. Sivaramakrishnan (Hong Kong: Hong Kong University Press, 2021), 138–58; Michael Goldman and Devika Narayan, "Water Crisis through the Analytic of Urban Transformation: An Analysis of Bangalore's Hydrosocial Regimes," *Water International* 44, no. 2 (2019): 95–114.

19 The New "Commons"

Eesha Kunduri

"Karmikara Colony" is a small residential area in Yeshwantpur, a former industrial hub of Bengaluru whose origins date back to the early 1960s (see chapter 11). The urban development authority at the time, the City Improvement Trust Board (CITB), had allotted house sites here to workers relocated from a nearby informal settlement, where mill workers, unorganized sector workers, and dairy farmers had built their homes on some open land. About 150 families out of nearly 200 that were living there had agreed (after some persuasion) to move to this new settlement. "Radha," a former garment factory worker who now works as a domestic worker in nearby apartment buildings, recollects that the allotment began from a road adjacent to a former factory in the area. This road was locally called "onti line" (solitary line) because it was separated from the rest of the houses in the locality by a small open space.

Older residents speak fondly about the *kere* (tank) next to which Karmikara Colony was built. Since several households in the colony owned cows and were supplying milk to nearby middle-class localities, the CITB built a cattle shed next to the *kere*, where residents could graze and water their cattle. The *kere* and its surroundings were used by the residents as a space of work, leisure, and sociality, where women would gather to wash clothes and young people would go to swim. Longtime residents recollect that the *kere* even attracted people from nearby areas for fishing.

The *kere* was not just a shared community resource that supported livelihoods; it was part of a larger, interconnected system of *keres* that supplied water to the city. "Ramakrishna," a seventy-three-year-old resident of Karmikara Colony who was earlier employed at

240

a nearby factory, recalled that the water from the *kere* flowed downstream to Juganahalli Lake, from where it connected further to Aane Park (Elephant Park)—an open space that also used to be a tank. These memories of the *kere* and its uses recall a time when the tanks were interconnected through the *rajakaluves* (channels) that had not yet been disrupted by the concretization of the city (see chapter 21).[1]

Like many of Bengaluru's *keres*, this one was probably seasonal. As urbanization and construction activities replaced what Harini Nagendra calls the "wetland-agricultural-grazing-orchard-landscape," which acted as a recharging basin around *keres*, tanks began to dry up (see chapter 2).[2] However, neighborhood memories narrate a story of declining water levels in Karmikara Colony without reference to the larger processes of land transformation in the areas around the tank. It is possible that the *kere* was deliberately drained. As the significance of the older *keres* in the city's water provision system declined, they began to be blamed for causing illnesses such as malaria as well as for flooding. In any case, residents narrate the transformation of a pristine and well-loved *kere* into a large, empty ground.

Even after the *kere* disappeared, the open ground continued to be a common space utilized by local people for livelihood needs such as grazing cows and for social activities such as celebrating festivals. Much like the *kere* which it replaced, this ground had functional, recreational, and cultural significance for the people of Karmikara Colony. As a resident recollected, until a few years ago the annual Ganesha festival was celebrated on this ground with orchestra shows, amusement rides for children, and small stalls selling snacks and cheap goods.

However, this community space came under threat when various actors tried to claim this "public" land for diverse uses: the local MLA wanted to build a school and a cowshed there, while officials of the Bangalore Development Authority (BDA, which superseded the CITB), supported by a few powerful individuals in the neighborhood, floated a plan to make house sites on the ground. These attempts to divert the land for other uses were strongly opposed by "Venkata Naidu," a resident of the nearby middle-class locality of Malleswaram and brother of a well-known community leader. Venkata Naidu wanted to develop this open space as a sports ground for the benefit of the local community.

Naidu, along with some residents of Karmikara Colony, led a successful struggle against these attempts to divert this common land for other uses. He claimed that a nexus of city planning officials, local politicians, and influential residents stood to gain financially from the proposed conversion of the ground into house sites. According to other older residents, the BDA had even carved out and allotted about two dozen house sites. Residents of Karmikara Colony staunchly opposed this appropriation of the ground by bringing various illegal actions of the BDA to the notice of the Lokayukta (ombudsman who receives complaints about corruption). The residents advocated against the proposed conversion by meeting with ministers and chief ministers to press their case and by filing a court case. They also formed a citizens collective led by "K. C. Ravi." One of the arguments advanced during the case was that the BDA's own rules mandated that every neighborhood should have a park, school, and other such public amenities.

Venkata Naidu, who was well into his eighties when we met him in 2017, had retired from his job at Bharat Heavy Electricals Limited (BHEL, a large public-sector enterprise) in 2009. He started his career in 1969, when he was about twenty-five years old, working at the Mysore Porcelain factory in Yeshwantpur (later acquired by BHEL). He was offered this job because he was a very good football (soccer) player. (Because public-sector companies sponsor sports teams and competitions, they often offer jobs to skilled sportspersons.) Naidu used to play football regularly at the nearby Malleswaram ground, and he was instrumental in developing and maintaining it as an open space accessible to everyone. His ambition was to develop a similar sports ground in Karmikara Colony—a neighborhood that he often visited because his siblings lived there. Several residents who knew Venkata Naidu supported his plan to develop a playground for the children of the locality.

When *galaate* (disputes) over the ground emerged, Venkata Naidu argued with the officials and politicians who wanted to put the land to other uses. The residents of Karmikara Colony were divided—while some stood by Naidu in his efforts to create a well-equipped sports ground, others considered him a nuisance getting in the way of these plans to "develop" the area. Venkata Naidu recollects spending several years "running from pillar to post" in his efforts to prevent the ground from being converted into house sites, negotiating with local officials and politicians, and refusing bribes (of cash and land) to stand down. He remarked, "I could have become very rich if I had accepted the money. But I did not want money. I wanted a playground for children."

In this struggle against the "land-grabbers," Venkata Naidu received support from a prominent local politician and a high-ranking bureaucrat who sent a bulldozer to level the land to make a sports ground. The bureaucrat even donated 25,000 rupees (about 3,000 USD in the late 1960s) to cover the costs. Having spent a lot of money out of his own pocket, Naidu was very grateful for this generous donation. Several senior residents of Karmikara Colony also credit the chief minister of Karnataka at the time for halting the plan to create house sites on the land.

Venkata Naidu has meticulously preserved an old sketch of the plan for the playground on a large piece of chart paper in his small office at the Malleswaram ground, which nearby schools now use for their sports classes. This office space, which is adorned with pictures of tournaments from Naidu's youth, was built by the local MLA, who also appointed Naidu as honorary secretary of the Young Boys' Football Club of the area. The chart paper, tearing at the folds, bears testimony to the fact that Naidu had come up with the plan for a sports ground at Karmikara Colony way back in 1981. The sketch has detailed descriptions of the boundaries of the land and a proposed division into various pitches—marking out areas with names and careful numerical measurements of the space needed for basketball and tennis courts and fields for football and *kabaddi* (an Indian-origin contact sport), among other amenities. Comparing this sketch with what the ground later became—an upscale urban park developed by the real estate company that built Golden Springs (see chapters 1 and 20)—"Anand," the assistant secretary of the Young Boys' Football Club (also Naidu's aide), exclaimed that the redeveloped park "does not even have a football field!"

Venkata Naidu envisioned a large sports ground open to people of all ages and from different social classes. A small room with sports supplies was constructed to house the Karmikara Colony Sports Club. When numerous letters to the Greater Bengaluru Metropolitan Corporation (BBMP) requesting them to donate sports equipment for the club brought no response, Naidu spent his own money to buy the equipment. Support from some well-wishers helped him in this pursuit. Numerous sports events and tournaments were organized by the sports club, while schools in the vicinity also made use of the grounds for their students' sports activities. The sports club also served as a resource center for local women—it housed sewing machines donated by a local charity where women could learn to sew and undertake tailoring work. Like the *kere* and the common ground that preceded it, Naidu's recollections of the Karmikara Colony playground and sports club suggest that it served as an important recreational space for children of the neighborhood, including young girls. Moreover, the ground was used for neighborhood festivities. While the old ground was a "commons" that provided various resources and amenities for the use of the local community, its transformation into a sports ground marks a purposive (re)imagining of the commons, even as it continued to be a space for neighborhood sociality that was open for collective use.

This long history of an urban commons was drastically disrupted in the early 2000s as Yeshwantpur was transformed from an industrial zone into one of Bengaluru's real estate "hot spots" (chapter 8). With the construction of "Golden Springs"—a high-end mixed-use development—next to Karmikara Colony, on land vacated by a relocated factory, the BBMP outsourced the redevelopment of the playground to the real estate company that built Golden Springs. While the exact modalities of this handover are unclear, it appears that the MLA and corporator of the area facilitated the "adoption" of the ground by the developer, reflecting the BBMP's post-1990s policy of inviting corporate sponsorship for the development and maintenance of public spaces such as road medians, traffic circles, and parks (leading to several protests against privatization). The ground was transformed into an upscale, gated urban park, with tracks for walking and jogging, a skating rink, a basketball court, and cricket nets. It also has restrooms, a facility providing purified drinking water, and steps on which people can sit under the trees to relax.

With this upgrade, the park began to be used by residents of the new apartment complexes in the area. Middle-class children attend paid sports classes, wearing uniforms and led by a coach (Figure 19.1), while children from lower-income Karmikara Colony and other nearby working-class localities play with sand and plastic buckets in another corner of the park. Unlike the ground in its former avatar as

Figure 19.1. Children from "Golden Springs" apartments taking roller-skating lessons in repurposed "Karmikara Colony" park. Photograph by Pierre Hauser.

a community space, which was open around the clock, the new park is shut and locked from 10 a.m. to 4 p.m. Like most parks in Bengaluru today, it is open to the public from 6 to 10 a.m. and from 4 to 8 p.m., guarded by security personnel who sometimes prevent children from relatively modest backgrounds from entering even when open.

As real estate and infrastructure investments refashion Bengaluru into a "world-class" city, urban commons like the Karmikara Colony ground bear the brunt of this transition. When private companies step in to develop and manage these public spaces through "public-private partnerships," often using (mandatory) corporate social responsibility (CSR) funds (supposedly earmarked for social welfare and developmental activities), they are quietly converted into privatized or exclusionary spaces. Commenting on the seemingly inclusive yet visibly elite nature of the transformed ground, "Narayan"—an older resident of Karmikara Colony—said: "Anyone can come, they say, 'no problem.' [But] only people from Golden Springs come here!" Another resident said that they are no longer permitted to hold the Ganesha festival in the playground as they used to.

However, some residents of Karmikara Colony perceive these

changes as an improvement over the former playground, arguing that keeping it under surveillance is important to "value" the new park and maintain its facilities: "If they keep it open, people will damage the plants," a resident rationalized. Another remarked, "Well, parents should be able to set aside some 500 rupees per month for sports, right? Even that is very important for the child." Countering the perception that only affluent residents of the apartment complexes access the park, a senior resident of Karmikara Colony remarked that his grandchildren also attend skating classes there—reflecting changing aspirations, class identities, and household spending practices among the older residents (see chapter 11). However, some of the older residents mourn the loss of the commons—first of the *kere* and then of the open sports ground. As a senior resident remarked, "If you ask the new people, they may say this is an improvement. [But] I still remember the cool breeze that used to come all the way from the *kere* and hit our house."

The story of the transition of Karmikara Colony's *kere* and sports ground is not unique: it gestures to what many neighborhoods across Bengaluru have seen over the years: the disruption and eventual disappearance of their ecological commons by urbanizing processes, and subsequent moves to privatize them. Nonetheless, since urban commons have always witnessed heterogeneous users and multiple (often competing) claims, urbanization has simultaneously given rise to new struggles over the commons, ranging widely from restoration efforts to collaborative governance models—not without critiques.

Venkata Naidu mourns the destruction by the BBMP, in collaboration with the real estate company, of everything he had helped to create—playing fields and courts and the physical space of the sports club. He is deeply pained by the usurping of the neighborhood commons. He says he has not visited the park in several years because it distresses him to see what has happened to the space. "Nobody will remember people who do good work," he lamented. "Today, they would have not had the ground if I had kept quiet long back. There would just be more buildings there." His tone cannot hide the painful fact that the history of the struggle for an open-access, reasonably well equipped sports ground has been erased from the memories of Karmikara Colony residents. This forgotten history is also one of camaraderie and sociality, created through mutual struggle, contestations, and claims to the commons in a rapidly transforming city.

Such claims are increasingly difficult to sustain in the "world-class" city Bengaluru aspires to be. At their office at the Malleswaram ground, Naidu's aide Anand bemoans the failure of the city and the state government to provide funds to keep the sports ground afloat. Instead, to organize neighborhood tournaments they are made to pay fees to the BBMP. When asked whether they receive an honorarium for their services to the area's football club, Anand laughs and shakes his head: "*Anna* [older brother, referring to Venkata Naidu] has spent so much money on this ground and on that Karmikara Colony ground. If he still had all that money, he would have been a rich man today."

Notes

Kaveri Medappa and Swathi Shivanand contributed to this chapter.

1. Harini Nagendra, "Maps, Lakes and Citizens," *Seminar* 613 (2010), https://www.india-seminar.com/2010/613/613_harini_nagendra.htm.

2. Nagendra.

20

Leakages of Affluence

Swathi Shivanand

"Vani" invited us into her aging, multistory house on the "onti line" (solitary line) of "Karmikara Colony" to show the damage that had been inflicted on her building after "Golden Springs," a sprawling high-rise apartment complex, was built right behind her house (discussed in chapter 1). Water flowing down the slope from the parking lot of the complex had begun to stagnate against the ground floor of Vani's house. This had caused a persistent mold to develop on the walls of her kitchen and bathroom. Occasionally, the damp walls would even cause mild electric shocks to members of her household. Vani's troubles were further exacerbated by the overflowing sewage outside her house, which often flooded her house as well. This was again thanks to Golden Springs, which, she claimed, had connected its sewage system to the small pipeline running outside her house, which had been unable to bear the load of the excess sewage from the complex. Her complaints to the municipality had been to no avail. Finally, one day, extremely frustrated at having to clean her house repeatedly of sewage, she complained to the local corporator, "Kumar," telling him, "I am a Lingayat, and I am being made to clean the waste of other people. If this continues, I will commit suicide!" Whether it was Vani's invocation of caste honor, her threat to commit suicide, or both, the corporator finally swung into action. Changes were made to the sewage system such that it flowed away from Vani's house.

This apartment complex, which had caused Vani and other residents of the colony so much trouble, is part of an enclosed, high-end "integrated township" that also includes office towers, a hospital, and a shopping mall, built on forty acres of land purchased by the developer from an industry that had closed down. When asked how the area changed after this modern township came up, residents of Karmikara Colony waver between noncommittal responses, such as "the area has improved," and a detailed inventory of the troubles that it had caused. Land values and the rental market may have seen an upward surge, benefiting some residents (chapter 11), but discontent was also simmering. In the interval between the closure of the factory and the start of construction, residents recall, the area had become *kadu* (wild). Just before construction was to begin, an unexplained fire on the vacated plot had burned down plastic water tanks on the roofs of neighboring houses and caused panic. Residents suspect that the developers set fire to the woody areas as a way of quickly clearing the place. During the construction phase, dynamite blasts to crush boulders had caused intense noise and even led to cracks on the walls of nearby houses. In protest, angry residents of this colony threw stones at the construction site and even blocked trucks from entering the site. The local MLA had to step in to smooth frayed tempers.

Many residents hinted or openly speculated that connections between the MLA and the real estate company that built Golden Springs had allowed them to violate building codes and planning norms without consequence. Kumar, who belonged to the Indian National Congress when we first met him, had an antagonistic relationship with the developer as well as with the upper-middle-class residents of the new apartment complex. He laid out in detail all the problems the new development had caused to the colony, ranging from the escalating cost of living (higher rental prices) to overburdened sewage lines and increased traffic density. He mentioned in particular the waste recycling unit within the complex, which created bad odors and attracted mosquitoes. "I am not against development, but this is spoiling the peace [of mind] of people," he said.

While the worst-affected households were those located next to the compound wall that separates the colony from the apartment complex, this development also had wider neighborhood-level impacts. "Ganesh," Kumar's brother (who assisted him in managing the ward), said that groundwater depletion in the area had become a grave concern after the apartment complex was built. Earlier, bore wells could tap water at 150–300 feet, but now they needed to drill as much as 900 feet to find water. Although Ganesh's assertion that the apartments had dug nearly four hundred bore wells could not be verified, the claim gestures to the general sentiment that the apartment complex had overburdened and monopolized local resources.

What further bolstered this sentiment is the social distance that the residents and management of the apartment complex seem to maintain from the older settlements in the neighborhood. Kumar, for example, claimed that he had never set foot in the complex. According to Ganesh, the security guards were instructed not to allow anyone other than residents and authorized service providers to enter their premises. Nor do their new neighbors wish to interact with their local representative, the corporator. Ganesh said, "They're enclosed in their compound and live like they're in another city." Residents of this exclusive enclave did not figure in the corporator's electoral calculations, since even the small fraction of upper-middle-class residents who do vote in municipal elections generally do not support the party to which the corporator at that time belonged, the Indian National Congress. Even when the apartment management requires government assistance, they approach the area MLA, who belongs to the Bharatiya Janata Party, or other political representatives or government officials, bypassing the corporator and local government: "If we say anything, they say 'prime minister,' 'chief minister'—what can we do?," Kumar rued.

These remarks reflect the popular view that the large real estate companies that develop such middle-class and elite gated communities accrue power in the city by leveraging their connections with officials and politicians in the higher echelons of government. A common sentiment among residents who have faced the adverse impacts of the construction of a large apartment or commercial complex in their vicinity is that these "hi-fi" connections—a colloquial term to refer to elitism—allow developers and their customers to bypass rules and regulations with which more "ordinary" residents must comply.

"Suresh," the founder of a local NGO that had fought against encroachments on stormwater drains in Yeshwantpur, gave an example of this cronyism. He pointed out that in the case of Golden Springs, the developer had managed to get away with building over a stormwater drain, while other buildings had been demolished for the same violation. To him, this was a clear instance of how powerful business interests are favored by the city's governing elite. Severe flooding during the rains in recent years had compelled the Greater Bangalore Metropolitan Corporation (BBMP) to undertake a much-publicized "encroachment clearance drive," targeting buildings that had been built over these major drains, or *rajakaluve* (channels that in the past connected the city's tanks and absorbed runoff). In August 2016, in the area around the complex, 1,093 homes were identified for demolition for the same violation (although only 141 houses were demolished). "Of the 1,093 violations on that list, Golden Springs was also one of them. Why did the law apply to 141 houses but not to the apartments? When an SWD [stormwater drain] is also passing under the complex, why is it not subject to the same punishment borne by the 141 houses? Hundreds of JCBs [earthmoving machines] were brought in overnight, large numbers of administrative personnel, the BMTF [Bangalore Metropolitan Task Force], and the police were brought together to bring down the 141 houses, but where are they when it comes to Golden Springs? This is what we are asking," Suresh argued.

Suresh's NGO had filed a public interest litigation on the issue of stormwater drain encroachment in 2016, also naming the shopping mall next to Golden Springs. However, the BBMP commissioner declared that the stormwater drain had become "lifeless" and hence there was no merit in the complaint. Because so much "development" had already taken place, the BBMP refrained from taking action. "We knew the decision was already made," Suresh asserted, referring to the "hi-fi" connections that the builders of such complexes enjoy. He explained the nexus between real estate companies, politicians, and the municipal government in this way: "If a husband and wife are fighting with each other and a third person comes in, then the husband will support the wife and the wife will support the husband."

The stormwater drain issue came up regularly in our conversations with Kumar and his brother as well. Like Suresh, Kumar claimed that the apartment complex indeed had been built over a stormwater drain and that the builders had diverted the drain away from the complex. Further, although stormwater drains are meant to carry only the excess runoff from the rains and the overflow from tanks, Golden Springs had (illegally) linked their sewage network to the stormwater drain. The developers deny this allegation, but then "why is it that the stormwater drain close to Golden Springs has water flowing through it on all 365 days?," Kumar asked, laughing.

Golden Springs may or may not be guilty of the encroachments and other illegalities of which it is accused, but these conversations illustrate the general atmosphere of mistrust. It was perhaps because of local residents' mistrust of the real estate company's intentions that their offer to supply the local park with recycled water from their treatment plant was turned down: "Why do we need their water? Let them use it to wash their cars," Kumar said. Although the area MLA had supported the proposal to lay pipes to supply recycled water from the apartment complex to the local park, some residents opposed the scheme, claiming that such water had caused skin irritation when used on plants.

What was particularly galling for Kumar and his associates is the way in which the developer had imprinted its brand identity on the physical landscape of the neighborhood. Residents had begun to view several new developments—such as road works undertaken by the BBMP—as developer-led projects. Similarly, the old playground—which was "adopted" by the developer and transformed into a middle-class green park with a skating rink, walking track, and other sporting facilities—now displayed prominent signs crediting the developer with this makeover (see chapter 19). Because entry to the park was tightly controlled, some residents of Karmikara Colony demanded that the BBMP should resume its management. Ganesh said, "They would keep it locked most of the time. But we will leave it open to the public." Although most parks managed by the BBMP are also closed between 10 a.m. and 4 p.m., what is significant is the contention that public concerns are best addressed by local people such as himself and their local representative, the corporator.

The real estate developers and residents of the apartment complex stand outside this dense network of social and political relations that characterize the neighborhood. The antagonism expressed by the corporator and other residents is directed at this interloper status, which elite enclaves perhaps strive to retain by bypassing local government and remaking common spaces in their own class image.

Even as these conflicts play out over the space of Karmikara Colony, Vani grapples with the everyday difficulties of having powerful, inconsiderate neighbors all around her. Lacking the capacity to upgrade her home and build stronger walls, as several of her neighbors did to deal with the seepage, she struggles to retain tenants in the upper floors of her house. This problem is of great concern, because she and her husband are aged and are dependent on rental income. Vani often wonders if she should have sold their house in the early

Figure 20.1. Unpaved "onti line" road running along boundary wall separating "Karmikara Colony" and "Golden Springs." Photograph by Pierre Hauser.

2000s, when the developer offered to buy all the houses in her lane. (Acquiring all the properties on the onti line would have enabled direct access to the park on the other side of the lane for residents of the gated community, but the developer did not succeed in this effort; see Figure 20.1.)

This tense coexistence between the gated community and its lower-middle-class neighbors is a story that plays out in other parts of the global city as well. These frictions may not challenge the onward march of large real estate projects and the bureaucratic and political nexus that sustains it. But they do challenge the powerful urban visions, promoted by the state and finance capital, of large-scale developments as signs of progress *for all* by foregrounding the unequal negotiations that take place between the enclave elite, ordinary residents, and the local state in the speculative city.[1]

Notes

Kaveri Medappa contributed to this chapter.

1. For more on the experiences of Karmikara Colony and Golden Springs, see Hemangini Gupta, "In Bengaluru's Gated Communities, New Forms of

Civil Engagement Are Emerging," *Economic and Political Weekly* 53, no. 39 (2018), https://www.epw.in/engage/article/bengalurus-gated-communities-new-forms-civil; Hemangini Gupta and Kaveri Medappa, "Nostalgia as Affective Landscape: Negotiating Displacement in the 'World City,'" *Antipode* 52, no. 6 (2020): 1688–1709.

21
Guarding the Lake
Priyanka Krishna

"Purvapur," located at the far southeastern edge of Bengaluru, is in the throes of breakneck urbanization. Real estate development, property speculation, expropriation of rural lands, and a burgeoning rentier economy have upended the area's agrarian ecology and mode of life (see chapters 2 and 3). "Purvapur Lake," once central to life here, is in disrepair. The lake lies at the tail end of the three valleys comprising an interconnected drainage system of over one hundred lakes (or tanks) across the city. It is one of the few lakes remaining in Bengaluru that has not dried up, only to be encroached on by private developers or used by the city government to create public facilities. But it is not uncommon for residents to have to wade through cottony froth on the road that runs along the lake's embankment, as the lake now and then bubbles from a toxic overload of sewage, effluents, and pollution—as if resurrecting itself from the dead to make its abuse known. This doesn't deter a resident of one of the new luxury highrises nearby from posting on her social media handles about how wonderful it is to wake up to the "view" of Purvapur Lake.

The dystopia is palpable. Even as everything is breaking down—shortage of clean water, no drainage, poor sanitation, a sense of apprehension among locals about the dizzying pace of change—there is a thrill of anticipation mixed with anxiety about what the future holds for Purvapur. Will I lose my land to the government for lower compensation if I don't sell it now to a private buyer? Instead of toiling in my fields for an uncertain income, isn't it smarter to sell my land now, to have money in hand for my children's marriages or to buy a car? Attempts to resurrect an ailing lake are symptomatic of the tensions tugging at Purvapur's fraying rural fabric.

The tale pivots around struggles that have sprung up around the lake as it transforms from a rural tank that was once the lifeblood of a

256 Priyanka Krishna

thriving agrarian economy into an urban lake claimed by new constituencies. This momentous shift involves changing sensibilities about the lake as well as an attempt to install a new regime of access and governance. At the center of this contestation around who "owns" the lake are sometimes converging but often diverging claims—by those who side with the lake's traditional guardian, the lake goddess Devi Duggalamma, and those allied with its new guardian, "Sriramu," a locally powerful landowner and environmental activist.

Devi Duggalamma, as the legend goes, was brought to contain the lake after several attempts to do so by building embankments failed. The temple dedicated to her, where once multiple paddy fields were fed by an outlet from the lake, suggests that she arose from the lake. As a Shakti goddess, Duggalamma is both beneficent and punitive—indeed, an embodiment of the lake. In the popular imagination of Purvapur's residents, the material realities of water and its governance have long been associated with her and ancillary goddesses. Numerous cultural rituals have anchored what local residents view as their collective duty to a life-sustaining force. The frothy turbulence, the frequent mishaps in recent years due to the overflowing sewage on the road along the lake's embankment, and deaths by drowning, among other adverse incidents, are read by many as signs of Duggalamma's ire about the lake's ill treatment. It is as though Duggalamma is expressing the wider unease with ongoing transformations in Purvapur.

This is not to say these urbanizing transformations are unwelcome, especially when traditional livelihoods like farming and fishing have already become increasingly unviable, if not impossible, due to growing water scarcity and the systematic decimation of the lake. "The Peripheral Ring Road will be built very soon and will come right here, and that's when I will sell my land," says "Palani," a native of Purvapur. And with the infusion of real estate capital—in the form of luxury apartments, commercial properties, "villa" developments, and new roads and infrastructure—the stage has been set for the emergence of a fast-growing peri-urban middle class. Sriramu, the local lake activist and a software engineer, is upwardly mobile but also armed with the traditional vestments of caste power. Emblematic of this burgeoning rural middle class, Sriramu embodies the larger shift from an agrarian ecology to a commercial economy, and a lake in transition from an earlier relationship based on water's collective use values to a now more privatized relationship centered around middle-class aspirations, property values, and speculative gains from land-related transactions.

The Arrival of Duggalamma Devi

Picture, if you will, Purvapur: a land of abundance, functioning as the principal commercial and hydrological node of a constellation of thirty-six villages around it. A lake bursting at its seams was the nucleus for these agrarian settlements. In a depression of nearly twenty feet, downstream from the lake, stands the temple of Keri Eerie Banda Duggalamma (Duggalamma Who Rose from the Lake). According to the legend, after it proved impossible to contain the lake's overflow during the rains despite raising the height of the *bandhs* (embankments), residents brought Devi Duggalamma from Davangere, 285 kilometers away, to keep the lake from flooding the village. Duggalamma, as an embodiment of the lake, is revered as well as feared. The lake was the primary source of sustenance for the village, providing for a variety of rural livelihoods and operating as a place of thick sociality. A wide range of crops was cultivated in the village, including water-intensive paddy, several types of vegetables, and fodder for dairy farming. "Shyamili" and her sisters remember how as children, when they needed quick money for sweets, they would go to the lake, catch fish with their bare hands, and sell it in the market. "Ammu" remembers swimming in the lake. With eyes brightened by memories of yesteryear's defiance, she told me, "My mother would warn me not to go to the lake. But in the evenings, I had to take cattle to graze, so I would not heed her warnings and would go to the lake and dive into the canal flowing next to the lake and frolic with my friends." Others remember taking a dip in its crystal-clear waters—so transparent one could see a coin on the lake's bottom clearly. Women remember washing clothes and chatting until late by the lake.

Every year, the village community would come together to desilt the lake. "Rehman" tells me about how the villagers would work to remove the silt each summer when the lake dried up. He explains that had the silt been left to accumulate the lake would have lacked the capacity to sequester water, risking flooding in the monsoons. Also, farmers used silt from the lake (and to some extent, still do) as manure.

258 Priyanka Krishna

Without provocation, as if it needed to be said, he tells me that in those days Muslims weren't discriminated against but that Dalits did face prejudice and ill-treatment in the village.

Even today, the Dalit settlement in the village is located far from the lake, illustrating how spatial arrangements mark and reinforce relations of dominance and hierarchy within the agrarian landscape. Ammu, a Dalit woman, spoke of how the labor of desilting fell mostly on Dalits. She recalls being paid a sum of 5 rupees for each load of silt. She adds that Dalits were not allowed to fetch water from the wells and that water would be poured into their hands by the upper castes rather than offered to them in drinking vessels. Yet the lakes remained accessible to all.

Silt was also collected from the lakebed to be sent to nearby brick factories, one of the main nonagricultural enterprises in the area. Such uses of the lake reflect its status as a rural commons. The local community cultivated a strong affective relationship with the lake. Even Sriramu, the self-styled environmental activist and upper-caste landowner, addresses the lake as "Mother." Every year, villagers would gather for a celebration in honor of Devi Duggalamma. A goat would be sacrificed, and a meal featuring the goat's meat would be offered to devotees. The lake's use and governance were steeped in a sense of collective duty and deep spiritual entwinement. The lake was imbued with agency through Duggalamma as nurturer, provider, and punisher.

On one of our walks around the lake, Sriramu explains to me with pride and in elaborate detail how his grandfather, who was the president of a temple, had successfully reinstalled the idols now celebrated during the festival by the villagers. Both of Sriramu's parents had at different times held the position of president of the village governing body, the gram panchayat. Rehman reiterated this association between divine and political power, observing that everybody listened to only one person concerning the lake—the panchayat president, who normally belonged to the Reddy community (an upper caste).

A longtime resident, while explaining to me about the goddess, said that I should think of Duggalamma as the village's "security guard." This observation reflects how the goddess has been absorbed into the vocabulary of the world-class city. Security guards have become ubiquitous in apartment complexes and office buildings in Bengaluru, and the once thriving paddy fields close to the Duggalamma temple are now heavily secured real estate. One day, when I entered the Devi Duggalamma temple, I was surprised to find a man locked inside. "I have the key," he declared. Telling me that he came from Uttar Pradesh, he claimed that he had been hired as a watchman for the temple.

Indeed, the fields that were fed by the lake were among the very first to be sold to developers. They are now owned by land aggregators, real estate companies, and private investors. These lands, like Duggalamma's temple, are all gated and guarded.

"Bengaluru's Bathroom Water"

"After real estate came, the farmer died," says "Rajneesh." It is not clear when the deterioration of the lake began. But in Purvapur, Bengaluru's dramatic changes over the last several decades have had significant consequences for the lake and consequently for the villagers. "Arnav," another local resident, claims that it was after the Intermediate Ring Road was built in the city that the lake started to get polluted. For many villagers, Bengaluru is their nemesis, which decimated the lake and their livelihoods. For them, the first signs of the deterioration of the lake was the infiltration of *neer soppu* (water hyacinth) and the arrival of catfish (a threat to other species in the lake). "When they started to allow water from Bangalore to enter the lake, it started dying," says Arnav. This started close to fifty years ago, according to the villagers. Sriramu half-jokingly tells me that if anybody in Majestic (in central Bengaluru) flushes the toilet, the waste reaches Purvapur Lake in exactly five minutes! The pollution in the lake is compounded by its location at the tail end of Bengaluru's network of interconnected tanks.

Several factors have contributed to the lake's ill health—sewage ejected by upstream restaurants and apartment complexes lacking the mandatory sewage treatment plants, factories releasing effluents, and developers dumping construction waste. At times, quick fixes for lakes upstream, fueled by middle-class activism, end up diverting sewage downstream, which compounds problems for lakes at the system's lower ends. The insufficient sanitation infrastructure of an expanding city aggravates the issue. In 2005, all fishing in the lake stopped. This was also the year that developers and land aggregators began buying up land in the area, in collusion with local politicians and brokers, speculating that prices would soar as the real estate market heated up (see chapters 3 and 7). Many residents, particularly those from marginalized communities, parted with their lands at low prices, through compulsion, ignorance, or trickery. By some accounts, by 2012 Purvapur was already plagued by water scarcity. Without even one foot of clean water in the lake and a falling water table, growing a water-intensive crop like paddy became impossible. A few farmers who continued to cultivate paddy spoke of developing skin allergies. The remaining farmers who hadn't sold their lands increasingly came to rely on borewell water supplied by tankers to grow crops. An acre of land, depending on the crop in question, required three tanker loads of water per week at a cost of 1,200 rupees, which proved unsustainable for most. No wonder many of Purvapur's cultivators say there is no "use" of the lake anymore—it is just "Bengaluru's bathroom water."

Resistance and Co-optation

The unease of villagers with the lake's degradation finds expression in incidents they attribute to Duggalamma's ire. Several deaths by drowning in the lake and the growing number of accidents on Purvapur's narrow main road are blamed on the goddess's wrath. There is palpable discomfort and a lingering feeling among villagers that they have not fulfilled their duty of protecting and preserving the lake. An older resident, narrating a drowning incident that took place during the immersion of Ganesha idols in the lake (during an annual festival), told me, "How can we expect the gods to remain silent when immersed in sewage water?"

However, many view the ongoing social changes in the village, the proliferation of real estate projects, the rise of rentier and service economies, and the water tanker business as necessary signs of progress. "Sunil" is among the many local farmers who sold their land early, drastically limiting the gains he could have made from the new real estate market. He comes at dawn to collect "fodder" (actually invasive weeds—not a traditional source of cattle feed!) from the lake to feed his cattle, from which he makes a living selling milk (Figure 21.1). I asked him if he regrets having sold the land when he did,

Figure 21.1. Collecting hyacinth from polluted "Purvapur Lake" to use as fodder for cattle. Photograph by Pierre Hauser.

and about what has become of the lake. He shrugs, saying, "We can't be stuck in time. We have to move forward."

A yellow Porsche whizzes down the main road. "Palaniamma" has converted her single-story house to four stories with ten rental units, at a cost of nearly 8.5 million rupees (about 115,000 USD). The construction was financed through her share of the proceeds from the sale of her father's land as well as a loan from her son-in-law. The family has taken out a bank loan to purchase a tractor to ferry water to supply the building; they tell me the tractor will soon be seized if they are not able to clear their bank debt. Despite trying to capitalize on the new economy by diversifying their source of income, they lament, "Perhaps it would have been best had we remained farmers."

I watch apprehensively as Duggalamma herself is co-opted into these furious changes, traversing the city by way of water tankers that announce the new borewell economy with the name "Duggalamma Water Supply."

A new crop of high-rise apartments and several smaller multi-story apartment buildings boast views of the forlorn lake. A motley set of modest three-story buildings on a deserted street desperately mimic their richer cousins—the high-end apartments developed by well-known real estate firms—with names such as "Lakeview Apartments." The apartments strain to catch a glimpse of Purvapur Lake, frothing at a distance.

Reimagining the Lake

While Devi Duggalamma is revered as the protector of the lake and the village, after the incorporation of Purvapur into Bengaluru municipality it is city government agencies—such as the Bangalore Development Authority (BDA), the Bruhat Bengaluru Mahanagara Palike (BBMP), and the Bangalore Water Supply and Sewerage Board (BWSSB)—that were assigned joint responsibility for management of the lake, under the supervision of a lake warden. The current warden of Purvapur Lake is Sriramu, who also heads the lake-rejuvenation efforts through a local citizens' group called "Purvapur Rising."

Sriramu belongs to an influential landowning family of Purvapur. As mentioned above, his parents had both served as president of the gram panchayat and were key political figures in the locality, giving him generational authority. Sriramu is well educated, working as an IT professional in a city software firm. He thus holds both old caste and class power as well as the modern cultural capital of a higher degree and a professional occupation. He is upwardly mobile, with the ability to comport himself in the English language and urban middle-class society, which other villagers see as aspirational. In many ways, Sriramu can easily identify with the new residents of the area who live in the new apartment complexes—largely IT workers and middle-class professionals (see chapter 4).

Sriramu attributes the dismal state of Purvapur Lake to several factors—including sewage flowing from the city, unregulated disposal of waste by local vendors, and the changing demography of the village—and with it, a diminishing sense of connection to the lake. The untenability of using the lake for agriculture, along with the official absorption of Purvapur into the city, the rampant conversion of land into real estate, and the imposition of various regulations (such as prohibition on the construction of durable structures within a certain distance of the lake boundary), have created a new social ecology around the lake. Purvapur's proximity to key IT hubs such as

Whitefield has drawn IT employees to the area—some as residents and others who buy apartments or land here as an investment. This movement in turn has spurred the emergence of a new service economy, drawing migrants who are employed as low-end service workers and live in rented accommodations in nearby villages.

This explains the mushrooming of squatter settlements around Purvapur Lake—the only sites where poor migrant workers can afford to live on their paltry incomes. Local landowners rent out uncultivated agricultural land to waste pickers and other service workers, where they stay in plastic tents and are given access to water for around 500 rupees (6 USD) a month. Since the National Green Tribunal has mandated that permanent structures cannot be built within seventy-five meters of a water body, this strategy allows landowners to generate income from land that cannot be sold or used otherwise. Several such settlements can be seen around the lake, some of which resemble small villages with their own shops. Sriramu claims that one such camp of waste workers, some employed by the BBMP to separate dry waste, dispose of some of the waste that cannot be sold in the lake. He also claims that many of these settlers are illegal Bangladeshi migrants (see chapter 3).

Even as Sriramu decries the newer middle-class residents' lack of connection with the lake, his ideas for its development borrow directly from the imaginaries espoused by middle-class activists across Bengaluru. His revitalization plan includes fencing the lake to keep out "encroachers" (including villagers who are still engaged in livelihood activities around the lake, such as collecting fodder) and constructing a jogging path around it. But most of his negotiations with the authorities to get his plans approved have failed. For instance, the Detailed Project Report that he submitted to the BDA for consideration was rejected. Sriramu complains that the planning authorities do not understand that Purvapur's water body is now an "urban lake" and should be managed as such. Although his plan for converting the lake into a middle-class recreational site risks marginalizing the few remaining traditional users of the lake, he is unconcerned: "If people want to use the lake, they will find ways to use it anyway." He cites an instance when, after fencing the lake, fodder collectors broke the fence at several places to gain access.

Now that the lake's diverse livelihood functions have been flattened out—and with rent becoming a major source of income for local residents—its value for many these days is its contribution to local property values. Like Sriramu, many of Purvapur's older residents also imagine a lake with boating and a park around it. They would like their children to have access to urban parks and playgrounds like the ones they see in the city. According to a villager, their local MLA had promised to turn the lake into a tourist spot like Ulsoor Lake, with boating and other recreational activities—a proposal they endorse. Others, referring to the IT workers living in the nearby apartment complexes, tell me earnestly, "Won't they get tired after working long hours? It will be good [for them] to have a lake to run along after their tiring days."

Sriramu's leadership of lake-rejuvenation efforts must be viewed against the social power he wields in the village. Purvapur Rising, the collective he heads, is an offshoot of the civic action group Whitefield Rising—a group of well-meaning middle-class and affluent residents (many employed in the software industry) who work together to solve civic problems such as poor solid waste management. "Abel," who started rejuvenation efforts at Purvapur Lake in 2013, explained that he was distressed to see the sorry state of the lake every day while passing by.

The efforts of these voluntary associations have been wide-ranging, requiring them to engage with various city agencies such as the BDA, BWSSB, BBMP, and the state government's Minor Irrigation Department—which themselves are embroiled in jurisdictional conflicts over the management of the city's peri-urban lakes. Dealing with multiple departments and cognizant of a funding crisis adversely affecting the upkeep of lakes, Purvapur Rising mobilized funds from private sources, established connections with relevant NGOs, and solicited CSR (corporate social responsibility) funds from private companies to help in the rejuvenation efforts. Abel initially identified Sriramu as a "volunteer" who ensured that the silt trap installed in the lake was maintained. Later, he called Sriramu and his allies partners in the common cause of rejuvenating the lake. While a leader of Whitefield Rising described fencing the lake as their group's first success, Abel noted that the fencing excludes the lake's multiple stakeholders. He also characterized the jogging path as a "noose" around the lake that blocks water inlets.

The vision of the lake itself is a source of constant debate within the group, with some members holding up Marina Beach in Singapore as a model. Abel's position is that as long as the water quality is maintained, lake-rejuvenation efforts should be transferred to local residents, which will ensure that their vision is realized through consensus. While Abel says that Whitefield Rising avoids "conflict" situations, Sriramu asserts that the people of Purvapur only know how to access government services *through* politics. In his view, "the challenge of Whitefield Rising is [precisely] that it is apolitical." Here we witness the collision of two different political sensibilities, one distinctly urban and middle class, the other peri-urban and still rooted in agrarian sentiments and modes of collective action.

The proposed transfer of responsibility for the management of the lake to local people through a collective is fraught with challenges. For one, social power in the village is still distributed along existing structures of caste and class. Sriramu, for instance, speaks of inviting all the villagers to meetings to discuss the future of the lake. However, for many the social profile of Purvapur Rising, and especially the prospect of debating the English-speaking Sriramu in a public forum, is intimidating: "Sriramu continued his postsecondary school education in an English medium college, but I dropped out because I always imagined tilling land is my destiny as a farmer," said Rajesh, elaborating on why he had to leave the meeting convened to discuss the lake issue when the language of discussion changed from Kannada to English.

As debates swirl around the lake's future, the effort to widen the road adjoining the lake and adjacent to the Duggalamma temple led to another proposal—to shift the idol and abode of the goddess to a different site. This move, which would divorce her from the lake, provoked ongoing protests. And, in a surreal twist, the president of the temple society proposed installing a borewell on the premises of the Duggalamma temple—built for a goddess who was originally brought to the village to stem the abundance of overflowing water!

Note

This chapter is based on field research carried out by Priyanka Krishna.

22
Reinventing the City

Michael Goldman

Untangling the multiple influences to understand Bengaluru's current predicament—of a rapidly degrading environment marked by floods and intensifying water scarcity, growing social inequalities and exclusions, and unsustainable urban growth—is not an easy task. Instead of data-driven analyses of these changes, in this book we have explored Bengaluru's urban crisis through the stories and voices of people who have shaped the new Bengaluru, as well as those of ordinary citizens trying to live and survive in the speculative city. Indeed, it is only through the experiences and perceptions of the city's residents that we can come to understand the significance of what we have called "speculative urbanism" (see introduction).

Our final chapter delves into the assortment of processes that have dragged the once verdant city to an environmental precipice, and how we might reimagine Bengaluru's urban future, through a conversation with two researcher/activists who have a deep grassroots appreciation of its social ecology—the evolving entanglements of nature and society as Bangalore underwent its "Great Transformation."

Bhargavi Rao and Leo Saldanha are well known to Bangaloreans as allies, advocates, and nemeses. They helm the research, campaign, and advocacy organization Environment Support Group (ESG), which works on a range of environmental and social justice issues in Bengaluru and beyond. Given the centrality of water in Bengaluru's ecological crisis, we asked them how water has shaped the way in which they apprehend the city and their work as activists.[1] The conversation recounted below was edited for clarity.

266

Michael Goldman [MG]: How would you say water has shaped your lives?

Bhargavi Rao [BR]: I was born and raised in a neighborhood very close to Jayanagar. When I was a child we used to go to Lal Bagh Botanical Garden every Sunday, as it was almost in our backyard. The neighborhood was cosmopolitan, and my neighbors were Hindus, Christians, and Muslims. Many different languages were spoken—so, as a child, I easily picked up all these languages as I played with other children in the neighborhood. Apart from Kannada [my mother tongue] and English [the language of my schooling], I could interact in Hindi, Tamil, Telugu, even a bit of Malayalam.

I was schooled in Christian institutions, lived amid Muslims in a Hindu-dominated neighborhood, and grew up in a religious Hindu family. During my youth, people of all religions lived freely together and celebrated one another's festivals and cultural traditions. I fondly remember the midnight Christmas carol singing, which was a regular practice in the neighborhood, and also receiving sweets during Ramzan. That spirit, however, has died since 2014. It is deeply disconcerting now to see how neighbors in an area respond to an existential crisis through the lenses of religion, caste, and class.

Though my initial inclination was toward humanities, I ended up studying biological sciences. My first job was at the Indian Institute of Science, where I was employed as a research assistant in a lab working on rotavirus, trying to come up with a vaccine that would cure diarrhea in neonates. This is where enlightenment happened for me. I remember saying [to myself] that a vaccine is not the answer to diarrhea; clean drinking water is!

So, I thought: Should I spend the rest of my life sitting in a laboratory looking into test tubes and running sequencing gels, or should I work to ensure people get safe drinking water? That's when I realized that the pure science track had led me to the lab life, but not to real life. Rather than the endless pursuit of the right vaccine, we needed to solve serious problems such as access to clean drinking water. What was needed was to build up public health systems, offer more holistic education that brings science together with the social sciences, environment, and law, and to fight social issues such as casteism and sexism. While all people deserve the right to water, that doesn't come through the sciences alone. It needs a much more interdisciplinary effort at the intersections of religion, caste, class, language, and more.

After my stint at the lab, I worked as a college lecturer and high school teacher for some time. But soon an interesting little pamphlet announcing a workshop called "Environmental Challenges of Bangalore" reached me through a friend. I noticed that it was organized by my former [college] classmate, Leo. So, I attended the workshop, which was an experiential one, and soon found myself volunteering with the organization. I worked with ESG as a volunteer for about two years, and slowly found myself fully engaged in the many issues that they were dealing with at that time.

By looking at water and sanitation problems in Bangalore, you quickly come to see that everything is so connected. Housing, access to education, recreation, public health, mobility, green spaces, and more are all issues that reveal how governance works, or not, in a city. Governance is something which we don't focus on at the school level, apart from lessons in civics which is not taught well. I feel that the work we do at ESG, or any civil society organization, is a live laboratory for understanding issues of governance. We learn by doing, and this perhaps is the best way to learn how the world really works and fix prevailing gaps in justice and access to resources and services.

MG: How about you, Leo. How has water shaped your life?

Leo Saldanha [LS]: In so many fundamental ways, my life has been shaped by water, or water *stress* to be precise.

As a kid, I grew up in a working-class neighborhood where we did not have piped water for quite a long while. Our morning ritual was to go and fetch water from the only public fountain, which was over two hundred meters away. In these circumstances, you learn to use water very carefully. We also had access to a community open well, but you couldn't drink from it—it was not at all tasty.

Our home was at the end of a cul-de-sac in one of the alleys of Gavipuram, an erstwhile village of Bangalore of the nineteenth century. Across the road from our poorly serviced neighborhood was the well-laid-out Chamrajpet suburb, which developed along with Malleswaram and Basavanagudi as a refuge for the population of the old *pete*[2] after it was ravaged by the bubonic plague at the end of the nineteenth century [see chapter 1]. Almost a century after the expansion of the city, our neighborhood still reflected a rural character in terms of its resident population and the occupation of some—cattle rearing was the most indicative.

As the city did not really care to extend services to the erstwhile village, which was heavily built up and provided cheap housing for the working classes and the poor, the woeful inadequacy of civic infrastructure and services showed up every time it rained. Our street flooded, and I recall our house half full of dirty and smelly floodwaters, multiple times over the years.

As kids we would joyfully celebrate all our schoolbooks getting ruined in the floodwaters. But really, it destroyed my parents' feeble resources, which they had painfully built over years of hard work. To them, water was a curse—both because of the everyday struggle to have enough good water to raise healthy kids, and to ensure the kids stayed alive through the floods!

When we moved out of this neighborhood to the locality where my parents now live, in peri-urban Bangalore, a key reason was to get into a better house and a healthier neighborhood. Here, too, there was no piped water supply, but at least it did not flood. Luckily for us, the open well we dug provided good drinking water. The morning ritual was to draw from the well and ensure all pots were full of water for the rest of the day. The intermittent power supply ensured that pumping water up from a well was quite a luxury.

When I had my own family, we moved further out into the peri-urban region, way south of the city. The massive Cauvery Project water pipes that run right past this neighborhood to feed the thirsty city are a metaphor for us—of our lack of access to water that flows past us in massive pipes.

So, we have built our house to harvest every drop of rainwater that falls on our roof and in the garden. And with that we manage for about six to eight months of the year. It is the healthiest water there is—free from the sky. For the other months, we rely on a community borewell which we share with our neighbors.

When it does not rain, which is quite often, we really have a tough time. The local borewell dries up. To drill our own bore would be expensive and environmentally a terrible idea. So, we rely on an expensive supply of water from private tankers, who in turn draw it out of borewells on farmlands [see chapter 5]. Over the past twenty years we have lived here, we have seen the cost of a tanker of water rise from 125 rupees for six thousand liters to almost 600 rupees now. Even with all our calculated struggles for water, we never could imagine there would be a future without water. But now, it's real. For the hundreds of massive apartment complexes that are rising all over peri-urban Bengaluru, the main source of water is from borewells or private tankers. Most of these projects advertise fancy lifestyles, but water is a serious limiting factor to sustain that dream, which they simply do not reveal to the buyers [see chapter 4].

Yes, water scarcity was always endemic when we were growing up. But we had no idea the whole city would run out of water, or that water would become a commodity that people are forced to buy in bottles or tankers. Or that it would be so politicized as a resource that people would kill each other over who has more rights to it. This is especially the case over the sharing of Kaveri River waters between the states of Karnataka and Tamil Nadu.

This violence is strange, since I recall growing up in a city where it was a tradition to keep water cisterns at every other street corner. Someone would fill it up for anyone to drink from. The Jain community in particular built water fountains in several public places and even installed coolers. Never could we have predicted that the people who shared water so, who lived interdependently, would one day riot over the sharing of Cauvery water—conflicts that are colored, unfortunately, by linguistic differences, Tamil versus Kannada, stoked by politicians who use the river to promise a greater share of the Kaveri waters for their electorate, knowing well they cannot deliver on the promise!

This city is expanding as though there are no environmental limits. There is no thought about sustainability. It is all about return on investment, highly speculative, without a thought to the repercussions. We see the fanciest new apartment buildings have private swimming pools on each floor, and then the village by it has long lines of women, men, and children with pots waiting for a municipal tanker to supply water. We see just about everywhere good, clean, living streams that not too long before fed our lakes, recharging groundwater aquifers that nourished open wells and borewells, are all polluted and encroached [see chapter 21].

This vicious cycle of water scarcity and the contamination of the abundant water we receive from rain all about us leads eventually to political grandstanding—with demands to build bigger dams across the Kaveri River, most recently at Mekedatu, a project that will destroy forever an extraordinary riverine forest and gorge.[3] This to supply more water to an insatiable city that only manages to muck it all up and throw it all, extremely dirty, back into the river. This approach can only worsen the water scarcity, and water sharing between riparian states can only become more complex in the years to come.

MG: Yes, didn't Bengaluru just get ranked close behind Cape Town as the second large city in the world that is predicted to run out of water in the near future? How do we reconcile this water crisis with the fact that the city is also suffering from extreme flooding? Can you explain this odd irony?

BR: Yes, I can answer this question as it relates to what is happening at the household level. I grew up in a home with a lot of green space around it. We had a front yard and a backyard, and on either side of the house there was plenty of space—full of trees. We always played in the dirt and grass, which became muddy when it rained. And we built mud houses. My mother would get so angry with us when we came inside all covered in mud. There was no cementing of the front or back yards; it didn't exist. There was a beautiful home garden all around with a variety of flowering and fruiting plants. This little garden around every home provided the much-needed habitat to the urban biodiversity, too, and helped rainwater percolate to the ground.

When I went to college, newer homes and newer layouts mushroomed. At the same time, people started to buy cars. So, builders would create cement driveways. There was a cultural shift where people started feeling that cementing the front gardens and backyards of homes and driveways was much sturdier, classier, cleaner, and nicer, and that less dust came into the house. Soon, the city began to build footpaths from cement and stones, removing the grass and other greenery that used to grow around them. Eventually, this stopped the rainwater from percolating down into the groundwater aquifers. Instead, all the water is allowed to flow into the roads and the stormwater drainage network, which is not continuous. This means that flooded streets and overflowing stormwater drains have become the norm.

In the 1950s, civic agencies first introduced the underground drainage system in Bangalore, and that became the new way of dealing with runoff. The Bangalore Development Authority was busy building new layouts and neighborhoods, and without thinking they just went on expanding the underground drainage system. It was a system run by civil engineers who knew nothing but pouring cement everywhere, without a thought to the implications.

The result? All the sewage from the new layouts and homes would pour into these cement drains and flow right into the age-old water channels—the *raja kaluve*—which collected all that drainage and dumped it all across hundreds of kilometers of canals, directly into the city's lakes. At this point, the water systems were taken over by city agencies staffed exclusively by engineers, who knew nothing about hydrology or the age-old complex system of water capture, percolation, filtration, which gently guided its movements and helped to create all our clean and ecologically sound lakes [see chapter 2]. This old system built the city, and yet the people who are building nonstop now don't consider the importance of the lake-and-channel system for the city's survival. This eventually killed the two rivers that take birth in the city and were largely fed by the lake systems. The Vrushabhavathi and Arkavathi River systems are today carriers of the city's sewage.

The new luxury complexes sell property based on the fantasy that water supply is limitless in the city. These complexes further add exorbitant amounts of untreated and partially treated sewage into these canal systems. It's shocking that the city administrators did not consider the fact that Bangalore sits on a plateau where there is no water source close by, that the city and its countryside completely depended on this complex system of water tanks and water canals for its well-being.

Science and technology have helped Bangalore in so many ways. We managed to write [software] code for the rest of the world. Did nobody ever think about the science and technology of water that was integrated into our cultural systems? It's such a shame that we did not take care of our waste and sewage in a scientific manner. We have also failed to understand the landscape of the city that is on a plateau and at a height of a thousand meters above sea level. We just keep on building, in blind faith, to please the real estate sector and construction industry, promoting the interests of developers and the cement industry, without a thought to how the city has survived over the centuries.

MG: And you, Leo, what are your thoughts on this matter?

LS: The government has been working closely with major contractors in town to convert the city's major lakes into concrete symbols of growth. For example, the city's major bus stand—Majestic—is in Dharmabudhi Lake, which was filled in during the 1970s. The National Games Village and Stadium complex came up on the Koramangala Lake in the mid-1990s. Hundreds of kilometers of canals have been concretized and encroached. There simply is no space for rainwater to flow, soak the soil, feed the groundwater aquifers, and stay a bit longer in the lakes, [thereby] creating excellent wetlands. Consequently, and predictably, numerous housing layouts have been flooded repeatedly over the years.

During the latest floods in Bangalore, the government's response was to carpet-bomb the canals with cement. And their oft-repeated assurance of desilting the lakes is an excuse to generate massive contracts. All this results in the destruction of wetlands, creation of water scarcity in summer, and flooding during the monsoons.

The city's major investment strategy is to convert public spaces such as lakes and canals into high-value private property. Land is becoming financialized, and the city's flooding is the result. This water crisis is a crisis by design. It is the product of a class and caste struggle, where the erstwhile feudal lords have amassed massive wealth in trading their farms to real estate developers, and now have turned on small and marginal farmers, pressuring them to trade away their lands [see chapters 5 and 7]. There is so much money flowing into this sector that planning of any sort, particularly rational, transparent, and democratic planning, is perceived as an impediment to this "progress." Which is why we have neighborhoods such as the Bellandur-Varthur-Whitefield-Sarjapur region—a massive and critical wetland—that is now all built up and floods every time it rains. And guess what, this is where much of the IT/BT [information technology/biotechnology] sector is located.

MG: What has ESG been doing about this crisis by design?

BR: We have been working at multiple levels to resolve the situation. Our major advantage is that we work with local communities and various civic agencies. From 2008, we campaigned to protect the lakes of Bengaluru from being privatized. This was an outstanding campaign as we had prominent citizens such as retired judges, MPs, and film actors participating in it. This effort helped highlight the fact that the city is divided by a ridge that runs north to south, carving the city into three valleys into which a network of lakes has been built over centuries. The initiative helped people understand how this network of lakes is now being disturbed by the poor planning and reckless expansion of the city, resulting in the loss of many lakes. This was also at a time when the city had set up an agency exclusively to focus on lakes—the Lake Development Authority [LDA]—which even before understanding the challenges blindly commenced with a grand plan of privatizing the lakes to ensure they were "developed" and maintained. "Development" to the LDA meant commercializing these water bodies such that eventually the general public would be kept away.

Despite efforts to dialogue and explain the importance of not privatizing the lakes, the city authorities went ahead and handed over four massive lakes of the city to private companies for "development" and maintenance. Privatization would have been a death knell for the lakes of the city, which play a crucial role in safeguarding the water cycles. Since the government did not abandon the policy of privatizing lakes, ESG was compelled to file a PIL [public interest litigation] in the High Court of Karnataka. We took this step because all our efforts to stop the privatization of lakes through campaigns, workshops, and conversations with bureaucracy had failed. The PIL resulted in an excellent court order that laid out specific guidelines to protect city lakes and also ensure safeguarding of the city's drainage pattern. This order is also applicable statewide and is being adopted nationwide as well. This is key to stopping the unprecedented floods that the city has seen over the last decade, and it could well serve as a model for other metropolises which are similarly suffering.

LS: While the city at large suffers from such urbanization, it has not been so bad for the feudal lords who either influenced the politics of the past two decades or have themselves seized political power. At present, all twenty-eight MLAs from the city have a background in the real estate sector. They all work closely with contractors and real estate developers, whose interest is in turning land into real estate, any which way. In this context, it is extremely difficult to gain government support to conserve and restore the water infrastructure. A major challenge is in overcoming the paradigm of development that these political leaders believe in, which is far removed from the sensitivity required to make Bangalore water secure.

Now this is a work in progress. The litigation we started in 2008 ended with an unprecedented directive in April 2012, one that incorporated two reports of the Justice N. K. Patil Committee that was appointed by the High Court to look into the matter. Justice Patil's first report provided clear pathways on how each and every little pond, stretch of *kaluve* [canal], and every lake needed to be protected and rehabilitated in socially inclusive and ecologically wise ways. The aim was not only to support the drinking water needs of a thirsty city, but also to revive functional wetland ecosystems so the metropolis would be replete with biodiversity—including the magical winter visitors, waterfowl that migrate over the Himalayas from Mongolia, Siberia, and Eurasia. The second report specifically addressed the pitfalls of privatization of water commons. While rejecting the idea as corporate colonization for profit, the report did encourage responsible corporate investment into a common pool fund to rehabilitate the water commons—a fund that would be utilized with direct oversight from local government and communities. To ensure local oversight and regulatory controls, the court also directed the state to organize lake protection committees at the local, district, and state levels whose functioning would be regularly reported to the court. This order was made applicable statewide.

However, because this order was not implemented, ESG has had to go back to the court. We managed to get orders to set up the committees by filing a contempt of court petition in 2013. But the next challenge was to ensure that these committees were made to work—there is so much resistance in the system against any kind of transparency or accountability. Therefore, we interjected in 2019 in another PIL, originally filed in 2014 by Citizens Action Group. We have argued through this strategy to secure directions from the High Court to ensure not only that the lake protection committees would function but that they would also be the bodies that will plan our way out of the prevailing mess.

The good news is that lakes can no longer be encroached, and those that have been encroached are being systematically tackled—a laborious and painful process, testing your patience. When we initiated our first PIL in 2008, the government claimed that there were only thirty-five thousand lakes across the state. A recent court-mandated survey reveals that five thousand more have been discovered and are in various stages of rehabilitation. In time we may "discover" five thousand more! Which is all very good, as this might be the pathway to ensure that there is water security for all, even in a bad rainfall year, and that we don't have to destroy rivers, forests, and hundreds of villages, submerging them in dams, to bring water to cities and villages.

BR: Again, on the positive side, we are conducting training programs for local taluk-level officials across Bengaluru District and all other districts of Karnataka. Governance has collapsed, and large expenses like for the Bangalore Metro project have bankrupted the city [see chapter 9]. So, we're helping local governments understand the old water system and the key provisions in the High Court order that can be effectively used to protect these water bodies. This will ensure that every village, town, and city will be water secure and that rural communities can still have some hope of being able to continue with their agropastoral lives, even as urban livelihoods thrive. The workshops we are conducting on lake protection have been very well received. Today everyone is keen to do something in their neighborhoods, knowing well that the state has failed them.

LS: But tensions remain as the state authorities still believe they can rule from above. ESG and other groups worked collectively to produce a People's Climate Action Plan for the region, through a lengthy and highly participative collaborative process, during the first Covid wave. But the state government recently hired two international NGO entities—WRI and C40[4]—to come in and draft a Climate Action Plan, ignoring the due role of local communities and elected representatives in the process. Top-down enforced "sovereignty"?!

MG: Any final thoughts on how we might reimagine Bengaluru's future for a more sustainable city? This question seems particularly urgent now, in the wake of the recent floods![5]

BR: It is such a shame that a city that boasts of its science and technology has failed to understand the science of its landscape. And the result is that a part of the city is under water. The process of urbanization disregards normative laws, especially fairly thoughtful guidelines of the Town and Country Planning Act, in planning its expansion. Problematically, to aid such urban expansions, apartment and commercial complexes were also removed from the purview of public consultations mandated under the federal environmental impact assessment processes in the mid-2000s. Obtaining clearances for such buildings was thereby made easy, for it was delegated to the State Environment Impact Assessment Authority. Moreover, only constructions that exceed twenty thousand square meters of built-up area are required to get clearance from this authority. The result we can now see: the cumulative impact of hundreds of buildings that were perhaps less than twenty thousand square meters, coming up without any regard to the city's water regime, several in and around lake beds, are causing the flooding. This is particularly the case in the eastern part of the city—which was transformed rapidly and without any planning into the IT/BT sprawl—which floods every time it rains.

The IT and BT sectors got special attention from the state government because they contribute significantly to the GDP. Unfortunately, with all the access these industries have to science, technology, and information, they have failed to conduct due diligence of the structures that have come up in a wetland landscape—buildings they occupy for work, living, and playing.

The IT/BT companies also helped their employees to avail themselves of a variety of interest-free loans to buy homes and cars. The result is that apartment buildings have basements for parking ranging from one to three floors below ground, resulting in deep cementing of the area. This has also prevented water from percolating into the ground and made way for the floods. Building bylaws have been violated, magnifying the current crisis.

The entire eastern region of the city is so poorly planned that it even lacks an effective network of good roads. This is because these IT/BT campuses came up just about anywhere—in villages, turning them into built-up areas rapidly. As a result, the Outer Ring Road is the only artery—which also serves as an evacuation route for flood water, adding to the woes of terribly slow-moving traffic.

To top all this, we have CSR [corporate social responsibility]–

driven lake rejuvenation programs which began in 2013. These began after the company laws were amended to make this contribution mandatory.[6] Under this program, most lakes that were "rejuvenated" have been turned into soup bowl structures, without making any provisions for the overflow of lake waters from one lake to the other, as in the old network of lakes.

All court orders with respect to lakes, and recommendations of court-appointed committees on lake issues, have been disregarded in the planning of new neighborhoods since the [early] 2000s, and that has left these areas completely inundated with water during the monsoon.

LS: Importantly, the entire approach to bringing sanity to the prevailing madness of reckless expansion of Bangalore has fallen on the shoulders of petitioners like ESG and judges of the High Court. It is mainly due to unprecedented directions issued by the Karnataka High Court in response to ESG's submissions that civic and state agencies are now compelled to invest efforts in granular planning and public engagements. This is resulting in a renewed effort to identify all water bodies and their legal limits and mark out encroachments for removal—with the caveat that poor communities who may have settled in such places out of sheer necessity of securing some kind of "housing"— usually shanties—must be relocated locally at government expense. Overall, the only sustainable and viable way forward for this intensely built metropolis to function and survive is to promote rehabilitation of the water landscape, with the idea of arresting water where it falls and utilizing it locally.

This effort has also spread across the state due to court directions. Every district is now required to come up with its own lake protection plans. Karnataka Chief Minister Siddaramaiah, in his Independence Day address in 2023, committed to spending 3,400 crore [34 billion] rupees on lake rehabilitation. One does hope this expenditure will follow the progressive guidelines mandated by the court. It is plausible to imagine a future when such efforts can result in making the metropolis water secure. But this demands ground-up, community-based planning and rehabilitation of age-old water systems, without being lured by dependence on faraway Kaveri River, a strategy that is not only financially expensive but also disastrous for the river and its extraordinary riverine forests. The future of Bangalore's sustainability, therefore, lies more in how prudently and intelligently the city builds its water security. On this wise choice rests the future of the astonishing economic growth that IT/BT sectors have fostered.

MG: Thank you both. There's a lot more to be said, obviously! We look forward to continuing this conversation.

Notes

1. Michael Goldman interviewed Bhargavi Rao and Leo Saldanha over Zoom on June 23, 2022, and followed up with an email exchange on September 20, 2022, and again in early September 2023. For details on ESG's activities, see https://esgindia.org.

2. *Pete* is the Kannada word for "market center" or "market town." Here it refers to the "Indian" part of Bangalore that was segregated from the British cantonment during the colonial period.

3. See, for example, T. Krishnan, "Dam over Troubled Waters: Why the Mekedatu Water Project Continues to Divide Karnataka and Tamil Nadu," *The Hindu*, June 4, 2022, https://www.thehindu.com/news/national/why-the-mekedatu-water-project-continues-to-divide-karnataka-and-tamil-nadu/article65493653.ece.

4. WRI (World Resources Institute) is an entity based in Washington, D.C., that describes itself as a "global research organization that works with governments, businesses, multilateral institutions, and civil society groups to develop practical solutions that improve people's lives and ensure nature can thrive" (https://www.wri.org). C40 (Cities Climate Leadership Group, Inc.) is a Delaware incorporated, non-stock, nonprofit corporation (https://www.c40.org/privacy-policy/).

5. This section of the conversation took place over email on September 20, 2022, after the recent episodes of massive flooding in Bengaluru.

6. In 2014, India made it mandatory for companies above a certain size to spend at least 2 percent of their average net profit (of the previous three years) on "corporate social responsibility" activities. In Bengaluru, many of these interventions have been cosmetic rather than addressing serious social or environmental issues. See Nicole Rigillo, "'Islands of Excellence': On the Emergence of Corporate Socials in India," *Economic Anthropology* 9, no. 1 (2022): 99–111.

Afterword
Malini Ranganathan

A sea of *pourakarmikas* (sanitation workers) sit cross-legged in their faded green-and-orange sari uniforms at Bengaluru's Freedom Park, chanting slogans and singing revolutionary songs. Some hold posters in Kannada and English, "Workers of the World Unite, You Have Nothing to Lose but Your Chains," and "Oppose the Caste Discrimination That Workers Face." Red hammer-and-sickle flags and blue Ambedkar flags flutter side by side. Thousands of municipal sanitation workers strike that July 2022, abandoning their jobs as street sweepers, garbage collectors, loaders, and drivers. Mounds of garbage are left unattended in a bid to convince the city and state governments to respond to the workers' calls for more dignified working conditions.

Despite having the insignia of the BBMP (Bruhat Bengaluru Mahanagara Palike, the municipal corporation) emblazoned on their uniforms, over the past three decades of neoliberalism's steady creep, sanitation workers have been strategically removed from the ambit of permanent employment and accountability that was once nominally guaranteed by the government. The majority are Dalits, sitting near the bottom of a labor pyramid that reinforces caste and gender hierarchies. Women workers are insulted on the job and do not have access to toilets or drinking water. Across Bengaluru's 198 wards, approximately ten thousand sanitation workers who perform essential door-to-door garbage collection and drive auto-rickshaw tippers remain at the whim of exploitative contractors and *mestris* (labor managers). They are denied a regular salary, social security benefits, and gloves and boots, forcing them to segregate waste with their bare hands. Another 16,500 "direct payment system" street sweepers receive salaries from the BBMP thanks to union efforts since 2017, which managed to abolish the contract system for this group of workers. But drivers, helpers, loaders, and other nonsweepers still work under an exploitative and precarious contract system. And for all workers in the sanitation sector, stagnant wages barely cover monthly rent and other expenses.

"*Karmikarendu gulaamaralla! (Gulaamaralla! Gulaamaralla!)*" (Workers are not slaves! [Are not slaves! Are not slaves!]) and "*Jai Jai Jai Jai Jai Bhim! (Jai Bhim Jai Bhim!)*" (Victory to Bhim! [i.e., Ambedkar]) come call-and-response rallying cries over the loudspeaker. Leaders of the BBMP Pourakarmika Sangha (affiliated with the Karnataka All-India Central Council of Trade Unions), along with Dalit activists from across the state, appeal to the workers over three days of rousing speeches, songs, and drumming to persevere with the strike. After all, the city's wealthier classes cannot clean up after themselves, and the state's political establishment cannot stomach another garbage crisis.

One year later, Chandrayaan-3 is about to land on the south pole of the moon. Scientists at the Bengaluru-based Indian Space Research Organization hold their breath as the spaceship makes its final descent. For over six decades, Bengaluru has served as the government's laboratory for heavy engineering, defense, computing, and space research, making India's space program one of the most elite in the world. With massive public investments in land acquisition, scientific education, and the research enterprise, this city was built on a nationalist technoscientific fantasy. The final moments of Chandrayaan-3's landing in August 2023 are live-streamed to millions of people across the world on a split screen, with the rocket landing occupying one half and Prime Minister Narendra Modi's face occupying the other. The future is here, it seems. But it wears a saffron garb.

To Modi, space exploration symbolizes an *amrit kaal,* a Vedic astrological term translating as "golden era," used by the BJP to portend—and own—India's futuristic arrival on the world stage. Within seconds of the landing, the Hindu nationalist leader seizes the opportunity to remind viewers, "In the first light of *amrit kaal,* this is *amrit varsha* of success" (idiomatically, the moon landing augurs a coming golden age). Never mind that in the same city that moon-roving technology was developed, sanitation workers still lack basic safety equipment. Never mind that after a decade of a national program ostensibly dedicated to safe sanitation technology and policy, namely, Swachh Bharat Abhiyan (Clean India Campaign), Dalit manual scavengers and underground drain cleaners—the most ostracized of Hindu society—are still asphyxiated to death from poisonous sewer gases. In this technospiritual, speculative golden age, these are but small prices of progress.

The chapters in *Chronicles of a Global City* lay bare the underside of a city high on a speculative rush—in a nation (and, more recently, a state) high on a nationalist rush. The authors in this volume demonstrate that there are at least four axes along which speculative city-making in Bengaluru is unfolding. First is the steady refashioning of a once relatively secular city into one in which Muslim tenants, businesses, street vendors, and cattle traders are being more openly targeted by communal forces. The Indian National Congress trounced the BJP in Karnataka's 2023 elections, but the BJP won the following year's Lok Sabha elections in the state, consolidating its Hindu nationalist agenda among dominant castes, particularly in Bengaluru. Journalists covering Karnataka's politics warn of the infiltration of far-right Sanghi (affiliated with far-right Hindu organizations known as the Sangh Parivar) ideology in numerous spheres of social, political, and cultural life, especially along the state's coast. There is good reason to believe that Karnataka will continue to be a southern gateway to hindutva politics in the years to come. Several chapters of the book show that "cosmopolitan" Bengaluru has not been immune to communal tensions. "No owner likes to give houses on rent to Muslims," says a Bengaluru-based Hindu tailor-cum-realtor in chapter 11. While meat-eating Muslims and Dalits have long been denied rentals in cities across India due to a pervasive brahminism (upper-caste ideology), such discriminatory rhetoric, emboldened by the rise of communalism, is more naked now. The threat of boycotting Muslim street vendors looms large, as we learn in chapter 16, and can easily be stoked by politicians with one click of disinformation. Muslims are being pitted against one another, too: migrant Muslim rag pickers in peripheral Bengaluru are divided between those who are perceived as legitimate and "Indian" and those who are perceived as "illegal Bangladeshis," as we see in chapter 3. These are divisive narratives that the BJP's leaders are only too eager to exploit. Finally, we see how hindutva ideologues are targeting progressive activists and journalists in the city. When environmental activist Leo Saldanha tried to salvage land belonging to a heritage church from acquisition by the state for the metro project, and a lake from takeover by a garish BBMP-installed Shiva (Hindu god) statue, he was targeted by right-wing agitators because of his Christian name. One of the agitators, Puneet Karehalli, a self-proclaimed cow vigilante of the far-right Rashtra Rakshana Pade (National Protection Force), was later arrested in April 2023 for murdering a Muslim cow trader in Ramanagara, about seventy kilometers from Bengaluru. These are just a few instances of how speculative city-making cannot be divorced from speculative nation-making.

Second is the centrality of caste to the workings of Bengaluru's land relations, what I am calling "the urbanization of caste power" in a book manuscript I am writing with Bengaluru-based activist-scholars Issac Arul Selva and Siddharth K. J. When academics started to turn to Bengaluru to theorize Indian urbanism two decades ago, there was an overreliance on Western Marxian frameworks to decipher late-twentieth- and early-twenty-first-century strategies of accumulation, enclosure, dispossession, and market-oriented reform. Class analysis took precedence over caste analysis. Today we cannot think the city without simultaneously thinking caste, class, and gender. Several chapters speak to the agrarian middle-caste networks leveraged by landowners, brokers, and aggregators. We find ourselves in the archetypical peripheral locality of "Purvapur," a pseudonym for an area on the southeastern fringes of Bengaluru, where Reddy (the dominant landowning caste) landlords like "Somnath" utilize their caste status to convince fellow villagers to sell their agricultural land. Euphemistically, Somnath refers to his ability to cut deals with villagers as his "inheritance," or as chapter 7 puts it, "the family and caste connections he enjoys because he belongs to a landowning Reddy family."

Throughout the book, we see that it is such inheritance wrought by kinship, family, and "community" (another code word for caste) that drives all manner of speculative transactions. Affective bonds based on trust, patronage, deference, stature, reputation, superstition, and clout—things that do not inhabit a bygone rural past but very much animate the modern urban present—lubricate access to the state, land, and other resources. Inherited caste capital makes it possible for Somnath and his Bunt caste (traditionally landowning, like Reddys) land aggregator, "Nitin," to value-add at each step of the chain, from an initial purchase of three acres of land on which millet (*ragi*) was once cultivated to the aggregation of one hundred acres for

Afterword **285**

a profitable high-end project. Towering gated apartments catering to wealthy residents dot Bengaluru's rural-urban peripheries, thanks to actors like Somnath and Nitin. In older areas of the city, Brahmins used their "inheritance" in the late nineteenth and twentieth centuries to corner formal-sector jobs and self-segregate in vegetarian-only state-planned upper-caste localities (urban *agraharas*, as Selva refers to them). Working-class localities or Dalit *keris* (ghettos or slums) often sprang up next to *agraharas* as a labor reserve for the latter. Today at the periphery, the *agrahara-keri* binary is reproduced by the private real estate market via processes of caste-laden and speculative agrarian urbanism.

Third, the speculative gaming of land, real estate, and finance is not simply the domain of the elite and landed castes, nor does it result simply in a caste-polarized *agrahara-keri* landscape. This book shows us that speculative logics are deployed by a range of lower- and middle-income groups. Everyone in Bengaluru does "real estate *kelasa*" (work), even those with relatively less inheritance. As chapter 11's study on "Karmikara Colony" shows, public-sector factory workers have gradually transformed into rentier landlords because "the belief that easy money can be made from property circulates widely in Bengaluru's speculative economy." These modest forms of speculation can depend, as chapter 6 shows, on "vernacular architectures of finance," as in the case of the *cheeti* fund, an informal pooled credit mechanism used by contract laborers and auto-rickshaw drivers, for instance, to pay for the "lease amount" (up-front payment) on a one-bedroom rental. While enabling a source of quick cash, poorer groups risk much when they turn to ad hoc forms of microcredit, informal lending (often at usurious interest rates), and land speculation. This is part of the slippery allure of the speculative city: the prospect of "making it" would seem to be available to everyone, yet only those who truly know and run the system come out on top.

Fourth, and finally, here is a collection of essays that delve into the realities of Bengaluru's old and new labor precariat. Most people who know Bengaluru's labor history know of its textile mill (earlier in the twentieth century) and, later, public-sector factory workers. The city has a long history of "trade union militancy," as a former Indian Telephone Industries union organizer, Fernandes, puts it in chapter 8. Most people know, too, of Bengaluru's "techies" and call center workers who have gotten rich since the late 1990s. But people do not know about how public-sector workers, following massive worker retrenchment and downsizing in the 1990s, including those at ITI, are now dubbed "contract" workers, with degraded wages, benefits, and job security. The contractualization of public-sector labor over the past four decades is an assault on the working classes and oppressed castes that has accompanied Bengaluru's speculative city-making. In addition, new types of labor precarity have arisen with the gig economy. In chapter 17 we follow the grueling schedule of Ajay, a "delivery boy," or, more positively, a "platform worker," who drives a motor scooter for Zomato, a popular food delivery app. Fifteen orders, fourteen hours of work, legs and back aching in pain, body covered in soot—all for 700 rupees earned in a day after expenses are deducted: not quite minimum wage if you count overtime. Yet for workers like Ajay this is a necessary but temporary hardship, or *vanavaasa* (literally, a kind of penance or banishment, from the Hindu epic Ramayana), in order to "make it" in a city with few other secure employment opportunities. Each must spin their own speculative tale.

On July 4, 2022, the sanitation strike in Bengaluru was called off following four days of accumulated garbage and negative press. Union leaders managed to squeeze a deal in writing from Chief Minister Bommai, including promises to regularize workers (by bringing contract workers under the direct payment system and making sweepers permanent), provide equal pay for equal work, and guarantee retirement and other benefits. These promises were partially met by the Congress government, which won the 2023 Assembly election in Karnataka. But the workers' struggle still has a long way to go. Genuine social transformation is rarely achieved overnight or in a linear manner. But the ground is shifting. Sanitation workers are more organized and share their experiences and strategies across regions. Public discourse critiquing the deeply caste- and class-stratified housing and labor geographies of Bengaluru has grown in recent years. Students, workers, lawyers, activists, journalists, and academics have taken to streets, community halls, sit-ins outside factories, and universities to contest communalism, caste bigotry, and labor injustices. These are everyday reminders that the exclusionary and speculative city has been, and can be, disrupted periodically and collectively to build toward a more just, ethical, and humane one.

Acknowledgments

It is in the nature of acknowledgments to be incomplete, and for authors to be haunted by this specter of incompletion. The deliberate and chance conversations, the past encounters that now exist only as vague body memories, the affective experiences of urban life and rural peripheries, the ideas quietly assimilated and the arguments discursively processed—these are all part of the collective inheritance that suffuses any writing endeavor, but particularly this one. It is impossible to remember all the attributions that deserve mention here. Know, however, that any omissions are unwitting, and unintended.

Most immediately, this book is an outcome of "Speculative Urbanism: Land, Labor, and Finance Capital," a collaborative research project funded by the National Science Foundation (grant no. BCS-1636437). We sincerely thank our research collaborators, Helga Leitner and Eric Sheppard, for their intellectual leadership and stimulating contributions to this project.

We would especially like to acknowledge the commitment and efforts of members of the Bengaluru research team, without whose hard work and creative inputs the project (and this collaborative volume) could not have been completed: postdoctoral associate Hemangini Gupta, who led the research team from 2017 to 2019, and whose creative sensibilities and contributions shaped the project in countless ways; research associates Kaveri Medappa, Sachinkumar Rathod, and Juwairia Mehkri, who conducted much of the fieldwork and also contributed significantly to our thinking and writing; Deeksha M. Rao, B. Manjunatha, Priyanka Krishna, Revathi Kondur, Swathi Shivanand, Harsha Anantharaman, Anuradha Sajjanhar, Harpreet Kaur, Amay Narayan, and Devika Narayan, whose work on different aspects of the project was invaluable; and H. S. Sudhira of Gubbi Labs, our remote sensing consultant, who provided the spatial images and census data for the project. We also thank Eesha Kunduri and Swathi Shivanand for their courage in stepping in to write chapters of this volume based on field notes that were mostly not their own!

The inputs of our expert consultant Sanjiv Aundhe, who enthusiastically researched and wrote two in-depth reports for the project on the history and structuring of the Indian real estate industry, have been formative to our understanding of Bengaluru's urban transformation. Sanjiv shared with us key insights and lively stories about Bengaluru real estate over the course of many entertaining conversations and was also extremely helpful in putting us in touch with potential interviewees.

Pierre Hauser deserves special mention here. Pierre joined us over three summers, participating in public workshops, academic presentations, and numerous field interview sessions, often following up on his own with people with whom he developed a rapport, photographing them in their daily routines—such as street vendors going from their predawn wholesale market visits to the streets where they sold their goods. Through his remarkable photographic prowess, he captured places, people, and events in ineffable ways that words alone cannot. We featured his work in two public multimedia exhibitions held in Bengaluru and do so here throughout the book.

A multimedia exhibition titled "Speculative Urbanism," at Rangoli (a public gallery located, appropriately for this book, in a metro station in Bengaluru) from July 27 to August 8, 2019, presented creative expressions of our research that included photographs, poetry, videos, soundtracks, soils, and contaminated water samples from our field sites, as well as plenty of explanatory texts in English and Kannada. The exhibition was curated by Hemangini Gupta and Michael Goldman, with the assistance of Anisha Baid. The exhibition then traveled to the Indian Institute of Human Settlements, Bengaluru, where it was on display from September 26 to October 5, 2019, with the assistance of Mallika Joshi. We are grateful to curious visitors whose vigorous engagements with our work enriched our understanding of the city.[1]

We would like to thank the National Science Foundation and our home institutions, the University of Minnesota Twin Cities and the National Institute of Advanced Studies (NIAS), Bengaluru, for their generous support. We are grateful to the Directors of NIAS, (late) Dr. Baldev Raj and Dr. Shailesh Nayak; Sri Srinivasa P. Aithal, Head of Administration; and all the administrative and other staff of NIAS for their support over the years.

We would also like to acknowledge members of the Jakarta research team, especially Dr. Suryono Herlambang and Dr. Liong Ju Tjung of Universitas Tarumanagara Jakarta, for energetic discussions and helpful input during our annual meetings and for their gracious hospitality during our visit to Jakarta in 2018.

As part of the project, we organized a stimulating workshop on Housing and Rental Economy at NIAS on July 20, 2019. We are grateful to the participants who shared their experiences and ideas during the workshop, especially Sri A. Narasimhamurthy, state convenor of Slum Janandolana-Karnataka. In addition, we thank Leo F. Saldanha and Bhargavi Rao of Environment Support Group, Bengaluru, for organizing a public dialogue with our team members on July 29, 2019, and to the participants in that event for their critical engagement with our work.

A panel on Speculative Urbanism organized by Eric Sheppard at the 2021 Annual Meeting of the Association of American Geographers provided an opportunity for several members of the project team to present their work. We thank the attendees for their participation and responses to our work.[2]

The idea for the Speculative Urbanism project germinated during an earlier research project titled "The Great Transformation: Urban Land Markets, Livelihoods, and the Growing Ecological Crisis in Asia's Cities," a collaboration with, and funded through a Global Spotlights award by, the Interdisciplinary Center for the Study of Global Change, University of Minnesota. We are grateful to the leaders and team members of Environment Support Group, Bengaluru, and Vinay K. Sreenivasa of the Alternative Law Forum for undertaking fieldwork and helping us with that study. A workshop titled "Bangalore's 'Great Transformation,'" funded by the same grant, was held at NIAS on June 24–25, 2016. We thank the participants for their brilliant contributions, which led to an issue of *Seminar* (694, June 2017) of the same title.[3]

Apart from our collaborators on the project and the contributors to this volume, several friends, colleagues, and interlocutors who have contributed to our thinking on Bengaluru over the years include Vinay Baindur, Sai Balakrishnan, Curt Gambetta, Lalitha Kamath, Janaki Nair, Seema Purushothaman, Champaka Rajagopal, Malini Ranganathan, Sharidini Rath, and Supriya RoyChowdhury.

290 Acknowledgments

Vinay extends his thanks to Harsha Anantharaman, Lalit Batra, Amita Baviskar, Bruce Braun, Cesare Casarino, Tom Cowan, George Henderson, the late Qadri Ismail and the late Ashok Kotwal (both sorely missed), Sunil Kumar, Eesha Kunduri, Anant Maringanti, Priti Ramamurthy, and Ajay Skaria, incidental or sustained conversations with whom over the years have enlivened his understanding of political economy, uneven development, caste patriarchy, social reproduction, and the thick, intimate relations that bind city and country. Divya Karan has listened to, discussed, and read bits and bytes from this project throughout its long gestation, influencing his thinking in ineffable ways. Their son Aseem provided unvarnished views and spirited company during a 2018 research visit to Bengaluru and Jakarta. The consistent display of interest and indifference to his research endeavors by Aseem's younger brother, Aman, has forced Vinay to ponder how we can communicate academic ideas in more publicly accessible ways.

Michael would like to thank the American Institute of Indian Studies for financial support for one leg of the research and the Institute for Social and Economic Change (Bengaluru) and its endowed VKRV Rao Chair Professor position that he held from 2016 to 2018, during which he learned immensely from faculty and PhD students. He would also like to thank the National Institute of Advanced Studies, which affiliated him as adjunct faculty during this project, and whose staff, faculty, and students have nourished him in so many intangible ways over the past fifteen years. Finally, he would like to thank Rachel Schurman, whose support during these years of research, writing, and life has been so pivotal and wonderful.

Carol would like to reiterate her appreciation to NIAS and its staff for their support over many years. She also thanks the NIAS PhD students for keeping her current and engaged through many discussions and debates, inside and outside class. Special mention to Neesha Dutt, Rashmi M., Krupa Rajangam, Sumithra Sunder, Savitha Suresh, Sahana Udupa, and Vijayashree C. S., whose own work on Bengaluru and Karnataka has enriched Carol's understanding of the city and the region. At NIAS she has been fortunate to have supportive and brilliant colleagues: A. R. Vasavi, Shivali Tukdeo, Smriti Haricharan, and Ritajyoti Bandyopadhyay, among others. Carol acknowledges with thanks the Swedish Collegium for

Advanced Study (Uppsala), where she worked on this book as a visiting fellow during spring term 2022–23. Special thanks to the principal, Christina Garsten, for creating such a collegial and generative atmosphere. Finally, Carol would like to express her deep gratitude for the unwavering support of her extended family, in India and the United States. Her son, Vivek, in his multifaceted interests and pursuits, constantly reminds her that academics is not the only pathway to understanding the world. And his commitment to egalitarian and life-affirming principles, like so many of his generation, offers hope that all is not yet lost.

We thank the anonymous reviewers of the manuscript, who subsequently revealed themselves as D. Asher Ghertner and Malini Ranganathan, for their thorough, perceptive, and productive comments, which helped us sharpen the book's analytical focus.

Finally, we are grateful to Jason Weidemann and Zenyse Miller at the University of Minnesota Press, whose prompt and patient support throughout the publication process has been invaluable.

Above all, we express our deep gratitude to the numerous extraordinary people, most of whom go unnamed in this volume, for their generosity, insights, patience, and time. We hope the chapters here are faithful to their stories of living the speculative city.

Notes

1. For images from the exhibition and an archive of publications from the project, see https://www.speculativeurbanism.net/.

2. The panel led to a theme issue of *Environment and Planning A: Economy and Space* on "Unleashing Speculative Urbanism" (vol. 55, no. 2, 2023), guest-edited by Helga Leitner and Eric Sheppard.

3. See https://www.india-seminar.com/cd8899/cd_frame8899.html.

Contributors

Vinay Gidwani is Distinguished University Teaching Professor of Geography and Global Studies at the University of Minnesota. He is author of *Capital, Interrupted: Agrarian Development and the Politics of Work in India* (Minnesota, 2008).

Michael Goldman is associate professor of sociology and global studies at the University of Minnesota. He is coeditor of *The Social Lives of Land* and author of *Imperial Nature: The World Bank and Struggles for Social Justice in the Age of Globalization* and *Privatizing Nature: Political Struggles for the Global Commons*.

Hemangini Gupta is lecturer in gender and global politics and associate director of GENDER.ED at the University of Edinburgh. She is author of *Experimental Times: Startup Capitalism and Feminist Futures in India* and coeditor of *Feminist Studies: Notes toward a Field*.

Pierre Hauser is a noted New York–based photographer whose work has been featured in *Town & Country, The Photo Review,* and the *Huffington Post* as well as in YourDailyPhotograph.com.

Priyanka Krishna is a PhD candidate at the Knowledge, Technology and Innovation Group in Wageningen University and Research.

Eesha Kunduri is a PhD candidate in the Department of Geography, Environment, and Society at the University of Minnesota Twin Cities.

Kaveri Medappa is a postdoctoral researcher in human geography at the University of Oxford.

Janaki Nair retired from the Centre for Historical Studies, JNU, New Delhi, as professor of modern history. She is author of *Mysore Modern: Rethinking the Region under Princely Rule* (Minnesota, 2011) and *The Promise of the Metropolis: Bangalore's Twentieth Century*.

294 Contributors

Malini Ranganathan is associate professor at the School of International Service, American University, Washington, D.C. She is coauthor of *Corruption Plots: Stories, Ethics, and Publics of the Late Capitalist City* and coeditor of *Rethinking Difference through Racialization in India: Caste, Tribe, and Hindu Nationalism in Transnational Perspective.*

Usha Rao is independent researcher, media maker, and visiting faculty at Azim Premji University, Bengaluru. She codirected the documentary film *Our Metropolis.*

Shaheen Shasa is a mobility activist based in Bengaluru and a founding member of Bengaluru Bus Prayanika Vedike, a people's collective advocating for equitable mobility in the city.

Swathi Shivanand is assistant professor at the Department of Liberal Arts, Humanities, and Social Sciences in Manipal Academy of Higher Education, Manipal, India.

Vinay K. Sreenivasa is an advocate who works in association with the Bengaluru Jilla Beedhi Vyapari Sanghatanegala Okkuta.

Carol Upadhya is visiting professor at the School of Social Sciences and Head of the Urban and Mobility Studies Programme, National Institute of Advanced Studies, Bengaluru, India. She is author of *Reengineering India: Work, Capital, and Class in an Offshore Economy* and coeditor of *Provincial Globalization in India: Transregional Mobilities and Development Politics.*

Index

Figures are indicated by "(fig.)" following the page number. Fictionalized names of people and places are in quotation marks at their main entries.

"Abdul" (street vendor), 213–14
"Abel" (Purvapur Lake activist), 264–65
accidents: construction workers, 204–6; delivery workers, 224
affirmative action, 119
affordable housing schemes, privatization of, 185
African students, 60–61
Aggarwal, Snehdeep, 33–35, 38, 41
aggregators. *See* land aggregation; *specific individuals*
agrarian urbanism, 23n20, 285
agricultural land: as ancestral property, 103; construction workers able to purchase in home village, 204; conversion to nonagricultural use, 5, 12, 47, 100, 103, 165, 167, 180–81, 188–95, 195n2, 255, Plate 1.12; Dalits countering illegal transfers of, 155, 189; eminent domain taking, 114, 167; family disputes over, 100, 103; land aggregation of, 64, 98–108, 259; selling to buy cheaper land elsewhere, 106. *See also* green belt; land-grabbing tactics
agricultural workers, 107, 165, 194. *See also* farmers
"Ahmed" (street vendor), 214
air pollution, 6, 19, 50, 71, 149, 221
Airport Road and Airport Metro Line, 132, 136n8, 147, 216

"Ajay" ("delivery boy"), 198, 218–28, 286; accidents and safety concerns, 224; addictive nature of work, 226; background of, 220; debt and expenses of, 222, 226–28; job's toll on his body, 223, 224, 227, 286; remuneration schedule and incentive pay, 218–19, 221, 226, 228; responsibility for his brother, 220, 222; security guards and, 222, 225; social support among fellow delivery workers, 224, 226; typical day of, 217–28
Akrama Sakrama scheme, 194, 195n6
All-India Central Council of Trade Unions, 119, 282
"Amba" (elderly former construction worker), 197, 200–203, 205–6
Ambedkar, B. R., 182, 192, 195n5, 220, 282
"Ammu" (Dalit woman in Purvapur), 258
"Ammu" (Purvapur villager), 257
Amritsar, 38
Amruthraj, Isaac, 149–50
"Anand" (local MLA of RP Colony), 169, 170
"Anand" (Naidu's aide), 243, 246
Andersen, Allan Kjaer, 33–34
Andhra Pradesh, migrants from, 201
anti-Muslim animus. *See* Muslims
apartment complexes: domestic

workers, 229–31, 234–35; food delivery, 222–25; high-end, 67, 79 (fig.); security systems and guards, 222, 225, 234–35, 235 (fig.), 250; underground parking, effect on groundwater, 278. *See also* rental market; *specific locations and names*

app-based work. *See* gig economy and workers

architects as city designers, 37

Arkavathi River, 273

"Arnav" (Purvapur villager), 259

"Ashok" (Halasuru Station controller), 132

Asian Development Bank, 7, 10, 17, 25n33, 133, 147

Asian financial crisis (1997), 17, 80

assetization of land and homes, 10, 11, 75, 153, 274

Atal Mission for Rejuvenation and Urban Transformation, 7–8

Atal Sarige (special transit service for poor), 141

auto-rickshaws, 61, 89, 90–91, 142, 162, 281

Babu, S. (street vendor union president), 208

bachelors as undesirable tenants, 161

Balakrishnan, C., 120

Bangalore Development Authority (BDA), 31; Bellandur and, 48–50; City Improvement Trust Board as former name, 157; criticism of planning process, 58, 63, 272; Hasiruhalli and, 104; Karmikara Colony common land dispute and, 241, 242; park mandate, 242; Purvapur development and, 55; Purvapur Lake management, 262–63, 264; slum land annexed by, 180

Bangalore (former name of Bengaluru). *See* Bengaluru

Bangalore Metropolitan Transport Corporation (BMTC), 112–13, 140–51, Plate 1.7; bus priority lane, 144, 146–47; citizen jury on bus service, 149–50; as cost-effective alternative to metro construction, 148; cost recovery approach, 142–43, 145; Covid-19 pandemic's impact, 146, 148; decline in ridership, 146; electric bus fleet, lease of, 146; fares and service issues, 139, 140–49; free day of service, 150; Majestic bus station built on former lake, 273; majority of population relying on, 133, 143; recommendations to improve, 144; staffing shortage, 146; state failure to provide support and offset losses, 143, 145–47; student passes, 149, 150; women and vulnerable persons as bus passengers, 142, 147, 148, 149–50, 151n4; worker strikes against, 146

Bangalore Metro Rail Corporation Limited (BMRCL), 112, 123–35; affordability and availability, 112–13; Anjanapura depot on Green Line to replace reserve forest, 135; construction and development of, 110 (fig.), 112, 124–26, 125 (fig.), 130, 134–35, 144, 147; corruption, 134; criticism of, 112, 123, 144, 147, 277; Delhi Metro as model for, 133–34, 136nn12–13; employees and management relations, 134; environmental impact, 112, 135; financing and revenues of, 25n33, 133–34, 136n10, 144, 277; Green Line, 2 (fig.), 132, 135; land acquisition practices, 124–25; less popular than buses, 133, 143; MG Road and, 110 (fig.), 112, 123, 125, 126–30; public land acquired by, 124–26, 135; retail

Index **297**

spaces in and around stations, 112, 129, 132–33; rules and restrictions, 127–28, 131; service problems due to cutting corners in construction, 134; as special purpose vehicle, 124; transformation of space and urban densification, 124–26, 133; transparency, lack of, 123, 125; worker productivity improved by riding metro, 124, 135n2. *See also* Namma Metro

Bangalore Transport Service, 142–43. *See also* Bangalore Metropolitan Transport Corporation

Bangalore Urban Agglomeration, 23n21

Bangalore Water Supply and Sewerage Board (BWSSB), 210, 262, 264

Bangladeshi migrants, 31–32, 61–62, 63n3, 263, 283

Barcelona, 38, 41

Baroda, 37

"Basava" (bonded laborer), 197, 203–5

Basavanagudi, 269

BBMP. *See* Bruhat Bengaluru Mahanagara Palike

BBMP Pourakarmika Sangha, 282

BBPV (Bengaluru Bus Prayanikara Vedike, Bengaluru Bus Commuter Forum), 144–50

BDA. *See* Bangalore Development Authority

Bear, Laura, 26n45, 113

Beckert, Jens, 15

Bellandur, 45–52; flooding, 45, 47, 50–51; as IT hub, 31, 45–51; land markets in, 31, 46–47; Outer Ring Road and, 45–46, 50; unauthorized development in, 48

Bellandur Lake, 45, 48, 50, 53

Bengaluru: among fastest-growing cities in Asia, 6, 10, 143; comparative research project on, 10–12;

formerly named Bangalore, 21n1; fringe areas, 53, 84, 134, 155; as global tech hub, 4–7, 14; as IT city, 12, 111, 120; location of, xi (map), 3; problems typical of other cities, 19–20, 143; as public-sector city in post-independence era, 111, 116; as "Science City," 116; as Silicon Plateau, 5, 14; as speculative city, 7–10, 12, 120, 283–86

Bengaluru Bus Prayanikara Vedike (BBPV, Bengaluru Bus Commuter Forum), 144–50

Bengaluru Jilla Beedhi Vyapari Sanghatanegala Okkuta (Federation of Street Vendors Unions of Bangalore District), 208–15

Bengaluru Revised Master Plan: (2015), 53, 55; (2031), 60, 124

Bettahalasur Metro station, 132

Bharatiya Janata Party (BJP), 57, 215, 250, 282, 283

Bhartiya City, 33–35; Chaman Bhartiya School, 33–34; electronic watch over city, 42; embodying both traditional and modern, 38; Financial Districts, 34; Nikoo Homes Phase 2, 35; as public realm, 41–42; as smart city, 34

"Bhaskar" ("delivery boy"), 225

billboard ads for real estate developments, 78, 79 (fig.)

biodiversity, 11, 19, 272, 276

BJP. *See* Bharatiya Janata Party

black money, 104, 105, 107

Blackstone, 16

BMRCL. *See* Bangalore Metro Rail Corporation Limited

BMTC. *See* Bangalore Metropolitan Transport Corporation

BOCW Board, 205

Bommai, Chief Minister, 286

boom times, 23n16, 59–60, 76, 80–82,

84; Dalits excluded from, 177–79, 185, 190; low-income residents excluded from, 154, 173, 177–78, 185; money laundering and, 104; slowdown ending, 23n16, 82, 84

borewells, 54–55, 59, 63n1, 70, 106, 172, 249, 260, 261, 270, 271

Brahmins (upper-caste community), 184, 284; *agrahara-keri* binary, 185, 285; domestic worker's relationship with, 229–30

bribes, 56–57, 188, 191, 208, 243

brickmaking, as cause of water scarcity, 59

Brigade Orchards, 34

Brigade's IPO, 83

brokers: criticism of, 105; Dalits as, 192–93; on land-grabbing, 188–92. *See also specific individuals*

Bruhat Bengaluru Mahanagara Palike (BBMP, Greater Bengaluru Metropolitan Corporation): bureaucratic problems of, 54; city planning by, 48; complaints about, 54; credit rating of, 180; DPA as help to Dalits with, 191–92; eviction of street vendors by, 209–11; Golden Springs and, 252; Karmikara Colony Sports Club and park, 243–44; Lakeview Haven road and, 70; Purvapur Lake management, 262; quasi-legal plots and, 57; resident welfare associations and, 41; RP Colony house construction and, 164, 168–70; sanitation workers and, 281; stormwater drain violation of Golden Springs allowed by, 251; subcontracting with migrants, 61–62

bubonic plague (1898), 37, 269

Building and Other Construction Workers (Regulation of Employment and Conditions of Service) Act (1996), 205

Bunt caste, 98, 284

buses. *See* Bangalore Metropolitan Transport Corporation

business parks, growth of, 1, 5, 6, 16

BWSSB. *See* Bangalore Water Supply and Sewerage Board

canals. See *rajakaluves*

capital: capital market regulations, 82; separating types of construction, 80. *See also* foreign direct investment; private equity capital

castes: affective bonds of, 284; agrarian middle-caste networks, 284–85; connections important in land relations, 6, 102–3, 155, 190, 284; ITI terminated workers from marginalized castes, 119; land struggles related to, 188–95; Purvapur Lake management and, 265; recent criticism of system of, 286; urbanization of caste power, 284; water crisis and, 274. *See also* Scheduled Castes and Scheduled Tribes (SC/ST) communities; *specific castes and communities*

Cauvery Water Supply Scheme, 22n7, 48, 54, 269

CDP. *See* Comprehensive Development Plan

cement, use of, 272–73, 278

Central Power Research Institute, 116

C40 (international NGO), 277, 280n4

Chalavadi community (Scheduled Caste), 193–94

Chamrajpet, 148, 269

Chandrayaan-3 (Indian lunar mission), 282

cheeti system (chit funds/revolving credit), 16, 76, 85–97, 285; functioning of various types, 86–88; group members, criteria for, 86, 94–95;

Karmikara Colony construction financing by, 160; RP Colony residents and, 88–92, 170–71; Sushma's *cheeti* enterprise, 92–96; trust as element of, 86, 88, 92, 94; value of participating in, 96

children: as construction workers, 201, 202 (fig.), 203; housing based on number of, 178; Karmikara Colony park used by, 244–46, 245 (fig.); transportation issues, 149. *See also* education of children

CIBIL scores, 226–27

CITB. *See* City Improvement Trust Board

Citizens Action Group, 276

City Improvement Trust Board (CITB), 157, 158, 240. *See also* Bangalore Development Authority

civil society groups, 112, 144, 150, 181, 202, 207, 268

clean title, 99

climate change, 2, 19, 149; People's Climate Action Plan, 277

cobblers, 171, 213–14

common land (commons, public realm), 33, 39, 41–43; development designed with allowance for open space, 68–69; *gomala* land (village common land), 188–90; Karmikara Colony dispute with Golden Springs over, 237, 240–47; Lake Purvapur as, 258; privatization of water commons, 276; types of, 237, Plate 1.5

commute times. *See* traffic congestion

Comprehensive Development Plan (CDP), 49, 55, 135n4

Comprehensive Mobility Plan (2020), 140

compulsory land acquisition, threat of, 104–5

"Comrade Chandan" (Minerva Mills union worker), 114, 120–21

concretization, 3, 241, 272, 273

construction workers, 18, 196 (fig.), 197, Plate 1.2; accidents and, 204–6; children as, 201, 202 (fig.), 203; Lakeview Haven, 65; *mestris* (labor contractors) and, 203, 204; migrants as, 60, 200–206, Plate 1.2; short work life, 205; wages, 140, 203–4; women as, 200–201

contractualization of labor, 112, 117, 118, 286; difficulty in organizing contractual workers, 117; essential services, 8; metro jobs, 134; software industry, 5, 14; subcontracting arrangements with migrants, 61–62

corporate executives as investors, 81

corporate social responsibility (CSR) funds, 245, 264, 276, 278–79, 280n6

corporate sponsorship to develop public spaces, 244, 276

corporate urbanization, 42

corporators (local representative), 54–55; Golden Springs residents circumventing, 250; replacement of slums and, 89, 169; RP Colony redevelopment and, 166–67; street vendor eviction and, 210, 212; windfall profits and, 174

corruption: BMRCL, 134; connivance of politicians and bureaucrats, 56, 189, 237, 249; designation of "no development" areas and, 58; land aggregation and, 105, 107; land-grabbing tactics, politicians participating in, 189, 195n3, 249, 260; legislation proposed on, 179. *See also* bribes

Cottonpet, 114

Covid-19 pandemic, 16, 118; domestic workers, impact on, 233–34; rental income, impact on, 160–61; RP Colony construction delay due to,

300 Index

170; transportation, impact on, 143, 146, 148

credit ratings, 180, 226–27

crime reduction, 41

cronyism, 6, 250–51, 260, 275. *See also* corruption

CSR. *See* corporate social responsibility

Dalal Street (Mumbai), 16

Dalits: activists and rights organizations, 89, 181–82, 187n13, 191–92, 195n3, 195n5, 282; *agrahara-keri* binary, 185, 285; as brokers, 192–93; as cobblers, 214; contesting illegal transfers of land, 155, 189, 190, 192; dispossession of, 184, 189; DPA movement, 191–92; employment of, 63, 282–83; equal property rights for, 153, 154; excluded from land ownership and boom real estate market, 177–79, 185, 190; as farm workers, 194; funding available for housing, 178; ill-treatment of, 258; land aggregation and, 103; money-lenders getting land from, 190; Purvapur and peri-urban villages, 63; Purvapur Lake desilting done by, 258; pushing back against marginalization, 194; real estate market and, 154–55, 184–85, 188–95, 285; rental discrimination, 185, 283; residential sites tied to labor opportunities, 285; as RP Colony residents, 88–92, 154, 166–67; sanitation worker strike and, 282; SJK and, 182; as slum residents, 187n13, 285; stigma, 91; subsidized housing schemes, 178; as victims of land-grabbing, 188–94; water access, 258. *See also* Scheduled Castes and Scheduled Tribes (SC/ST) communities

debt: *cheeti* groups and, 92, 96; construction workers and, 204; delivery workers and, 220, 226–28; farmers and, 204; increase between 2004 and 2014, 96n2; structured debt, 80, 83; suicide related to, 93

Defence Research and Development Organisation, 116

deindustrialization, 12, 111, 158

Delhi Metro, 133–34, 136nn12–13, 137n16, 147–48

Delhi–National Capital Region market, 81

delivery workers, 198, 217–28, 286. *See also* "Ajay"

democratization of city governance, 238

demonetization, 83

dense urbanism, 30, 39–40, 68; Karmikara Colony and, 156; metro availability and, 124

developers: debt-ridden, 8, 83; environmental clearances avoided by, 278; land aggregators becoming, 107–8; purchasing land with clean title, 99; small and medium, wiped out by regulatory and tax reforms, 84

Devi Duggalamma (lake goddess), 256–62, 265

"Devika" (RP Colony flower vendor), 165–66, 169

Dharmabudhi Lake, 273

Dirlik, Arif, 126

disinvestment of state-owned enterprises and utilities, 7, 8

displaced slum dwellers, 5, 18; in Karmikara Colony, 156–63; KSDB resettlement plans for, 176–77; from Netaji Slum, 141; relocation and redevelopment schemes vs. slum rehabilitation, 175n2; relocation to JB Nagar settlement, 200;

relocation when nearby water bodies undergo rehabilitation, 279; from RP Colony, 88–92, 91 (fig.), 154, 164–75; temporary apartment units and expenses, 89–92, 91 (fig.), 170–71

District Commissioner: corruption and land-grabbing, 189; land aggregators dealing with, 103; role in converting land from agricultural to nonagricultural use, 103

domestic workers, 13, 198–99, 229–35; advance loan as part of remuneration, 231–32; apartment residents as employers, 229–31, 234–35; bus as essential mode of transportation for, 139, 148; *cheeti* system and, 92–93; devaluation of labor and exploitation, 229, 232, 235; double burden as unpaid worker at home and as paid worker at employer's home, 233; employment choices of, 230–31; excluded from definition as "workers," 232; flexibility for worker's own home caregiving needs, 233; in Golden Springs, 229; illiteracy or low level of education, 231, 232; as informal employment, 231, 233, 235; in Karmikara Colony, 42, 159, 230–35; living in slums or informal settlements, 85; Muslims as, 62; new middle class vs. older middle class as employers, 234–35; no benefits and no employment rights, 233; number of employers, 230; part-time nature of work, 230; patronage relationships of, 229, 230, 232, 235; security systems of apartment complexes and, 234, 235 (fig.); typical tasks performed by, 230, 232; wages depressed due to being women's income, 232

"DPA" (Dalit organization in Karnataka), 191–92

drainage. *See* stormwater drains; wastewater and sewage leakage

dreams, 15, 42, 43, 84, 163, 177, 185, 219. *See also* good life/better future

drinking water. *See* water supply

drought (early 1970s), 200

Dubai, 14, 29, 38

ecologies and ecological concerns, 237–39; buffer zones for, 59; degradation of, 22n8; devaluation of, 238; interconnections with society and governance, 268; irreparable damage, 238; loss of commons by urbanizing processes and privatization, 246; mixed-use developments and, 35; speculative, 19; sustainability, 6; water as central to, 266–80

Ecospace (RMZ tech park), 47

education of children: bus transportation costs, 149, 150; Chaman Bhartiya School, 33; construction worker legislation and, 205; PSUs and, 119; school fees, 95, 139, 222; working-class children, 208

Electronic City, 45

Electronics and Radar Development Establishment, 116

elitism, 250, 252

Embassy Group, 132

Embassy Springs, 34–35

eminent domain, 104, 112, 114, 124, 167

environmental impact, 237–39, 266; due diligence lacking, 278; environment activists' interviews, 238, 266–80; Karmikara Colony, 237, 240–54; land-grabbing tactics and, 195n3; metro development, 112, 135; new construction's ability to avoid environmental clearances, 278.

302 Index

See also ecologies and ecological concerns; lakes; "Purvapur Lake"; sustainability

Environment Support Group (ESG), 125, 238, 266, 268, 274–77

equality, issues of. *See* castes; Muslims

equity capital. *See* initial public offerings; private equity capital

eucalyptus, 59, 188

"everyday, the," 20–21

evictions: no-eviction provisions, 157–58, 167; in RP Colony, 168; slum residents experiencing financial distress and, 184; street vendors, 198, 208–13

exclusion, 266; of Dalits from real estate boom market, 177–79, 185, 190; domestic workers excluded from definition as "workers," 232; of low-income/slum residents excluded from real estate boom market, 18, 154, 173, 177–78, 185; from public realm, 41–42; rejection of, 286

exclusive gated communities, 6, 9, 43, 75, 234. *See also specific locations and developments*

extreme weather, 19

factories. *See* industrial background of Bangalore; public sector undertakings

family disputes, 100, 103, 172–73

farmers: Bellandur land market and, 46–51; debt of, 204; land aggregators purchasing land from, 99–100; pledging land as collateral for private loans, 190; Purvapur land sales and, 59–60; tanker business run by, 55; tenant farmers, 107. *See also* water supply: scarcity

farm workers, 107, 165, 194

FDI. *See* foreign direct investment

Fernandes, Michael, 114, 116–20, 285

financialization of the city, 7–9, 20, 24n31, 111, 274. *See also* foreign direct investment; private equity capital

fires set to force out residents, 181, 201–2, 249

Fiscal Responsibility and Budget Management Act (2022), 180

flooding, 1–4, 6, 19; BBMP's encroachment clearance drive, 251; Bellandur, 45, 47, 50–51; concretization and loss of lakes, impact of, 273; government's response to, 274; inadequacy of infrastructure to deal with, 269; Outer Ring Road (ORR), 1, 46 (fig.), 278; runoff and, 272–73. *See also* stormwater drains

food order delivery. *See* delivery workers

foreign direct investment (FDI): Indian policies (early 2000s) aimed at, 76; in real estate ventures, 8–9, 82–83; "round-tripping" of capital, 82

Fraser Town (British settlement), 37

"futures past," 111

Gandhinagar, eviction of street vendors in, 211

"Ganesh" (brother of Kumar), 249–50, 252

"Ganesh" (resident of RP Colony), 166, 169, 171, 174–75

Ganesha shrine, 64

gantebattalu (bell and ladle for tax collection), 193–94

garment workers, 211, 214, 233

gated communities, 6, 7, 13, 42, 75, 96, 235, 250

"Gaurav" (real estate consultant), 82–84

Gavipuram, 269

GDP growth, between 1991 and 2001, 80

Geddes, Patrick, 37–38

General Electric, 39, 44n15

general power of attorney (GPA) and land transfer, 190, 195n4

gentrification, 159, 163n1, 176

Ghertner, D. Asher, 15, 26n39, 32n3, 155n5, 163n1

Gidwani, Vinay, 1, 33, 53, 78

gig economy and workers, 6, 18, 198, 217. *See also* delivery workers

global asset class, 16

"global city" model, 7, 10, 29, 38; change reaching to working-class level, 78; critics of, 42

global financial crisis (2008), 16, 17

"Golden Springs" (mixed-use development), 35–42; cronyism and, 249–51; domestic worker in, 229; elite residents (NRIs), 41; as gated community, 42; impact on Karmikara Colony, 237, 248–54; integrated development, 39, 248; mistrust concerning developers, 251–52; Mori Brothers's principles applied, 40; "onti line" road as boundary separating from Karmikara Colony, 248, 253 (fig.); playground conversion to fenced urban park, 237, 244–47; as public realm, 41–42; social distance and elitism of residents to neighbors in Karmikara Colony, 250; stormwater drain violation allowed to persist, 251; sustainability in, 40–41; Viren as architect-developer, 39–40; water offered to local park by, 251–52. *See also* public sportsground conversion to fenced urban park

Goldman, Michael, 1, 266

Golf Course Road (Gurgaon), 82

gomala land (village common land), 188–90

good life/better future, 68, 91, 154, 198

Goods and Services Tax (GST 2017), 83–84

Google Play Store loan apps, 227

goondaism (strong-arm tactics), 102, 105, 168, 201

"Gopal" (Karmikara Colony resident), 157

Gowdas (upper-caste community), 184

GPA. *See* general power of attorney

gram panchayat (village government) system, 54, 258

Greater Bengaluru Metropolitan Corporation (BBMP), 23–24n21, 54, 243

greed, 4, 29, 80, 105

green belt, 55–59, 66, 194, 237

greenhouse gas emissions. *See* climate change

green values, 35

Grofers (grocery delivery app), 221

groundwater depletion, 3, 19, 21–22n7; attempts to control, 54–55; construction's impact, 271–73; Karmikara Colony, 241, 249; Lakeview Haven, 70; Purvapur, 59

Gupta, Hemangini, 85

hakku patras (possession certificates), 175, 180, 183–84, 187n15

Halasuru Metro station, 131–33

happiness, 30, 33–34, 41

"Hasiruhalli" (village), 59, 100, 103, 104, 106

Hasiru Usiru, 125, 144

high finance, 75–76. *See also* foreign direct investment; private equity capital

Hindu nationalism, 31, 63n3, 163n2, 283. *See also* nativism

304 Index

Hiranandani, Niranjan, 35
history of city development, 35–37
Holeyas SC community, 184
home mortgages, 80
housekeeping staff, 85, 139–40. *See also* domestic workers
housing: healthy vs. excess stock, 84; PSUs and, 117–18, 120. *See also* exclusive gated communities; informal settlements; low-income residents; slum residents; *specific locations and developments*
hyacinth. See *neer soppu*

inclusion: lake rehabilitation and, 276; of Muslims and all non-Hindus, 258, 267
income. *See* low-income residents; precarious employment and income; *specific types of workers*
India Coffee House, 126–27, 130
Indian National Congress, 249, 250, 283, 286
Indian Space Research Organisation, 116, 119, 282
Indian Telephone Industries Limited (ITI), 111–12, 114, 116–19, 121, 286
Indore, 37
industrial background of Bangalore, 111, 114–16. *See also* public sector undertakings
inequality, 12, 21, 185, 193. *See also* castes; exclusion
informal employment, 7, 61, 76–77, 122n8, 167, 176, 197–98, 231, 233, 235
informal moneylending, 16, 18, 75, 92, 159–60, 170, 226–27, 285
informal settlements, 85, 175n1; Karmikara Colony's origins and, 240; RP Colony, 88–92, 91 (fig.), 154; RWAs leading legal battles against, 216n1. *See also* slum residents

Infosys, 45, 46–47
infrastructure: as global asset class, 16; global city's requirements, 7, 29; governmental financing of, 9–10; inadequacy revealed by flooding, 269; large projects, local impact of, 11; takeover by financially leveraged firms, 24n31, 75; tolls, tariffs, and user fees charged for, 24n31; water bodies and, 237
initial public offerings (IPOs), 16, 76, 80, 83
integrated development: future vision, 39, 66; Golden Springs, 39, 40, 248–49; India's history of, 35; Lakeview Haven, 66; townships, 6, 30, 33, 41, 117, 248
intermediaries: as part-time rental agents, 162; Reddy caste members as, 155
Intermediate Ring Road, 259
international development bank loans: Bengaluru Metro construction, 133–34; Delhi Metro construction, 137n16
International Monetary Fund, 17
investors: Bengaluru's, as salaried employees and executives, 81; categories of, 81; pre-launch to structural completion, 81. *See also* foreign direct investment; special purpose vehicles; speculation and speculative investment
IPOs (initial public offerings), 16, 76, 80, 83
Istanbul, 14, 19
IT/BT hubs and corridor, 1, 19, 278, 280; avoidance of environmental impact assessments, 278; Bellandur, 31–32, 45–51, 124; growth of IT sector enabled by PSUs, 118–20; Lakeview Haven marketing to workers in, 66; planning

Index **305**

viewed as impediment to, 274. *See also* Whitefield

ITES (IT Enabled Services) sector, 118

ITI. *See* Indian Telephone Industries Limited

Iyer, Seshadri, 35–37, 38

Jacobs, Jane, 41

Jagannath, K., 31–32, 45–51

Jain community, 270

"Jairam" (real estate agent in Karmikara Colony), 161, 162

Jakarta: comparative research project on, 10–12; speculative urbanism's ills in, 19

"Janaki" (street vendor), 208

Janasahayog (slum rights organization), 181, 203

Japan International Cooperation Agency (JICA), 17, 25n33, 133, 137n16

Jawaharlal Nehru National Urban Renewal Mission (JNNURM), 7, 177, 186n5

Jayanagar neighborhood, inclusion of, 267

JB Nagar settlement, 200–203

jeeta (bonded laborer), 203, 204

joint development agreements (JDAs), 99, 101, 108nn1–2

Joint Legislature Committee on Encroachments in Bangalore Urban District Committee, 179

Justice N. K. Patil Committee, 276

"Jyoti" (local corporator of Purvapur), 54–55

"Kalanagar" redevelopment, 88–89, 92, 169, 171–73

Karehalli, Puneet, 284

"Karmikara Colony," 153–54, 156–63, 240, 285; allotments of property,

157–58, 173, 177; bachelors as undesirable tenants, 161; *cheeti* system used to finance construction of rental units, 160; Covid-19 pandemic's impact on rental property, 160–61; creation of, 157–58; domestic workers in, 42, 230–35; environmental impact, 240–54; Ganesha festival in, 241, 245; garment industry in, 233; gentrification of, 159, 163n1; Golden Springs and, 42, 248; groundwater depletion, 241, 249; Karmikara Colony Sports Club, 243–44, 246; *kere* (tank) land, dispute over use of, 240–41, 246; migrant workers settling in, 156; no-eviction clause in lease agreements, 157–58; "onti line" road as boundary separating from Golden Springs, 248, 253 (fig.); public playground conversion to fenced urban park, 237, 240–47, 245 (fig.); public-sector factory workers as rentier landlords, 285; real estate makeover and rental market in, 153–63, 157 (fig.); security and advance deposits, 154, 159, 161; single women as undesirable tenants, 161; types of tenants, 159, 161; wastewater and sewage leakage coming from Golden Springs, 237, 248–52. *See also* public sportsground conversion to fenced urban park

Karnataka (state): boycott called against Muslim vendors in, 215; hindutva politics, 283; topographic contour map, x (map)

Karnataka All-India Central Council of Trade Unions, 282

Karnataka General Labour Union (KGLU)–ITI Unit, 118–19, 121

Karnataka High Court: Bellandur

Lake cleanup ordered (1999), 50; disregard of orders with respect to lakes, 279; ITI settlement upheld to reinstate terminated contract workers (2023), 119; protecting lakes and safeguarding city's drainage, 275–76, 277, 279; removal of vendors on footpath ordered by (2014), 209

Karnataka Industrial Areas Development Board (KIADB), 46–51, 51n3

Karnataka Land Reforms Act (1961), 58

Karnataka Land Revenue Act (1964), 182

Karnataka Slum Areas (Improvement and Clearance) Act (1973), 181, 182

Karnataka Slum Development Board (KSDB): JB Nagar residents, housing for, 203; name change from Karnataka Slum Clearance Board, 182; *parichaya patra* (identification certificate) issued by, 175n1; power to transfer land to slum residents, 182; quarters for displaced slum residents, 141–42; RP Colony redevelopment plan, 168–69; slum redevelopment schemes of, 176–77, 180

Karnataka State Road Transport Corporation, 142–43

"Karthik" (Purvapur Lake area resident), 59–61

"Karunakar" (transgender community representative), transportation challenges of, 149

"Kausalya" (community worker), transportation challenges of, 148

"Kaveri" (street vendor), 207

Kaverinagar, street vendor evictions in, 208–11, 214

Kaveri River, 3, 22n7, 48, 270–71, 279

"Kavita" (street vendor), 210

Kempegowda International Airport metro line, 132, 136n8, 147, 216

Keri Eerie Banda Duggalamma (temple), 257

KIADB (Karnataka Industrial Areas Development Board), 46–51, 51n3

kickbacks, 49, 134

"Kishore" (real estate broker), 162–63

Koramangala, eviction of street vendors in, 212–13

Koramangala Lake, 273

Korea Exim Bank, 25n33

Koselleck, Reinhart, 111

Krishna, Priyanka, 255

Krishna, S. M., 5, 47, 181

"Krishna" (school principal), 31, 55–57

Krishnanandanagar, street vendors in, 211–12

KSDB. *See* Karnataka Slum Development Board

"Kumar" (local corporator), 248–52

Kunduri, Eesha, 114, 240

labor, 285–86; affirmative action initiatives, 119; catchment areas for, 201; Marx on, 199n1; *mestris* (labor contractors), 203, 204, 281; metro workers, 134; PSUs as Bangalore's major employers, 116; wages, 139–40. *See also* delivery workers; domestic workers; informal employment; migrant workers; outsourcing; precarious employment and income; strikes; unions; waste collection workers

Laggere, 139, 200–202

Lahore, 37

Lake, Robert, 15

Lake Development Authority (LDA), 274–75

lakes: Bengaluru's loss of, 19, 48, 53,

55, 59, 273; CSR-driven rejuvenation programs, 278–79; desilting, 257, 258, 274; formation of, 3–4; government funding for rehabilitation, 279; hyacinths invading, 48, 238, 259, 261 (fig.); importance to Bengaluru's existence, 237, 272–73; jurisdictional conflicts over management of, 264; pollution of, 272; rehabilitation and protection plans, 274, 276–79; upstream fixes affecting lower lakes, 259. *See also specific lakes*

"Lakeview Haven," 64–72, 65 (fig.), 102 (fig.), Plate 1.3; land aggregation and, 101, 105

"Lakshmi" (sanitation worker), 139, 148

"Lakshmi" (street vendor), 207–8

"Lalitha" (domestic worker), 229–31, 233–35

land. *See* agricultural land; public land; real estate sector; speculation and speculative investment

land aggregation, 77, 80, 98–108; agricultural fields, 64, 98–108, 259; bureaucratic hurdles, 77, 99, 103–4, 107; corruption and, 105, 107; Dalits pushing back against, 194; Nitin's story, 98–108; process, 101–2; trust of landowners as factor, 100, 101. *See also specific aggregators*

land bankers and banking, 57, 84, 99, 107, 134, 182

land brokering. *See* brokers

land-grabbing tactics, 20, 80, 260; Dalit broker profiting from countering, 193; falsifying land records, 59, 188, 191; general power of attorney used as, 190; intentional fires, 181, 201–2, 249; open space development in Karmikara

Colony and, 242–43; politicians participating in, 189, 195n3, 249, 260; as public issue in 1990s, 195n3; by Reddy community, 188–89, 190, 194; regularization of properties acquired through, 194, 195n6; water crisis and, 274. *See also* bribes; corruption

landlordism, 153, 159–60. *See also* rental market

land recording, sub-registrar's role in, 56–57

land-use categorization: manipulation of, 59; maps as speculative devices for politically powerful, 56; reclassification in green belt for public purposes, 58

LDA (Lake Development Authority), 274–75

Lefebvre, Henri, 20

"Lehman lag," 83

loans: apps for, 227; "gold loans," 170; land as collateral for, 180, 190; long-term (lump-sum) leases as, 93–95, 160; state waiver of interest on installments paid by slum residents, 182. *See also cheeti* system; debt; informal moneylending; moneylending

local developers, 29, 83

local elites, 12, 15

"Lokayukta" (ombudsman for corruption complaints), 242

low finance, 16, 75–76, 154. *See also* informal moneylending

low-income residents: *cheeti* system, 76–77, 85–97; excluded from booming property market, 154, 173, 177–78, 185; mandatory beneficiary contributions and, 178–79; public transportation costs, 139–40. *See also* slum residents

Lucknow, 37

Madigas SC community, 184
Mahatma Gandhi Road. *See* MG Road metro
Malleswaram: demand for more bus services, 150; domestic workers in, 229–31, 234–35; evictions of slum residents, 184; history of, 269; Iyer and, 37; street vendors in, 213
"Mani" (local leader and activist), 88–92, 91 (fig.), 172
"Manjubai" (domestic worker), transportation challenges of, 139, 140, 143, 148, 150
"Manjunath" (RP Colony landowner), 154, 164, 167–71, 173–74
"Manjunath" (street vendor), 210
Manjunath ancestral home, replaced by Ulsoor Metro station, 131
"Manoranjan" (real estate broker), 162
Marx, Karl, 199n1, 284
mass transit, 17, 139–51; Atal Sarige (special transit service for poor), 141. *See also* Bangalore Metropolitan Transport Corporation; Bangalore Metro Rail Corporation Limited
master plans, as speculative devices for politically powerful, 56
McKinsey Global Institute, 15
McKinsey's Infrastructure Practice, 15
McMordie, Michael, 43n13
Medappa, Kaveri, 46, 188, 217
mestris (labor contractors), 203, 204, 281
metro development. *See* Bangalore Metropolitan Rail Corporation Limited
Metro Rangoli Center (MG Road), 127–28
MG Road metro, 110 (fig.), 112, 123, 125, 126–32; colonial and postindependence history of MG Road, 127, 129–30

microfinance institutions (MFIs), 96–97n2, 285
middle class: civic activism of, 22n9, 127; conflicting sensibilities of urban vs. peri-urban/agrarian, 265; flooding and, 1–4; housing sites catering to investors of, 155; public sector's role in shaping, 6, 111, 119; quasi-legal plots of land and, 57; spending by, 6; verticalization of residential housing for, 68
migrant workers: circular migration to return to home village, 204; as construction workers, 60, 200–206, Plate 1.2; distress migration and, 201; housing shelters, 16, 61, 62 (fig.), 152 (fig.); Muslims as, 31–32, 62, 63n3; Purvapur area, 60–62, 263; rental units for, 153, 156, Plate 1.4; subcontracting arrangements with, 61–62; as waste collection workers, 60, 61–62, 63n3, 89–92; women as heads of households, 201. *See also* Bangladeshi migrants
Minor Irrigation Department, 264
mixed-use developments, 13, 28 (fig.), 29–30; dense urbanism and, 39; future vision of, 43, 66; postindustrial imagination of, 35. *See also* "Golden Springs"; integrated development; "Purvapur"
MLAs (Members of the Legislative Assembly), 52n7; Bengaluru's representatives involved in real estate business, 49; corruption and land-grabbing, 189; cronyism with developers and real estate sector, 275; eviction of street vendors and, 209–11; Golden Springs and, 249, 250; land aggregators dealing with, 103; land speculation by, 56; public spaces, management of, 244;

RP Colony redevelopment and, 166–68, 174

MLCs (Members of the Legislative Council), 49, 52n7

mobility. *See* social mobility

Modi, Narendra, 282

Mohan, Dinesh, 133

money laundering, 104, 107

moneylending, 154; Dalit dispossession and, 190; delivery workers and, 227; for Karmikara Colony construction financing, 160; rental income and, 154, 159; for RP Colony residents during redevelopment, 171. *See also* informal moneylending

Mori Brothers/Mori Building Company, 40

mortgage-backed securities, 81

Mumbai market, 81

municipal entrepreneurialism, 8–10

"Munilakshmi" (street vendor), transportation challenges of, 148–49

Murthy, N. R. Narayana, 47

Muslims: anti-Muslim rhetoric and hostility, 31–32, 62, 215, 283–84; as migrant workers, 31–32, 62, 63n3; refusal to rent to, 161–62, 163n2, 283; social inclusion prior to rise of hindutva politics, 258, 267; as street vendors, 198, 215, 283; as waste collection workers, 62, 63n3

"mutation corridor zones," 124, 135n4

Mysore kingdom, 193

Mysuru, 1, 51

"Nagappa" (land broker), 188–89

Nagendra, Harini, 241

"Naidu, Venkata" (Malleswaram resident), 241–44, 246–47

Naidu caste, 95; land purchase of Old Airport Road slums, 184

Nair, Janaki, 116

"Nalini" (domestic worker), 231–33

Namma Metro (Our Metro), 112, 123, 125. *See also* Bangalore Metro Rail Corporation Limited

Narasimhamurthy, A., 154, 173, 177–79, 181–82, 184–85, 187n15, 194

"Narayan" (Karmikara Colony resident), 245

"Narayana" (corporator) negotiating with RP Colony residents, 169–70

National Aerospace Laboratories, 116

National Green Tribunal, 263

nativism, 61–62, 63n3, 163n2, 215, 267

neer soppu (water hyacinth), 48, 238, 259, 261 (fig.)

neoliberalism, 7, 15, 113, 122n8, 142, 281

Netaji Slum, 141

new urbanism, 35, 36 (fig.)

"Nitin" (land aggregator), 72n1, 98–108, 284–85; Lakeview Haven development, 68, 101, 102 (fig.), 284–85; political connections, 104; Somnath and, 100–106

no-eviction provisions, 157–58, 167

nonperforming assets (NPAs), 16

Old Airport Road slums, 184

organized labor. *See* unions

Outer Ring Road (ORR): Bellandur and, 45–46, 50; bus priority lane, 146, 147; flooding, 1, 46 (fig.), 278; as main artery to IT/BT campuses, 278; metro construction, 147; migrant settlement in Laggere at, 202; planning and land acquisition of, 49

Outer Ring Road Companies Association, 1

outsourcing. *See* contractualization of labor

"Palani" (Purvapur villager), 257

"Palaniamma" (Purvapur rentier), 261

310 Index

park conflict between Karmikara Colony and Golden Springs. *See* public sportsground conversion to fenced urban park

Parvez, Anjum, 136n8

Patil, N. K., Committee report on lake protection, 276

patriarchy, 200

patronage, 80, 120, 230, 232

People's Climate Action Plan, 277

Peripheral Ring Road, 55, 256

peri-urban villages, Plate 1.8; life in, 269; real estate development in, 188–95; upheaval in, 62–63. *See also* "Purvapur"

Phoenix Watch Works, 128–30

PIL. *See* public interest litigation

plague (1898), 37, 269

political economy of land, 6

political money, related to land transactions, 104

poor, the. *See* Dalits; low-income residents; Scheduled Castes and Scheduled Tribes (SC/ST) communities

pourakarmikas. See waste collection workers

"Praveena" (PSU public-relations manager), 118

precarious employment and income, 18–19; *cheeti* system and, 95–96; contract workers, 86, 92, 112; delivery workers, 198, 286; domestic workers, 93, 215, 231, 233; IT sector, 118; of Karmikara Colony residents, 153; of slum residents, 176; street vendors, 213; waste collection workers, 281–82; of women, 95–96

Prestige Lakeside Habitat, 34, 78

Prestige's IPO, 83

private equity capital, 7, 16, 20, 80, 111; dubious legality of, 82; Indian policies (early 2000s) aimed at, 76

privatization, 7, 244, 246, 257, 259, Plate 1.5; of affordable housing schemes, 185; of lakes, 274–75; opposition to, 274, 276; of water commons, 276. *See also* contractualization of labor

"Prominent Developers," 64, 70–71

"Prominent Ventures," 101

public interest litigation: over privatization of lakes, 275–76; over stormwater drain violation by Golden Springs, 251

public land: conversions, 111, 124–26, 135; disagreement over use of drained *keres* ground, 241; *gomala* land (village common land), 188–90; Ram Prakash's land as, 167; road space in front of middle-class and affluent homes, 212. *See also* common land

public-private partnerships, 182, 186n5, 245

public realm. *See* common land

public sector undertakings (PSUs), 111–12, 114, 116–22, 285; affirmative action initiatives, 119; high-paying jobs, 118; industrialization in colonial period, 114; infrastructure built and maintained by, 117–18; land of public-sector factories, 111, 114; role in shaping the city, 111–12; strike for wage revision, 116–17; urban growth fueled by, 117–18; worker training enabling growth of IT sector, 119–20

public services: financial performance as more important than quality of service, 142; reduction in, 17; state government failing to offset costs of, 113, 143, 145. *See also* Bangalore Metropolitan Transport Corporation

public space. *See* public land

public sportsground conversion to fenced urban park (Karmikara Colony), 237, 240–47; BBMP and, 252; children's use of, 244–46, 245 (fig.); gated park with limited hours and access, 244–45, 252; Golden Springs construction, effect of, 244; Golden Springs espousing control of converted park, 252; mourning loss of the commons, 246; Naidu's vision for open sports ground, 241–44, 246; privatization and, 244

public transport. *See* mass transit

Puravankara's IPO, 83

"Purvapur" (peri-urban mixed-use site), 30–31, 53–63; as alluring destination, 53–54; Chalavadi community and, 193; Comprehensive Development Plan (1995), 55; Jyoti as local corporator, 54–55; lake loss, 55; land aggregation, 100; land prices, 55–56, 255; mixed feelings of villagers toward development and social changes, 256, 259–61; rapid urbanization, 255–56; Reddy as dominant landowning caste, 191 (fig.), 258, 284; residential development of farmlands, 12, 100; water scarcity, 55, 59, 256, 260

"Purvapur Lake," Plate 1.10; Bengaluru as nemesis of, 259–60; caste and class as management issue for, 265; catfish as invasive species, 259; clear waters and annual desilting prior to development, 257; drownings, 256, 260; Duggalamma Devi (lake goddess) and, 256–62; fencing of, 264; fishing, cessation of, 259; hyacinths invading, 259, 261 (fig.); lakeview property, promotion of, 53, 255, 261–62, Plate 1.10; management after Purvapur's incorpora-

tion into Bengaluru, 262; omens over goddess's wrath at failure to protect, 256, 260; pollution, 53, 59, 64, 236 (fig.), 238, 255–65; property value contribution of, 264; recreational space, creation of, 238, 263–64; rejuvenation funding, 264; revitalization plan, 263, 264; rural livelihoods dependent on, 257; sewage and waste dumping reaching, 259; squatter settlements, 62 (fig.), 263; Sriramu as lake warden, 262–65; transformation from agrarian to urban lake, 255–56, 263; vision of, 265; waste segregation site near, 60

"Purvapur Rising" (local citizens' group), 262, 264, 265

racism, 60–62, 63n3. *See also* exclusion

"Radha" (Karmikara Colony resident), 240

"Raghu" (Zomato employee), 218–19

rag pickers, 283

Rajajinagar, 114, 115 (fig.), 139, Plate 1.1

rajakaluves (channels), 3–4, 241, 251, 272, 273

"Rajesh" (Hasiruhalli landowner), 106

"Rajesh" (non-English speaking Purvapur resident), 265

"Rajeswari" (water-bill collector in Kalangar), 171–72

"Rajiv" ("Prominent Development" chairman), 64–65, 67–72

"Rajiv" (self-proclaimed leader RP Colony slum), 164–65, 166, 169, 174

"Raju" (Karmikara Colony resident), 157–58 ·

Ramachandra, T. V., 22n8

"Ramakrishna" (Karmikara Colony

property owner and rentier), 158–60, 163, 240–41

Ramaswamy, A. T., 179, 195n3

Ramaswamy Committee Report, 179, 195n3

"Ramayana" (Hindu epic), 228, 286

"Ramesh" (land acquisition specialist), 58–59, 63

"Ram Prakash" as owner of farmland converted to RP Colony, 165, 167

"Ramu" (street vendor), 215

Randhawa, Pritpal, 136n6

Ranganathan, Malini, 3–4, 281

"Ranjeesh" (Purvapur villager), 259

Rao, Bhargavi, 238, 266–80; on ESG response to water crisis, 274–75; on ESG training programs for local officials, 277; imagining the future with a more sustainable city, 277–79; on water scarcity, 271–73; on water's role in shaping his life, 267–68

Rao, Usha, 123

Rashtra Rakshana Pade (National Protection Force), 284

Rathod, Sachinkumar, 188–89

Ravi, K. C., 242

real estate agents, 161–62, 192. *See also* brokers

real estate investment trusts (REITs), 16

Real Estate Regulation and Development Act (RERA, 2016), 76

Real Estate Regulation and Development Act (RERA, 2017), 84

real estate sector, 5–6, 11; *agraharas-keris* binary, 185, 285; boom, 23n16, 59–60, 76, 80–82, 104, 155; commissions and fees, 107; fantasy of limitless water and, 273; large scale investment, 11, 121; overproduction of housing units, 84; pervasive in Bengaluru life, 285; slowdown

post-boom, 23n16, 82, 84; sluggish vs. active market, 39–40. *See also* real estate agents; *specific locations and developments*

"Reddy, Prakash," 57–58

"Reddy, Subba," 190, 193

Reddy caste: as brokers, 63, 155, 192–93; *cheeti* groups and, 95; Dalits countering illegal land conversions and transfers of agricultural lands to, 155, 189; as dominant landowning caste, 191 (fig.), 258, 284; land aggregation role and, 100, 102–3; land-grabbing by, 188–89, 190, 193, 194; land purchase of Old Airport Road slums, 184; political connections of, 57; as Purvapur panchayat president, 258

regional planning, 39

"Rehman" (Purvapur villager), 257, 258

reinventing the city, 266–80; ESG response to water crisis, 274–77; ESG training programs for local officials, 277; imagining the future with a more sustainable city, 277–80; state authorities' failure to heed local communities and elected officials, 277; water scarcity and, 271–74; water's role in shaping lives of Rao and Saldanha, 267–71

REITs (real estate investment trusts), 16

relocation temporarily of slum/low-income residents. *See* displaced slum dwellers

rental market: anti-Muslim sentiment and, 161–62, 163n2, 283; in Bellandur, 50, 51; conversion of homes into middle-class apartments, 153, 158, 252, 261, Plate 1.4; Dalits and, 185, 283; failed rental ventures, 159–60; homeowner's caste, relevancy of, 184–85; informal lease arrangements, 93; in Karmikara Colony, 153, 156, 158–60; in Lakeview Haven, 67; long-term (lump-sum) leases, 93–95, 160; proceeds used to buy less expensive housing, 173; public-sector factory workers transformed into rentier landlords, 285; real estate agents and brokers, 161–63; in RP Colony, 90, 91 (fig.), 173; security and advance deposits, 89, 90, 92, 154, 159, 161. *See also* "Karmikara Colony"

research methodology, 12–13

residential segregation, 163n2, 185

resident welfare associations (RWAs), 208, 209, 212, 216n1

Revenue Department registers and procedures, 103, 191, 192, 195n2

"revenue layouts," 155, 189–90, 195n2

revolving credit groups. See *cheeti* system

Right to Information application, 210

right to the city, 176, 179

ripple effects: from Karmikara Colony owners selling sites, 158; from PSU job wages, 119; from small land sales, 106–7

RMZ tech park (Ecospace), 47

roads: bus priority lane, 144, 146–47; failure to plan in eastern region of Bengaluru, 278; Golden Springs and, 252; Lakeview Haven access, 70–71. *See also* Outer Ring Road; traffic congestion

Rogers, Gayle, 29

Roppongi Hills, Tokyo, 40

"round-tripping" of capital, 82

"RP Colony," Plate 1.6; *cheeti* system, 88–92; Covid pandemic delay in construction, 170; Dalits as residents, 166; demolition and redevelopment of, 154, 164–75, 165 (fig.); earlier Dalit settlement classified as slum, 167; history of, 165–66, 167–69; informal settlement, 88–89; notice of one week to residents to vacate, 170; as notified slum, rights of residents, 167, 168; opposition of some residents to redevelopment, 166, 169; restrictions on beneficiaries of allotments, 173, 177–78; temporary apartment units and expenses, 89–92, 91 (fig.), 170–71; trust lacking between Manjunath and residents, 170; value produced from windfall profits and construction, 174

rural existence, disruption of, 31

rural land. *See* agricultural land

Sadaramangala, transportation challenges of, 141–43

Safdie, Moshe, 39, 41; *The City after the Automobile*, 39, 43n13

Saldanha, Leo, 238, 266–80; "Environmental Challenges of Bangalore," 268; on ESG response to water crisis, 275–77; hindutva idealogues targeting, 283–84; on state authorities ignoring local communities and elected officials, 277; on water scarcity, 273–74; on water's role in shaping his life, 268–71

"Samir" (street vendor), 214

"Samuel" on RP Colony redevelopment, 166–67, 170, 174

Sangh Parivar, 283

"sanitary movement," 37, 282

sanitation workers. *See* waste collection workers

santhes (open village markets), 213

"Santosh" (Dalit activist), 190–92

"Santosh" (real estate investment executive), 80–83

314 Index

"Santosh" (street vendor), 212

Sarjapur Road, 66, 145, 274

Scheduled Castes and Scheduled Tribes (SC/ST) communities: excluded from property market boom, 185; funding available for housing, 170, 178; illegal transfer of lands assigned to, 189–90, 193; upper castes buying land from, 184–85

schools. *See* education of children

Selva, Isaac Arul, 185, 284, 285

"Selvi" (domestic worker), transportation challenges of, 148

service-oriented economy, 7, 263

services sector: catering to middle classes, 198; migrants coming to Yeshwantpur to work in, 156; rise of, 111, 118

servitude, 232

sewage and refuse, 19; Bellandur Lake and, 53; flowing into *rajakaluves*, 272; shortage of sewage treatment plants, 45; wastewater and sewage leakage from Golden Springs, 237, 248–52. *See also* "Purvapur Lake"

shadow bankers, 83

"Shamim" (migrant salvage seller), 31–32, 61–62

Shanghai, 29, 38

Shantakumari, Ms. (mayor of Bengaluru), 210

"Sharda" (domestic worker), 230–31

Sharma, Ramchander, 129–30

Shasa, Shaheen, 139

"Shekhar" (land broker), 188–90, 192–94

Shivajinagar, 141, 213–14

Shivanand, Swathi, 156, 176, 200, 229, 248

"Shyamili" (Purvapur resident), 257

Siddaramaiah, Chief Minister, 279

Siddharth K. J., 284

Singapore, 38, 40, 265

sites and services model, 173, 177, 186nn5–6

SJK. *See* Slum Janandolana Karnataka

Slum Development Board. *See* Karnataka Slum Development Board

Slum Dwellers of Karnataka Joint Action Committee, 181

Slum Janandolana Karnataka (SJK), 154, 177, 182–83, 183 (fig.)

Slum Janara Sanghatane, 149

slum rehabilitation schemes, 139, 141, 154, 168, 175n2, 179, 180, 186n5

slum residents: domestic workers as, 85; excluded from property market boom, 154, 173, 177–78; fires set to force out residents (early 2000s), 181, 201–2; *hakku patras* and, 175, 180, 183–84, 187n15; international events and games causing slum demolition and, 181; investing in vision of global city, 155n5; land rush to clear out, 5; law recognizing and granting possession of land, 182; notified slums, rights of residents, 167, 168, 175n1; recognized slums, rights of residents, 175n1; redevelopment projects, reactions to, 154, 170–74; representation in state negotiations over land, 181–82; right to the city and, 176; SJK getting state waiver of interest on installments paid by, 182; state funding for housing improvements, 182; use of term "slum," 23n18. *See also* displaced slum dwellers; "Kalanagar" redevelopment; "RP Colony"; slum rehabilitation schemes

slum rights organizations and movements, 154, 177–79, 183 (fig.), 185, 203. *See also specific organization names*

Smart Cities Mission, 8
smart city, 30, 34
Sobha's IPO, 83
socialism vs. capitalism, 80
social justice, 20, 191, 193, 266
social mobility, 6, 91, 95, 98, 119
"soft secession," 30
software industry. *See* ITES sector
"Somnath" (Hasiruhalli village
    resident), 64; Lakeview Haven villa
    ownership, 105; land aggregation
    and, 100–106, 284–85
space program (India), 282
special purpose vehicles (SPVs), 16,
    75, 76, 80, 82, 124
speculation and speculative invest-
    ment, 9, 29–30, 76; Bengaluru's
    vs. United States's bubble, 81;
    caste system and, 185, 285; heyday
    between 2000 and 2008, 80–81;
    land aggregators and, 99–100;
    land investment and, 20, 55, 67;
    land planners and manipulation
    of land-use categorization, 59;
    long-term, 81; persisting despite
    reality of slowdown, 84; perva-
    sive in Bengaluru life, 285; rental
    property, 67, 156, 161, 163, Plate 1.11;
    salaried professionals as inves-
    tors, 81; short-term, 81; slum land
    redevelopment, 174; as source of
    income, 154, 177–78, 285; underside
    of, 283. *See also* boom times; *specific
    development sites*
speculative city: becoming just, ethi-
    cal, and humane city, 286; Benga-
    luru as, 7–10, 12, 120, 283–86; as
    magnet for migrant laborers, 205,
    206; as part of speculative nation-
    making, 284; underside of, 286
speculative ecosystem, 19, 112
speculative governance, 17
speculative orientation, 17–18

speculative state planning, 113
speculative stories, 29–32; fictional
    expectations, 15
speculative urbanism, 11–12, 14–21, 77,
    266; creation of new financial tools,
    forms, and strategies, 16; discourse
    creating new urban mindset of,
    15, 29–32; finance of, 76; labor's
    precarious existence and, 18–19;
    speculative ecologies and, 19; specu-
    lative governance and, 17; specula-
    tive orientation and, 17–18
"Speculative Urbanism: Land, Labor,
    and Finance Capital" (research
    project), 10–11; comparison of
    Bengaluru and Jakarta, 11–12,
    25n36; principal investigators and
    researchers, 13, 25n36, 85, 195n1;
    research methodology, 12–13
SPVs. *See* special purpose vehicles
Sreenivasa, Vinay K., 207
"Sriramu" (landowner and environ-
    mental activist), 256, 258, 259,
    262–65
"Srivatsa" (real estate agent), 161–62
State Environment Impact Assess-
    ment Authority, 278
state-led industrialization, 114. *See
    also* public sector undertakings
stormwater drains, 2–4, 250–51, 272;
    court order on, 275
street sweepers, 281. *See also* waste
    collection workers
street vendors, 18, 197–98, 199n2,
    207–16, Plate 1.9; bus as essen-
    tial mode of transportation for,
    148–49; car-parking and, 212;
    economic boycotts against, 198,
    283; evictions of, 198, 208–13; goods
    and services offered by, 213, 214;
    harassment of, 208, 212; ID cards
    issued to, 215; law protecting, 198,
    210, 211, 213, 215; Muslim vendors,

198, 215, 283; police seeking bribes from, 208; as precarious livelihood, 213, 215; protective legislation (2014), 198, 210, 211, 213, 215; RWAs in opposition to, 208, 209, 212, 216n1; stationary vendors, 208–9, 209 (fig.), 213; union representing, 208, 209

Street Vendors (Protection of Livelihoods and Regulation of Street Vending) Act (2014), 198, 210, 211, 213, 215

strikes: bus system workers, 146; Indian Telephone Industries, 111–12, 116–17; sanitation workers, 281–82, 286

subsidized housing schemes, 178, 186n5

"Sunil" (Purvapur farmer), 260–61

supernormal profits. See windfall profits from land sales

"Suresh" (commuter), 123–24

"Suresh" (founder of local NGO), 250–51

survival strategies, 12

"Sushma's" *cheeti* enterprise, 92–96

sustainability: ecological, 6; environmental crises and, 19; failure to consider in city planning, 271; in mixed-use township, 40–41; rehabilitation of water landscape as essential to, 279–80; reimagining sustainable future, 266–80; technology-based solutions for, 8; transportation options, 144

Swachh Bharat Abhiyan (Clean India Campaign), 282

Swiggy (on-demand food delivery), 217, 223

Tamil Nadu, migrants from, 90, 92, 148, 165, 174, 201, 270

"tanker mafia," 22n7, 31, 50, 54, 66, 70, 75, 260, 270

taxes: *gantebattalu* (bell and ladle for tax collection), 193–94; new regime of GST, 83–84; treaties, 82

tenant farmers, 107

Texas Instruments, 4–5

textile mills of colonial period, 114

threats and strong-arm tactics to procure land, 102, 105, 168, 201. See *also* land-grabbing tactics

Tiwari, Geetam, 133

tolls and user fees, 7, 9, 24n31, 75

townships. See integrated development

traders as investors, 81

traditional heritage, retaining elements of, 38

traffic congestion, 6, 7, 30, 35, 42; elevated corridors proposal to alleviate, 145, 147, 166; Golden Springs causing for Karmikara Colony, 249; metro development as alternative to, 112, 124; no plans to curb vehicle use, 147; public buses as alternative to, 143, 149, 150; in Purvapur, 54; two-wheeled vehicles as alternative to, 146

train service. See Bangalore Metro Rail Corporation Limited

transgender community, transportation challenges for, 149, 151n4

transparency, lack of: BMRCL and, 123, 125; bureaucracy and, 48; government committees to rehabilitate and protect lakes, 276; IPOs ameliorating, 83

transportation options: auto-rickshaws, 61, 89, 90–91, 142; walking and cycling, 139, 140, 144, 148. See *also* Bangalore Metropolitan Transport Corporation; Bangalore Metro Rail Corporation Limited; traffic congestion

Uber Eats, 217, 219, 226

Ulsoor Lake, 264

Index **317**

Ulsoor Metro station, 131

unions: All-India Central Council of Trade Unions, 119, 282; Bengaluru's long history of, 285; BMRCL Employees Union, 134; contractualized jobs and, 118, 119, 121; Covid-19 lockdown and, 118–19; declining political power and influence of, 111, 117, 122n8; ITI Employees' Union, 116; Karnataka General Labour Union (KGLU)–ITI Unit, 118–19; during state-led economic development, 122n8; street sweepers, 281; strikes, 111–12, 116–17, 281; "trade union militancy," 285

United Progress Alliance, 186n5

Upadhya, Carol, 1, 45, 64, 98, 164, 188

Urban Development Department (UDD, Karnataka), 58

urbanism, 284. *See also* speculative urbanism

urbanization: imaginative geography and, 78; PSUs in Bangalore and, 118, 120; rapid urbanization, effects of, 11, 12, 60, 105, 107, 135n4, 237, 255. *See also* urban planning and administration

urban local bodies (ULBs), 180

urban planning and administration: criticism of planning process, 58, 63, 272; decentralization of, 8; roads, failure to plan for, 278; speculative state planning and, 113; sustainability, failure to plan for, 271; viewed as impediment to development, 274

urban poor. *See* low-income residents; slum residents

urban sprawl, 45, 68

Vaastu Shashtra, 185, 187n16

Valmiki Ambedkar Awas Yojana (housing scheme), 182

"Vani" (Karmikara Colony resident), 248, 252–53

"Varsha" (student), transportation challenges of, 149

"Vasavi" (RP Colony resident), 170–71

"Vedike" (Bengaluru Bus Prayanikara Vedike, BBPV), 144–50

"Vilas" (major private equity fund manager), 83

"Vinod" (former PSU chairman), 118, 119–20

"Viren" (architect), 29–30, 35–42, 107

Vrushabhavathi River, 273

Wall Street, 16

waste collection workers, 281–83; Dalits as, 91; living conditions of, 85, 89–90; migrants in Purvapur as, 60, 61–62, 63n3, 89–92; public transit use, 139; in Purvapur Lake area, 263; strike (2022), 281–82

wastewater and sewage leakage: from Golden Springs, 237, 248–52

water pollution: Bellandur Lake, 45, 53; Bengaluru's lakes, 48, 53; omnipresence of, 271; in Purvapur, 55

water supply: Bellandur and, 48, 50–51; central to Bengaluru's ecological crisis, 266, 267–80; conflict and violence over, 270; daily provision of water, 268, 269–70; dams, 271; drinking water, 19, 267, 268, 276; ESG response to water crisis, 274–77; eucalyptus and, 59; fantasy of limitless water, 273; future security of, 270, 277; Golden Springs's offer to provide water to local park, 251–52; Hasiruhalli and, 106; Kalanagar residents' responsibility for water bill, 171–72; Karmikara Colony, 240–41, 249; Lakeview Haven, 66, 70; price of, 66, 270; in Purvapur,

55, 59, 259–60; rainwater, 3, 41, 50, 70, 270–71, 273; scarcity, 3, 19, 41, 50, 70, 241, 256, 270–72; "tanker mafia," 22n7, 31, 50, 54, 66, 70, 75, 270. *See also* borewells; groundwater depletion; lakes; *rajakaluves*

wetlands, 4, 19, 47, 273–74, 276, 278

WhatsApp groups: *cheeti* groups, 86, 88, 95; delivery workers, 224; Lakeview Haven, 70

Whitefield, 45, 53, 66, 263, 274, Plate 1.7

"Whitefield Rising" (civic action group), 264, 265

windfall profits from land sales, 62, 76, 80, 81, 106–7, 174, Plate 1.11

Wipro, 46

women: bus travel, 142, 147, 148, 149–50, 151n4; *cheeti* system and, 76, 85–97; as construction workers, 200–201, 202 (fig.), 204; as domestic workers, 229–35; as effective heads of migrant households, 201, 205–6; as forgotten freedom fighters, 207–8; as garment workers, 233; in informal sector, 198; as ITI terminated workers, 119; Karmikara Colony Sports Club and, 244; as tenants when single and living alone, 161; wage inequality, 232

workers. *See* delivery workers; domestic workers; labor; migrant workers; precarious employment and income; waste collection workers

World Bank, 7, 10, 17

world cities. *See* "global city" model

World Economic Forum, 47

WRI (World Resources Institute), 277, 280n4

yellow belt/zone, 53, 56–60

Yeshwantpur: apartment complexes, 74 (fig.), 85; conversion from industrial zone to high-end real estate, 12, 169, 244; as core city site, 12; deindustrialization of, 12, 158; infrastructure projects in, 12; low-income residents and *cheetis*, 85–97; public sector industrialization in colonial period, 114. *See also* "Golden Springs"; "Karmikara Colony"; "RP Colony"

Y2K crisis, 80

Zomato (app-based delivery service), 217–28, 286

zones of sociality, 30

zoning as speculative device for politically powerful, 56